MACROMEDIA® DREAMWEAVER® 8
REVEALED
DELUXE EDUCATION EDITION

MACROMEDIA® DREAMWEAVER® 8
REVEALED
DELUXE EDUCATION EDITION

Sherry Bishop

Macromedia® Dreamweaver® 8—Revealed, Deluxe Education Edition

Sherry Bishop

Managing Editor:
Marjorie Hunt

Product Manager:
Jane Hosie-Bounar

Associate Product Manager:
Shana Rosenthal

Editorial Assistant:
Janine Tangney

Production Editor:
Pamela Elizian

Developmental Editor:
Ann Fisher

Marketing Manager:
Joy Stark

Composition House:
Integra—Pondicherry, India

QA Manuscript Reviewers:
Chris Carvalho, Susan Whalen

Text Designer:
Ann Small

Illustrator:
Philip Brooker

Cover Design:
Steve Deschene

For permission to use material from this text or product, submit a request online at **www.thomsonrights.com**

Any additional questions about permissions can be submitted by e-mail to **thomsonrights@thomson.com**

Trademarks
Some of the product names and company names used in this book have been used for identification purposes only and may be trademarks or registered trademarks of their respective manufacturers and sellers.

Macromedia, the Macromedia and Macromedia Education logos, Authorware, ColdFusion, Director, Dreamweaver, Fireworks, FreeHand, JRun, Macromedia Flash and Shockwave are trademarks or registered trademarks of Macromedia, Inc. in the United States and/or other countries. Third-party products, services, company names, logos, design, titles, words, or phrases within these materials may be trademarks of their respective owners.

Acknowledgment
Some of the information in Chapter 12, "Managing a Web Server and Files," is courtesy of Barbara M. Waxer, co-author of *Internet Surf and Turf Revealed: The Essential Guide to Copyright, Fair Use, and Finding Media*, published by Thomson Course Technology.

Disclaimer
Thomson Course Technology reserves the right to revise this publication and make changes from time to time in its content without notice.

ISBN-13: 978-1-4188-4308-3

ISBN-10: 1-4188-4308-3

Revealed Series Vision

The Revealed Series is your guide to today's hottest multimedia applications. These comprehensive books teach the skills behind the application, showing you how to apply smart design principles to multimedia products such as dynamic graphics, animation, Web sites, software authoring tools, and digital video.

A team of design professionals including multimedia instructors, students, authors, and editors worked together to create this series. We recognized the unique needs of the multimedia market and created a series that gives you comprehensive step-by-step instructions and offers an in-depth explanation of the "why" behind a skill, all in a clear, visually based layout.

It was our goal to create a book that speaks directly to the multimedia and design community—one of the most rapidly growing computer fields today. We feel that *Macromedia Dreamweaver 8—Revealed, Deluxe Education Edition* does just that—with sophisticated content and an instructive book design.

—The Revealed Series

Author's Vision

Can you hear my standing ovation for the many people who have contributed their time and talents to this project? I have never worked with a more talented and enthusiastic group of folks. Jane Hosie-Bounar is a superb project manager. She led the way with a gentle hand and strong spirit and was always available and ready to help. Ann Fisher is a most wonderful editor. She is creative and warm and has a great sense of humor. She edits my work so skillfully that I think I did it all by myself! I have enjoyed working with both of these ladies immensely and will miss our chats.

The designs from Deborah VanRooyen and her assistant graphic designer Andrew Huff made the Web sites fun for me to craft. Thank you, Deborah. The design advice from Dave Belden made my work much easier. Thank you, Dave. Barbara Waxer generously contributed her insight and knowledge about copyrights, and the information was much appreciated. Additional information on locating media on the Internet and determining its legal use is available in her Revealed Series book *Internet Surf and Turf Revealed: The Essential Guide to Copyright, Fair Use, and Finding Media*.

Susan Whalen and Chris Carvalho carefully tested each step to make sure that the end product was error-free. They gave exceptional feedback as they reviewed each chapter. This part of the publishing process is what truly sets Thomson Course Technology apart from other publishers. Pam Elizian, our production editor, kept the schedule on track to make sure that we all met our deadlines. Her attention to detail contributed much to the quality of our book.

Special thanks go to Marjorie Hunt, the Managing Editor, a very talented individual with clear vision. I owe a debt of gratitude to both Marjorie and Nicole Pinard, Vice President of End-User Publishing, who gave me my first opportunity to work with Course Technology.

The Beach Club (*www.beach-clubal.com*) in Gulf Shores, Alabama, generously allowed us to use several photographs of their beautiful property for The Striped Umbrella Web site. Florence Pruitt, the club director, was extremely helpful and gracious.

I hope you enjoy reading and working through the book. Dreamweaver is such an outstanding Web development tool. It plays easily with both the professional Web developer and the beginning student. We are all indebted to the inspired team at Macromedia.

Typically, your family is the last to be properly thanked. My husband, Don, continues to support and encourage me every day, as he has for the last thirty-five years. Our travels with our children and grandchildren provide happy memories for me and content for the Web sites. This book leans fairly strongly in the direction of my precious grandchildren Jacob, Emma, Thomas, and Caroline. You will see their faces peeking out from some of the pages.

—Sherry Bishop

Introduction to Macromedia Dreamweaver 8

Welcome to *Macromedia Dreamweaver 8—Revealed, Deluxe Education Edition*. This book offers creative projects, concise instructions, and complete coverage of basic to intermediate Dreamweaver skills, helping you to create and publish polished, professional-looking Web sites. Use this book as you learn Dreamweaver, and then use it later as your own reference guide.

This text is organized into twelve chapters. In these chapters, you will learn many skills you need to create dynamic Dreamweaver Web sites.

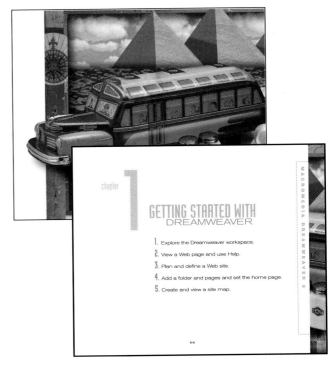

What You'll Do

A What You'll Do figure begins every lesson. This figure gives you an at-a-glance look at what you'll do in the chapter, either by showing you a page or pages from the current project or a tool you'll be using.

Comprehensive Conceptual Lessons

Before jumping into instructions, in-depth conceptual information tells you "why" skills are applied. This book provides the "how" and "why" through the use of professional examples. Also included in the text are tips and sidebars to help you work more efficiently and creatively, or to teach you a bit about the history or design philosophy behind the skill you are using.

Step-by-Step Instructions

This book combines in-depth conceptual information with concise steps to help you learn Dreamweaver 8. Each set of steps guides you through a lesson where you will create, modify, or enhance a Dreamweaver Web site. Step references to large colorful images and quick step summaries round out the lessons.

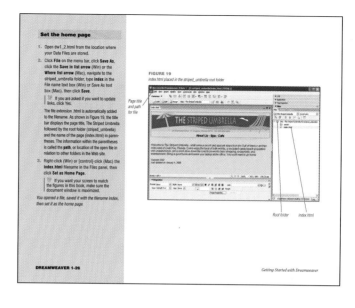

Projects

This book contains a variety of end-of-chapter materials for additional practice and reinforcement. The Skills Review contains hands-on practice exercises that mirror the progressive nature of the lesson material. Each chapter concludes with four projects: two Project Builders, one Design Project, and one Portfolio Project. The Project Builders and the Design Project require you to apply the skills you've learned in the chapter. Portfolio Projects encourage you to solve challenges based on the content explored in the chapter and to create a file for use in your portfolio.

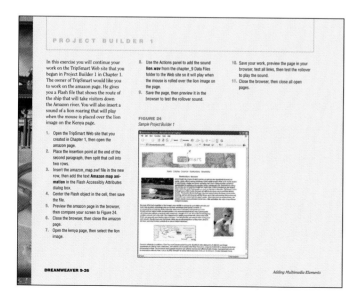

BRIEF CONTENTS

CONTENTS

CONTENTS

CHAPTER 4   WORKING WITH LINKS

CHAPTER 5   WORKING WITH TABLES

CONTENTS

CONTENTS

Intended Audience

This text is designed for the beginner or intermediate user who wants to learn how to use Dreamweaver 8. The book is designed to provide basic and in-depth material that not only educates, but also encourages you to explore the nuances of this exciting program.

Approach

The text allows you to work at your own pace through step-by-step tutorials. A concept is presented and the process is explained, followed by the actual steps. To learn the most from the use of the text, you should adopt the following habits:

- Proceed slowly: Accuracy and comprehension are more important than speed.
- Understand what is happening with each step before you continue to the next step.
- After finishing a skill, ask yourself if you could do it on your own, without referring to the steps. If the answer is no, review the steps.

Icons, Buttons, and Pointers

Symbols for icons, buttons, and pointers are shown in the step each time they are used.

Fonts

The Data Files contain a variety of commonly used fonts, but there is no guarantee that these fonts will be available on your computer. In a few cases, fonts other than those common to a PC or a Macintosh are used. If any of the fonts in use is not available on your computer, you can make a substitution, realizing that the results may vary from those in the book.

Windows and Macintosh

Macromedia Dreamweaver 8 works virtually the same on Windows and Macintosh operating systems. In those cases where there is a significant difference, the abbreviations (Win) and (Mac) are used.

System Requirements

For a Windows operating system, Dreamweaver 8 requires at least an 800 MHz Intel Pentium III processor (or equivalent); Windows 2000 or Windows XP; 256 MB RAM (1 GB recommended to run more than one Studio 8 product simultaneously); 1024 × 768, 16-bit display (32-bit recommended); and 1.8 GB available disk space.

For a Macintosh operating system, Dreamweaver 8 requires at least 600 MHz PowerPC G3; Mac OS X 10.3 or 10.4; 256 MB RAM (1 GB recommended to run more than one Studio 8 product simultaneously); 1024 × 768, thousands of colors display (millions of colors recommended); and 1.2 GB available disk space.

Dreamweaver 8 Workspace

If you are starting Dreamweaver for the first time after installing it, you will see the Workspace Setup dialog box, which asks you to choose between two workspace layouts. This text uses the Designer workspace layout throughout.

Building a Web Site

You will create and develop a Web site called The Striped Umbrella in the lesson material in this book. Because each chapter builds off of the previous chapter, it is recommended that you work through the chapters in consecutive order.

Data Files

To complete the lessons in this book, you need the Data Files on the CD in the back of this book. Your instructor will tell you where to store the files as you work, such as the hard drive, a network server, or a USB storage device. The instructions in the lessons will refer to "the drive and folder where your Data Files are stored" when referring to the Data Files for the book.

When you copy the Data Files to your computer, you may see lock icons that indicate that the files are read-only when you view them in the Dreamweaver Files panel. To unlock the files, right-click on the locked file name in the Files panel, then click Turn off Read Only.

Preference Settings

The learning process will be much easier if you can see the file extensions for the files you will use in the lessons. To do this in Windows, open Windows Explorer, click Tools, Folder Options, View, then uncheck the box Hide Extensions for Known File Types. To do this for a Mac, go to the Finder, click the Finder menu, and then click Preferences. Click the Advanced tab, then select the Show all file extensions check box.

To view the Flash content that you will be creating, you must set a preference in your browser to allow active content to run. Otherwise, you will not be able to view objects such as Flash buttons. To set this preference in Internet Explorer, click Tools, Internet Options, Advanced, then check the box Allow active content to run in files on My Computer. Your browser settings may be slightly different, but look for similar wording.

Creating a Portfolio

The Portfolio Project and Project Builders allow students to use their creativity to come up with original Dreamweaver designs. You might suggest that students create a portfolio in which they can store their original work.

chapter 1

GETTING STARTED WITH
DREAMWEAVER

1. Explore the Dreamweaver workspace.

2. View a Web page and use Help.

3. Plan and define a Web site.

4. Add a folder and pages and set the home page.

5. Create and view a site map.

Introduction

Macromedia Dreamweaver 8 is a Web
development tool that lets you create
dynamic, interactive Web pages containing
text, images, hyperlinks, animation, sounds,
video, and other elements. You can use
Dreamweaver to create individual Web
pages or complex Web sites consisting of
many Web pages. A **Web site** is a group of
related Web pages that are linked together
and share a common interface and design.
You can use Dreamweaver to create some
Web page elements such as text, tables,
and interactive buttons, or you can import
elements from other software programs.
You can save Dreamweaver files in many
different file formats including XHTML,
HTML, JavaScript, CSS, or XML to name a
few. **XHTML** is the acronym for eXtensible
HyperText Markup Language, the current
standard language used to create Web pages.
You can still use **HTML** (HyperText Markup
Language) in Dreamweaver; however, it is
no longer considered the standard language.
In Dreamweaver you can easily convert
existing HTML code to XHTML-compliant
code. You use a browser to view your Web
pages on the Internet. A **browser** is a program, such as Microsoft Internet Explorer

or Netscape Communicator, that lets you
display HTML-developed Web pages.

Using Dreamweaver Tools

Creating a good Web site is a complex task.
Fortunately, Dreamweaver has an impres-
sive number of tools that can help. Using
Dreamweaver's design tools, you can create
dynamic and interactive Web pages without
writing a word of code. However, if you
prefer to write code, Dreamweaver makes it
easy to enter and edit the code directly and
see the visual results of the code instantly.
Dreamweaver also contains organizational
tools that help you work with a team of
people to create a Web site. You can also use
Dreamweaver's management tools to help
you manage a Web site. For instance, you
can use the **Files panel** to create folders to
organize and store the various files for your
Web site, add pages to your Web site, and set
the **home page**, the first page that viewers
will see when they visit the site. You can
also use the **site map**, a graphical representation of how the pages within a Web site
relate to each other, to view and edit the
navigation structure of your Web site. The
navigation structure is the way viewers
navigate from page to page in your Web site.

Tools You'll Use

Property inspector

Browse for File icon

Refresh button

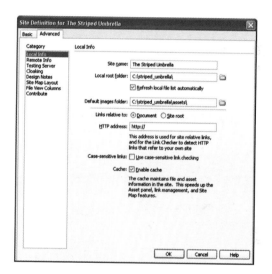

Show Code view button

Show Code and Design views button

Show Design view button

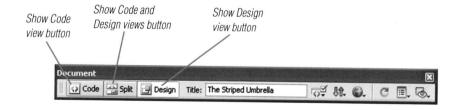

EXPLORE THE
DREAMWEAVER WORKSPACE

What You'll Do

 In this lesson, you will start Dreamweaver, examine the components that make up the Dreamweaver workspace, and change views.

Examining the Dreamweaver Workspace

The **Dreamweaver workspace** is designed to provide you with easy access to all the tools you need to create Web pages. Refer to Figure 1 as you locate the components described below.

The **document window** is the large white area in the Dreamweaver program window where you create and edit Web pages. The **menu bar**, located above the document window, includes menu names, each of which contains Dreamweaver commands. To choose a menu command, click the menu name to open the menu, then click the menu command. Directly below the menu bar is the Insert bar. The **Insert bar** includes eight groups of buttons displayed in a drop-down menu. They are Common, Layout, Forms, Text, HTML, Application, Flash elements, and Favorites. Clicking a group name on the Insert bar displays the buttons and menus associated with that group. For example, if you click Layout, you will find the Table button, used for

inserting a table, and the Frames menu, used for selecting one of thirteen different frame layouts.

> **QUICK**TIP
>
> You can also display the categories using tabs, as in previous versions of Dreamweaver, by clicking the current Insert bar list arrow, then clicking Show as Tabs.

The **Document toolbar** contains buttons and drop-down menus you can use to change the current work mode, preview Web pages, debug Web pages, choose visual aids, and view file-management options. The **Standard toolbar** contains buttons you can use to execute frequently used commands also available on the File and Edit menus. The Style Rendering toolbar contains buttons that can be used to render different media types. The Coding toolbar contains buttons that are used when working directly in the code. These, along with the Standard toolbar, are not part of the default workspace setup and might not show when you open Dreamweaver.

To hide or display the Standard, Document, Style Rendering, or Insert toolbars, click View on the menu bar, point to Toolbars, then click Document, Standard, Style Rendering, or Insert. The Coding toolbar is available only in Code view and appears vertically in the document window.

The **Property inspector**, located at the bottom of the Dreamweaver window, lets you view and change the properties of a selected object. The Property inspector is context sensitive, which means it changes according to what is selected in the document window. The **status bar** is located below the document window. The left end of the status bar displays the **tag selector**, which shows the HTML tags used at the insertion point location. The right side displays the window size and estimated download time for the current

page as well as the Select tool used for page editing, the Hand tool used for panning, and the Zoom tool used for magnifying.

A **panel** is a window that displays information on a particular topic or contains related commands. **Panel groups** are sets of related panels that are grouped together. To view the contents of a panel in a panel group, click the panel. Panel groups can be collapsed and docked on the right side of the screen, or undocked by dragging the gripper on the left side of the panel group title bar. To collapse or expand a panel group, click the expander arrow on the left side of the panel group title bar, as shown in Figure 2, or just click the name of the panel group. When you use Dreamweaver for the first time, the CSS Application, Tag Inspector, and Files panel groups are displayed by default. Panels can

be opened using the Window menu commands or the corresponding shortcut keys.

Working with Dreamweaver Views

A **view** is a particular way of displaying page content. Dreamweaver has three working views. **Design view** shows the page as it would appear in a browser and is primarily used for designing and creating a Web page. **Code view** shows the underlying HTML code for the page; use this view to read or edit the underlying code. **Code and Design view** is a combination of Code view and Design view. Code and Design view is the best view for **debugging** or correcting errors because you can immediately see how code modifications change the appearance of the page. The view buttons are located on the Document toolbar.

FIGURE 1
Dreamweaver 8 workspace

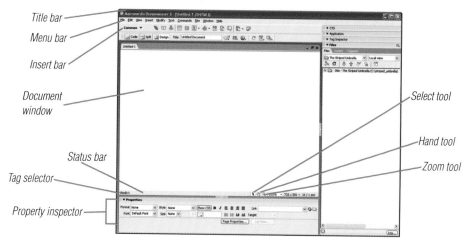

Title bar
Menu bar
Insert bar
Document window
Status bar
Tag selector
Property inspector

Select tool
Hand tool
Zoom tool

FIGURE 2
Panels in Files panel group

Expander arrow
Gripper
Active panel tab

Start Dreamweaver (Windows)

1. Click the **Start button** 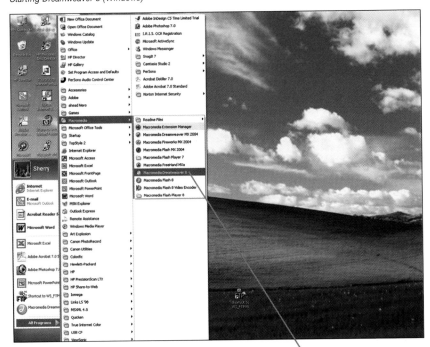 on the taskbar.

2. Point to **Programs** or **All Programs**, point to **Macromedia**, then click **Macromedia Dreamweaver 8**, as shown in Figure 3.

You started Dreamweaver 8 for Windows.

FIGURE 3
Starting Dreamweaver 8 (Windows)

Click Macromedia Dreamweaver 8

Choosing a workspace layout (Windows)

If you are starting Dreamweaver in Windows for the first time after installing it, you will see the Workspace Setup dialog box, which asks you to choose between the Designer or Coder layout. Both layouts are built with an integrated workspace using the Multiple Document Interface (MDI). The **Multiple Document Interface** means that all document windows and panels are positioned within one large application window. In the Designer workspace layout, the panels are docked on the right side of the screen and the Design view is the default view. In the Coder workspace layout, the panels are docked on the left side of the screen and the Code view is the default view. To change the workspace layout, click Window on the menu bar, point to Workspace Layout, then click the desired layout.

Getting Started with Dreamweaver

FIGURE 4

Starting Dreamweaver 8 (Macintosh)

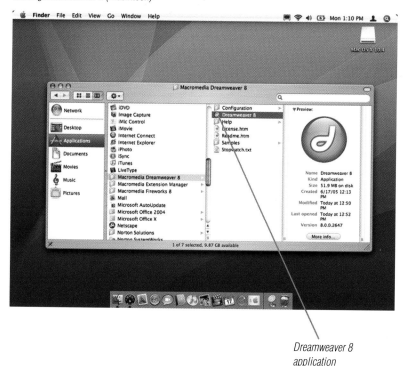

Dreamweaver 8
application

1. Click **Finder** in the Dock, then click **Applications**.

2. Click the **Macromedia Dreamweaver 8 folder**, then double-click the **Dreamweaver 8 application,** as shown in Figure 4.

   TIP Once Dreamweaver is running, you can add it to the Dock permanently by [control]-clicking the Dreamweaver icon, then clicking Keep In Dock.

You started Dreamweaver 8 for Macintosh.

Change views and view panels

1. Click the **HTML link** in the Create New category on the Dreamweaver Start page.

   The Dreamweaver Start page provides shortcuts for opening files or for creating new files or Web sites.

   TIP If you do not want the Dreamweaver Start page to appear each time you start Dreamweaver, click the Don't show again check box on the Start page or remove the check mark next to Show start page in the General category of the Preferences dialog box.

2. Click the **Show Code view button** on the Document toolbar.

   The default code for a new document appears in the document window, as shown in Figure 5.

   TIP The Coding toolbar is available only in Code view.

3. Click the **Show Code and Design views button** on the Document toolbar.

4. Click the **Show Design view button** on the Document toolbar.

(continued)

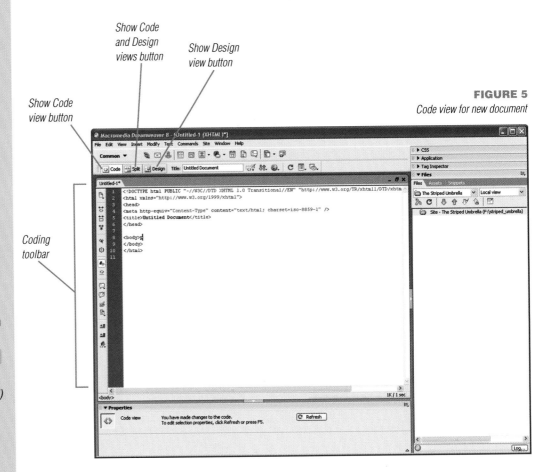

Show Code and Design views button

Show Design view button

Show Code view button

FIGURE 5
Code view for new document

Coding toolbar

FIGURE 6
Displaying a panel group

Expander arrow

Drag to undock or
"float" panel group

Application
panel group with
four panels

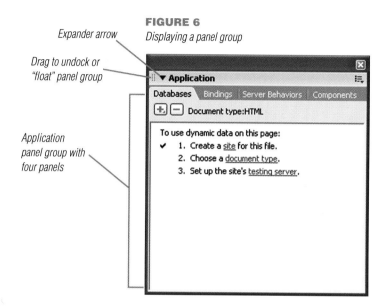

5. Click **Application** on the panel group title
   bar, then compare your screen to Figure 6.

   TIP If the Application panel group is not
   displayed, click Window on the menu bar,
   then click Server Behaviors.

6. Click each panel name tab to display the
   contents of each panel.

7. Click **Application** on the panel group title bar
   to collapse the Application panel group.

8. View the contents of the CSS and Files panel
   groups, then collapse the CSS panel group.

   TIP If you are a Mac user, you first need to
   open the panel groups. To open each panel
   group, click Window on the menu bar, then
   click Server Behaviors (for the Application
   panel group) or Assets (for the Files panel
   group).

9. Close the open XHTML document.

*You viewed a new Web page using three views,
opened panel groups, viewed their contents, then
closed panel groups.*

VIEW A WEB PAGE
AND USE HELP

What You'll Do

 In this lesson, you will open a Web page, view several page elements, and access the Help system.

Opening a Web Page

After starting Dreamweaver, you can create a new Web site, create a new Web page, or open an existing Web site or Web page. The first Web page that appears when viewers go to a Web site is called the **home page**. The home page sets the look and feel of the Web site and directs viewers to the rest of the pages in the Web site.

Viewing Basic Web Page Elements

There are many elements that make up Web pages. Web pages can be very simple and designed primarily with text, or they can be media-rich with text, graphics, sound, and movies. Figure 7 is an example of a Web page with several different page elements that work together to create a simple and attractive page.

Most information on a Web page is presented in the form of **text**. You can type text directly onto a Web page in Dreamweaver or import text created in other programs. You can then use the Property inspector to format text so that it is attractive and easy

to read. Text should be short and to the point to prevent viewers from losing interest and leaving your site.

Hyperlinks, also known as **links**, are graphic or text elements on a Web page that users click to display another location on the page, another Web page on the same Web site, or a Web page on a different Web site.

Graphics add visual interest to a Web page. The saying that "less is more" is certainly true with graphics, though. Too many graphics will cause the page to load slowly and discourage viewers from waiting for the page to download. Many pages now have **banners**, which are graphics displayed across the top of the screen that can incorporate a company's logo, contact information, and links to the other pages in the site.

Navigation bars are bars that contain multiple links that are usually organized in rows or columns. Sometimes navigation bars are used with an image map. An **image map** is a graphic that has been divided into sections, each of which contains a link.

Getting Started with Dreamweaver

Flash button objects are Flash objects that can be created in Dreamweaver that can serve as links to other files or Web pages. You can insert them onto a Web page without requiring the Macromedia Flash program to be installed. They add "pizzazz" to a Web page.

Getting Help

Dreamweaver has an excellent Help feature that is both comprehensive and easy to use.

When questions or problems arise, you can use the commands on the Help menu to find the answers you need. Clicking the Using Dreamweaver command opens the Dreamweaver 8 Help window that contains four tabs you can use to search for answers in different ways. The Contents tab lists Dreamweaver Help topics by category. The Index tab lets you view topics in alphabetical order, and the Search tab lets you enter a keyword to search for a specific topic. You can use the Favorites tab to bookmark topics that you might want to view later. On a Macintosh you can choose between Index or Table of Contents view, and the Search field is always present at the top of the window. You can also use the Getting Started and Tutorials command on the Help menu to get step-by-step instructions on how to complete various tasks. Context-specific help can be accessed by clicking the question mark button on the Property inspector.

FIGURE 7
Common Web page elements

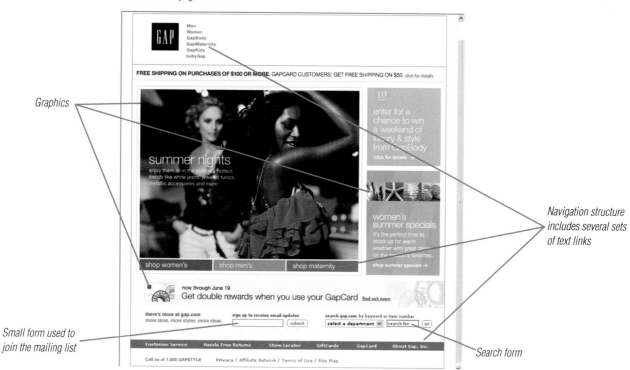

Graphics

Navigation structure includes several sets of text links

Small form used to join the mailing list

Search form

Open a Web page and view basic page elements

1. Click the **Open link** at the bottom of the first column on the Dreamweaver Start page.

2. Click the **Look in list arrow** (Win), or **navigation list arrow** (Mac), locate the drive and folder where your Data Files are stored, then double-click the **chapter_1 folder** (Win), or click the **chapter_1 folder** (Mac).

3. Click **dw1_1.html**, then click **Open**.

4. Locate each of the Web page elements shown in Figure 8.

5. Click the **Show Code view button** ◁▷ Code to view the code for the page.

6. Scroll down to view all the code, then click the **Show Design view button** ▱ Design to return to Design view.

> TIP To view the code for a particular page element, select the page element in Design view, then click the Show Code view button.

7. Click **File** on the menu bar, then click **Close** to close the page without saving it.

You opened a Web page, located several page elements, viewed the code for the page, then closed the Web page without saving it.

FIGURE 8
Striped Umbrella Web page elements

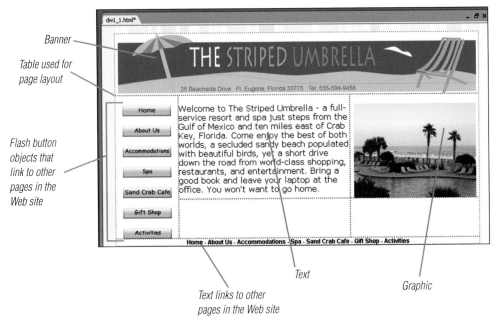

Banner

Table used for page layout

Flash button objects that link to other pages in the Web site

Text links to other pages in the Web site

Text

Graphic

FIGURE 9
Dreamweaver 8 Help window

Keywords

Click to
see topics

Topics found
with keywords

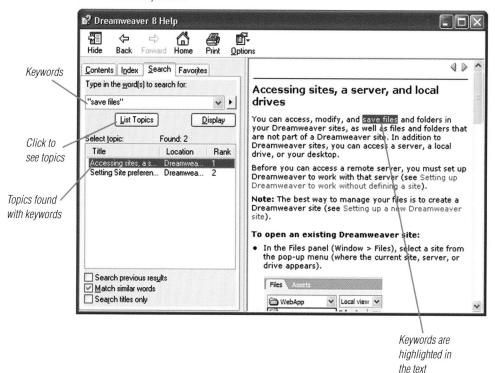

Keywords are
highlighted in
the text

1. Click **Help** on the menu bar, then click **Using Dreamweaver**.

2. Click the **Search tab** (Win).

3. Type **saving** in the Type in the word(s) to search for text box (Win) or the Ask a Question text box (Mac).

4. Press **[Enter]** or click **List Topics** (Win) or press **[return]** (Mac), then scroll down to view the topics.

5. Continue to Step 6 (Win) or close the Dreamweaver 8 Help window (Mac).

6. If necessary, select **saving** in the Type in the word(s) to search for text box, type **"save files"** (be sure to type the quotation marks), then press **[Enter]** or click **List Topics**.

    Because you placed the keywords in quotation marks, Dreamweaver shows only the topics that contain the exact phrase "save files".

7. Double-click the first topic in the topic list.

    Information on accessing sites, a server, and local drives appears in the right frame, as shown in Figure 9.

8. Scroll down and scan the text.

    The search words you used are highlighted in the Help text.

9. Close the Dreamweaver 8 Help window.

You used the Dreamweaver Help files to read information about connecting to a server to edit files.

PLAN AND DEFINE A
WEB SITE

What You'll Do

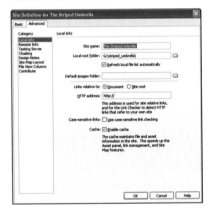

 In this lesson, you will review a Web site plan for The Striped Umbrella, a full-service beach resort and spa. You will also create a root folder for The Striped Umbrella Web site, and then define the Web site.

Understanding the Web Site Creation Process

Creating a Web site is a complex process. It can often involve a large team of people working in various roles to ensure that the Web site contains accurate information, looks good, and works smoothly. Figure 10 illustrates the phases in a Web site development project.

Planning a Web Site

Planning is probably the most important part of any successful project. Planning is an *essential* part of creating a Web site, and is a continuous process that overlaps the subsequent phases. To start planning your Web site, you need to create a checklist of questions and answers about the site. For example, what are your goals for

FIGURE 10
Phases of a Web site development project

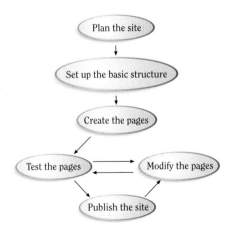

Getting Started with Dreamweaver

the Web site? Who is the audience you want to target? Teenagers? Senior citizens? How can you design the site to appeal to the target audience? The more questions you can answer about the site, the more prepared you will be when you begin the developmental phase. Because of the public demand for "instant" information, your plan should include not just how to get the site up and running, but how to keep it current. Table 1 lists some of the basic questions you need to answer during the planning phase for almost any type of Web site. From your checklist, you should create a statement of purpose and scope, a timeline for all due dates, a budget, a task list with work assignments, and a list of resources needed. You should also include a list of deliverables such as a preliminary storyboard, page drafts, and art work for approval. The due dates for each deliverable should be included in the timeline.

Setting Up the Basic Structure

Once you complete the planning phase, you need to set up the structure of the site by creating a storyboard. A **storyboard** is a small sketch that represents every page in a Web site. Like a flowchart, a storyboard shows the relationship of each page in the Web site to all the other pages. Storyboards are very

TABLE 1: Web Site Planning Checklist

question	examples
1. Who is the target audience?	Seniors, teens, children
2. How can I tailor the Web site to reach that audience?	Specify an appropriate reading level, decide the optimal amount of multimedia content, use formal or casual language
3. What are the goals for the site?	Sell a product, provide information
4. How will I gather the information?	Recruit other company employees, write it myself, use content from in-house documents
5. What are my sources for multimedia content?	Internal production department, outside production company, my own photographs
6. What is my budget?	Very limited, well financed
7. How long do I have to complete the project?	Two weeks, 1 month, 6 months
8. Who is on my project team?	Just me, a complete staff of designers
9. How often should the site be updated?	Every 10 minutes, once a month
10. Who is responsible for updating the site?	Me, other team members

helpful when planning a Web site, because they allow you to visualize how each page in the site is linked to others. You can sketch a storyboard using a pencil and paper or using a graphics program on a computer. The storyboard shown in Figure 11 shows all the pages that will be contained in The Striped Umbrella Web site that you will create in this book. Notice that the home page appears at the top of the storyboard, and that it has four pages linked to it. The home page is called the **parent page**, because it is at a higher level in the Web hierarchy and has pages linked to it. The pages linked to it below are called **child pages**. The Activities page, which is a child page to the home page, is also a parent page to the Cruises and Fishing pages. You can refer to this storyboard as you create the actual links in Dreamweaver. More detailed storyboards will also include all document names, images, text files, and link information.

QUICKTIP
You can create a storyboard on a computer using a software program such as Word, PowerPoint, Paint, Paintshop Pro, or Macromedia Freehand. You might find it easier to make changes to a computer-generated storyboard than to one created on paper.

In addition to creating a storyboard for your site, you should also create a folder hierarchy for all of the files that will be used in the Web site. Start by creating a folder for the Web site with a descriptive name, such as the name of the company.

This folder, known as the **root folder** or **local root folder**, will store all the Web pages or HTML files for the site. Then create a subfolder called **assets** in which you store all of the files that are not Web pages, such as images and video clips. You should avoid using spaces, special characters, or uppercase characters in your folder names to ensure that all your files can be read and linked successfully on all Web servers.

After you create the root folder, you need to define your Web site. When you **define** a Web site, the root folder and any folders and files it contains appear in the **Files**

panel, the panel you use to manage your Web site's files and folders. Using the Files panel to manage your files ensures that the site links work correctly when the Web site is published. You also use the Files panel to add or delete pages.

Creating the Web Pages and Collecting the Page Content

This is the fun part! After you create your storyboard, you need to gather the files that will be used to create the pages, including text, graphics, buttons, video, and animation. Some of these files will come

FIGURE 11
The Striped Umbrella Web site storyboard

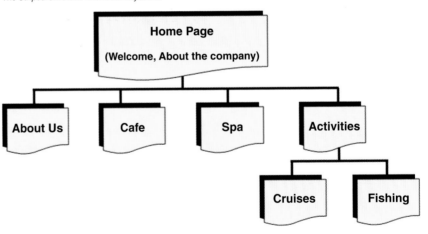

from other software programs, and some will be created in Dreamweaver. For example, you can create text in a word-processing program and insert it into Dreamweaver, or you can create and format text in Dreamweaver. Graphics, tables, colors, and horizontal rules all contribute to making a page attractive and interesting. In choosing your elements, however, you should always carefully consider the file size of each page. A page with too many graphical elements might take a long time to load, which could cause visitors to leave your Web site. Before you actually add content to each page, however, it is a good idea to use the Files panel to add all the pages to the site according to the structure you specified in your storyboard. Once all the blank pages are in place, you can add the content you collected. This will allow you to create and test the navigation links you will need for the site. The blank pages will act as placeholders. Some designers prefer to add pages as they are created and build the links as they go. It is a personal preference.

Testing the Pages

Once all your pages are completed, you need to test the site to make sure all the links work and that everything looks good.

It is important to test your Web pages using different browser software. The two most common browsers are Microsoft Internet Explorer and Netscape Navigator, although the Firefox browser is quickly gaining popularity. You should also test your Web site using different versions of each browser. Older versions of Internet Explorer and Netscape Navigator do not support the latest Web technology. You should also test your Web site using a variety of screen sizes. Some viewers may have small monitors, while others may have large, high-resolution monitors. You should also consider modem speed. Although more people use cable modems or DSL (Digital Subscriber Line) these days, some still use slower dial-up modems. Testing is a continuous process, for which you should allocate plenty of time.

Modifying the Pages

After you create a Web site, you'll probably find that you need to keep making changes to it, especially when information on the site needs to be updated. Each time you make a change, such as adding a new button or graphic to a page, you should test the site again. Modifying and testing pages in a Web site is an ongoing process.

Publishing the Site

Publishing a Web site means that you transfer all the files for the site to a **Web server**, a computer that is connected to the Internet with an IP (Internet Protocol) address, so that it is available for viewing on the Internet. A Web site must be published or users of the Internet cannot view it. There are several options for publishing a Web site. For instance, many Internet Service Providers (ISPs) provide space on their servers for customers to publish Web sites, and some commercial Web sites provide limited free space for their viewers. Although publishing happens at the end of the process, it's a good idea to set up Web server access in the planning phase. Use the Files panel to transfer your files using the FTP (File Transfer Protocol) capability. **FTP** is the process of uploading and downloading files to and from a remote site. Dreamweaver 8 also gives you the ability to transfer files using the FTP process without creating a Web site first. You simply enter login information to an FTP site to establish a connection by clicking New in the Manage Sites dialog box, then clicking the FTP & RDS Server option.

Create a root folder (Windows)

1. Click the **Start button** 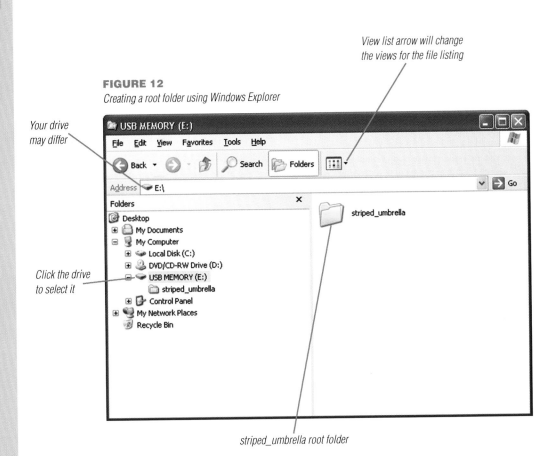 on the taskbar, point to **All Programs**, point to **Accessories**, then click **Windows Explorer**.

2. Navigate to the drive and folder where you will create a folder to store your files for The Striped Umbrella Web site.

3. Click **File** on the menu bar, point to **New**, then click **Folder**.

4. Type **striped_umbrella** to rename the folder, then press **[Enter]**.

   The folder is renamed striped_umbrella as shown in Figure 12.

   TIP Your desktop will look different than Figure 12 if you are not using Windows XP.

5. Close Windows Explorer.

   TIP You can also use the Files panel to create a new folder by clicking the Site list arrow, selecting the drive and folder where you want to create the new folder, right-clicking, selecting New Folder, then typing the new folder name.

You created a new folder to serve as the root folder for The Striped Umbrella Web site.

FIGURE 12
Creating a root folder using Windows Explorer

View list arrow will change the views for the file listing

Your drive may differ

Click the drive to select it

striped_umbrella root folder

Getting Started with Dreamweaver

FIGURE 13

Creating a root folder using a Macintosh

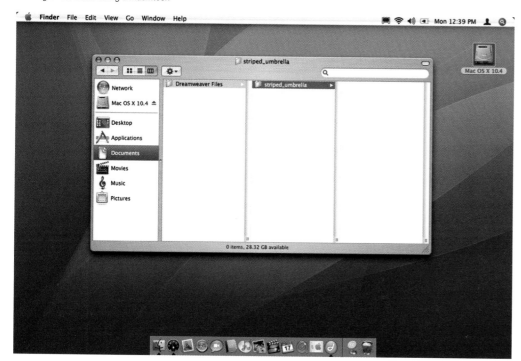

Create a root folder (Macintosh)

1. Double-click the **hard drive icon**, then navigate to the drive and folder where you will create a folder to store your files for The Striped Umbrella Web site.

2. Click **File** on the menu bar, then click **New Folder**.

3. Type **striped_umbrella** to rename the folder, as shown in Figure 13.

   TIP   If you cannot type a new folder name, click the current folder name once to highlight it, then type a new folder name.

You created a new folder to serve as the root folder for The Striped Umbrella Web site.

Define a Web site

1. Return to Dreamweaver, then click the **Dreamweaver Site link** in the Create New category on the Start page.

2. Click the **Advanced tab** (if necessary), then type **The Striped Umbrella** in the Site name text box.

   The Basic tab can be used instead of the Advanced tab if you prefer to use a wizard approach.

   TIP It is acceptable to use uppercase letters in the site name because it is not the name of a folder or a file.

3. Click the **Browse for File icon** next to the Local root folder text box, click the **Select list arrow** (Win) or the **navigation list arrow** (Mac) in the Choose local root folder for site The Striped Umbrella dialog box, click the drive and folder where your Web site files will be stored, then click the **striped_umbrella folder**.

4. Click **Open** (Win) or **Choose** (Mac), then click **Select** (Win).

5. Verify that the Refresh local file list automatically and the Enable cache check boxes are both checked, as shown in Figure 14.

6. Verify that the Links relative to option button is set to Document.

   This is very important to make sure your links work correctly.

You created a Web site and defined it with the name The Striped Umbrella. You then verified that the correct options were selected in the Site Definition dialog box.

FIGURE 14
Site Definition for The Striped Umbrella dialog box

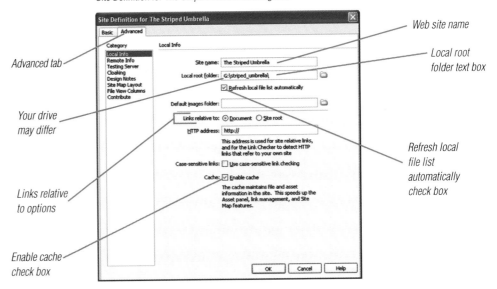

Understanding IP addresses and domain names

To be accessible over the Internet, a Web site must be published to a Web server with a permanent IP address. An **IP address** is an assigned series of numbers, separated by periods, that designate an address on the Internet. To access a Web page, you can enter either an IP address or a domain name in the address text box of your browser window. A **domain name** is a Web address that is expressed in letters instead of numbers and usually reflects the name of the business represented by the Web site. For example, the domain name of the Macromedia Web site is *www.macromedia.com*, but the IP address would read something like 123.456.789.123. Because domain names use descriptive text instead of numbers, they are much easier to remember. Compare an IP address to your Social Security number and a domain name to your name. Both your Social Security number and your name are used to refer to you as a person, but your name is much easier for your friends and family to use than your Social Security number. You can type the IP address or the domain name in the address text box of the browser window to access a Web site. The domain name is also referred to as a URL, or Uniform Resource Locator.

FIGURE 15
Setting the remote access for The Striped Umbrella Web site

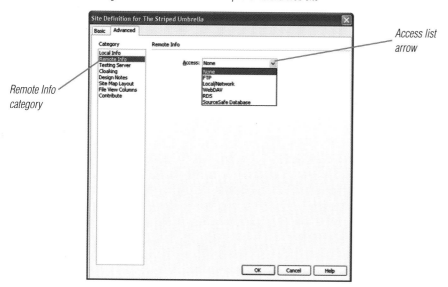

Access list arrow

Remote Info category

1. Click **Remote Info** in the Category list, click the **Access list arrow**, then choose the method you will use to publish your Web site, as shown in Figure 15.

   TIP If you do not have the information to publish your Web site, choose None. You can specify this information later.

2. Enter any necessary information in the Site Definition dialog box based on the setting you chose in Step 1, click **OK**, then click **Done**.

You set up the remote access information to prepare you for publishing your Web site.

Understanding the process of publishing a Web site

Before publishing a Web site so that viewers of the Web can access it, you should first create a local root folder, called the **local site**, to house all the files for your Web site. This folder usually resides on your hard drive. Next, you need to gain access to a remote server. A **remote server** is a Web server that hosts Web sites and is not directly connected to the computer housing the local site. Many Internet Service Providers, or ISPs, provide space for publishing Web pages on their servers. Once you have access to a remote server, you can then use the Remote Info category in the Site Definition dialog box to enter information such as the FTP host, host directory, login, and password. After entering this information, you can then use the Put File(s) button in the Files panel to transfer the files to the designated remote server. Once the site is published to a remote server, it is called a **remote site**.

ADD A FOLDER AND PAGES
AND SET THE HOME PAGE

What You'll Do

 In this lesson, you will set the home page. You'll also create a new folder and new pages for the Web site, using the Files panel.

Adding a Folder to a Web Site

After defining a Web site, you need to create folders to organize the files that will make up the Web site. Creating a folder called **assets** is a good beginning. You can use the assets folder to store all non-HTML files, such as images or sound files. After you create the assets folder, it is a good idea to set it as the default location to store the Web site images. This saves a step when you import new images into the Web site.

DESIGNTIP **Creating an effective navigation structure**

When you create a Web site, it's important to consider how your viewers will navigate from page to page within the site. A navigation bar is a critical tool for moving around a Web site, so it's important that all text, buttons, and icons used in a navigation bar have a consistent look across all pages. If a complex navigation bar is used, such as one that incorporates JavaScript or Flash, it's a good idea to include plain text links in another location on the page for accessibility. Otherwise, viewers might become confused or lost within the site. A navigation structure can include more links than those included in a navigation bar, however. For instance, it can contain other sets of links that relate to the content of a specific page and which are placed at the bottom or sides of a page in a different format. No matter what navigation structure you use, make sure that every page includes a link back to the home page. Don't make viewers rely on the Back button on the browser toolbar to find their way back to the home page. It's possible that the viewer's current page might have opened as a result of a search and clicking the Back button will take the viewer out of the Web site.

Setting the Home Page

The home page of a Web site is the first page that viewers see when they visit your Web site. Most Web sites contain many other pages that all connect back to the home page. Dreamweaver uses the home page that you have designated as a starting point for creating a **site map**, a graphical representation of the Web pages in a Web site. When you **set** the home page, you tell Dreamweaver which page you have designated to be your home page. The home page filename usually has the name index.html (.htm), or default.html (.htm).

Adding Pages to a Web Site

Web sites might be as simple as one page or might contain hundreds of pages. When you create a Web site, you need to add all the pages and specify where they should be placed in the Web site folder structure in the root folder. Once you add and name all the pages in the Web site, you can then add the content, such as text and graphics, to each page. It is better to add as many blank pages as you think you will need in the beginning, rather than adding them one at a time with all the content in place. This will enable you to set up the navigation structure of the Web site at the beginning of the development process and view how each page is linked to others. When you are satisfied with the overall structure, you can then add the content to each page. This is strictly a personal preference, however. You can also choose to add and link pages as they are created, and that will work just fine, too.

You have a choice of several default document types you can generate when you create new HTML pages. The default document type is designated in the Preferences dialog box. XHTML 1.0 Transitional is the default document type when you install Dreamweaver and will be used throughout this book. It's important to understand the terminology— the pages are still called HTML pages and the file extension is still HTML, but the document type will be XHTML 1.0 Transitional.

Using the Files panel for file management

You should definitely use the Files panel to add, delete, move, or rename files and folders in a Web site. It is very important that you perform these file maintenance tasks in the Files panel rather than in Windows Explorer (Win) or in the Finder (Mac). Working outside of Dreamweaver, such as in Windows Explorer, will cause linking errors. You cannot take advantage of Dreamweaver's simple yet powerful site-management features unless you use the Files panel for all file-management activities. You may choose to use Windows Explorer (Win) or the Finder (Mac) only to create the root folder or to move or copy the root folder of a Web site to another location. If you move or copy the root folder to a new location, you will have to define the Web site again in the Files panel, as you did in Lesson 3 of this chapter. Defining a Web site is not difficult and will become routine for you after you practice a bit.

Add a folder to a Web site (Windows)

1. Right-click **The Striped Umbrella site** in the Files panel, then click **New Folder**.

2. Type **assets** in the folder text box, then press **[Enter]**.

3. Compare your screen with Figure 16.

You used the Files panel to create a new folder in the striped_umbrella folder and named it assets.

Add a folder to a Web site (Macintosh)

1. Click **Window** on the menu bar, click **Files** to open the Files panel (if necessary), press and hold **[control]**, click the **striped_umbrella folder**, then click **New Folder**.

2. Click the triangle to the left of the striped_umbrella folder to open it (if necessary), then click untitled on the new folder, type **assets** as the folder name, then press **[return]**.

   TIP You will not see the new folder until you expand the striped_umbrella folder by clicking the triangle to the left of the striped_umbrella folder.

3. Compare your screen with Figure 17.

You used the Files panel to create a new folder under the striped_umbrella folder and named it assets.

FIGURE 16
The Striped Umbrella site in Files panel with assets folder created (Windows)

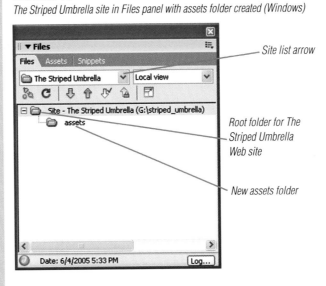

Site list arrow

Root folder for The Striped Umbrella Web site

New assets folder

FIGURE 17
The Striped Umbrella site in Files panel with assets folder created (Macintosh)

Getting Started with Dreamweaver

FIGURE 18

Site Definition for The Striped Umbrella with assets folder set as the default images folder

Default images
folder text box

Browse
for File
icon

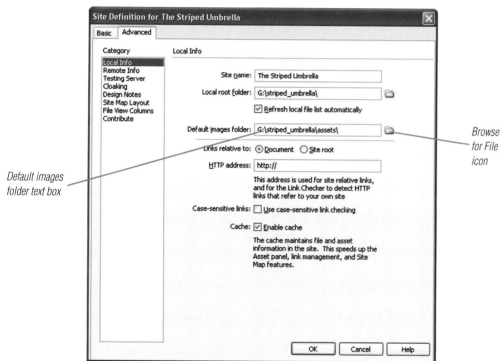

1. Click the **Site list arrow** next to The Striped Umbrella in the Site text box on the Files panel, click **Manage Sites**, then click **Edit**.

2. Click the **Browse for File icon** next to the Default images folder text box.

3. Navigate to the folder where your Web site files will be stored, double-click the **striped_umbrella folder** (Win) or click the **striped_umbrella folder** (Mac), double-click the **assets folder** (Win) or click the **assets folder** (Mac), then click **Select** (Win) or **Choose** (Mac).

   Compare your screen to Figure 18.

4. Click **OK**, then click **Done**.

You set the assets folder as the default images folder so that imported images will be automatically saved in it.

Set the home page

1. Open dw1_2.html from the location where your Data Files are stored.

2. Click **File** on the menu bar, click **Save As**, click the **Save in list arrow** (Win) or the **Where list arrow** (Mac), navigate to the striped_umbrella folder, type **index** in the File name text box (Win) or Save As text box (Mac), then click **Save**.

   TIP If you are asked if you want to update links, click Yes.

   The file extension .html is automatically added to the filename. As shown in Figure 19, the title bar displays the page title, The Striped Umbrella followed by the root folder (striped_umbrella) and the name of the page (index.html) in parentheses. The information within the parentheses is called the **path**, or location of the open file in relation to other folders in the Web site.

3. Right-click (Win) or [control]-click (Mac) the **index.html filename** in the Files panel, then click **Set as Home Page**.

   TIP If you want your screen to match the figures in this book, make sure the document window is maximized.

You opened a file, saved it with the filename index, then set it as the home page.

FIGURE 19

index.html placed in the striped_umbrella root folder

Page title and path for file

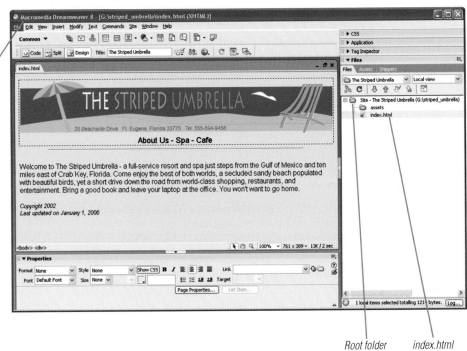

Root folder   index.html

Getting Started with Dreamweaver

FIGURE 20
Property inspector showing properties of The Striped Umbrella banner

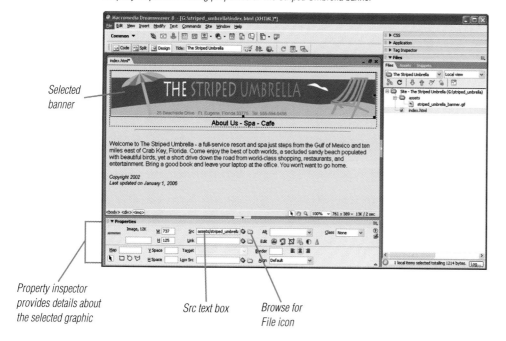

Selected banner

Property inspector provides details about the selected graphic

Src text box

Browse for File icon

Save a graphic in the assets folder

1. Click **The Striped Umbrella banner** to select it.

   The Src text box in the Property inspector displays the current location of the selected banner. The banner is linked to the data files folder, which is the original source for this file. You need to copy the banner to your assets folder and reset the link to your site. Otherwise, you will have linking problems when you publish the Web site.

2. Click the **Browse for File icon** 📁 next to the Src text box in the Property inspector, click the **Look in list arrow** (Win) or **navigation list arrow** (Mac), navigate to the assets folder in your Data Files folder for this chapter, click **striped_umbrella_banner.gif**, then click **OK** (Win) or **Choose** (Mac).

   The Striped Umbrella banner is automatically copied to the assets folder of The Striped Umbrella Web site, the folder that you designated as the default images folder. The Src text box now shows the path of the banner to the assets folder in the Web site.

3. Compare your screen to Figure 20.

   TIP If you do not see the striped_umbrella_banner.gif file listed in the Files panel, click the Refresh button 🔁 on the Files panel toolbar.

   Until you copy a graphic from an outside folder to your Web site, the graphic is not part of the Web site and the image will appear as a broken link on the page when the Web site is copied to a remote site.

You saved The Striped Umbrella banner in the assets folder.

Add pages to a Web site (Windows)

1. Click the **plus sign** to the left of the assets folder (if necessary) to open the folder and view its contents, striped_umbrella_banner.gif.

   TIP If you do not see any contents in the assets folder, click the Refresh button C on the Files panel toolbar.

2. Right-click the **striped_umbrella root folder**, click **New File**, type **about_us.html** to replace untitled.html, then press **[Enter]**.

   TIP If you create a new file in the Files panel, you must type the filename extension (.html) manually. If you create a new file using the File menu or the Start page, the filename extension will be added automatically.

3. Repeat Step 2 to add five more blank pages to The Striped Umbrella Web site, then name the new files **spa.html**, **cafe.html**, **activities.html**, **cruises.html**, and **fishing.html**.

   TIP Make sure to add the new files to the root folder, not the assets folder. If you accidentally add them to the assets folder, just drag them to the root folder.

4. Click the **Refresh button** C on the Files panel to list the files alphabetically, then compare your screen to Figure 21.

You added the following six pages to The Striped Umbrella Web site: about_us, activities, cafe, cruises, fishing, index, and spa.

FIGURE 21
New pages added to The Striped Umbrella Web site (Windows)

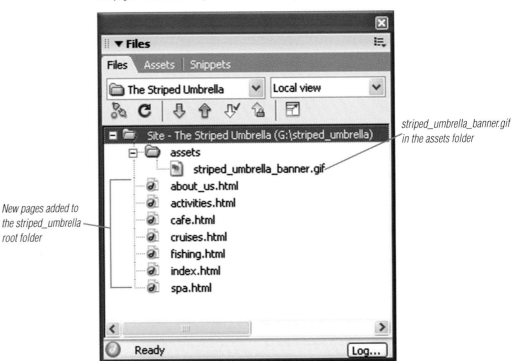

striped_umbrella_banner.gif in the assets folder

New pages added to the striped_umbrella root folder

FIGURE 22

New pages added to The Striped Umbrella Web site (Macintosh)

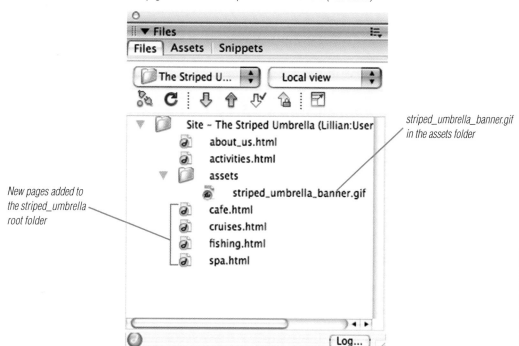

New pages added to the striped_umbrella root folder

striped_umbrella_banner.gif in the assets folder

CREATE AND VIEW
A SITE MAP

What You'll Do

 In this lesson, you will create and view a site map for The Striped Umbrella Web site.

Creating a Site Map

As you add new Web pages to a Web site, it is easy to lose track of how they all link together. You can use the site map feature to help you keep track of the relationships between pages in a Web site. A **site map** is a graphical representation of the pages in the Web site and shows the folder structure for the Web site. You can find out details about each page by viewing the visual clues in the site map. For example, the site map uses icons to indicate pages with broken links, e-mail links, and links to external Web sites. It also indicates which pages are currently **checked out,** or being used by other team members.

Viewing a Site Map

You can view a site map using the Map view in the Files panel. You can expand the Files panel to display both the site map and the Web site file list. You can specify that the site map show a filename or a page title for each page. You can also edit page titles in the site map. Figure 23 shows the site map and file list for The Striped Umbrella Web site. Only the home page and pages that are linked to the home page will display in the site map. As more child pages are added, the site map will display them using a **tree structure**, or a diagram that visually represents the way the pages are linked to each other.

DESIGNTIP **Verifying page titles**

When you view a Web page in a browser, its page title is displayed in the browser window title bar. The page title should reflect the page content and set the tone for the page. It is especially important to use words in your page title that are likely to match keywords viewers may enter when using a search engine. Search engines compare the text in page titles to the keywords typed into the search engine. When a title bar displays "Untitled Document", the designer has neglected to give the page a title. This is like giving up free "billboard space" and looks very unprofessional.

Using Site Map Images in Web Pages

It is very helpful to include a graphic of the site map in a Web site to help viewers understand the navigation structure of the site. Using Dreamweaver, you have the options of saving a site map for printing purposes or for displaying a site map on a page in a Web site. Windows users can save site maps as either a BMP (bitmapped) file or as a PNG (Portable Network Graphics) file. The BMP format is the best format to use for printing the site map or inserting it into a page layout program or slide show. The PNG format is best for inserting the site map on a Web page. Macintosh users can save site maps as PICT or JPEG file. The PICT format is the best format for printing the site map and inserting it into a page layout program or a slide show. The JPEG format is best for inserting the site map on a Web page. Though gaining in popularity, PNG files are not supported by older versions of browsers. However, they are capable of showing millions of colors, are small in size, and compress well without losing image quality.

FIGURE 23
The Striped Umbrella site map

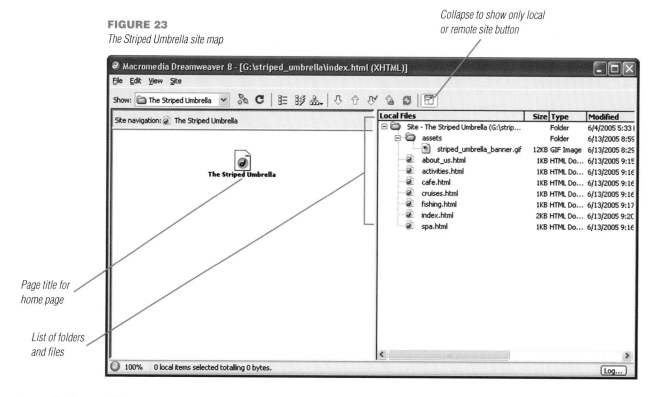

Collapse to show only local or remote site button

Page title for home page

List of folders and files

Select site map options

1. Click the **Site list arrow** next to The Striped Umbrella in the Files panel, click **Manage Sites**, click **The Striped Umbrella** (if necessary), then click **Edit** to open the Site Definition dialog box.

2. Click **Site Map Layout** in the Category list.

3. Verify that index.html is specified as the home page in the Home page text box, as shown in Figure 24.

   TIP If the index.html file is not specified as your home page, click the Browse for File icon next to the Home page text box, then locate and double-click index.html.

4. Click the **Page titles option button**.

5. Click **OK**, then click **Done**.

You designated index.html as the home page for The Striped Umbrella Web site to create the site map. You also specified that page titles display in the site map instead of filenames.

FIGURE 24
Options for the site map layout

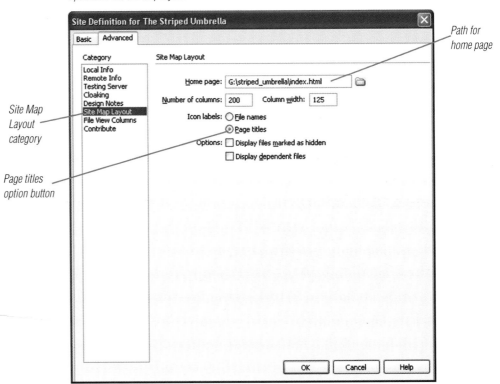

Site Map Layout category

Page titles option button

Path for home page

FIGURE 25
Expanding the site map

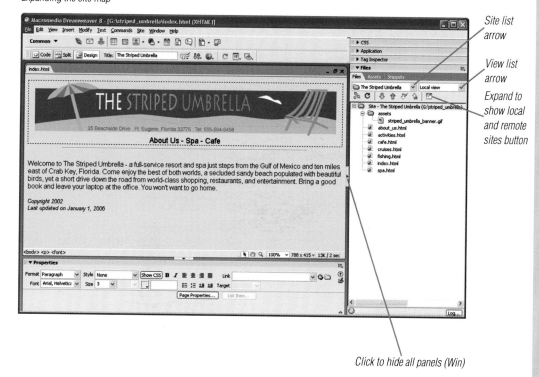

Site list arrow

View list arrow

Expand to show local and remote sites button

Click to hide all panels (Win)

1. Click the **Expand to show local and remote sites button** 🗗 on the Files panel toolbar, as shown in Figure 25, to display the expanded site map.

   The site map shows the home page and pages that are linked to it. Because there are no pages linked to the home page, the site map shows only the home page.

   TIP You can drag the border between the two panes on the screen to resize them.

2. Click the **Site map button**, then click **Map and Files** if you don't see the index page icon on the site map.

3. Click the **Collapse to show only local or remote site button** 🗗 on the toolbar to collapse the site map.

   The file list appears again in the Files panel.

4. Click **File** on the menu bar, then click **Exit** (Win) or click **Dreamweaver** on the menu bar, and then click **Quit Dreamweaver** (Mac).

   TIP If you are prompted to save changes, click No.

You opened and closed The Striped Umbrella site map in the Files panel.

Explore the Dreamweaver workspace.

1. Start Dreamweaver.
2. Create a new HTML document.
3. Change the view to Code view.
4. Change the view to Code and Design views.
5. Change the view to Design view.
6. Expand the Application panel group.
7. View each panel in the Application panel group.
8. Collapse the Application panel group.
9. Close the page without saving it.

View a Web page and use Help.

1. Open dw1_3.html from the folder where your Data Files are stored.
2. Locate the following page elements: a table, a banner, a graphic, and some formatted text.
3. Change the view to Code view.
4. Change the view to Design view.
5. Use the Dreamweaver Help feature to search for information on panel groups.
6. Display and read one of the topics you find.
7. Close the Dreamweaver 8 Help window.
8. Close the page without saving it.

Plan and define a Web site.

1. Select the drive and folder where you will store your Web site files using Windows Explorer or the Macintosh Finder.
2. Create a new root folder called **blooms**.
3. Close Windows Explorer or the Finder (Mac), then activate the Dreamweaver window.
4. Create a new site called **blooms & bulbs**.
5. Specify the blooms folder as the Local root folder.
6. Verify that the Refresh local file list automatically and the Enable cache check boxes are both selected.
7. Use the Remote Info category in the Site Definition for blooms & bulbs dialog box to set up Web server access. (Specify None if you do not have the necessary information to set up Web server access.)
8. Click OK, then click Done to close the Site Definition for blooms & bulbs dialog box.

Add a folder and pages and set the home page.

1. Create a new folder in the blooms root folder called **assets**.
2. Edit the site to set the assets folder as the default location for the Web site graphics.

3. Open dw1_4.html from the folder where your Data Files are stored, save this file in the blooms root folder as **index.html**, then click Yes to update the links.
4. Set index.html as the home page.
5. Select the blooms & bulbs banner on the page.
6. Use the Property inspector to browse for blooms_banner.jpg, then save it in the assets folder of the blooms & bulbs Web site.
7. Create seven new pages in the Files panel, and name them: **plants.html**, **classes.html**, **newsletter.html**, **annuals.html**, **perennials.html**, **water_plants.html**, and **tips.html**.
8. Refresh the view to list the new files alphabetically.

Create and view a site map.

1. Use the Site Definition dialog box to verify that the index.html file is shown as the home page.
2. View the expanded site map for the Web site.
3. Show the page titles.
4. Compare your screen to Figure 26.
5. Collapse the site map, save your work, then close index.html.

FIGURE 26
Completed Skills Review

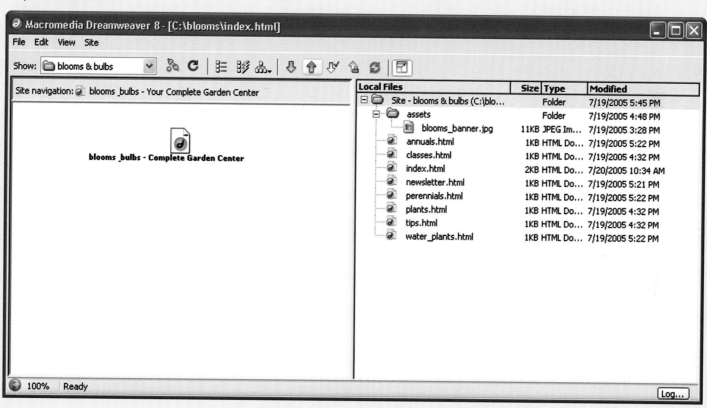

You have been hired to create a Web site for a travel outfitter called TripSmart. TripSmart specializes in travel products and services. In addition to selling travel products, such as luggage and accessories, they sponsor trips and offer travel advice. Their clients range from college students to families to vacationing professionals. The owner, Thomas Howard, has requested a dynamic Web site that conveys the excitement of traveling.

1. Using the information in the paragraph above, create a storyboard for this Web site, using either a pencil and paper or a software program such as Microsoft Word. Include the home page with links to four child pages named **catalog.html**, **newsletter.html**, **services.html**, and **destinations.html**. Include two child pages under the destinations page named **amazon.html** and **kenya.html**.

2. Create a new root folder named **tripsmart** in the drive and folder where you store your Web site files.

3. Start Dreamweaver, then create a Web site with the name **TripSmart**.

4. Create an assets folder and set it as the default location for images.

5. Open dw1_5.html from the location where your Data Files are stored, then save it in the tripsmart root folder as **index.html**.

6. Save the tripsmart_banner.jpg file in the assets folder.

7. Set index.html as the home page.

8. Create six additional pages for the site, and name them as follows: **catalog.html**, **newsletter.html**, **services.html**, **destinations.html**, **amazon.html**, and **kenya.html**. Use your storyboard and Figure 27 as a guide.

9. Refresh the Files panel.

10. View the site map for the Web site.

FIGURE 27
Completed Project Builder 1

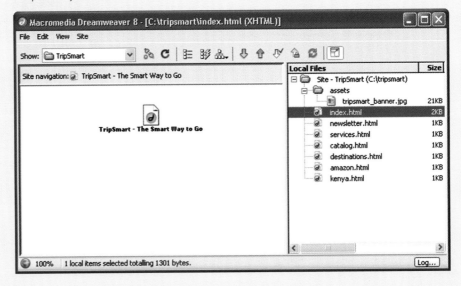

Your company has been selected to design a Web site for "emma's book bag," a small bookstore in rural Virginia. The owner of the bookstore, Emma Claire, specializes in children's books, although she stocks a large variety of other books. She has a small cafe in the store that serves drinks and light snacks.

1. Create a storyboard for this Web site that includes a home page and child pages named **events.html**, **books.html**, **cafe.html**, and **corner.html**. Create two more child pages under the events.html page called **signings.html** and **seasonal.html**.

2. Create a new root folder for the Web site in the drive and folder where you save your Web site files, then name it **book_bag**.

3. Create a Web site with the name **emma's book bag**.

4. Create an assets folder for the Web site and set the assets folder as the default location for images.

5. Open dw1_6.html from the chapter_1 Data Files folder, then save it as **index.html** in the book_bag folder.

6. Save the book_bag_banner.jpg file in the assets folder.

7. Set index.html as the home page, then add the title **emma's book bag** to the page.

8. Using Figure 28 and your storyboard as guides, create the additional pages shown for the Web site.

9. View the site map that displays page titles.

FIGURE 28
Completed Project Builder 2

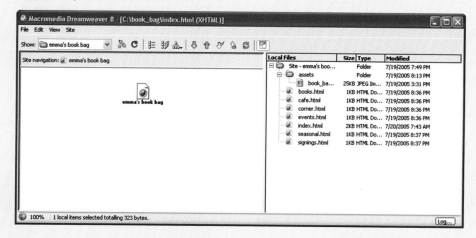

Figure 29 shows the Audi Web site, a past selection for the Macromedia Site of the Day. To visit the current Audi Web site, connect to the Internet, go to *www.course.com*, navigate to the page for this book, click the Online Companion link, then click the link for this chapter. The current page might differ from the figure because dynamic Web sites are updated frequently to reflect current information. If you are viewing the Web page on a screen whose resolution is set to 800 × 600, you will see that the design fits very well. The main navigation structure is accessed through the images along the right side of the page. The page title is Audi World Site.

Go to the Macromedia Web site at *www.macromedia.com*, click the Showcase link, then click the current Site of the Day. Explore the site and answer the following questions:

1. Do you see page titles for each page you visit?
2. Do the page titles accurately reflect the page content?
3. View the pages using more than one screen resolution, if possible. For which resolution does the site appear to be designed?

4. Is the navigation structure clear?
5. How is the navigation structure organized?

6. Why do you think this site was chosen as a Site of the Day?

FIGURE 29
Design Project

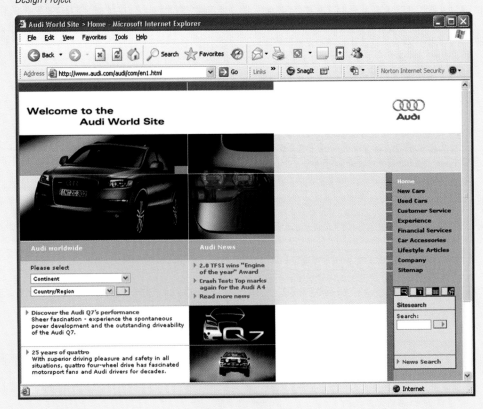

The Portfolio Project will be an ongoing project throughout the book, in which you will plan and create an original Web site without any data files. The focus of the Web site can be on any topic, organization, sports team, club, or company that you would like. You will build on this Web site from chapter to chapter, so you must do each Portfolio Project assignment in each chapter to complete your Web site. When you finish, you should have a completed Web site that would be an excellent addition to a professional portfolio.

1. Decide what type of Web site you would like to create. It can be a personal Web site about you, a business Web site that promotes a fictitious or real company, or an informational Web site that provides information about a topic, cause, or organization.

2. Write a list of questions and answers about the Web site you have decided to create.

3. Create a storyboard for your Web site to include at least four pages. The storyboard should include the home page with at least three child pages under it.

4. Create a root folder and an assets folder to house the Web site assets, then set it as the default location for images.

5. Create a blank page named **index.html** as a placeholder for the home page, then set it as the home page.

6. Begin collecting content, such as pictures or text to use in your Web site. You can use a digital camera to take photos, scan pictures, or create your own graphics using a program such as Macromedia Fireworks. Gather the content in a central location that will be accessible to you as you develop your site.

2

DEVELOPING A
WEB PAGE

1. Create head content and set page properties.

2. Create, import, and format text.

3. Add links to Web pages.

4. Use the History panel and edit code.

5. Modify and test Web pages.

Introduction

The process of developing a Web page requires several steps. If the page is a home page, you need to decide on the head content. The head content contains information used by search engines to help viewers find your Web site. You also need to choose the colors for the page background and the links. You then need to add the page content and format it attractively, and add links to other spages in the Web site or to other Web sites. To ensure that all links work correctly and are current, you need to test them regularly.

Understanding Page Layout

Before you add content to a page, consider the following guidelines for laying out pages:

Use White Space Effectively. A living room crammed with too much furniture makes it difficult to appreciate the individual pieces. The same is true of a Web page. Too many text blocks, links, and images can be distracting. Consider leaving some white space on each page. White space, which is not necessarily white, is the area on a Web page that contains no text or graphics.

Limit Multimedia Elements. Too many multimedia elements, such as graphics, video clips, or sounds, may result in a page that takes too much time to load. Viewers may leave your Web site before the entire page finishes loading. Use multimedia elements only if you have a good reason to.

Keep It Simple. Often the simplest Web sites are the most appealing and are also the easiest to create and maintain. A simple Web site that works well is far superior to a complex one that contains errors.

Use an Intuitive Navigation Structure. Make sure the navigation structure is easy to use. Viewers should always know where they are in the site and be able to find their way back to the home page. If viewers get lost, they may leave the site rather than struggle to find their way around.

Apply a Consistent Theme. To help give pages in your Web site a consistent appearance, consider designing your pages using elements that relate to a common theme. Consistency in the use of color and fonts, the placement of the navigation links, and the overall page design gives a Web site a unified look and promotes greater ease-of-use and accessibility. Template-based pages make this task much easier.

Tools You'll Use

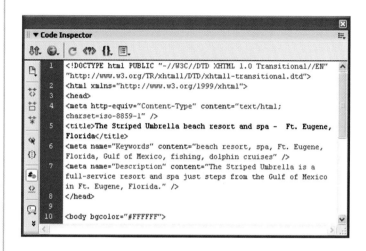

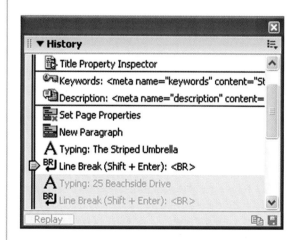

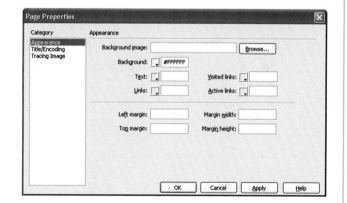

CREATE HEAD CONTENT AND
SET PAGE PROPERTIES

What You'll Do

 In this lesson, you will learn how to enter titles, keywords, and descriptions in the head content section of a Web page. You will also change the background color for a Web page.

Creating the Head Content

A Web page is composed of two distinct sections: the head content and the body. The **head content** includes the page title that is displayed in the title bar of the browser and some important page elements, called meta tags, that are not visible in the browser. Page titles are not to be confused with filenames, the name used to store each file on the server. **Meta tags** are HTML codes that include information about the page, such as keywords and descriptions. Meta tags are read by screen readers and are also used to provide the server information such as the PICS rating for the page. PICS is the acronym for **Platform for Internet Content Selection**. This is a rating system for Web pages that is similar to rating systems used for movies. **Keywords** are words that relate to the content of the Web site.

DESIGNTIP **Using Web-safe colors**

Before 1994, colors appeared differently on different types of computers. For instance, if a designer chose a particular shade of red in a document created on a Windows computer, he or she could not be certain that the same shade of red would appear on a Macintosh computer. In 1994, Netscape developed the first **Web-safe color palette**, a set of colors that appears consistently in all browsers and on Macintosh, Windows, and UNIX platforms. If you want your Web pages to be viewed across a wide variety of computer platforms, choose Web-safe colors for all your page elements. Dreamweaver has two Web-safe color palettes, Color Cubes and Continuous Tone, each of which contains 216 Web-safe colors. Color Cubes is the default color palette. To choose a different color palette, click Modify on the menu bar, click Page Properties, click the Appearance category, click the Background, Text, or Links color box to open the color picker, click the color picker list arrow, then click the color palette you want. This issue has become much less important today, however, with most computers capable of displaying millions of colors.

A **description** is a short paragraph that describes the content and features of the Web site. For instance, "beach" and "resort" would be appropriate keywords for The Striped Umbrella Web site. It is important to include concise, useful information in the head content, because search engines find Web pages by matching the title, description, and keywords in the head content of Web pages with keywords that viewers enter in search engine text boxes. The **body** is the part of the page that appears in a browser window. It contains all the page content that is visible to viewers, such as text, graphics, and links.

Setting Web Page Properties

When you create a Web page, one of the first design decisions that you should make is choosing the **background color**, or the color that fills the entire Web page. The background color should complement the colors used for text, links, and graphics that are placed on the page. Many times images are used for backgrounds for either the entire page or a part of the page, such as a table background. A strong contrast between the text color and the background color makes it easier for viewers to read the text on your Web page. You can choose a light background color and a dark text color, or a dark background color and a light text color. A white background with dark text, though not terribly exciting, provides good contrast and is the easiest to read for most viewers. Another design decision you need to make is whether to change the **default font** and **default link colors**, which are the colors used by the browser to display text, links,

and visited links. The default color for **unvisited links**, or links that the viewer has not clicked yet, is blue. In Dreamweaver, unvisited links are simply called **links**. The default color for **visited links**, or links that have been previously clicked, is purple. You change the background color, text, and link colors using the color picker in the Page Properties dialog box. You can choose colors from one of the five Dreamweaver color palettes, as shown in Figure 1.

QUICK TIP

Many design decisions are implemented through the use of Cascading Style Sheets, or CSS. We will initially use the Page Properties dialog box to set page properties such as the background color. Later we will learn to do this through the use of Cascading Style Sheets.

FIGURE 1
Color picker showing color palettes

Click list arrow to choose a color palette

Color Cubes
Continuous Tone
Windows OS
Mac OS
Grayscale
Snap to Web Safe

Web-safe palettes

DESIGNTIP   **Making pages accessible to viewers of all abilities**

Not all of your viewers will have perfect vision and hearing or full use of both hands. There are several techniques you can use to ensure that your Web site is accessible to individuals with disabilities. These techniques include using alternate text with graphic images, avoiding certain colors on Web pages, and supplying text as an alternate source for information that is presented in an audio file. Macromedia provides much information about Web site compliance with Section 508 accessibility guidelines. For more information, visit the Macromedia Web site at *www.macromedia.com/resources/accessibility/*.

Edit a page title

1. Start Dreamweaver, click the **Site list arrow** on the Files panel, then click **The Striped Umbrella** (if necessary).

2. Double-click **index.html** in the Files panel to open The Striped Umbrella home page, click **View** on the menu bar, then click **Head Content**.

   The Title icon ⁺▦ and Meta icon 🐾 are now visible in the head content section, as shown in Figure 2.

3. Click the **Title icon** ⁺▦ in the head content section.

   The page title The Striped Umbrella appears in the Title text box in the Property inspector.

4. Click at the end of The Striped Umbrella in the Title text box in the Property inspector, press **[Spacebar]**, type **beach resort and spa, Ft. Eugene, Florida**, then press **[Enter]** (Win) or **[return]** (Mac).

   Compare your screen with Figure 3. The new title is better, because it incorporates the words "beach resort" and "spa" and the location of the resort—words that potential customers might use as keywords when using a search engine.

   | TIP You can also change the page title using the Title text box on the Document toolbar.

   You opened The Striped Umbrella Web site, opened the home page in Design view, opened the head content section, and changed the page title.

FIGURE 2
Viewing the head content

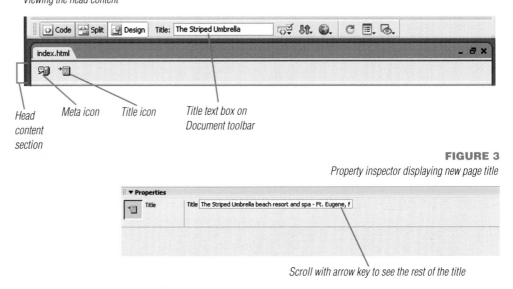

Head content section   Meta icon   Title icon   Title text box on Document toolbar

FIGURE 3
Property inspector displaying new page title

Scroll with arrow key to see the rest of the title

DESIGNTIP   Planning the page layout

When you begin developing the content for your Web site, you need to decide what content to include and how to arrange each element on each page. You must design the content with the audience in mind. What is the age group of your audience? What reading level is appropriate? Should you use a formal or informal tone? Should the pages be simple, containing mostly text, or rich with images and multimedia files? Your content should fit your target audience. Look at the font sizes used, the number and size of graphics used, the reading level, and the amount of technical expertise needed to navigate your site, then evaluate them to see if they fit your audience. If they do not, you will be defeating your purpose. Usually the first page that your audience will see when they visit your Web site is the home page. The home page should be designed so that viewers will feel "at home" and comfortable finding their way around the pages in your site. To ensure that viewers do not get lost in your Web site, make sure you design all the pages with a consistent look and feel. You can use templates to maintain a common look for each page. **Templates** are Web pages that contain the basic layout for each page in the site, including the location of a company logo or a menu of buttons.

FIGURE 4
Insert bar displaying the HTML category

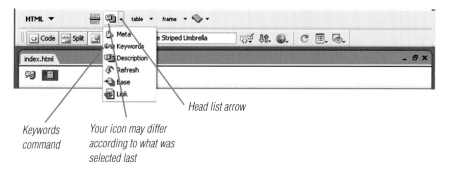

Head list arrow

Keywords command

Your icon may differ according to what was selected last

1. Click the **Insert bar list arrow**, then click **HTML**.

2. Click the **Head list arrow**, as shown in Figure 4, then click **Keywords**.

   TIP Some buttons on the Insert bar include a list arrow indicating that there is a menu of choices beneath the current button. The button that you select last will appear on the Insert bar until you select another.

3. Type **beach resort, spa, Ft. Eugene, Florida, Gulf of Mexico, fishing, dolphin cruises** in the Keywords text box, as shown in Figure 5, then click **OK**.

You added keywords relating to the beach to the head content of The Striped Umbrella home page.

FIGURE 5
Keywords dialog box

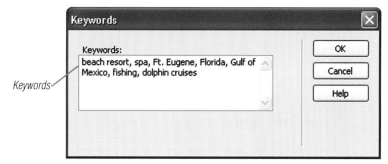

Keywords

DESIGNTIP **Entering keywords and descriptions**

Search engines use keywords, descriptions, and titles to find pages after a user enters search terms. Therefore, it is very important to anticipate the search terms your potential customers would use and include these words in the keywords, description, and title. Many search engines display page titles and descriptions in their search results. Some search engines limit the number of keywords that they will index, so make sure you list the most important keywords first. Keep your keywords and description short and concise to ensure that all search engines will include your site.

Enter a description

1. Click the **Head list arrow** on the Insert bar, then click **Description**.

2. Type **The Striped Umbrella is a full-service resort and spa just steps from the Gulf of Mexico in Ft. Eugene, Florida**.

   Your screen should resemble Figure 6.

3. Click **OK**.

4. Click the **Show Code view button** `< > Code`
   on the Document toolbar.

   Notice the title, keywords, and description appear in the HTML code in the document window, as shown in Figure 7.

   | TIP   You can also enter and edit the meta tags directly in the code in Code view.

5. Click the **Show Design view button** `Design`
   to return to Design view.

6. Click **View** on the menu bar, then click **Head Content** to close the head content section.

You added a description of The Striped Umbrella resort to the head content of the home page. You then viewed the home page in Code view and examined the HTML code for the head content.

FIGURE 6
Description dialog box

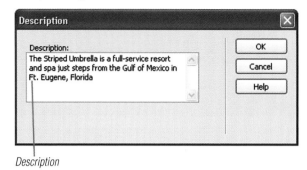

Description

FIGURE 7
Head content displayed in Code view

Opening HTML tag

Title tags

Head tag

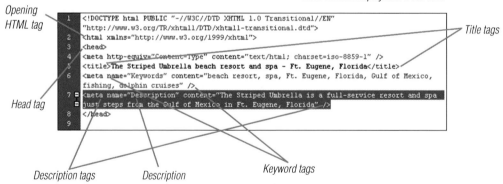

Description tags   Description   Keyword tags

FIGURE 8

Page Properties dialog box

Strikethrough
button

Background
color box

Hexadecimal
number for
white

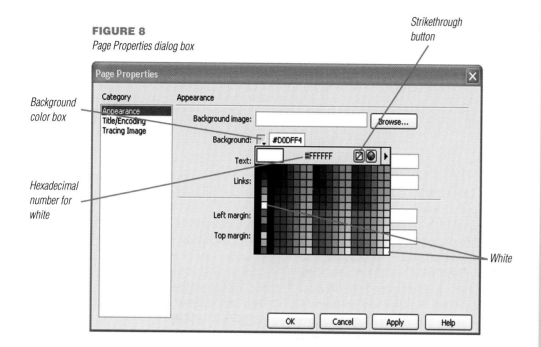

White

1. Click **Modify** on the menu bar, then click **Page Properties** to open the Page Properties dialog box.

2. Click the **Background color box** □ to open the color picker, as shown in Figure 8.

3. Click the last color in the bottom row (white).

4. Click **Apply**, then click **OK**.

    Clicking Apply lets you see the changes you made to the Web page without closing the Page Properties dialog box.

    TIP If you don't like the color you chose, click the Strikethrough button ⌧ in the color picker to switch back to the default color.

    The background color of the Web page is now white. The black text against the white background provides a nice contrast and makes the text easy to read.

You used the Page Properties dialog box to change the background color to white.

Understanding hexadecimal values

Each color is assigned a **hexadecimal value**, a value that represents the amount of red, green, and blue present in the color. For example, white, which is made of equal parts of red, green, and blue, has a hexadecimal value of FFFFFF. Each pair of characters in the hexadecimal value represents the red, green, and blue values. The hexadecimal number system is based on 16, rather than 10 in the decimal number system. Because the hexadecimal number system includes only numbers up to 9, values after 9 use the letters of the alphabet. "A" represents the number 10 in the hexadecimal number system. "F" represents the number 15.

CREATE, IMPORT, AND
FORMAT TEXT

What You'll Do

In this lesson, you will apply HTML heading styles and HTML text styles to text on The Striped Umbrella home page. You will also import an XHTML file and set text properties for the text on the new page.

Creating and Importing Text

Most information in Web pages is presented in the form of text. You can type text directly in Dreamweaver or copy and paste it from another software program. To import text from a Microsoft Word file, you use the Import Word Document command. Not only will the formatting be preserved, but clean HTML code will be generated. When you import text, it is important to keep in mind that visitors to your site must have the same fonts installed on their computers as the fonts applied to the imported text. Otherwise, the text may appear incorrectly. Some software programs may be able to convert text into graphics so that the text retains the same appearance no matter what fonts are installed. However, text converted into graphics is no longer editable. If text does

Using keyboard shortcuts

When working with text, the standard Windows keyboard shortcuts for Cut, Copy, and Paste are very useful. These are [Ctrl][X] (Win) or ⌘ [X] (Mac) for Cut, [Ctrl][C] (Win) or ⌘ [C] (Mac) for Copy, and [Ctrl][V] (Win) or ⌘ [V] (Mac) for Paste. You can view all Dreamweaver keyboard shortcuts using the Keyboard Shortcuts dialog box, which lets you view existing shortcuts for menu commands, tools, or miscellaneous functions, such as copying HTML or inserting an image. You can also create your own shortcuts or assign shortcuts that you are familiar with from using in other software programs. To view or modify keyboard shortcuts, click the Keyboard Shortcuts command on the Edit menu (Win) or Dreamweaver menu (Mac), then select the shortcut key set you want. The Keyboard Shortcuts feature is also available in Macromedia Fireworks and Flash. A printable version of all Dreamweaver keyboard shortcuts can be downloaded from the Dreamweaver Support Center at *www.macromedia.com/support/ dreamweaver/documentation/dwmx_shortcuts/.*

not have a font specified, the default font will apply. This means that the default font on the user's computer will be used to display the text. Keep in mind that some fonts may not be displayed the same on both a Windows and Macintosh computer. It is wise to stick to the standard fonts that work well with both systems.

Formatting Text Using the Property Inspector

Because text is more difficult and tiring to read on a computer screen than on a printed page, you should make the text in your Web site attractive and easy to read. You can format text in Dreamweaver by changing its font, size, and color, just as you would in other software programs. To apply formatting to text, you first select the text you want to enhance, and then use the Property inspector to apply formatting attributes, such as font type, size, color, alignment, and indents.

Changing Fonts

You can format your text with different fonts by choosing a font combination from the Font list in the Property inspector. A **font combination** is a set of three fonts that specify which fonts a browser should use to display the text of your Web page. Font combinations are used so that if one font is not available, the browser will use the next one specified in the font combination. For example, if text is formatted with the font combination Arial, Helvetica, sans serif, the browser will first look on the viewer's system for Arial. If Arial is not available, then it will look for Helvetica. If Helvetica is not available, then it will look for a sans-serif font to apply to the text. Using fonts within the default settings is wise, as fonts set outside the default settings may not be available on all viewers' computers.

Changing Font Sizes

There are two ways to change the size of text using the Property inspector. You can select a font size between 1 and 7 (where 1 is the smallest and 7 is the largest), or you can change the font size relative to the default base font. The **default base font** is size 3. For example, choosing +1 in the Size list increases the font size from 3 to 4. Choosing −1 decreases the font size from 3 to 2. Font sizes on Windows and Macintosh computers may differ slightly, so it's important to view your page on both platforms, if possible.

Formatting Paragraphs

You can format blocks of text as paragraphs or as different sizes of headings. To format a paragraph as a heading, click anywhere in the paragraph, then select the heading size you want from the Format list in the Property inspector. The Format list contains six different heading formats. Heading 1 is the largest size, and Heading 6 is the smallest size. Browsers display text formatted as headings in bold, setting them off from paragraphs of text. You can also align paragraphs with the alignment buttons on the Property inspector and indent paragraphs using the Text Indent and Text Outdent buttons on the Property inspector.

QUICKTIP

Avoid mixing too many different fonts and formatting attributes on a Web page. This can result in pages that are visually confusing and that may be difficult to read.

Using HTML Tags or Using CSS

The standard practice today is to use Cascading Style Sheets (CSS) to handle most of the formatting and placement of Web page objects. In fact, the default preference in Dreamweaver is to use CSS rather than HTML tags. However, this is a lot to learn when you are just beginning, so we are going to disable this preference temporarily until we study CSS in depth. At that point, we will select the default preference by clicking Edit (Win) or Dreamweaver (Mac) on the menu bar, then clicking Preferences.

Enter text

1. Position the insertion point directly after "want to go home." at the end of the paragraph, press **[Enter]** (Win) or **[return]** (Mac), then type **The Striped Umbrella**.

   Pressing [Enter] (Win) or [return] (Mac) creates a new paragraph. The HTML code for a paragraph break is <p>. The tag is closed with </p>.

2. Press and hold **[Shift]**, press **[Enter]** (Win) or **[return]** (Mac), then type **25 Beachside Drive**.

   Pressing and holding [Shift] while you press [Enter] (Win) or [return] (Mac) creates a line break. A line break places a new line of text on the next line down without creating a new paragraph. Line breaks are useful when you want to add a new line of text directly below the current line of text and keep the same formatting.

3. Add the following text below the 25 Beachside Drive text, using line breaks after each line:

   Ft. Eugene, Florida 33775

   (555) 594-9458

4. Compare your screen with Figure 9.

   You entered text for the address and telephone number on the home page.

FIGURE 9

Entering the address and telephone number on The Striped Umbrella home page

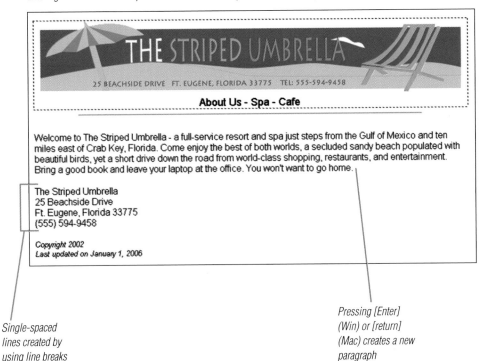

THE STRIPED UMBRELLA

25 BEACHSIDE DRIVE   FT. EUGENE, FLORIDA 33775   TEL: 555-594-9458

About Us - Spa - Cafe

Welcome to The Striped Umbrella - a full-service resort and spa just steps from the Gulf of Mexico and ten miles east of Crab Key, Florida. Come enjoy the best of both worlds, a secluded sandy beach populated with beautiful birds, yet a short drive down the road from world-class shopping, restaurants, and entertainment. Bring a good book and leave your laptop at the office. You won't want to go home.

The Striped Umbrella
25 Beachside Drive
Ft. Eugene, Florida 33775
(555) 594-9458

Copyright 2002
Last updated on January 1, 2006

Single-spaced lines created by using line breaks

Pressing [Enter] (Win) or [return] (Mac) creates a new paragraph

FIGURE 10

Formatting the address on The Striped Umbrella home page

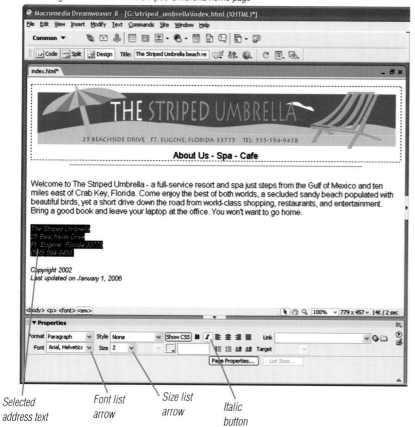

Selected
address text

Font list
arrow

Size list
arrow

Italic
button

1. Select the entire address and telephone number, as shown in Figure 10, then click the **Italic button** *I* in the Property inspector to italicize the text.

   When you have applied the italic style to selected text, the HTML code is <em>.

   > TIP To create bold text, the HTML tag is <strong></strong>; to underline text the HTML code is <u></u>.

2. With the text still selected, click the **Size list arrow**, click **2**, then compare your screen to Figure 10.

3. Save your work, then close the document.

You formatted the address and phone number for The Striped Umbrella by changing the font style to Italic and changing the size to 2.

Preventing data loss

When you are ready to stop working with a file in Dreamweaver, it is a good idea to save your changes, close the page or pages on which you are working, and exit Dreamweaver. Doing this will prevent the loss of data if power is interrupted. In some cases, loss of power can corrupt an open file and render it unusable.

Save graphics in the assets folder

1. Open dw2_1.html from your Data Files folder, save it as **spa.html** in the striped_umbrella folder, overwriting the existing file, then click **No** in the Update Links dialog box.

2. Select The Striped Umbrella banner.

   If you update the links, any links to graphics or hyperlinks on the page will remain linked to the data files location. Because you have the banner file in your Web site, the banner will correctly link to your folder, instead.

3. Click the broken link placeholder to select it, click the **Browse for File icon** [icon] next to the Src text box in the Property inspector, navigate to the chapter_2 assets folder, click **the_spa.jpg**, then click **OK** (Win) or **Choose** (Mac).

   Because you did not have this graphic in your Web site, it displayed as a broken link. You must use the Browse for File icon to select the source of the original graphic file. The file will automatically be copied to the assets folder of the Web site and be displayed on the page. You may have to deselect the new graphic to see it replace the broken placeholder.

4. Click the **Refresh button** [icon] on the Files panel toolbar, then click the **plus sign** (Win) or **expander arrow** (Mac) next to the assets folder in the Files panel, (if necessary).

   A copy of the_spa.jpg file is now in the assets folder, as shown in Figure 11.

You opened a new file and saved it as the new spa page. You changed the path of the new graphic to The Striped Umbrella assets folder.

FIGURE 11

Graphic file added to The Striped Umbrella assets folder

Expanded assets folder

The Spa graphic selected

Correct path for spa.jpg file

Choosing filenames for Web pages

When you choose a name for a Web page, you should use a descriptive name that reflects the contents of the page. For example, if the page is about your company's products, you could name it products.html. You should also follow some general rules for naming Web pages. For example, you should name the home page **index.html**. Most file servers look for the file named index.html to use as the initial page for a Web site. Do not use spaces, special characters, or punctuation in Web page filenames or the names of any graphics that will be inserted in your Web site. Spaces in filenames can cause errors when a browser attempts to read a file, and may cause your graphics to load incorrectly. You should also never use a number for the first character of a filename. To ensure that everything will load properly on all platforms, including UNIX, assume the filenames are case-sensitive and use lowercase characters. Files are saved with the .htm or .html file extension. Although either file extension is appropriate, the default file extension is .html. Use underscores in place of spaces. Forbidden characters include * & ^ % $ # @ ! / and \.

FIGURE 12
Clean Up Word HTML dialog box

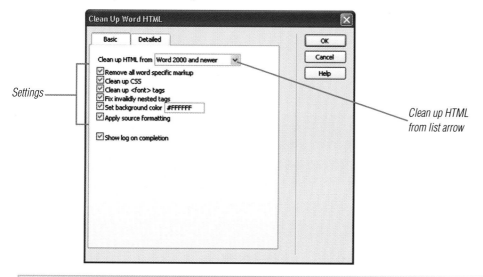

Settings

Clean up HTML
from list arrow

1. Click **Edit** (Win) or **Dreamweaver** (Mac) on the menu bar, click **Preferences**, then click **General** on the left (if necessary).

2. Verify that the Use CSS instead of HTML tags check box is not checked, then click **OK**.

   TIP It is very important to remove the check mark in the Use CSS instead of HTML tags check box at this time. After we explore CSS, we will restore this default preference. This is not a recommended practice. It is being suggested only to facilitate the learning process for a beginning Web designer.

3. Click to the right of the spa graphic on the spa.html page, then press **[Enter]** (Win) or **[return]** (Mac).

4. Click **File** on the menu bar, point to **Import**, click **Word Document**, navigate to the drive and folder where your Data Files are stored, double-click the **chapter_2 folder** (Win), then double-click **spa.doc** (Win), or navigate to the chapter_2 folder, double-click **spa.doc**, select all, copy, close spa.doc, and paste the copied text on the spa page in Dreamweaver (Mac).

5. Click **Commands** on the menu bar, then click **Clean Up Word HTML**.

   TIP If a dialog box appears stating that Dreamweaver was unable to determine the version of Word used to generate this document, click OK, click the Clean up HTML from list arrow, then choose a version of Word.

6. Make sure each check box in the Clean Up Word HTML dialog box is checked, as shown in Figure 12, click **OK**, then click **OK** again to close the Clean Up Word HTML Results window.

You imported a Word document then used the Clean Up Word HTML command.

Importing and Linking Microsoft Office documents

Macromedia has made enormous strides in providing for easy transfer of data between Microsoft Office documents and Dreamweaver Web pages. When importing a Word or Excel document, you click File on the menu bar, point to Import, then click either Word Document or Excel Document. Select the file you want to import, then click the Formatting list arrow to choose between importing Text only (unformatted text); Text with structure (unformatted text with structure intact); Text, structure, basic formatting (retains structure and simple HTML-formatted text); and Text, structure, full formatting (formatted text with structure intact and CSS styles) before you click Open. The option you choose depends on the importance of the original structure and formatting. Always use the Clean Up Word HTML command after importing a Word file. You can also create a link to a Word or Excel document on your Web page. To do so, drag the Word or Excel document from its current location to the location on the Web page where you would like the link to appear. (If the document is located outside the Web site, you can browse for it using the Site list arrow on the Files panel.) Next, select the Create a link option button in the Insert Document dialog box, then save the file in your root folder so it will be uploaded when you publish your site. If it is not uploaded, the link will be broken.

Set text properties

1. Click the **Insert bar list arrow**, click **Common**, then place the insertion point anywhere within the words "Spa Services".

2. Click the **Format list arrow** in the Property inspector, then click **Heading 4**.

   The Heading 4 format is applied to the paragraph. Even a single word is considered a paragraph if there is a hard return, or paragraph break, after it. The HTML code for a Heading 4 tag is <h4>. The tag is then closed with </h4>. The level of the heading tag follows the h, so the code for a Heading 1 tag is <h1>.

3. Click the **Align Center button** in the Property inspector to center the heading.

   When the paragraph is centered, the HTML code align="center" is added to the <p> tag.

4. Select the words "Spa Services", click the **Font list arrow**, then click **Arial, Helvetica, sans-serif**.

   Because setting a font is a character command, you must select all the characters you want to format before applying a font.

   | TIP   You can modify the font combinations in the Font list by clicking Text on the menu bar, pointing to Font, then clicking Edit Font List.

5. With the heading still selected, click the **Text Color button** in the Property inspector to open the color picker, then click the dark blue color in the third row of the first column (#000066). The HTML code

   (continued)

FIGURE 13
Formatted Spa Services text

added when the font color is designated is <font color="#000066">. The tag is closed with </font>.

> TIP You can also type #000066 in the color text box in the Property inspector to select the color in Step 5.

6. Click to the left of the O in Our spa services, press and hold **[Shift]**, scroll to the end of the text, click to place the insertion point after the end of the last sentence on the page, then release **[Shift]**.

7. Click the **Font list arrow** in the Property inspector, click **Arial, Helvetica, sans-serif**, click the **Size list arrow** in the Property inspector, then click **3**.

> TIP To change the size of selected text, use either the Format list arrow or the Size list arrow, but not both.

8. Click anywhere on the page to deselect the text, save your work, then compare your screen to Figure 13.

9. Close the spa page.

You formatted the Spa Services text using the Heading 4 style and the Arial, Helvetica, sans-serif font combination. Next, you centered the heading on the page and changed the text color to a dark blue. You then selected the rest of the text on the page and changed it to the Arial, Helvetica, sans-serif font combination with a text size of 3.

DESIGNTIP **Choosing fonts**

There are two classifications of fonts: sans-serif and serif. **Sans-serif fonts** are block-style characters that are often used for headings and subheadings. The headings in this book use a sans-serif font. Examples of sans-serif fonts include Arial, Verdana, and Helvetica. **Serif fonts** are more ornate and contain small extra strokes at the beginning and end of the characters. Some people consider serif fonts easier to read in printed material, because the extra strokes lead your eye from one character to the next. This paragraph you are reading uses a serif font. Examples of serif fonts include Times New Roman, Times, and Georgia. Many designers feel that a sans-serif font is preferable when the content of a Web site is primarily intended to be read on the screen, but that a serif font is preferable if the content will be printed. When you choose fonts, you need to keep in mind the amount of text each page will contain and whether most viewers will read the text on-screen or print it out. A good rule of thumb is to limit each Web site to no more than three font variations. Using more than three may make your Web site look unprofessional and suggest the "ransom note effect." The phrase **ransom note effect** implies that fonts have been randomly used in a document without regard to style, similar to a ransom note made up of words cut from various sources and pasted onto a page.

ADD LINKS TO
WEB PAGES

What You'll Do

 In this lesson, you will open the home page and add links to the navigation bar that link to the About Us, Spa, Cafe, and Activities pages. You will then insert an e-mail link at the bottom of the page and create page titles for the untitled pages in the site map.

Adding Links to Web Pages

Links provide the real power for Web pages. Links make it possible for viewers to navigate through all the pages in a Web site and to connect to other pages anywhere on the Web. Viewers are more likely to return to Web sites that have a user-friendly navigation structure. Viewers also enjoy Web sites that have interesting links to other Web pages or other Web sites.

To add links to a Web page, first select the text or graphic that you want to serve as a link, then specify a path to the page to which you want to link in the Link text box in the Property inspector. After you add all your links, you can open the site map to see a diagram of how the linked pages relate to each other.

When you create links on a Web page, it is important to avoid **broken links**, or links that cannot find their intended destinations. You can accidentally cause a broken link by typing the incorrect address for the link in the Link text box. Broken links are often caused by companies merging, going out of business, or simply moving their Web site addresses.

In addition to adding links to your pages, you should provide a **point of contact**, or a place on a Web page that provides viewers with a means of contacting the company. A common point of contact is a **mailto: link**, which is an e-mail address that viewers with questions or problems can use to contact someone at the company's headquarters.

Using Navigation Bars

A **navigation bar** is an area on a Web page that contains links to the main pages of a Web site. Navigation bars are usually located at the top or side of the main pages of a Web site and can be created with text, graphics, or a combination of the two. To make navigating through a Web site as easy as possible, you should place navigation bars in the same position on each Web page. Navigation bars are the backbone of a Web site's navigation structure, which includes all navigation aids for moving around a Web site. You can, however, include additional links to the main pages of the Web site elsewhere on the page. The Web page in Figure 14 shows an example of a navigation bar that contains both text and graphic links that use JavaScript. Notice that when the mouse is placed on an item at the top of the navigation bar, a menu appears.

Navigation bars can also be simple and contain only text-based links to the pages in the site. You can create a simple navigation bar by typing the names of your Web site's pages at the top of your Web page, formatting the text, and then adding links to each page name. It is always a good idea to provide plain text links for accessibility regardless of the type of navigation structure you choose to use.

FIGURE 14
Coca-Cola Web site

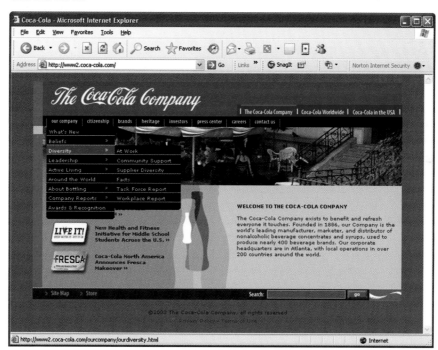

Create a navigation bar

1. Open index.html (the home page).

2. Position the insertion point to the left of "A" in About Us then drag to select About Us - Spa - Cafe.

3. Type **Home - About Us - Spa - Cafe - Activities,** as shown in Figure 15.

   These five text labels will serve as a navigation bar. You will add the links later.

You created a new navigation bar using text, replacing the original navigation bar.

Format a navigation bar

1. Select **Home - About Us - Spa - Cafe - Activities**, click the **Size list arrow** in the Property inspector, then click **None**.

   None is equal to size 3, the default text size. The None setting eliminates any prior size formatting that was applied to the text.

   TIP If your Property inspector is not displayed, click Window on the menu bar, then click Properties to open it.

2. Click the **Format list arrow** in the Property inspector, then click **Heading 4**.

3. Click the **Font list arrow** in the Property inspector, click **Arial, Helvetica, sans-serif** (if necessary), deselect the text, then compare your screen to Figure 16.

   TIP An asterisk after the filename in the title bar indicates that you have altered the page since you last saved it. After you save your work, the asterisk will disappear.

You formatted the new navigation bar, using a heading and a font combination.

FIGURE 15
Viewing the new navigation bar

New navigation bar

FIGURE 16
Formatting the navigation bar

New navigation bar

Format list arrow

Font list arrow

Property inspector

Size list arrow

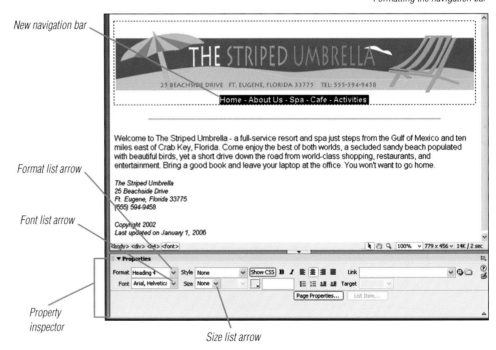

Developing a Web Page

FIGURE 17
Selecting the Home link

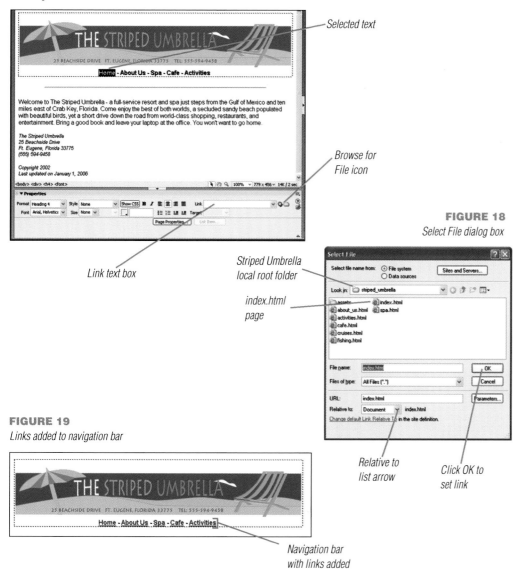

Selected text

Browse for
File icon

Link text box

FIGURE 19

Links added to navigation bar

Navigation bar
with links added

FIGURE 18

Select File dialog box

Striped Umbrella
local root folder

index.html
page

Relative to
list arrow

Click OK to
set link

Add links to Web pages

1. Double-click **Home** to select it, as shown in Figure 17.

2. Click the **Browse for File icon** 🗁 next to the Link text box in the Property inspector, then navigate to the striped_umbrella root folder (if necessary).

3. Verify that the link is set Relative to Document in the Select File dialog box.

4. Click **index.html** as shown in Figure 18, click **OK** (Win) or **Choose** (Mac), then click anywhere on the page to deselect Home.

   Home now appears in blue with an underline, indicating it is a link. However, clicking Home will not open a new page because the link is to the home page. It might seem odd to create a link to the same page on which the link appears, but this will be helpful when you copy the navigation bar to other pages in the site. Always provide viewers a link to the home page.

5. Repeat Steps 1–4 to create links for About Us, Spa, Cafe, and Activities to their corresponding pages in the striped_umbrella root folder.

6. When you finish adding the links to the other four pages, deselect all, then compare your screen to Figure 19.

You created a link for each of the five navigation bar elements to their respective Web pages in The Striped Umbrella Web site.

Create an e-mail link

1. Place the insertion point after the last digit in the telephone number, then insert a line break.

2. Click the **Insert bar list arrow**, click **Common** (if necessary), then click the **Email Link button** ☐ on the Insert bar to insert an e-mail link.

3. Type **Club Manager** in the Text text box, type **manager@stripedumbrella.com** in the E-Mail text box, as shown in Figure 20, then click **OK** to close the Email Link dialog box.

4. Save your work.

   Notice that the link in the Property inspector for the e-mail link shows mailto: manager@striped_umbrella.com. When clicked, this link will automatically open the default e-mail software on the viewer's computer for him to type his e-mail message. See Figure 21.

   > TIP   You must enter the correct e-mail address in the E-Mail text box for the link to work. However, you can enter any descriptive name, such as customer service or Bob Smith in the Text text box. You can also enter the e-mail address as the text if you want to show the actual e-mail address on the Web page.

You inserted an e-mail link to serve as a point of contact for The Striped Umbrella.

FIGURE 20
Email Link dialog box

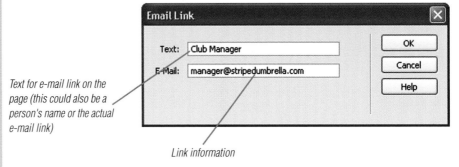

Text for e-mail link on the page (this could also be a person's name or the actual e-mail link)

Link information

FIGURE 21
mailto: link on the Property inspector

mailto: link

FIGURE 22

The Striped Umbrella site map

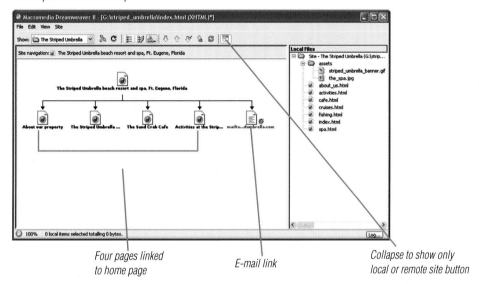

*Four pages linked
to home page*   *E-mail link*   *Collapse to show only
local or remote site button*

View the linked pages in the site map

1. Click the **Expand to show local and remote sites button** on the Files panel to expand the site map.

    The site map shows the home page, the four pages that are linked to it, and the e-mail link on the home page.

    > TIP If you don't see the site map on the left window, click the Site Map button, then click Map and Files.

2. Click **View** on the Files panel menu bar, point to **Site Map Options**, then click **Show Page Titles** (Win), or click the **Files panel list arrow**, point to **View**, point to **Site Map Options**, then click **Show Page Titles** (Mac) (if necessary).

3. Select the first Untitled Document page in the site map, click the words **Untitled Document**, type **About our property**, then press **[Enter]** (Win) or **[return]** (Mac).

    When you select a page title in the site map, the corresponding file is selected in the Local Files panel. Be careful before entering a new page title in the Site map. If the option is set to file names rather than page titles, you will accidentally change the filename.

4. Repeat Step 3 for the other two Untitled Document pages, naming them **The Sand Crab Cafe** and **Activities at The Striped Umbrella**, as shown in Figure 22.

5. Click the **Collapse to show only local or remote site button** on the toolbar to collapse the site map.

You viewed the site map and added page titles to the untitled pages.

USE THE HISTORY
PANEL AND EDIT CODE

What You'll Do

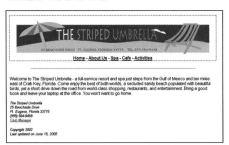

 In this lesson, you will use the History panel to undo formatting changes you make to a horizontal rule. You will then use the Code Inspector to view the HTML code for the horizontal rule. You will also insert a date object and then view its code in the Code Inspector.

Using the History Panel

Throughout the process of creating a Web page, it's likely that you will make mistakes along the way. Fortunately, you have a tool named the History panel to undo your mistakes. The **History panel** records each editing and formatting task performed and displays them in a list in the order in which they were completed. Each task listed in the History panel is called a **step**. You can drag the **slider** on the left side of the History panel to undo or redo steps, as shown in Figure 23. You can also click in the gray bar to the left of a step to undo all steps below it. If you click on the step itself, you will select that step. By default, the History panel records 50 steps. You can change the number of steps the History panel records in the General category of the Preferences dialog box. However, keep in mind that setting this number too high might require additional memory and could hinder the way Dreamweaver operates.

Understanding other History panel features

Dragging the slider up and down in the History panel is a quick way to undo or redo steps. However, the History panel offers much more. It has the capability to "memorize" certain tasks and consolidate them into one command. This is a useful feature for steps that are executed repetitively on Web pages. Some Dreamweaver features, such as drag and drop, cannot be recorded in the History panel and have a red "x" placed next to them. The History panel does not show steps performed in the Files panel.

Viewing HTML Code in the Code Inspector

If you enjoy writing code, you occasionally might want to make changes to Web pages by entering the code rather than using the panels and tools in Design view. You can view the code in Dreamweaver using Code view, Code and Design views, or the Code Inspector. The **Code Inspector**, shown in Figure 24, is a separate window that displays the current page in Code view. The advantage of using the Code Inspector is that you can see a full-screen view of your page in Design view while viewing the underlying code in a floating window that you can resize and position wherever you want.

You can add advanced features, such as JavaScript functions, to Web pages by copying and pasting code from one page to another in the Code Inspector. A **JavaScript** function is a block of code that adds dynamic content such as rollovers or interactive forms to a Web page. A **rollover** is a special effect that changes the appearance of an object when the mouse "rolls over" it.

QUICK TIP

If you are new to HTML, you can use the Reference panel to find answers to your HTML questions. The Reference panel is part of the Code panel group and contains many resources besides HTML help, such as JavaScript help.

FIGURE 23
The History panel

Slider

Click in the gray bar next to a step to undo to that step

FIGURE 24
Code Inspector

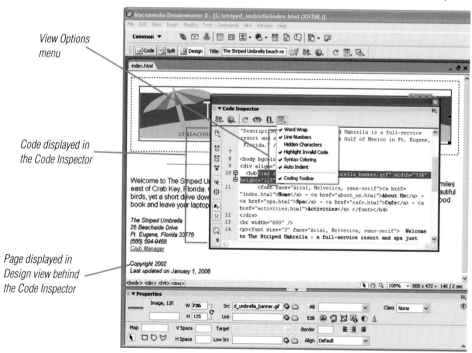

View Options menu

Code displayed in the Code Inspector

Page displayed in Design view behind the Code Inspector

Use the History panel

1. Click **Window** on the menu bar, then click **History**.

   The History panel opens and displays steps you have recently performed.

2. Click the **History panel list arrow**, click **Clear History**, as shown in Figure 25, then click **Yes** to close the warning box (if necessary).

3. Select the horizontal rule on the home page.

   A **horizontal rule** is a line used to separate page elements or to organize information on a page.

4. Select the number in the W text box, type **90**, click the list arrow next to the W text box, click **%**, press **[Tab]**, then compare your screen to Figure 26.

5. Using the Property inspector, change the width of the horizontal rule to 80%, click the **Align list arrow**, then click **Left**.

6. Drag the **slider** on the History panel up to Set Width: 90%, as shown in Figure 27.

   The bottom two steps in the History panel appear gray, indicating that these steps have been undone.

7. Click the **History panel list arrow**, then click **Close panel group** to close the History panel.

   You formatted the horizontal rule, made changes to it, then used the History panel to undo some of the changes.

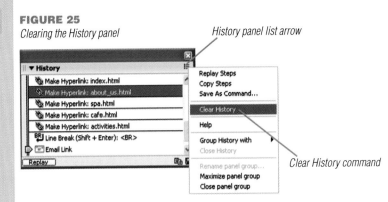

FIGURE 25
Clearing the History panel

History panel list arrow

Clear History command

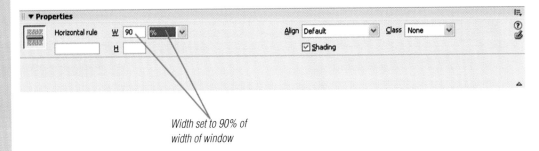

FIGURE 26
Property inspector settings for horizontal rule

Width set to 90% of width of window

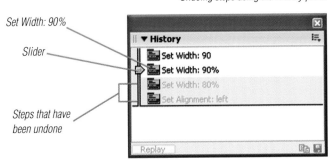

FIGURE 27
Undoing steps using the History panel

Set Width: 90%

Slider

Steps that have been undone

Developing a Web Page

FIGURE 28
Viewing the View Options menu in the Code Inspector

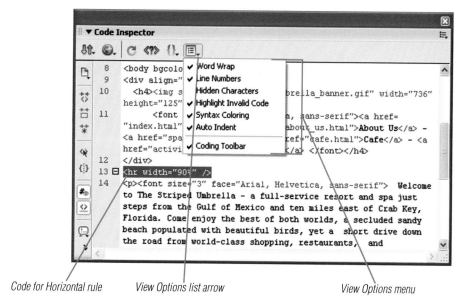

Code for Horizontal rule   View Options list arrow   View Options menu

1. Click the **horizontal rule** to select it (if necessary), click **Window** on the menu bar, then click **Code Inspector**.

   The Code Inspector highlights the code for the horizontal rule.

   > TIP   You can also press [F10] to display the Code Inspector.

2. Click the **View Options list arrow** on the Code Inspector toolbar to display the View Options menu, then click **Word Wrap** (if necessary), to activate Word Wrap.

   The Word Wrap feature forces text to stay within the confines of the Code Inspector window, allowing you to read without scrolling sideways.

3. Click the **View Options list arrow**, then verify that the Word Wrap, Line Numbers, Highlight Invalid Code, Syntax Coloring, Auto Indent, and the Coding Toolbar menu items are checked, as shown in Figure 28.

4. Replace the 90% horizontal rule width in the code with 80%.

5. Click **Refresh** in the Property inspector.

   After typing in the Code Inspector, you must refresh your changes to see them.

You changed the width of the horizontal rule by changing the code in the Code Inspector.

Use the Reference panel

1. Click the **Reference button** <?> on the Code Inspector toolbar, as shown in Figure 29, to open the Results panel group with the Reference panel displayed.

   TIP Verify that the horizontal rule is still selected, or you will not see the horizontal rule description in the Reference panel.

2. Read the information about horizontal rules in the Reference panel, as shown in Figure 30, right-click the **Results panel group title bar**, then click **Close panel group** (Win) or click the **Results panel option list** in the Results panel title bar, then click **Close panel group** (Mac) to close the Results panel group.

3. Close the Code Inspector.

You read information about horizontal rule settings in the Reference panel.

FIGURE 29
Reference button on the Code Inspector toolbar

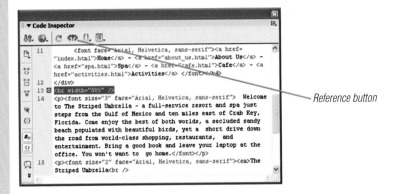

Reference button

FIGURE 30
Viewing the Reference panel

Information on HR (horizontal rule) tag

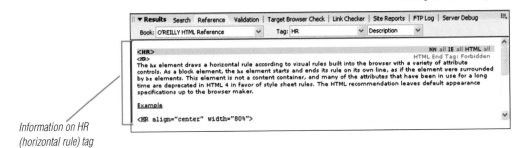

Inserting comments

A handy Dreamweaver feature is the ability to insert comments into HTML code. Comments can provide helpful information describing portions of the code, such as a JavaScript function. You can create comments in any Dreamweaver view, but you must turn on Invisible Elements to see them in Design view. To create a comment, click the Insert bar list arrow, click Common, click the Comment button, type a comment in the Comment dialog box, then click OK. Comments are not visible in browser windows.

Developing a Web Page

FIGURE 31
Insert Date dialog box

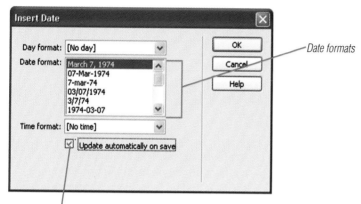

Date formats

Update automatically
on save check box

FIGURE 32
Viewing the date object in Code view

```
21  <p><em><font size="2" face="Arial, Helvetica, sans-serif">Copyright 2002<br />
22     Last updated on
23        <!-- #BeginDate format:Am1 -->June 13, 2005<!-- #EndDate -->
24  </font></em></p>
25  </body>
26  </html>
27
```

Code for date object

Insert a date object

1. Scroll down, if necessary, to select January 1, 2006, then press **[Delete]** (Win) or **[delete]** (Mac).

2. Click the **Date button** 🔲 on the Insert bar, then click **March 7, 1974** in the Date format text box.

3. Click the **Update automatically on save check box**, as shown in Figure 31, then click **OK**.

4. Click the **Show Code and Design views button** 🔲 Split.

   Notice that the code has changed to reflect the date object, which is set to today's date, as shown in Figure 32. (Your date will be different.)

5. Return to Design view.

You inserted a date object that will be updated automatically when you open and save the home page.

MODIFY AND TEST
WEB PAGES

What You'll Do

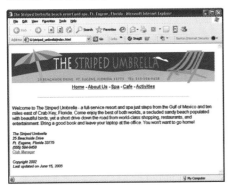

In this lesson, you will preview the home page in the browser to check for typographical errors, grammatical errors, broken links, and overall appearance. After previewing, you will make slight formatting adjustments to the page to improve its appearance.

Testing and Modifying Web Pages

Testing Web pages is a continuous process. You never really finish a Web site, as there are always additions and corrections to make. As you add and modify pages, you must test each page as part of the development process. The best way to test a Web page is to preview it in a browser window to make sure that all text and graphic elements appear the way you expect them to. You should also test your links to make sure they work properly. You also need to proofread your text to make sure it contains all the necessary information for the page and no typographical or grammatical errors. Designers typically view a page in a browser, return to Design view to make necessary changes, then view the page in a browser again. This process may be repeated many times before the page is ready for publishing. In fact, it is sometimes difficult to stop making improvements to a page and move on to another project. You need to strike a balance among quality, creativity, and productivity.

DESIGNTIP **Using "Under Construction" pages**

Many people are tempted to insert an unfinished page as a placeholder for a page that will be finished later. Rather than have real content, these pages usually contain text or a graphic that indicates the page is not finished, or "under construction." You should not publish a Web page that has a link to an unfinished page. It is frustrating to click a link for a page you want to open only to find an "under construction" note or graphic displayed. You want to make the best possible impression on your viewing audience. If you cannot complete a page before publishing it, at least provide enough information on it to make it "worth the trip."

Testing a Web Page Using Different Browsers

Because users access the Internet using a wide variety of computer systems, it is important to design your pages so that all browsers and screen sizes can display them well. You should test your pages using different browsers and a wide variety of screen sizes and resolutions to ensure the best view of your page by all types of computer equipment. Although the most common screen size that designers use today is 800×600, many viewers view at 1024×768. A page that is designed for a screen resolution of 800×600 will look much better at that setting than at a higher one. Many designers place a statement such as "this Web site is best viewed at 800×600" on the home page. To view your page using different screen sizes, click the Window Size pop-up menu in the middle of the status bar (Win) or at the bottom of the document window (Mac), then choose the setting you want to use. Table 1 lists the Dreamweaver default window screen sizes. Remember also to check your pages using Windows and Macintosh platforms. Some page elements such as fonts, colors, table borders, layers, and horizontal rules may not appear consistently in both.

TABLE 1: Dreamweaver Default Window Screen Sizes

window size (inside dimensions of the browser window without borders)	monitor size
592W	
536×196	640×480, default
600×300	640×480, maximized
760×420	800×600, maximized
795×470	832×624, maximized
955×600	1024×768, maximized
544×378	Web TV

Modify a Web page

1. Click the **Restore Down button** on the index.html title bar to decrease the size of the home page window (Win) or skip to Step 2 (Mac).

2. Click the **Window Size list arrow** on the status bar, as shown in Figure 33, then click **600 × 300 (640 × 480, Maximized)**, if necessary.

   A viewer using this setting will be forced to use the horizontal scroll bar to view the entire page. This should be avoided, but very few people view at this resolution anymore.

   TIP You cannot use the Window Size options if your document window is maximized (Win).

3. Click the **Window Size list arrow**, click **760 × 420 (800 × 600, Maximized)**.

4. Replace the period after the last sentence, "You won't want to go home." with an exclamation point.

5. Shorten the horizontal rule to 75%.

6. Click the **Maximize button** on the index.html title bar to maximize the home page window.

7. Save your work.

You viewed the home page using two different window sizes and you made simple formatting changes to the page.

FIGURE 33
Window screen sizes

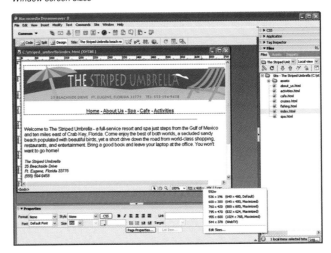

Using design principles in Web page layout

As you view your pages in the browser, take a critical look at the symmetry of the page. Is it balanced? Are there too many graphics compared to text or vice versa? Does everything "heavy" seem to be on the top or bottom of the page, or do the page elements seem to balance with the weight evenly distributed between the top, bottom, and sides of the page? There are many design principles that will help guide you to create a site-wide consistency for your pages. Horizontal symmetry means that the elements are balanced across the page. Vertical symmetry means that they are balanced down the page. Diagonal symmetry balances page elements along the invisible diagonal line of the page. Radial symmetry runs from the center of the page outward, like the petals of a flower. These principles all deal with balance; however, too much balance is not good, either. Sometimes it adds interest to place page elements a little off center or to have an asymmetric layout. Color, white space, text, and graphics should all complement each other and provide a natural flow across and down the page. The rule of thirds—dividing a page into nine squares like a tic-tac-toe grid—states that interest is increased when your focus is on one of the intersections in the grid.

FIGURE 34
Viewing The Striped Umbrella home page in the Firefox browser

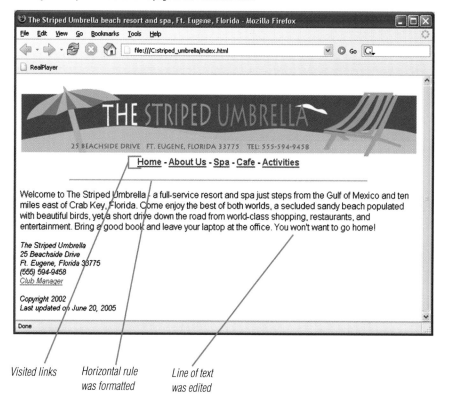

Visited links   Horizontal rule   Line of text
             was formatted   was edited

Test Web pages by viewing them in a browser

1. Click the **Preview/Debug in browser button** 🌐. on the Document toolbar, then choose your browser from the menu that opens.

   The Striped Umbrella home page opens in your default browser.

2. Click all the links on the navigation bar, then after each click, use the Back button on the browser toolbar to return to the home page.

   Pages with no content at this point will appear as blank pages. Compare your screen to Figure 34.

3. Close your browser window.

You viewed The Striped Umbrella home page in your browser and tested each link on the navigation bar.

DESIGNTIP **Choosing a window size**

The 640 × 480 window size is not used by many viewers today. The 800 × 600 window setting is used on 15-inch monitors and some 17-inch monitors. Most consumers have at least a 15-inch monitor at their homes or offices, making this window size a good choice for a Web page. However, because more viewers are viewing at a 1024 resolution or higher, even if you are designing to an 800 × 600 window size, you can make sure that the pages will still view well at a higher resolution by placing the page content in a table with a fixed width. This will keep the content from spreading out too much when viewed in a larger window.

Create head content and set Web page properties.

1. Open the blooms & bulbs Web site.
2. Open the index page and view the head content.
3. Change the page title to **blooms & bulbs - Your Complete Garden Center**.
4. Insert the following keywords: **garden, plants, nursery, flowers, landscape**, and **blooms & bulbs**.
5. Insert the following description: **blooms & bulbs is a premier supplier of garden plants for both professional and home gardeners.**
6. Switch to Code view to view the HTML code for the head content, then switch back to Design view.
7. Open the Page Properties dialog box to view the current page properties.
8. Change the background color to a color of your choice.
9. Change the background color to white again, then save your work.

Create, import, and format text.

1. Select the current navigation bar and replace it with **Home, Featured Plants, Garden Tips**, and **Classes**. Use the [Spacebar] and a hyphen to separate the items.
2. Using the Property inspector, apply the Heading 4 format to the navigation bar.

3. Create a new paragraph after the paragraph of text and type the following text, inserting a line break after each line.
   blooms & bulbs
   Highway 43 South
   Alvin, Texas 77511
   (555) 248-0806
4. Italicize the address and phone number lines and change the font to Arial, Helvetica, sans-serif and the size to 2.
5. Change the copyright and last updated statements to size 2.
6. Save your work, then close the home page.
7. Open dw2_2.html and save it as **tips.html** in the blooms & bulbs Web site, overwriting the existing file, but not updating links.
8. Click the broken image link below the blooms & bulbs banner, browse to the chapter_2 Data Files folder, find the garden_tips.jpg in the assets folder of the blooms folder, then click OK to save it in the blooms & bulbs Web site.
9. Place the insertion point under the Garden Tips graphic.
10. Import gardening_tips.doc from the drive and folder where your chapter 2 Data Files are stored, using the Import Word Document command, then use the Clean Up Word HTML command. (*Hint*: The Use CSS instead of HTML tags should be turned off before executing the following steps.)
11. Format all of the text on the page using the following attributes: Font: Arial, Helvetica, sans-serif, Alignment: Align Left, and Style: None.

12. Select the Seasonal Gardening Checklist heading, then use the Property inspector to center the text.
13. Use the Property inspector to format the selected text with a Heading 3 format.
14. Apply the color #003366 (the second color in the third row) to the text.
15. Select the rest of the text on the page except for the Seasonal Gardening Checklist heading, then set the size to 3.
16. Select the Basic Gardening Tips heading, then format this text in bold, with the color #003366.
17. Save your work and close the tips page.

Add links to Web pages.

1. Open the index page, then use the Property inspector to link Home on the navigation bar to the index.html page in the blooms & bulbs Web site.
2. Link Featured Plants on the navigation bar to the plants.html page.
3. Link Garden Tips on the navigation bar to the tips.html page.
4. Link Classes on the navigation bar to the classes.html page.
5. Using the Insert bar, create an e-mail link under the telephone number.
6. Type **Customer Service** in the Text text box and **mailbox@blooms.com** in the E-Mail text box.
7. Open the plants.html page, add a page title called **Our Featured Plants**, then save the page.
8. Open the classes.html page and add the page title **Classes Offered**, then save your work.

Developing a Web Page

Use the History panel and edit code.

1. Open the History panel, then clear its contents.
2. Delete the current date in the Last updated on statement on the home page and replace it with a date that will update automatically when the file is saved.
3. Change the font for the last updated on statement using the font of your choice.
4. Use the History panel to go back to the original font and style settings for the last updated on statement.
5. Close the History panel.

6. Examine the code for the last updated on statement.
7. Save your work.

Modify and test Web pages.

1. Using the Window Size pop-up menu, view the home page at 600×300 (640×480, Maximized) and 760×420 (800×600, Maximized), then maximize the document window.
2. View the page in your browser.

3. Verify that all links work correctly, then close the browser.
4. On the home page, change the text "Stop by and see us soon!" to **We ship overnight**.
5. Save your work, then view the pages in your browser, comparing your screens to Figure 35 and Figure 36.
6. Close your browser.
7. Adjust the spacing (if necessary), save your work, then preview the home page in the browser again.
8. Close the browser, then close all open pages.

FIGURE 35
Completed Skills Review, home page

Home - Featured Plants - Garden Tips - Classes

Welcome to blooms & bulbs. We carry a variety of plants and shrubs along with a large inventory of gardening supplies. Our four greenhouses are full of healthy young plants just waiting to be planted in your yard. Our staff includes a certified landscape architect, three landscape designers, and six master gardeners. We offer detailed landscape plans tailored to your location as well as planting and regular maintenance services. We ship overnight.

blooms & bulbs
Highway 43 South
Alvin, Texas 77511
(555) 248-0806
Customer Service

©Copyright 2001
Last updated on July 20, 2005

FIGURE 36
Completed Skills Review, tips page

Garden Tips

We have some planting tips we would like to share with you as you prepare your gardens this season. Remember, there is always something to be done for your gardens, no matter what the season. Our experienced staff is here to help you plan your gardens, select your plants, prepare your soil, assist you in the planting, and maintain your beds. Check out our calendar for a list of our scheduled classes. All classes are free of charge and on a first-come, first-served basis!

Seasonal Gardening Checklist:

Fall – The time to plant trees and spring blooming bulbs.
Winter – The time to prune fruit trees and finish planting your bulbs.
Spring – The time to prepare your beds, plant annuals, and apply fertilizer to established plants.
Summer – The time to supplement rainfall so that plants get one inch of water per week.

Basic Gardening Tips

Developing a Web Page

You have been hired to create a Web site for a TripSmart, a travel outfitter. You have created the basic framework for the Web site and are now ready to format and edit the home page to improve the content and appearance.

1. Open the TripSmart Web site, then open the home page.

2. Enter the following keywords: **travel**, **traveling**, **trips**, and **vacations**.

3. Enter the following description: TripSmart is a comprehensive travel store. We can help you plan trips, make travel arrangements, and supply you with travel gear.

4. Change the page title to **TripSmart - Serving All Your Travel Needs**.

5. Create a centered navigation bar below the TripSmart logo with the following text links: **Home**, **Catalog**, **Services**, **Destinations**, and **Newsletter**. Place hyphens between each text link.

6. Apply the Arial, Helvetica, sans-serif font combination to the text links.

7. Type the following address two lines below the paragraph about the company, using line breaks after each line:
TripSmart
1106 Beechwood
Fayetteville, AR 72704
(555) 848-0807

8. Insert an e-mail link in the line below the telephone number, using **Customer Service** for the Text text box and **mailbox@tripsmart.com** for the E-mail text box in the Email Link dialog box.

9. Italicize the address, phone number, and e-mail link and format it to size 2, Arial, Helvetica, sans-serif.

10. Link the navigation bar entries to index.html, catalog.html, services.html, destinations.html, and newsletter.html.

11. View the HTML code for the page.

12. View the page using two different window sizes, then test the links in your browser window.

13. View the site map.

14. Create the following page titles:
catalog.html = **TripSmart Catalog**
services.html = **TripSmart Services**
destinations.html = **TripSmart Featured Destinations**
newsletter.html = **TripSmart Newsletter**

15. Verify that all the page titles are entered correctly, then save your work.

16. Preview the home page in your browser, then test all the links.

17. Compare your page to Figure 37, close the browser, then close all open pages.

FIGURE 37
Completed Project Builder 1

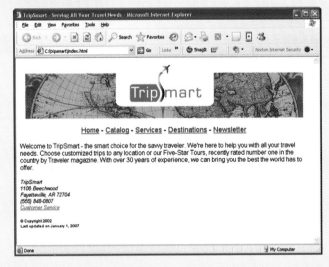

Developing a Web Page

Your company has been selected to design a Web site for emma's book bag, a small bookstore that specializes in children's books. You are now ready to add content to the home page and apply formatting options to improve the page appearance, using Figure 38 as a guide.

1. Open the emma's book bag Web site, then open the home page.
2. Enter a line break after "emma's book bag - a unique bookshop", then add the following sentence: **Store hours - Monday through Saturday from 9:00 til 5:00**.
3. Center the two lines of text.
4. Change the navigation bar to the Heading 5 format.
5. Add the following address below the store hours text using line breaks after each line:
   emma's book bag
   496 Maple Street
   Seven Falls, Virginia 52404
   (555) 958-9684
6. Enter another line break after the telephone number and type **E-mail**, then add an e-mail link using **Emma Claire** for the text and **mailbox@emmasbookbag.com** for the e-mail address.

7. Apply the Verdana, Arial, Helvetica, sans-serif font to the contact information then apply any other formatting of your choice.
8. Create links from each navigation bar element to its corresponding Web page.
9. Replace the date that follows the text "Last updated on" with a date object, then save your work.

10. View the completed page in your default browser, then test each link.
11. Close your browser.
12. View the site map, then title any untitled pages with appropriate titles.
13. Save your work, then close all pages.

FIGURE 38
Completed Project Builder 2

Developing a Web Page

Angela Lou is a freelance photographer. She is searching the Internet looking for a particular type of paper to use in processing her prints. She knows that Web sites use keywords and descriptions in order to receive "hits" with search engines. She is curious about how they work. Follow the steps below and write your answers to the questions.

1. Connect to the Internet, go to *www.course.com,* navigate to the page for this book, click the Online Companion link, then click the link for this chapter to see the Kodak Web site's home page, as shown in Figure 39.
2. View the page source by clicking View on the menu bar, then clicking Source (Internet Explorer) or Page Source (Netscape Navigator or Communicator).
3. Can you locate a description and keywords? If so, what are they?
4. How many keywords do you find?
5. Is the description appropriate for the Web site? Why or why not?
6. Look at the numbers of keywords and words in the description. Is there an appropriate number? Or are there too many or not enough?

7. Use a search engine such as Google at *www.google.com* and search for "photography" and "paper" in the Search text box.

FIGURE 39
Design Project

8. Click the first link in the list of results and view the source code for that page. Do you see keywords and a description? Do any of them match the words you used in the search?

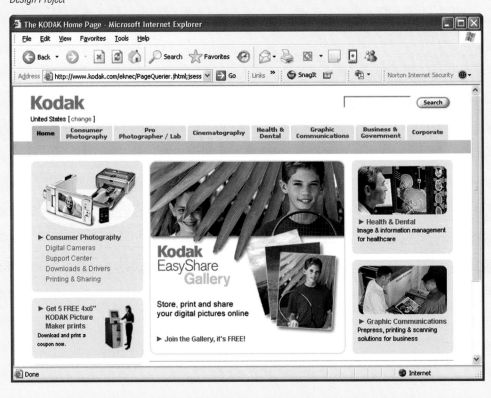

In this assignment, you will continue to work on the Web site you defined in Chapter 1. In Chapter 1, you created a storyboard for your Web site with at least four pages. You also created a local root folder for your Web site and an assets folder to store the Web site asset files. You set the assets folder as the default storage location for your images. You began to collect information and resources for your Web site and started working on the home page.

1. Add the title, keywords, and description. Think about to the head content for the home page.

2. Create the main page content for the home page and format it attractively.

3. Add the address and other contact information to the home page, including an e-mail address.

4. Consult your storyboard and design the navigation bar.

5. Link the navigation bar items to the appropriate pages.

6. Add a last updated on statement to the home page with a date that will automatically update when the page is saved.

7. Edit and format the page content until you are satisfied with the results.

8. Verify that each page has a page title by viewing the site map.

9. Verify that all links, including the e-mail link, work correctly.

10. When you are satisfied with the home page, review the check list questions shown in Figure 40, then make any necessary changes.

11. Save your work.

FIGURE 40
Portfolio Project check list

Web Site Check List

1. Do all pages have a page title?
2. Does the home page have a description and keywords?
3. Does the home page contain contact information, including an e-mail address?
4. Do all completed pages in the Web site have consistent navigation links?
5. Does the home page have a "last updated on" statement that will automatically update when the page is saved?
6. Do all pages have attractively formatted text?
7. Do all paths for links and images work correctly?
8. Does the home page view well using at least two different screen resolutions?

3

WORKING WITH TEXT
AND GRAPHICS

1. Create unordered and ordered lists.

2. Create, apply, and edit Cascading Style Sheets.

3. Add styles and attach Cascading Style Sheets.

4. Insert and align graphics.

5. Enhance an image and use alternate text.

6. Insert a background image and perform site maintenance.

chapter **3** WORKING WITH TEXT
AND GRAPHICS

Introduction

Most Web pages contain a combination of
text and graphics. Dreamweaver provides
many tools for working with text and
graphics that you can use to make your
Web pages attractive and easy to read.
Dreamweaver also has tools that help you
format text quickly and ensure a consistent appearance of text elements across all
your Web pages.

Formatting Text as Lists

If a Web page contains a large amount
of text, it can be difficult for viewers to
digest it all. You can break up the monot-
ony of large blocks of text by creating
lists. You can create three types of lists in
Dreamweaver: unordered lists, ordered
lists, and definition lists.

Using Cascading Style Sheets

You can save time and ensure that all your
page elements have a consistent appearance by using Cascading Style Sheets
(CSS). You can use Cascading Style Sheets
to define formatting attributes for page
elements such as text and tables. You can

then apply the formatting attributes you
define to any element in a single document or to all of the pages in a Web site.

Using Graphics to Enhance Web Pages

Graphics make Web pages visually stimu-
lating and more exciting than pages that
contain only text. However, you should use
graphics sparingly. If you think of text as
the meat and potatoes of a Web site, the
graphics would be the seasoning. You
should add graphics to a page just as you
would add seasoning to food. A little seasoning enhances the flavor and brings out
the quality of the dish. Too much seasoning overwhelms the dish and masks the
flavor of the main ingredients. Too little
seasoning results in a bland dish. There
are many ways to work with graphics so
that they complement the content of pages
in a Web site. There are specific file formats that should be used to save graphics
for Web sites to ensure maximum quality
with minimum file size. You should store
graphics in a Web site's assets folder in an
organized fashion.

Tools You'll Use

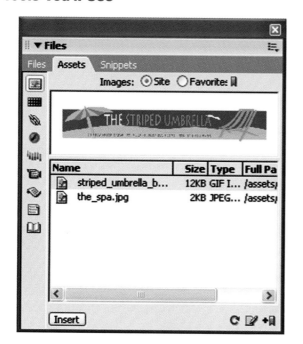

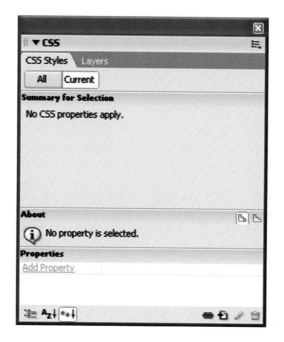

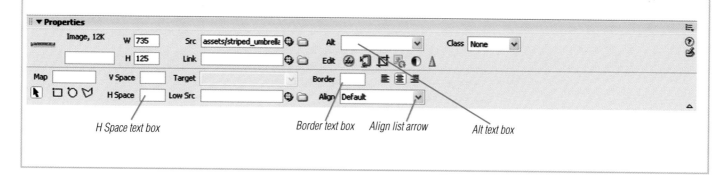

H Space text box

Border text box

Align list arrow

Alt text box

CREATE UNORDERED AND
ORDERED LISTS

What You'll Do

Massages

- Sports Massage
  Our deepest massage for tense and sore muscles.
- Swedish Massage
  A gentle, relaxing massage.
- Hot Stone Massage
  Good for tight, sore muscles. Advance notice required.

Packages

- Spa Sampler
  Mix and match any three of our services.
- Girl's Day Out
  One hour massage, a facial, a manicure, and a pedicure.
- Call the Spa desk for prices and reservations. Our desk is open from 7:00 a.m. until 5:00 p.m.

Questions you may have

1. How do I schedule Spa services?
   Please make appointments by calling The Club desk at least 24 hours in advance. Please arrive 15 minutes before your appointment to allow enough time to shower or use the sauna.
2. Will I be charged if I cancel my appointment?
   Please cancel 24 hours before your service to avoid a cancellation charge. No-shows and cancellations without adequate notice will be charged for the full service.
3. Are there any health safeguards I should know about?
   Please advise us of medical conditions or allergies you have. Heat treatments like hydrotherapy and body wraps should be avoided if you are pregnant, have high blood pressure, or any type of heart condition or diabetes.
4. What about tipping?
   Gratuities are at your sole discretion, but are certainly appreciated.

 In this lesson, you will create an unordered list of spa services on the spa page. You will also import text with questions and format them as an ordered list.

Creating Unordered Lists

Unordered lists are lists of items that do not need to be placed in a specific order. A grocery list that lists items in a random order is a good example of an unordered list. Items in unordered lists are usually preceded by a **bullet**, or a small raised dot or similar icon. Unordered lists that contain bullets are sometimes called **bulleted lists**. Though you can use paragraph indentations to create an unordered list, bullets can often make lists easier to read. To create an unordered list, first select the text you want to format as an unordered list, then use the Unordered List button in the Property inspector to insert bullets at the beginning of each paragraph of the selected text.

Formatting Unordered Lists

In Dreamweaver, the default bullet style is a round dot. To change the bullet style to square, you need to expand the Property inspector to its full size, as shown in Figure 1, click List Item in the Property inspector to open the List Properties dialog box, then set the style for bulleted lists to Square. Be aware, however, that not all browsers display square bullets correctly, in which case the bullets will appear as round dots.

Creating Definition Lists

Definition lists are similar to unordered lists but do not have bullets. They are often used with terms and definitions, such as in a dictionary or glossary. To create a definition list, select the text to use for the list, click Text on the menu bar, point to List, then click Definition List.

Creating Ordered Lists

Ordered lists, which are sometimes called **numbered lists**, are lists of items that are presented in a specific order and that are preceded by numbers or letters in sequence. An ordered list is appropriate for a list in which each item must be executed according to its specified order. A list that provides numbered directions for driving from Point A to Point B or a list that provides instructions for assembling a bicycle are both examples of ordered lists.

Formatting Ordered Lists

You can format an ordered list to show different styles of numbers or letters using the List Properties dialog box, as shown in Figure 2. You can apply numbers, Roman numerals, lowercase letters, or capital letters to an ordered list.

FIGURE 1

Expanded Property inspector

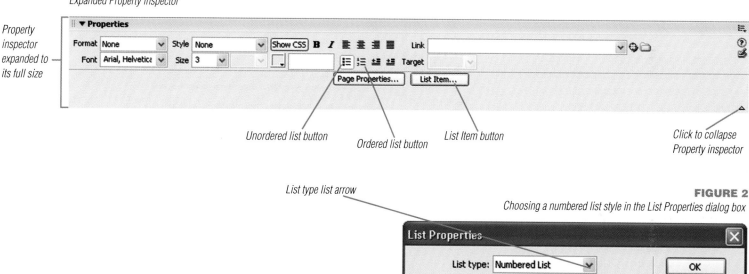

Property inspector expanded to its full size

Unordered list button

Ordered list button

List Item button

Click to collapse Property inspector

List type list arrow

FIGURE 2

Choosing a numbered list style in the List Properties dialog box

Numbered list styles

Create an unordered list

1. Open the spa page in The Striped Umbrella Web site.

2. Select the three items under the Skin Care Treatments heading.

3. Click the **Unordered List button** ≣ in the Property inspector to format the selected text as an unordered list, click anywhere to deselect the text, then compare your screen to Figure 3.

   Each spa service item and its description is separated by a line break. That is why each description is indented under its corresponding item, rather than creating a new list item. You must enter a paragraph break to create a new list item.

4. Repeat Step 3 to create unordered lists of the items under the Body Treatments, Massages, and Spa Packages headings.

   TIP Be careful not to include the last sentence on the page as part of your list. It is the contact information.

   TIP Pressing [Enter] (Win) or [return] (Mac) once at the end of an unordered list creates another bulleted item. To end an unordered list, press [Enter] (Win) or [return] (Mac) twice.

You opened the spa page in Design view and formatted four spa services lists as unordered lists.

FIGURE 3
Creating an unordered list

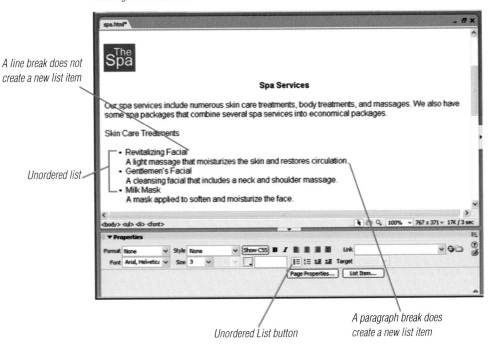

A line break does not create a new list item

Unordered list

Unordered List button

A paragraph break does create a new list item

FIGURE 4
List Properties dialog box

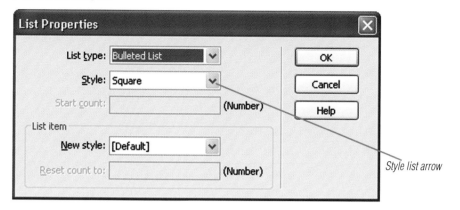

Style list arrow

FIGURE 5
HTML tags in Code view for unordered list

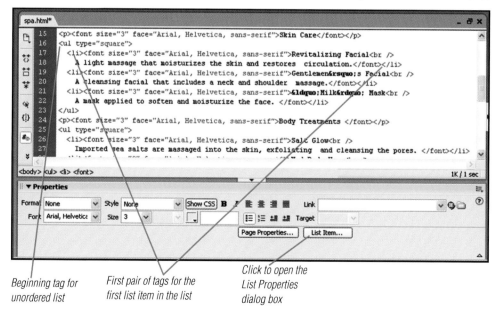

Beginning tag for unordered list

First pair of tags for the first list item in the list

Click to open the List Properties dialog box

Format an unordered list

1. Click any of the items in the first unordered list to place the insertion point in the list.

2. Expand the Property inspector (if necessary), click **List Item** in the Property inspector to open the List Properties dialog box, click the **Style list arrow**, click **Square**, as shown in Figure 4, then click **OK**.

   The bullets in the unordered list now have a square shape.

3. Repeat Step 2 to format the other three unordered lists.

4. Position the insertion point to the left of the first item in the first unordered list, then click the **Show Code view button** ⟨⟩ Code on the toolbar to view the code for the unordered list, as shown in Figure 5.

   Notice that there is a pair of HTML codes, or tags, surrounding each type of element on the page. The first tag in each pair begins the code for a particular element, and the last tag ends the code for the element. For instance, the tags <ul></ul> surround the unordered list. The tags <li> and </li> surround each item in the list.

5. Click the **Show Design view button** 🔲 Design on the toolbar.

   TIP To ensure that you do not have trouble with your lists being displayed correctly, it is wise to stick to unordered or ordered lists. This assures that you will have backward and forward compatibility with different versions of HTML.

You used the List Properties dialog box to apply the Square bullet style to the unordered lists. You then viewed the HTML code for the unordered lists in Code view.

Create an ordered list

1. Place the insertion point at the end of the page.

2. Use the Import Word Document command to import questions.doc from the chapter_3 folder where your Data Files are stored (Win) or open questions.doc from the chapter_3 folder, select all, copy, then paste the copied text on the page (Mac).

   TIP Remember to remove the check mark in the Use CSS instead of HTML tags check box in the General section of the Preferences dialog box before importing Word text.

3. Click the **Insert bar list arrow**, click **HTML**, place the insertion point to the left of the text "Questions you may have", then click the **Horizontal Rule button** 📖 on the Insert bar.

   A horizontal rule appears and helps to separate the unordered list from the text you just imported.

4. Select the text beginning with "How do I schedule" and ending with the last sentence on the page.

5. Click the **Ordered List button** ☷ in the Property inspector to format the selected text as an ordered list.

6. Deselect the text, then compare your screen to Figure 6.

You imported text onto the spa page. You also added a horizontal rule to help organize the page. Finally, you formatted selected text as an ordered list.

FIGURE 6

Creating an ordered list

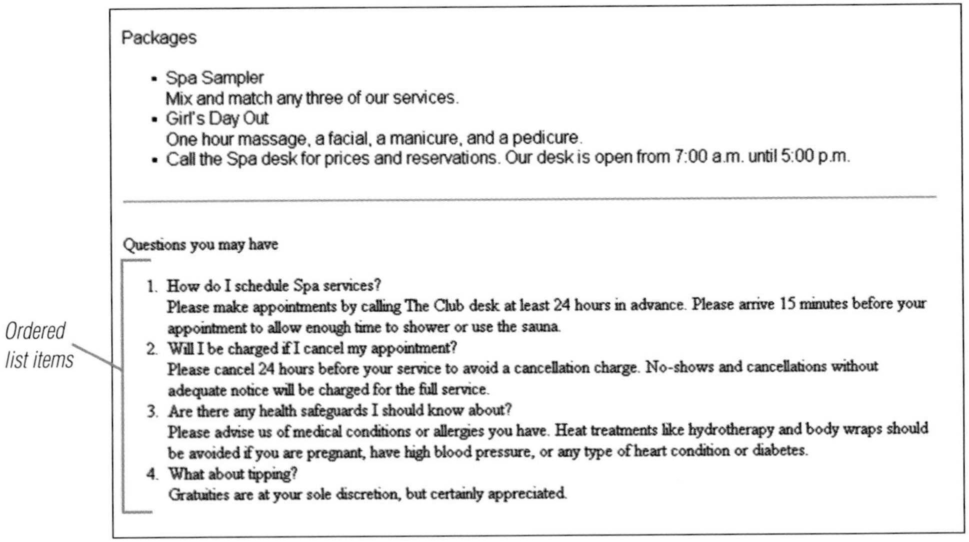

Packages

- Spa Sampler
  Mix and match any three of our services.
- Girl's Day Out
  One hour massage, a facial, a manicure, and a pedicure.
- Call the Spa desk for prices and reservations. Our desk is open from 7:00 a.m. until 5:00 p.m.

Questions you may have

Ordered list items →

1. How do I schedule Spa services?
   Please make appointments by calling The Club desk at least 24 hours in advance. Please arrive 15 minutes before your appointment to allow enough time to shower or use the sauna.
2. Will I be charged if I cancel my appointment?
   Please cancel 24 hours before your service to avoid a cancellation charge. No-shows and cancellations without adequate notice will be charged for the full service.
3. Are there any health safeguards I should know about?
   Please advise us of medical conditions or allergies you have. Heat treatments like hydrotherapy and body wraps should be avoided if you are pregnant, have high blood pressure, or any type of heart condition or diabetes.
4. What about tipping?
   Gratuities are at your sole discretion, but certainly appreciated.

1. Select all the text below the horizontal rule, then change the font to Arial, Helvetica, sans-serif, size 3.

2. Select the heading "Questions you may have", then click the **Bold button B** in the Property inspector.

3. Click the **Text Color button** in the Property inspector to open the color picker, click the first square in the third row, color #000066, deselect, then compare your screen to Figure 7.

   TIP If you want to see more of your Web page in the document window, you can collapse the Property inspector.

5. Save your work.

You applied a new font and font size to the ordered list. You also formatted the "Questions you may have" heading.

FIGURE 7
Spa page with ordered list

Formatted heading

Formatted body text

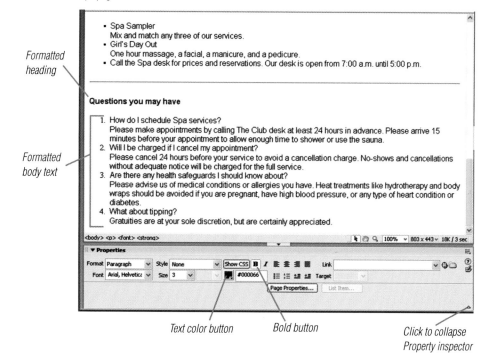

Text color button   Bold button

Click to collapse
Property inspector

CREATE, APPLY, AND EDIT
CASCADING STYLE SHEETS

What You'll Do

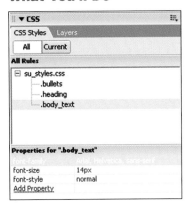

 In this lesson, you will create a Cascading Style Sheet file for The Striped Umbrella Web site. You will also create styles called bullets and heading and apply them to the spa page.

Using Cascading Style Sheets

When you want to apply the same formatting attributes to page elements such as text, objects, and tables, you can save a significant amount of time by using Cascading Style Sheets. A **Cascading Style Sheet (CSS)** is made up of sets of formatting attributes called rules and are either saved with a descriptive name as a separate file or are part of the code for an individual page. External CSS style sheets are saved as individual files with the .css extension and stored in the directory structure of a Web site, as shown in Figure 8. Internal CSS style sheets are embedded in the code on an individual page. CSS style sheets contain **styles**, or **rules**, which are formatting attributes that can be applied to page elements.

You use the buttons on the CSS Styles panel to create, edit, and apply styles. To add a style, use the New CSS Rule dialog box to name the style and specify whether to add it to a new or existing style sheet. You then use the CSS Rule definition dialog box to set the formatting attributes for the style. Once you add a new style to a style sheet, it appears in a list in the CSS Styles panel. To apply a style, you select the text to which you want to apply the style, then choose a style from the Style list in the Property inspector. You can apply CSS styles to any element on a Web page or to all of the pages in a Web site. When you make a change to a style, all page elements formatted with that style are automatically updated. Once you create a CSS style sheet, you can attach it to other pages in your Web site.

The CSS Styles panel is used for managing styles. If you select a style in the CSS Styles panel, the properties are displayed in the Properties pane, the bottom part of the panel. A drop-down list can be accessed next to each property value to enable you to make quick changes, such as increasing the font size.

You can use CSS styles to save an enormous amount of time. Being able to define a rule and then apply it to page elements on all the pages of your Web site means that you can make hundreds of formatting changes in a few minutes. Be aware, however, that not all browsers can read CSS styles. Versions of Internet Explorer that are 4.0 or lower do not support CSS styles. As for Netscape Navigator, version 6.0 or higher supports CSS styles.

QUICKTIP

You can also use CSS styles to format other page content such as backgrounds, borders, lists, and boxes.

Understanding CSS Style Sheet Settings

If you open a style sheet file, you will see the code for the CSS styles. A CSS style consists of two parts: the selector and the declaration. The **selector** is the name of the tag to which the style declarations have been assigned. The **declaration** consists of the property and the value. For example, Figure 9 shows the code for the su_styles.css style sheet. In this example,

the first property listed for the .bullets style is font-family. The value for this property is Arial, Helvetica, sans-serif. When you create a new Cascading Style Sheet, you will see it as an open document in the Dreamweaver document window. Save this file as you make changes to it.

QUICKTIP

For more information about Cascading Style Sheets, visit *www.w3.org.*

FIGURE 8

Cascading Style Sheet file created in striped_umbrella root folder

FIGURE 9

su_styles.css style sheet file

New Cascading
Style Sheet file

```
1   .bullets {
2       font-family: Arial, Helvetica, sans-serif;
3       font-size: 14px;
4       font-style: normal;
5       font-weight: bold;
6       color: #000066;
7   }
8   .heading {
9       font-family: Arial, Helvetica, sans-serif;
10      font-size: 16px;
11      font-style: normal;
12      font-weight: bold;
13      color: #000066;
14      text-align: center;
15  }
16  .body_text {
17      font-family: Arial, Helvetica, sans-serif;
18      font-size: 14px;
19      font-style: normal;
20  }
21
```

Lesson 2   Create, Apply, and Edit Cascading Style Sheets

Create a Cascading Style Sheet and a style

1. Click **Edit** (Win) or **Dreamweaver** (Mac) on the menu bar, click **Preferences**, click the **General category**, if necessary, click the **Use CSS instead of HTML tags check box**, then click **OK** to turn this default option back on.

   From this point forward, we will use CSS rather than HTML tags to format text. The Property inspector font sizes will be shown in pixels rather than HTML text sizes, as shown in Figure 10.

2. Expand the CSS panel group, then click the **CSS Styles panel tab** (if necessary).

3. Click the **Switch to All (Document) Mode button** , click the **New CSS Rule button** in the CSS Styles panel to open the New CSS Rule dialog box, verify that the Class option button is selected, then type **bullets** in the Name text box.

   TIP Class names are preceded by a period. If you don't enter a period when you type the name, Dreamweaver will add the period for you.

4. Click the **Define in list arrow**, click **(New Style Sheet File)**, if necessary, compare your screen with Figure 11, then click **OK**.

5. Type **su_styles** in the File name text box (Win) or the Save As text box (Mac), then click **Save** to open the CSS Rule Definition for .bullets in su_styles.css dialog box.

   The .bullets rule will be stored within the su_styles.css file.

(continued)

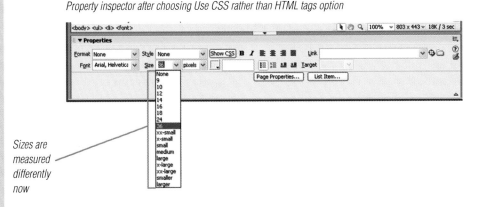

Sizes are measured differently now

FIGURE 11
New CSS Rule dialog box

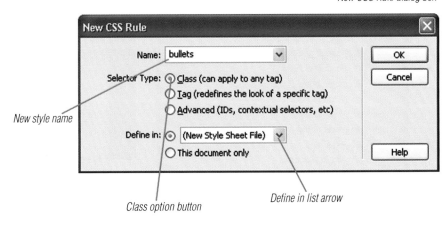

New style name

Class option button

Define in list arrow

FIGURE 12

CSS Rule Definition for .bullets in su_styles.css dialog box

Type category selected

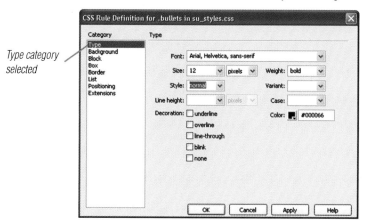

6. Verify that Type is selected in the Category list, set the Font to Arial, Helvetica, sans-serif, set the Size to 12 pixels, set the Weight to bold, set the Color to #000066, set the Style to normal, compare your screen to Figure 12, then click **OK**.

7. Click the **plus sign** (Win) or the **expander arrow** (Mac) next to su_styles.css in the CSS Styles panel (if necessary) to list the .bullets rule.

The CSS rule named .bullets appears in the CSS Styles panel, as shown in Figure 13.

You created a Cascading Style Sheet file named su_styles.css and a rule called .bullets.

FIGURE 13

CSS Styles panel with .bullets style added

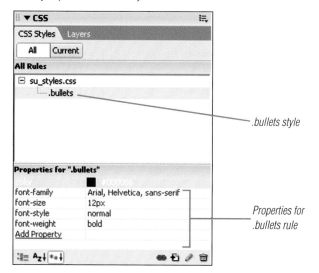

.bullets style

Properties for .bullets rule

Apply a Cascading Style Sheet

1. Click **View** on the menu bar, point to **Toolbars**, then click **Style Rendering**.

2. Verify that the **Toggle Displaying of CSS Styles button**  on the Style Rendering toolbar is activated, as shown in Figure 14.

   The Toggle Displaying of CSS Styles button can be used to see how your styles are affecting your page.

3. Select the text "Revitalizing Facial" as shown in Figure 15, then use the Property inspector to set the Font to Default Font, the Size to None, and the Style to bullets.

   TIP Before you apply a style to selected text, you need to remove all formatting attributes such as font and color from it, or the style will not be applied correctly.

4. Repeat Step 1 to apply the bullets style to each of the spa services names in the unordered lists, then compare your screen to Figure 16.

You applied the bullets style to each item in the Spa Services category lists.

FIGURE 14

Style Rendering toolbar

Toggle Displaying of CSS Styles button

FIGURE 15

Applying a CSS style to selected text

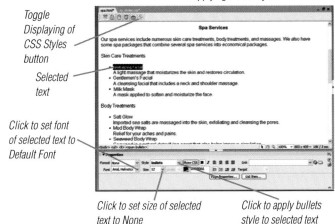

Toggle Displaying of CSS Styles button

Selected text

Click to set font of selected text to Default Font

Click to set size of selected text to None

Click to apply bullets style to selected text

FIGURE 16

Unordered list with bullets style applied

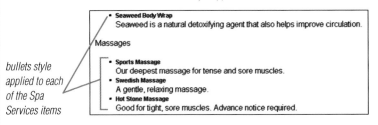

bullets style applied to each of the Spa Services items

Using the Style Rendering toolbar

The Style Rendering toolbar is a new Dreamweaver 8 feature. It can be displayed by clicking View on the menu bar, pointing to Toolbars, then clicking Style Rendering, when a page is open. The buttons on the Style Rendering toolbar allow you to render your page as different media types, such as print or handheld. The last button on the toolbar is the Toggle Displaying of CSS Styles button. Its purpose is to show you how styles applied to your page will display. It works independently from the other buttons and acts as a toggle between viewing and not viewing the styles.

FIGURE 17

Editing a CSS style

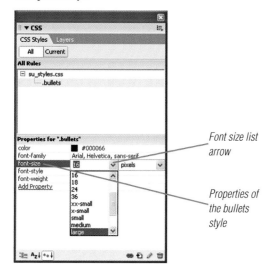

Font size list
arrow

Properties of
the bullets
style

1. Click **.bullets** in the CSS Styles panel.

    The style's properties and values are displayed in the Properties pane, the bottom part of the CSS Styles panel, as shown in Figure 17. You can also click the **Edit Style button** 🖉 in the CSS Styles panel to open the CSS Rule Definition for .bullets dialog box.

    TIP Click the plus sign (Win) or expander arrow (Mac) to the left of su_styles.css in the CSS Styles panel if you do not see .bullets. Click the plus sign (Win) or expander arrow (Mac) to the left of <style> if you do not see su_styles.css

2. Click **12px** in the CSS Styles panel, click the **font-size list arrow**, click **14**, then compare your screen to Figure 18.

    The text is much bigger than before, reflecting the changes you made to the bullets style.

    TIP If you position the insertion point in text that has a CSS style applied to it, that style is displayed in the Style text box on the Property inspector.

You edited the bullets style to change the font size to 14 pixels. You then viewed the results of the edited style in the unordered list.

FIGURE 18

Viewing the changes made to the bullets style

Text that has
the bullets style
applied to it is
now larger

Spa Services

Our spa services include numerous skin care treatments, body treatments, and massages. We also have some spa packages that combine several spa services into economical packages.

Skin Care Treatments

- **Revitalizing Facial**
  A light massage that moisturizes the skin and restores circulation.
- **Gentlemen's Facial**
  A cleansing facial that includes a neck and shoulder massage.
- **Milk Mask**
  A mask applied to soften and moisturize the face.

Body Treatments

- **Salt Glow**
  Imported sea salts are massaged into the skin, exfoliating and cleansing the pores.
- **Mud Body Wrap**
  Relief for your aches and pains.
- **Seaweed Body Wrap**
  Seaweed is a natural detoxifying agent that also helps improve circulation.

Massages

ADD STYLES AND ATTACH
CASCADING STYLE SHEETS

What You'll Do

 In this lesson, you will add a style to a Cascading Style Sheet. You will then attach the style sheet file to the index page and apply one of the styles to text on the page.

Understanding External and Embedded Style Sheets

When you are first learning about Cascading Style Sheets, the terminology can be very confusing. In the last lesson, you learned that external style sheets are a separate file in a Web site saved with the .css file extension. You also learned that Cascading Style Sheets can be part of an html file, rather than a separate file. These are called embedded style sheets. External CSS files are created by the Web designer. Embedded style sheets are created automatically by Dreamweaver when the Preference is set to Use CSS instead of

HTML tags. When this preference is set, any formatting choices you make using the Property inspector will automatically create a style. The code for these styles will reside in the head content for that page. These styles will be named style1, style2, etc. You can rename the styles as they are created to make them more recognizable for you to use such as body, heading, or address. Embedded style sheets apply only to a single page. Remember that style sheets can be used to format much more than text objects. They can be used to set the page background, link properties, tables, or almost any object on the page. Figure 19 shows the code for some

Working with Text and Graphics

embedded styles. The code resides in the head content of the Web page.

When you have several pages in a Web site, you will probably want to use the same CSS style sheet for each page to ensure that all your elements have a consistent appearance. To attach a style sheet to another doc-ument, click the Attach Style Sheet button on the CSS Styles panel to open the Attach External Style Sheet dialog box, make sure the Add as Link option is selected, browse to locate the file you want to attach, then click OK. The styles contained in the attached style sheet will appear in the CSS Styles panel, and you can use them to apply styles to text on the page. External style sheets can be attached, or linked, to any page. This is an extremely powerful tool. If you decide to make a change in a style, it will automatically be made to every object that it formats.

FIGURE 19

Code for embedded styles shown in Code view

```
1   <!DOCTYPE html PUBLIC "-//W3C//DTD XHTML 1.0 Transitional//EN"
    "http://www.w3.org/TR/xhtml1/DTD/xhtml1-transitional.dtd">
2   <html xmlns="http://www.w3.org/1999/xhtml">
3   <head>
4   <meta http-equiv="Content-Type" content="text/html; charset=iso-8859-1" />
5   <title>Welcome to the Striped Umbrella</title>
6   <style type="text/css">
7   <!--
8   .style1 {
9       font-size: 18px;
10      font-family: Arial, Helvetica, sans-serif;
11  }
12  .style2 {
13      font-family: Verdana, Arial, Helvetica, sans-serif;
14      font-size: 16px;
15  }
16  body {
17      background-color: #FFFFFF;
18  }
19  a:link {
20      color: #0033CC;
21  }
22  -->
23  </style>
24  </head>
```

Add a style to a Cascading Style Sheet

1. Click the **New CSS Rule button** in the CSS Styles Panel.

2. Type **heading** in the Name text box, as shown in Figure 20, then click **OK**.

3. Set the Font to Arial, Helvetica, sans-serif, set the Size to 16, set the Style to normal, set the Weight to bold, set the Color to #000066, compare your screen to Figure 21, then click **OK**.

4. Click the **Edit Style button** .

5. Click the **Block category** in the CSS Rule Definition for .heading in su_styles.css dialog box, click the **Text align list arrow**, click **center**, as shown in Figure 22, then click **OK**.

6. Select the heading "Spa Services" then use the Property inspector to set the Format to None and the Font to Default Font.

7. With the heading still selected, click the **Text Color button** to open the color picker, then click the **Strikethrough button** .

8. Click the **Style list arrow** in the Property inspector, then click **heading** to apply it to the Spa Services heading.

9. Repeat Steps 1 through 3 to add another style called **body_text** with the Arial, Helvetica, sans-serif font, size 14, and normal style.

10. Repeat Steps 5 through 7 to apply the body_text style to the rest of the text on the page except for the text that already has the bullets style applied to it and the text "Questions you may have".

FIGURE 20
Adding a style to a CSS style sheet

New style name

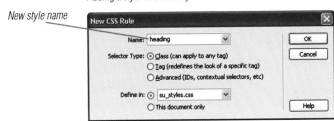

FIGURE 21
Formatting options for heading style

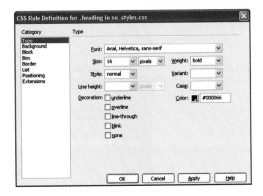

FIGURE 22
Setting text alignment for heading style

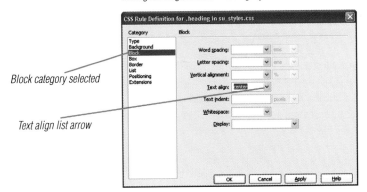

Block category selected

Text align list arrow

FIGURE 23

Attaching a style sheet to a page

Link option
button

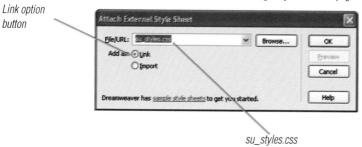

su_styles.css

FIGURE 24

Viewing the code to link the CSS style sheet file

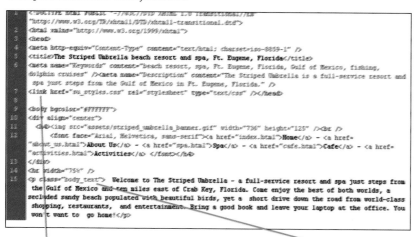

Code linking external style sheet file to the index page   Code that applies the body_text style to the paragraph

11. Click **File** on the menu bar, then click **Save All**, to save both the spa page and the su_styles.css file.

TIP You must save the open su_styles.css file after editing it, or you will lose your changes.

You added two new styles called heading and body_text to the su_styles.css file. You then applied the two styles to selected text.

Attach a style sheet

1. Close the spa page and open the index page.
2. Click the **Attach Style Sheet button** ⊞ on the CSS Styles panel.
3. Click the **Link option button**, if necessary, as shown in Figure 23, then click **OK**.
4. Select the paragraph of text and set the Font to Default and the Size to None to clear prior formatting.
5. Click the **Style list arrow**, then click **body_text**.
6. Click the **Show Code view button** ⟨⟩ Code and view the code that links the su_styles.css file to the index page as shown in Figure 24.
7. Click the **Show Design view button** ⊞ Design, then save your work.

You attached the su_styles.css file to the index.html page.

INSERT AND ALIGN
GRAPHICS

What You'll Do

 In this lesson, you will insert five graphics on the about us page in The Striped Umbrella Web site. You will then stagger the alignment of the images on the page to make the page more visually appealing.

Understanding Graphic File Formats

When you add graphics to a Web page, it's important to choose the appropriate graphic file format. The three primary graphic file formats used in Web pages are **GIF** (Graphics Interchange Format), **JPEG** (Joint Photographic Experts Group), and **PNG** (Portable Network Graphics). GIF files download very quickly, making them ideal to use on Web pages. Though limited in the number of colors they can represent, GIF files have the ability to show transparent areas. JPEG files can display many colors. Because they often contain many shades of the same color, photographs are often saved in JPEG format. Files saved with the PNG format share advantages of both GIFs and JPEGs, but are not universally recognized by older browsers.

QUICKTIP

The status bar displays the download time for the page. Each time you add a new graphic to the page, you can see how much additional time is added to the total download time.

Understanding the Assets Panel

When you add a graphic to a Web site, it is automatically added to the Assets panel. The **Assets panel**, located in the Files panel group, displays all the assets in a Web site. The Assets panel contains nine category buttons that you use to view your assets by category. These include Images, Colors, URLs, Flash, Shockwave, Movies, Scripts, Templates, and Library. To view a particular type of asset, click the appropriate category button. The Assets panel is split into two panes. When you click the Images button, as shown in Figure 25, the lower pane displays a list of all the images in your site and contains four columns. The top pane displays a thumbnail of the selected image in the list. You can view assets in each category in two ways. You can use the Site option button to view all the assets in a Web site, or you can use the Favorites option button to view those assets that you have designated as **favorites**, or assets that you expect to use repeatedly while you work on the site. You can use the Assets panel to add an asset to a Web page by dragging the asset from the Assets panel to the page or by using the Insert button on the Assets panel.

QUICKTIP
You might need to resize the Assets panel to see all four columns when it is docked. To resize the Assets panel, undock the Files panel group and drag the window borders as needed or drag the left border of the panel.

Aligning Images

When you insert an image on a Web page, you need to position it in relation to other elements on the page. Positioning an image is referred to as **aligning** an image. By default, when you insert an image in a paragraph, its bottom edge aligns with the baseline of the first line of text or any other element in the same paragraph. When you select an image, the Align text box in the Property inspector displays the

alignment setting for the image. You can change the alignment setting using the options in the Align menu in the Property inspector.

QUICKTIP
The Align menu options function differently than the Align buttons in the Property inspector. You use the Align buttons to center, left-align, or right-align an element without regard to how the element is aligned in relation to other elements.

FIGURE 25
The Assets panel

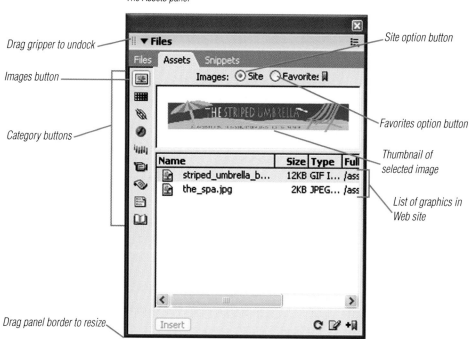

Drag gripper to undock

Images button

Category buttons

Drag panel border to resize

Site option button

Favorites option button

Thumbnail of selected image

List of graphics in Web site

Insert a graphic

1. Open dw3_1.html from the chapter_3 folder where your Data Files are stored, then save it as **about_us.html** in the striped_umbrella root folder.

2. Click **Yes** (Win) or **Replace** (Mac) to overwrite the existing file, then click **No** to Update Links.

   Clicking No to Update Links will keep the links from linking to the original Data Files location.

3. Click the **Attach Style Sheet button** in the CSS Styles panel, attach the su_styles.css style sheet, then apply the body_text style to all of the paragraph text on the page.

4. Position the insertion point in front of "When" in the first paragraph, click the **Insert bar list arrow**, click **Common**, click the **Images list arrow**, then click **Image** to open the Select Image Source dialog box, navigate to the chapter_3 assets folder, double-click **club_house.jpg**, insert the alternate text **The Striped Umbrella Club House**, then verify that the file was copied to your assets folder in the striped_umbrella root folder.

   Compare your screen to Figure 26.

5. Click the **Assets panel tab** in the Files panel group, click the **Images button** on the Assets panel (if necessary), then click the **Refresh Site List button** on the Assets panel to update the list of images in The Striped Umbrella Web site.

   The Assets panel displays a list of all the images in The Striped Umbrella Web site, as shown in Figure 27. A thumbnail of the club house image appears above the list.

   (continued)

FIGURE 26
The Striped Umbrella about us page with inserted image

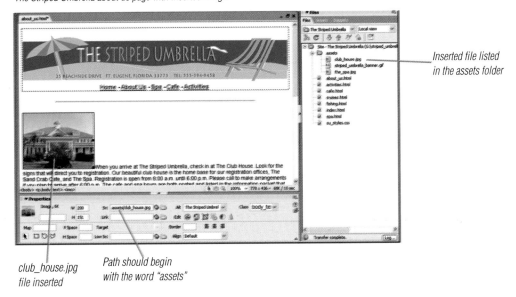

Inserted file listed in the assets folder

club_house.jpg file inserted

Path should begin with the word "assets"

FIGURE 27
Image files for The Striped Umbrella Web site listed in the Assets panel

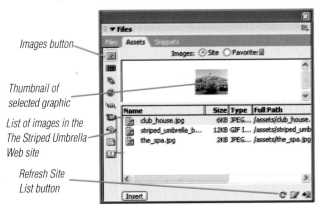

Images button

Thumbnail of selected graphic

List of images in the The Striped Umbrella Web site

Refresh Site List button

Working with Text and Graphics

FIGURE 28

Assets panel with seven images

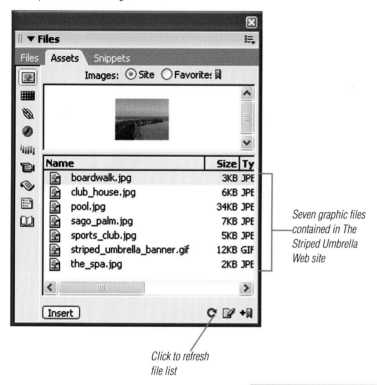

Seven graphic files
contained in The
Striped Umbrella
Web site

Click to refresh
file list

6. Insert boardwalk.jpg to the left of "After" at the beginning of the second paragraph, then refresh the Assets panel to verify that the boardwalk.jpg file was copied to the assets folder of The Striped Umbrella Web site.

   TIP The file boardwalk.jpg is located in the assets folder in the chapter_3 folder where your Data Files are stored.

7. Repeat Step 5 to insert the pool.jpg, sago_palm.jpg, and sports_club.jpg files at the beginning of each of the next paragraphs.

   After refreshing, your Assets panel should resemble Figure 28.

You inserted five images on the about us page and copied each image to the assets folder of The Striped Umbrella Web site.

Using Favorites in the Assets panel

The assets in the Assets panel can be listed two ways: Site and Favorites. The Site option lists all of the assets in the Web site in the selected category in alphabetical order. As your list of assets grows, you can designate some of the assets that are used more frequently as Favorites for quicker access. To add an asset to the Favorites list, right-click (Win) or [control]-click (Mac) the asset name in the Site list, then click Add to Favorites. When an asset is placed in the Favorites list, it is still included in the Site list. To delete an asset from the Favorites list, select the asset you want to delete, then press [Delete] or the Remove from Favorites button on the Assets panel. You can further organize your Favorites list by creating folders for similar assets and grouping them inside the folders.

Align a graphic

1. Scroll to the top of the page, click the **club house image**, then expand the Property inspector (if necessary).

   Because an image is selected, the Property inspector displays tools for setting the properties of an image.

2. Click the **Align list arrow** in the Property inspector, then click **Left**.

   The club house photo is now left-aligned and the paragraph text flows around its right edge, as shown in Figure 29.

   (continued)

FIGURE 29
Left-aligned club house image

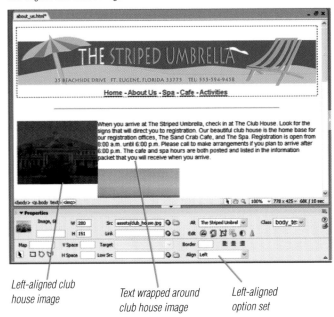

Left-aligned club
house image

Text wrapped around
club house image

Left-aligned
option set

Working with Text and Graphics

FIGURE 30

Aligned images on the about us page

3. Select the boardwalk image, click the **Align list arrow** in the Property inspector, then click **Right**.

4. Align the pool image, using the Left Align option.

5. Align the sago palm image, using the Right Align option.

6. Align the sports club image, using the Left Align option.

7. Save your work.

8. Preview the Web page in your browser, compare your screen to Figure 30, then close your browser.

You used the Property inspector to set the alignment for the five images. You then previewed the page in your browser.

ENHANCE AN IMAGE AND
USE ALTERNATE TEXT

What You'll Do

In this lesson you will add borders to images, add horizontal and vertical space to set them apart from the text, and then add alternate text to each image on the page.

Enhancing an Image

After you place an image on a Web page, you have several options for **enhancing** it, or improving its appearance. To make changes to the image itself, such as removing scratches from it, or making it lighter or darker, you need to use an image editor such as Macromedia Fireworks or Adobe Photoshop. To edit a graphic directly in Fireworks from Dreamweaver, first select the graphic, then click Edit on the Property inspector. This will open the Fireworks program. Complete your editing, then click Done to return to Dreamweaver. However, you can use Dreamweaver to enhance certain aspects of how images appear on a page. For example, you can add borders around an image or add horizontal and vertical space. **Borders** are frames that surround an image. Horizontal and vertical space is blank space above, below, and on the sides of an image that separates the image from text or other elements on the page. Adding horizontal or vertical space, which is the same as adding white space, helps images

---

DESIGNTIP   **Resizing graphics using an external editor**

Each image on a Web page takes a specific number of seconds to download, depending on the size of the file. Larger files (in kilobytes, not width and height) take longer to download than smaller files. It's important to figure out the smallest acceptable size for an image on your Web page. Then, if you need to resize an image to reduce the file size, use an external image editor to do so, *instead* of resizing it in Dreamweaver. Although you can adjust the width and height settings of an image in the Property inspector to change the size of the image as it appears on your screen, these settings do not affect the file size. Decreasing the size of an image using the H (height) and W (width) settings in the Property inspector does *not* reduce the time it will take the file to download. Ideally you should use graphics that have the smallest file size and the highest quality possible, so that each page downloads in eight seconds or less.

---

stand out on a page. In the Web page shown in Figure 31, the horizontal and vertical space around the images in the center column helps make these images more prominent. Adding horizontal or vertical space does not affect the width or height of the image. Spacing around Web page objects can also be created by using "spacer" images, or clear images that act as placeholders.

Using Alternate Text

One of the easiest ways to make your Web page viewer-friendly and handicapped-accessible is to use alternate text. **Alternate text** is descriptive text that appears in place of an image while the image is downloading or when the mouse pointer is placed over it. You can program some browsers to display only alternate text and to download images manually. Alternate text can be "read" by a **screen reader**, a device used by the visually impaired to convert written text on a computer monitor to spoken words. Screen readers and alternate text make it possible for visually impaired viewers to have an image described to them in detail. You can also set up Dreamweaver to prompt you to enter alternate text whenever you insert an image on a page.

The use of alternate text is the first checkpoint listed in the World Wide Web Consortium (W3C) list of Priority 1 checkpoints. The Priority 1 checkpoints dictate the most basic level of accessibility standards to be used by Web developers today. The complete list of these and the other priority level checkpoints are listed on the W3C Web site, *www.w3.org*. You should always strive to meet these criteria for all Web pages.

FIGURE 31
Lands' End Web site

Add a border

1. Select the club house image, then expand the Property inspector (if necessary).

2. Type **1** in the Border text box, then press **[Tab]** to apply the border to the club house image, as shown in Figure 32.

3. Repeat Step 2 to add borders to the rest of the images.

You added a 1-pixel border to each image on the about us page.

Add horizontal space

1. Select the club house image, type **7** in the V Space text box in the Property inspector, press **[Tab]**, type **7** in the H Space text box, then compare your screen to Figure 33.

   The text is more evenly wrapped around the image and is easier to read, because it is not so close to the edge of the image.

2. Repeat Step 1 to set the V Space and H Space to 7 for the other four images.

   The spacing under each picture differs because of the difference in the lengths of the paragraphs.

You added horizontal spacing and vertical spacing around each image on the about us page.

FIGURE 32
Using the Property inspector to add a border

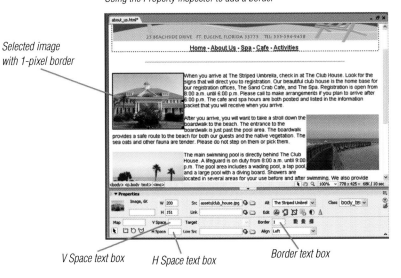

Selected image with 1-pixel border

V Space text box   H Space text box   Border text box

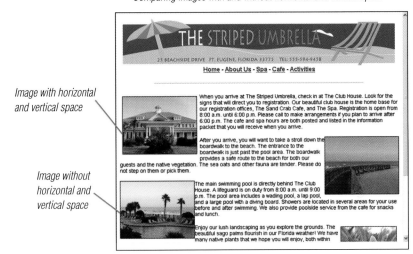

Image with horizontal and vertical space

Image without horizontal and vertical space

Working with Text and Graphics

Apply the Brightness/Contrast feature to graphics

1. Select the boardwalk image.

2. Click the **Brightness and Contrast button** in the Property inspector, then click **OK** to close the warning dialog box and open the Brightness/Contrast dialog box.

3. Compare your screen to Figure 34, then drag the **Brightness slider** slightly to the right to lighten the image, as shown in Figure 34.

4. Repeat Step 3 to adjust any of the other images if desired, then click **OK**.

   TIP To scale an image, first select the image, then drag one of the borders toward the center of the image to reduce it, or drag away from the center of the image to enlarge it.

You used the Brightness/Contrast dialog box to lighten an image.

FIGURE 34

Brightness and contrast settings for the boardwalk image

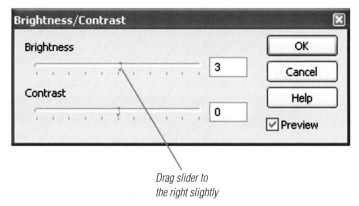

Drag slider to
the right slightly

Use alternate text

1. Select the club house image, type **The Striped Umbrella Club House** in the Alt text box in the Property inspector, as shown in Figure 35, then press **[Enter]** (Win) or **[return]** (Mac).

2. Save your work, preview the page in your browser, then point to the **club house image** until the alternate text appears, as shown in Figure 36.

3. Close your browser.

4. Select the boardwalk image, type **The board-walk to the beach** in the Alt text box in the Property inspector, then press **[Enter]** (Win) or **[return]** (Mac).

5. Repeat Step 4 to add the alternate text **The pool area** to the pool image.

6. Repeat Step 4 to add the alternate text **Sago palm** to the sago palm image.

7. Repeat Step 4 to add the alternate text **The Sports Club** to the sports club image.

8. Save your work.

9. Preview the page in your browser, view the alternate text for each image, then close your browser.

You added alternate text to five images on the page, then you viewed the alternate text in your browser.

FIGURE 35

Alternate text setting in the Property inspector

Alt text box

FIGURE 36

Alternate text displayed in browser

Alternate text displayed on top of image

FIGURE 37
Preferences dialog box with Accessibility category selected

Accessibility
category

Check boxes for
Form objects,
Frames, Media,
and Images

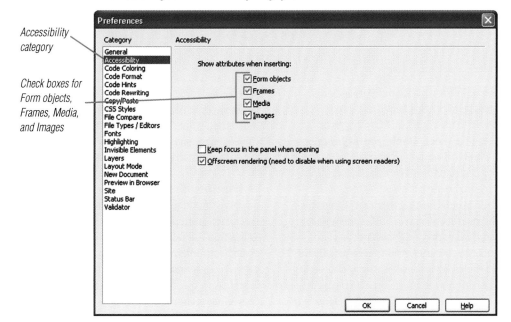

1. Click **Edit** (Win) or **Dreamweaver** (Mac) on the menu bar, click **Preferences** to open the Preferences dialog box, then click the **Accessibility category**.

2. Click the **four check boxes**, if necessary, as shown in Figure 37, then click **OK**.

   TIP Once you set the Accessibility preferences, they will be in effect for all Web sites that you develop, not just the one that's open when you set them.

You set the Accessibility preferences to prompt you to enter alternate text each time you insert a form object, frame, or media or image object on a Web page.

INSERT A BACKGROUND IMAGE
AND PERFORM SITE MAINTENANCE

What You'll Do

 In this lesson, you will insert two types of tiled background images. You will then use the Assets panel to delete them both from the Web site. You will also check for Non-Websafe colors in the Assets panel and delete one that you locate on the home page.

Inserting a Background Image

You can insert a background image on a Web page to provide depth and visual interest to the page, or to communicate a message or mood. **Background images** are graphic files used in place of background colors. Although you can use background images to create a dramatic effect, you should avoid inserting them on Web pages that have lots of text and other elements. Even though they might seem too plain, standard white backgrounds are usually the best choice for Web pages. If you choose to use a background image on a Web page, it should be small in file size, and preferably in GIF format. You can insert either a small graphic file that is tiled, or repeated, across the page or a larger graphic that is not repeated across the page. A tiled image will download much faster than a large image. A **tiled image** is a small graphic that repeats across and down a Web page, appearing as individual squares or rectangles. When you create a Web page, you should use either a background color or a

background image, but not both, unless you have a need for the background color to be displayed while the background image finishes downloading. The background in the Web page shown in Figure 38 contains several images arranged in a table format.

Managing Graphics

As you work on a Web site, you might find that you accumulate files in your assets folder that are not used in the site. To avoid accumulating unnecessary files, it's a good idea to look at a graphic on a page first, before you copy it to the assets folder. If you inadvertently copy an unwanted file to the assets folder, you should delete it or move it to another location. This is a good Web-site management practice that will prevent the assets folder from filling up with unwanted graphics.

Removing a graphic from a Web page does not remove it from the assets folder in the local root folder of the Web site. To remove an asset from a Web site, you first locate the file you want to remove in the Assets panel. You then use the Locate in Site command to open the Files panel with the unwanted file selected. You then use the Delete command to remove the file from the site.

QUICKTIP

You cannot use the Assets panel to delete a file. You must use the Files panel to delete files and perform all file-management tasks.

Removing Colors from a Web Site

You can use the Assets panel to locate Non-Websafe colors in a Web site. **Non-Websafe** colors are colors that may not be displayed uniformly across computer platforms. After you remove colors from a Web site, you should use the Refresh Site List button on the Assets panel to verify that these colors have been removed. Sometimes it's necessary to press [Ctrl] (Win) or ⌘ (Mac) while you click the Refresh Site List button. If refreshing the Assets panel does not work, try recreating the site cache, then refreshing the Assets panel again

QUICKTIP

To recreate the site cache, click Site on the menu bar, point to Advanced, then click Recreate Site Cache.

FIGURE 38
The Mansion on Turtle Creek home page

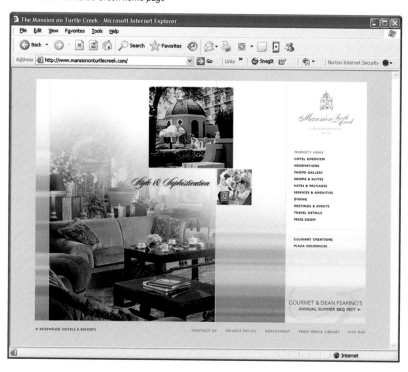

Insert a background image

1. Click **Modify** on the menu bar, then click **Page Properties** to open the Page Properties dialog box.

2. Click the **Appearance category**, if necessary.

3. Click **Browse** next to the Background image text box, navigate to the chapter_3 assets folder, then double-click **umbrella_back.gif**.

   The umbrella_back.gif file is automatically copied to The Striped Umbrella assets folder.

4. Click **OK** to close the Page Properties dialog box, then click the **Refresh Site List button** [icon] to refresh the file list in the Assets panel.

   A file with a single umbrella forms a background made up of individual squares, replacing the white background, as shown in Figure 39. It is much too busy and makes it difficult to read the page.

5. Repeat Steps 1 through 4 to replace the umbrella_back.gif background image with stripes_bak.gif, located in the chapter_3 assets folder.

   As shown in Figure 40, the striped background is still being tiled, but with vertical stripes you aren't aware of the small squares making up the pattern. It is still too busy, though.

You applied a tiled background to the about us page. Then you replaced the tiled background with another tiled background that was not as busy.

FIGURE 39
The about us page with a busy tiled background

Each umbrella is a small square that forms a tiled background

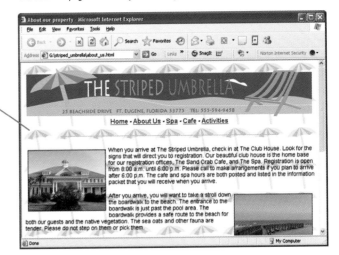

FIGURE 40
The about us page with a more subtle tiled background

It is harder to tell where each square ends

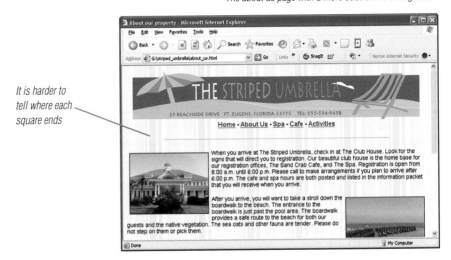

Working with Text and Graphics

FIGURE 41

Removing a background image

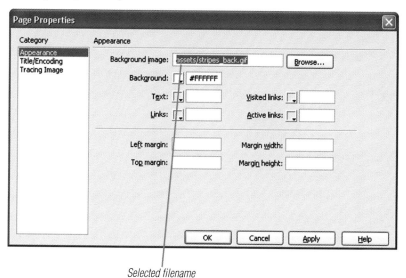

Selected filename

Remove a background image from a page

1. Click **Modify** on the menu bar, click **Page Properties**, then click **Appearance**.

2. Select the text in the Background image text box, as shown in Figure 41, press **[Delete]**, then click **OK**.

   The background of the about us page is white again.

You deleted the link to the background image file to change the about us page background back to white.

Understanding HTML body tags

When you are setting page preferences, it is handy to understand the HTML tags that are being generated. Sometimes it's much easier to make changes to the code, rather than through menus and dialog boxes. The <body> </body> tags define the beginning and end of the body section of a Web page. The page content falls between those two tags. If you want to change the page properties, additional codes will be added to the <body> tag. The tag to add a color to the page background is bgcolor, so the tag will read <body bgcolor="#000000">, where the numbers following the pound sign indicate a color. If you insert an image for a background, the code will read <body background="assets/stripes.gif">. The filename between the quotes is the name of the graphic file used for the background.

Delete files from a Web site

1. Click the **Assets panel tab** (if necessary).

2. Right-click (Win) or [control]-click (Mac) **stripes_back.gif** in the Assets panel, click **Locate in Site** to open the Files panel, click the **Refresh button** [C], select **stripes_back.gif** in the Files panel (if necessary), press **[Delete]**, then click **Yes** in the dialog box that appears.

3. Repeat Step 2 to remove umbrella_back.gif from the Web site, open the Assets panel, then refresh the Assets panel.

   TIP   If you delete a file in the Files panel that has an active link to it, you will receive a warning message. If you rename a file in the Files panel that has a link to it, the Files panel will update the links to correctly link to the renamed file. To rename a file, right-click (Win) or [control]-click (Mac) the file you want to rename, point to Edit, click Rename, then type the new name.

   Your Assets panel should resemble Figure 42.

You removed two image files from The Striped Umbrella Web site, then refreshed the Assets panel.

FIGURE 42
Images listed in Assets panel

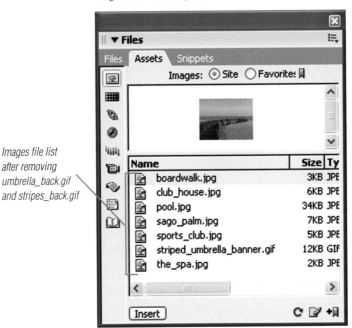

Images file list after removing umbrella_back.gif and stripes_back.gif

Managing graphic files

It is a good idea to store copies of your original Web site graphic files in a separate folder, outside the assets folder of your Web site. If you edit the original files, save them again using different names. Doing this ensures that you will be able to find a file in its original, unaltered state. You might have no need for certain files now, but you might need them later. Storing currently unused files also helps to keep your assets folder free of clutter. Storing copies of original Web site graphic files in a separate location also ensures that you have back-up copies in the event that you accidentally delete a file from the Web site that you need later.

FIGURE 43

Colors listed in Assets panel

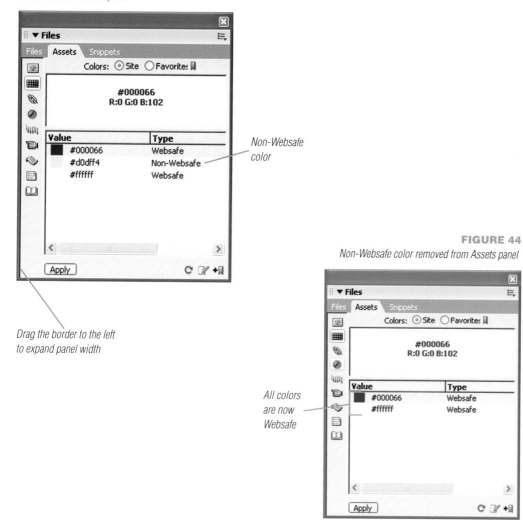

Non-Websafe color

Drag the border to the left to expand panel width

FIGURE 44

Non-Websafe color removed from Assets panel

All colors are now Websafe

Remove Non-Websafe colors from a Web site

1. Click the **Colors button** ⬚ in the Assets panel to display the colors used in the Web site, then drag the left border of the Assets panel (if necessary) to display the second column.

   The Assets panel shows that color d0dff4 is Non-Websafe, as shown in Figure 43. This color was the original background color on the home page. We removed it, but it is still listed in the list of colors used in the Web site.

   > TIP If you do not see any Non-Websafe colors in your Assets panel, your cache has already been cleared and you can skip Steps 2 and 3.

2. Click the **Refresh Site List button** ⟳.

3. Press and hold [**control**] (Win) or ⌘ (Mac) while you click the **Refresh Site List button**.

   The color is removed, as shown in Figure 44. Sometimes the Refresh Site List button doesn't work. If it doesn't, try pressing and holding [control] (Win) or ⌘ (Mac). If that doesn't work, recreate the site cache.

4. Save your work, preview the page in your browser, close your browser, then close all open files.

You removed one Non-Websafe color from the Assets panel list of colors.

Create unordered and ordered lists.

1. Open the blooms & bulbs Web site.
2. Open the tips page.
3. Select the four lines of text below the Seasonal Gardening Checklist heading and format them as an unordered list. (*Hint*: If each line does not become a separate list item, enter a paragraph break between each line, then remove any extra spaces.)
4. Select the lines of text below the Basic Gardening Tips heading and format them as an ordered list.
5. Save your work.

Create, apply, and edit Cascading Style Sheets.

1. Create a new CSS rule named **seasons**, making sure that the Class option button is selected in the Selector Type section and that the (New Style Sheet File) option button is selected in the Define in section of the New CSS Rule dialog box.
2. Click OK, name the style sheet file **blooms_styles** in the Save Style Sheet File As dialog box, then click Save.
3. Choose the following settings for the seasons style: Font = Arial, Helvetica, sans-serif, Size = 12 pixels, Style = normal, Weight = bold, and Color = #003366.
4. Change the Font setting to Default Font and the Size setting to None for the following words in the Seasonal Gardening Checklist: Fall, Winter, Spring, and Summer. Then, apply the seasons style to Fall, Winter, Spring, and Summer.
5. Edit the seasons style by changing the font size to 16 pixels.
6. Add an additional style called **headings** in the blooms_styles.css file and define this style choosing the following type settings: Font = Arial, Helvetica, sans-serif, Size = 18 pixels, Style = normal, Weight = bold, and Color = #003366.
7. Apply the headings style to the two sub-headings on the page: Seasonal Gardening Checklist and Basic Gardening Tips. (Make sure you remove any manual formatting before applying the style.)
8. Click File on the menu bar, click Save All, view the page in the browser, then compare your screen to Figure 45.
9. Close the browser and all open pages.

Insert and align graphics.

1. Open dw3_2.html from the chapter_3 Data Files folder, save it as **plants.html** in the blooms & bulbs Web site, overwriting the existing plants.html file, and do not update links.
2. Verify that the path of the blooms & bulbs banner is set correctly to the assets folder in the blooms root folder.
3. Set the Accessibility preferences to prompt you to add alternate text to images (if necessary).
4. Insert the petunias.jpg file from the assets folder located in the chapter_3 Data Files folder to the left of the words Pretty petunias and add **Petunias** as alternate text.
5. Insert the verbena.jpg file from the chapter_3 Data Files folder in front of the words Verbena is one and add **Verbena** as alternate text.
6. Insert the lantana.jpg file from the chapter_3 assets folder in front of the words Dramatic masses and add **Lantana** as alternate text.
7. Refresh the Files panel to verify that all three images were copied to the assets folder.
8. Left-align the petunias image.
9. Right-align the verbena image.
10. Left-align the lantana image.
11. Save your work, then compare your screen to Figure 46.

Enhance an image and use alternate text.

1. Apply a 1-pixel border and horizontal spacing of 20 pixels around the petunias image.
2. Apply a 1-pixel border and horizontal spacing of 20 pixels around the verbenas image.
3. Apply a 1-pixel border and horizontal spacing of 20 pixels around the lantanas image.
4. Open the index page and add appropriate alternate text to the banner.
5. Save your work.

Insert a background image and manage graphics.

1. Switch to the plants page, then insert the daisies.jpg file from the chapter_3 assets folder as a background image.
2. Save your work.
3. Preview the Web page in your browser, then close your browser.
4. Remove the daisies.jpg file from the background.
5. Open the Assets panel, then refresh the Files list.
6. Use the Files panel to delete the daisies.jpg file from the list of images.
7. Refresh the Assets panel, then verify that the daisies.jpg file has been removed from the Web site.
8. View the colors used in the site in the Assets panel, then verify that all are Websafe.
9. Save your work, then close all open pages.

FIGURE 45
Completed Skills Review

We have some planting tips we would like to share with you as you prepare your gardens this season. Remember, there is always something to be done for your gardens, no matter what the season. Our experienced staff is here to help you plan your gardens, select your plants, prepare your soil, assist you in the planting, and maintain your beds. Check out our calendar for a list of our scheduled classes. All classes are free of charge and on a first-come, first-served basis!

Seasonal Gardening Checklist:

- **Fall** – The time to plant trees and spring blooming bulbs.
- **Winter** – The time to prune fruit trees and finish planting your bulbs.
- **Spring** – The time to prepare your beds, plant annuals, and apply fertilizer to established plants.
- **Summer** – The time to supplement rainfall so that plants get one inch of water per week.

Basic Gardening Tips

1. Select plants according to your climate.
2. In planning your garden, consider the composition, texture, structure, depth, and drainage of your soil.
3. Use compost to improve the structure of your soil.
4. Choose plant foods based on your garden objectives.
5. Generally, plants should receive one inch of water per week.
6. Use mulch to conserve moisture, keep plants cool, and cut down on weeding.

FIGURE 46
Completed Skills Review

Drop by to see our Featured Spring Plants

Pretty petunias blanket your beds with lush green leaves and bright blooms in assorted colors. Shown is the Moonlight White Petunia (Mini-Spreading). This variety is fast-growing and produces spectacular blooms. Cut them back in July for blooms that will last into the fall. Full sun to partial shade. Great for border plants or hanging baskets.

Verbena is one of our all-time favorites. The variety shown is Blue Silver. Verbena grows rapidly and is a good choice for butterfly gardens. The plants can spread up to two feet wide, so it makes excellent ground cover. Plant in full sun. Heat resistant. Beautiful also in rock gardens. We have several other varieties equally as beautiful.

Dramatic masses of Lantana display summer color for your beds or containers. The variety shown is Golden Dream. Blooms late spring through early fall. This variety produces outstanding color. Plant in full sun with well-drained soil. We carry tall, dwarf, and trailing varieties. You can also overwinter with cuttings.

Stop by to see us soon. We will be happy to help you with your selections.

Use Figures 47 and 48 as guides to continue your work on the TripSmart Web site that you began in Project Builder 1 in Chapter 1. You are now ready to format text on the newsletter page and begin work on the destinations page that showcases one of the featured tours to Kenya. You want to include some colorful pictures and attractively formatted text on the page.

1. Open the TripSmart Web site.
2. Open dw3_3.html from the chapter_3 Data Files folder and save it in the tripsmart root folder as **newsletter.html**, overwriting the existing newsletter.html file and do not update the links.
3. Verify that the path for the banner is correctly set to the assets folder of the TripSmart Web site. Create an unordered list from the text beginning "Expandable clothesline" to the end of the page.
4. Create a new CSS Rule called **bodytext**, making sure that the Class option button is selected in the Selector Type section and that the (New Style Sheet File) option button is selected in the Define in section of the New CSS Rule dialog box.
5. Save the style sheet file as **tripsmart_styles.css** in the TripSmart Web site root folder.
6. Choose a font, size, style, color, and weight of your choice for the bodytext style.
7. Apply the bodytext style to all of the text on the page except the "Ten Packing Essentials" heading on the newsletter page.

8. Create another style called **heading** with a font, size, style, color, and weight of your choice and apply it to the "Ten Packing Essentials" heading.
9. Type **Travel Tidbits** in the Title text box on the Document toolbar, then save and close the newsletter page.
10. Open dw3_4.html from the chapter_3 Data Files folder and save it in the tripsmart root folder as **destinations.html**, overwriting the existing destinations.html file, and do not update links.
11. Insert zebra_mothers.jpg from the chapter_3 assets folder to the left of the sentence beginning "Our next", then add appropriate alternate text.
12. Insert lion.jpg from the chapter_3 assets folder to the left of the sentence beginning "This lion", then add appropriate alternate text.

13. Align both images using the Align list arrow in the Property inspector, then add horizontal spacing, vertical spacing, or borders if desired.
14. Apply the heading style to the "Destination: Kenya" heading and the bodytext style to the rest of the text on the page.
15. Apply any additional formatting to enhance the page appearance, then add the page title **Destination: Kenya**.
16. Verify that the Accessibility Preference option is turned on.
17. Save your work, then preview the destinations page in your browser.
18. Close your browser, then close all open files.

FIGURE 47
Sample Project Builder 1

FIGURE 48
Sample Project Builder 2

In this exercise you will continue your work on the emma's book bag Web site that you started in Project Builder 2 in Chapter 1. You are now ready to add two new pages to the Web site. One page will display a list of featured books and another page will describe the story hour that the bookstore sponsors each Saturday morning. Figures 49 and 50 show possible solutions for this exercise. Your finished pages will look different if you choose different formatting options.

1. Open the emma's book bag Web site.
2. Open dw3_5.html from the chapter_3 Data Files folder, save it to the book_bag root folder as **books.html**, overwriting the existing file and not updating the links.
3. Format the list of books as an ordered list.
4. Create a CSS rule named **bodytext** and save the style sheet file as **book_bag_styles.css** in the emma's book bag Web site root folder. Use any formatting options that you like, and then apply the bodytext style to the first paragraph and the list of books.
5. Create another style called **heading** using appropriate formatting options and apply it to the line of text beginning with "Featured books".

6. Add appropriate alternate text to the banner, then save and close the file.
7. Open dw3_6.html from the chapter_3 Data Files folder and save it as **corner.html**, over-writing the existing file and not updating the links.
8. Apply the bodytext style to the paragraph text.

FIGURE 49
Completed Project Builder 1

9. Insert the reading.jpg image from the chapter_3 assets folder next to the paragraph, choosing an alignment and spacing of your choice and adding appropriate alternate text.
10. Add the page title **Caroline's Corner** to the page, save all pages, then preview both new pages in the browser.
11. Close your browser, then close all open pages.

FIGURE 50
Completed Project Builder 2

Don Chappell is a new sixth-grade history teacher. He is reviewing educational Web sites for information he can use in his classroom.

1. Connect to the Internet, navigate to the Online Companion, then select the link for this chapter. The Library of Congress Web site is shown in Figure 51.
2. Which fonts are used for the main content on the home page? Are the same fonts used consistently on the other pages in the Web site?
3. Do you see ordered or unordered lists on any pages in the Web site? If so, how are they used?
4. Use the Source command on the View menu to view the source code to see if a set of fonts was used. If so, which one?
5. Do you see the use of Cascading Style Sheets noted in the source code?
6. Select another site from the list and compare the use of text on the two sites.

FIGURE 51
Design Project

In this assignment, you will continue to work on the Web site that you started in Chapter 1. There will be no data files supplied. You are building this Web site from chapter to chapter, so you must do each Portfolio Project assignment in each chapter to complete your Web site.

You will continue building your Web site by designing and completing a page that contains a list, headings, body text, graphics, and a background. During this process, you will develop a style sheet and add several styles to it. You will insert appropriate graphics on your page and enhance them for maximum effect. You will also check for Non-Websafe colors and remove any that you find.

1. Consult your storyboard and decide which page to create and develop for this chapter.
2. Plan the page content for the page and make a sketch of the layout. Your sketch should include at least one ordered or unordered list, appropriate headings, body text, several graphics, and a background color or image. Your sketch should also show where the body text and headings should be placed on the page and what styles should be used for each type of text. You should plan on creating at least two styles.
3. Create the page using your sketch for guidance.

4. Create a Cascading Style Sheet for the Web site and add to it the styles you decided to use. Apply the styles to the appropriate content.
5. Access the graphics you gathered in Chapter 1, and place the graphics on the page so that the page matches the sketch you created in Step 2. Add a background image if you want to and appropriate alternate text for each graphic.
6. Remove any Non-Websafe colors.
7. Identify any files in the Assets panel that are currently not used in the Web site. Decide which of these assets should be removed, then delete these files.

8. Preview the new page in a browser, then check for page layout problems and broken links. Make any necessary fixes in Dreamweaver, then preview the page again in the browser. Repeat this process until you are satisfied with the way the page looks in the browser.
9. Use the check list in Figure 52 to check all the pages in your site.
10. Close the browser, save your changes to the page, then close the page.

FIGURE 52
Portfolio Project check list

Web Site Check List

1. Does each page have a page title?
2. Does the home page have a description and keywords?
3. Does the home page contain contact information?
4. Does every page in the Web site have consistent navigation links?
5. Does the home page have a last updated statement that will automatically update when the page is saved?
6. Do all paths for links and images work correctly?
7. Do all images have alternate text?
8. Are all colors Websafe?
9. Are there any unnecessary files you can delete from the assets folder?
10. Is there a style sheet with at least two styles?
11. Did you apply the styles to page content?
12. Do all pages view well using at least two different browsers?

4 WORKING WITH
LINKS

MACROMEDIA DREAMWEAVER 8

1. Create external and internal links.

2. Create internal links to named anchors.

3. Insert rollovers with Flash text.

4. Create, modify, and copy a navigation bar.

5. Manage Web site links.

Introduction

What makes Web sites so powerful are the links that connect one page to another within a Web site or to any page on the Web. Though you can add graphics, animations, movies, and other enhancements to a Web site to make it visually attractive, the links you include are often the most essential components of a Web site. Links that connect the pages within a Web site are always very important because they help viewers navigate between the pages of the site. However, if one of your goals is to keep viewers from leaving your Web site, you might want to avoid including links to other Web sites. For example, most e-commerce sites include only links to other pages in the site to discourage shoppers from leaving the site. In this chapter you will create links to other pages in The Striped Umbrella Web site and to other sites on the Web. You will also insert a navigation bar that contains graphics instead of text, and check the links in The Striped Umbrella Web site to make sure they all work correctly.

Understanding Internal and External Links

Web pages contain two types of links: internal links and external links. **Internal links** are links to Web pages in the same Web site, and **external links** are links to Web pages in other Web sites or to e-mail addresses. Both internal and external links have two important parts that work together. The first part of a link is the element that viewers see and click on a Web page, for example, text, a graphic, or a button. The second part of a link is the **path**, or the name and location of the Web page or file that will open when the element is clicked. Setting and maintaining the correct paths for all your links is essential to avoid having broken links in your site.

Tools You'll Use

Named Anchor button

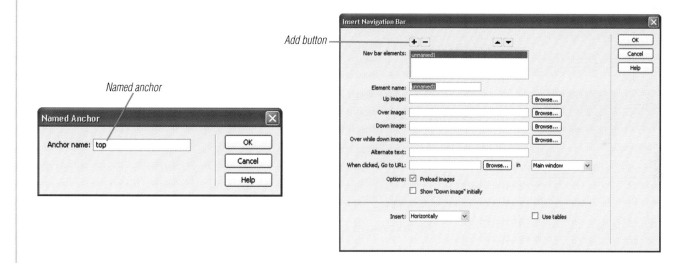

Add button

Named anchor

CREATE EXTERNAL AND
INTERNAL LINKS

What You'll Do

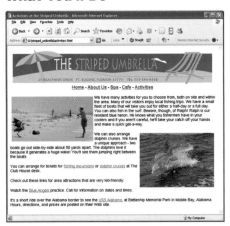

In this lesson, you will create external links on The Striped Umbrella activities page that link to Web sites related to area attractions. You will also create internal links to other pages within The Striped Umbrella Web site.

Creating External Links

A good Web site usually includes a variety of external links to other related Web sites so that viewers can get more information on a particular topic. To create an external link, you first select the text or object that you want to serve as a link, then you type the absolute path to the destination Web page in the Link text box in the Property inspector. An **absolute path** is a path used for external links that includes the complete address for the destination page, including the protocol (such as http://) and the complete **URL** (Uniform Resource Locator), or address, of the destination page. When necessary, the Web page filename and folder hierarchy are also part of an absolute path. Figure 1 shows an example of an absolute path showing the protocol, URL, and filename. After you enter external links on a Web page, you can view them in the site map. An example for the code for an external link would be <a href="http://www.macromedia.com" Macromedia Web site </a>.

FIGURE 1
An example of an absolute path

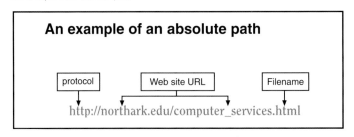

An example of an absolute path

protocol	Web site URL	Filename

http://northark.edu/computer_services.html

Creating Internal Links

Each page in a Web site usually focuses on an individual category or topic. You should make sure that the home page provides links to each page in the site, and that all pages in the site contain numerous internal links so that viewers can move easily from page to page. To create an internal link, you first select the text element or graphic object that you want to make a link, then you use the Browse for File icon next to the Link text box in the Property inspector to specify the relative path to the destination page. A **relative path** is a type of path used to reference Web pages and graphic files within the same Web site. Relative paths include the filename and folder location of a file. Figure 2 shows an example of a relative path. Table 1 describes absolute paths and relative paths. Relative paths can either be site root relative or document relative. You can also use the Point to File icon in the Property inspector to point to the file you want to use for the link, or drag the file you want to use for the link from the Files panel into the Link text box on the Property inspector.

You should take great care in managing your internal links to make sure they work correctly and are timely and relevant to the page content. You should design the navigation structure of your Web site so that viewers are never more than three or four clicks away from the page they are seeking. An example for the code for an internal link would be <a href="activities.html" Activities page </a>.

FIGURE 2

An example of a relative path

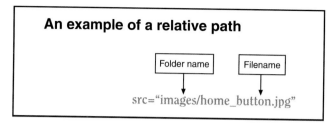

TABLE 1: Description of absolute and relative paths

type of path	description	examples
Absolute path	Used for external links and specifies protocol, URL, and filename of destination page	*http://www.yahoo.com/recreation*
Relative path	Used for internal links and specifies location of file relative to the current page	spa.html or assets/heron.gif
Root-relative path	Used for internal links when publishing to a server that contains many Web sites or where the Web site is so large it requires more than one server	/striped_umbrella/activities.html
Document-relative path	Used in most cases for internal links and specifies the location of file relative to current page	cafe.html or assets/heron.gif

Create an external link

1. Open The Striped Umbrella Web site that you completed in Chapter 3, open dw4_1.html from the chapter_4 folder where your Data Files are stored, then save it as **activities** in the striped_umbrella root folder, overwriting the existing activities page, but not updating links.

2. Attach the su_style.css file, then apply the body text style to the paragraphs of text on the page (not to the navigation bar).

3. Select the first broken image, click the **Browse for File icon** next to the Src text box, then select the heron_waiting_small.jpg in the Data Files folder to save the graphic in your assets folder.

4. Repeat Step 3 for the second image, two_dolphins_small.jpg.

5. Scroll down, then select the text "Blue Angels".

6. Click in the Link text box in the Property inspector, type **http://www.blueangels. navy.mil**, press [**Enter**] (Win) or [**return**] (Mac), then compare your screen to Figure 3.

7. Repeat Steps 5 and 6 to create a link for the USS Alabama site in the next paragraph: http://www.ussalabama.com.

8. Save your work, preview the page in your browser, test all the links to make sure they work, then close your browser.

   TIP   You must have an active Internet connection to test the links. If clicking a link does not open a page, make sure you typed the URL correctly in the Link text box.

You opened The Striped Umbrella Web site, replaced the existing activities page, attached the su_styles.css.file, applied the body text style to the text, then added two external links to other sites on the page. You also tested each link in your browser.

FIGURE 3
Creating an external link to the Blue Angels Web site

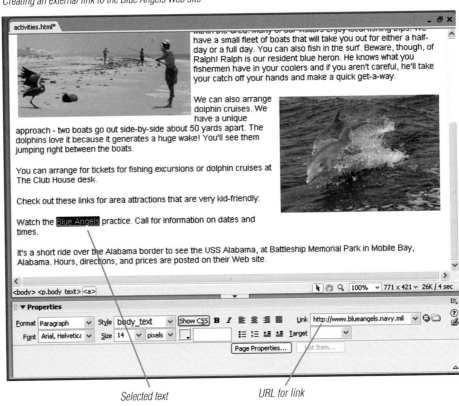

Selected text   *URL for link*

FIGURE 4

Site map displaying external links on the activities page

Click to collapse
window

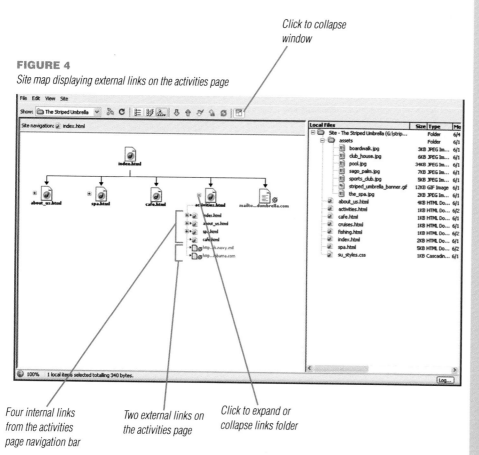

Four internal links
from the activities
page navigation bar

Two external links on
the activities page

Click to expand or
collapse links folder

View external links in the site map

1. Click the **Expand to show local and remote sites button** ⊡ on the Files panel to expand the Files panel.

2. Click the **Site Map list arrow** on the toolbar then click **Map and Files**.

   Four links from the navigation bar appear as internal links.

   > TIP If you want to view or hide page titles in the site map, click View on the menu bar, point to Site Map Options, then click Show Page Titles (Win) or click the Options button in the Files panel group title bar, point to View, then click Show Page Titles (Mac).

3. Click the **plus sign** to the left of the activities page icon in the site map (if necessary) to view a list of the two external links you created, as shown in Figure 4.

4. Click the **minus sign** to the left of the activities page icon in the site map to collapse the list of links.

5. Click the **Collapse to show only local or remote site button** ⊡ , on the toolbar.

You viewed The Striped Umbrella site map and expanded the view of the activities page to display the two external links you added.

Create an internal link

1. Select the text "fishing excursions" in the third paragraph.

2. Click the **Browse for File icon** 📁 next to the Link text box in the Property inspector, then double-click **fishing.html** in the Select File dialog box to set the relative path to the fishing page.

    Notice that fishing.html appears in the Link text box in the Property inspector, as shown in Figure 5.

    > TIP To collapse all open panels below the document window, such as the Link Checker or the Property inspector, click the expander arrow in the center of the bottom border of the Document window. Pressing [F4] will hide all panels, including the ones on the right side of the screen.

3. Select the text "dolphin cruises" in the same sentence.

4. Click the **Browse for File icon** 📁 next to the Link text box in the Property inspector, then double-click **cruises.html** in the Select File dialog box to specify the relative path to the cruises page.

    The words "dolphin cruises" are now a link to the cruises page.

5. Save your work, preview the page in your browser to verify that the internal links work correctly, then close your browser.

    The fishing and cruises pages do not have page content yet, but serve as placeholders until they do.

    You created two internal links on the activities page, and then tested the links in your browser.

FIGURE 5
Creating an internal link on the activities page

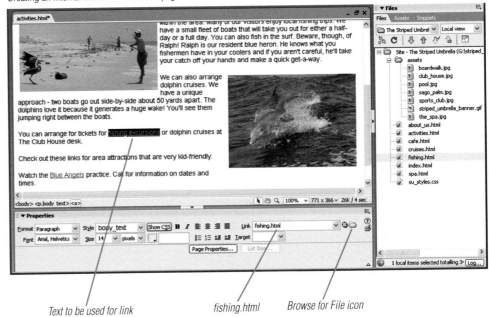

Text to be used for link   fishing.html   Browse for File icon

Typing URLs

Typing URLs in the Link text box in the Property inspector can be very tedious. When you need to type a long and complex URL, it is easy to make mistakes and create a broken link. You can avoid such mistakes by copying and pasting the URL from the Address text box (Internet Explorer) or Location text box (Netscape Navigator and Communicator) to the Link text box in the Property inspector. Copying and pasting a URL ensures that the URL is entered correctly.

FIGURE 6

Site map displaying external and internal links on the activities page

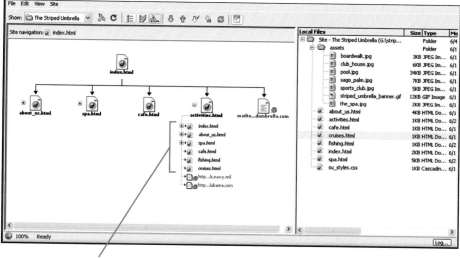

Six internal links, four from the navigation
bar and two from text links

Lesson 1   Create External and Internal Links

View internal links in the site map

1. Click the **Expand to show local and remote sites button** ⊞ on the Files panel.

2. Click the **Site Map list arrow**, then click **Map and Files**, if necessary.

3. Click the **plus sign** to the left of the activities page icon.

   A list of eight links appears below the activities page icon, as shown in Figure 6. Two are external links, and six are internal links.

   TIP If your links do not display correctly, recreate the site cache. To recreate the site cache, click Site on the menu bar, click Advanced, then click Recreate Site Cache.

4. Click the **Collapse to show only local or remote site button** ⊞ .

5. Close the activities page.

You viewed the links on the activities page in the site map.

CREATE INTERNAL LINKS
TO NAMED ANCHORS

What You'll Do

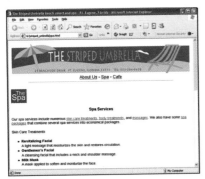

In this lesson, you will insert five named anchors on the spa page: one for the top of the page and four for each of the spa services lists. You will then create internal links to each named anchor.

Inserting Named Anchors

Some Web pages have so much content that viewers must scroll repeatedly to get to the bottom of the page and then back up to the top of the page. To make it easier for viewers to navigate to specific areas of a page without scrolling, you can use a combination of internal links and named anchors. A **named anchor** is a specific location on a Web page that has a descriptive name. Named anchors act as targets for internal links and make it easy for viewers to jump to a particular place on the same page quickly. A **target** is the location on a Web page that a browser displays when an internal link is clicked. For example, you can insert a named anchor called "top" at the top of a Web page, then

create a link to it at the bottom of the page. You can also insert named anchors in strategic places on a Web page, such as at the beginning of paragraph headings.

You insert a named anchor using the Named Anchor button on the Common category of the Insert bar, as shown in Figure 7. You then enter the name of the anchor in the Named Anchor dialog box. You should choose short names that describe the named anchor location on the page. Named anchors are represented by yellow anchor icons on a Web page. Selected anchors are represented by blue icons. You can show or hide named anchor icons by clicking View on the menu bar, pointing to Visual Aids, then clicking Invisible Elements.

Creating Internal Links to Named Anchors

Once you create a named anchor, you can create an internal link to it using one of two methods. You can select the text or graphic on the page that you want to make a link, then drag the Point to File icon from the Property inspector to the named anchor icon on the page. Or, you can select the text or graphic to which you want to make a link, then type # followed by the named anchor name (such as #top) in the Link text box in the Property inspector.

QUICKTIP

To avoid possible errors, you should create a named anchor before you create a link to it.

FIGURE 7

Named Anchor button on the Insert bar

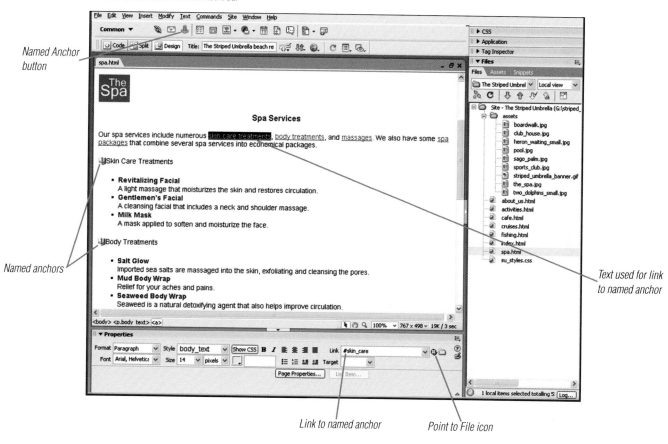

Named Anchor button

Named anchors

Text used for link to named anchor

Link to named anchor

Point to File icon

Insert a named anchor

1. Open the spa page, click the **banner** to select it, then press [←] to place the insertion point to the left of the banner.

2. Click **View** on the menu bar, point to **Visual Aids**, then verify that Invisible Elements is checked.

   TIP If there is no check mark next to Invisible Elements, this feature is turned off. Click Invisible Elements to turn this feature on.

3. Click the **Insert bar list arrow**, then click **Common**, if necessary.

4. Click the **Named Anchor button** ⚓ on the Insert bar to open the Named Anchor dialog box, type **top** in the Anchor name text box, compare your screen with Figure 8, then click **OK**.

   An anchor icon now appears before The Striped Umbrella banner.

   TIP Use lowercase letters, no spaces, and no special characters in named anchor names. You should also avoid using a number as the first character in a named anchor name.

   (continued)

FIGURE 8
Named Anchor dialog box

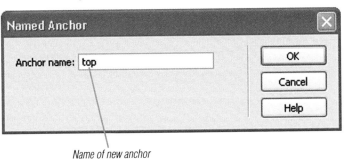

Name of new anchor

FIGURE 9

Named anchors on the spa page

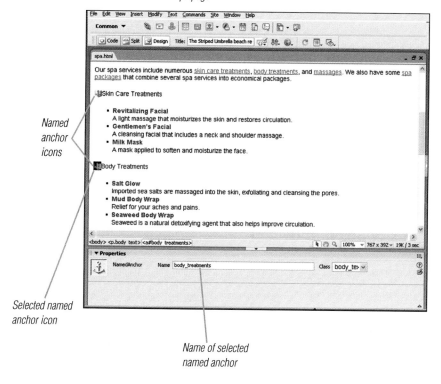

Named anchor icons

Selected named anchor icon

Name of selected named anchor

5. Click to the left of the Skin Care Treatments heading, then insert a named anchor called **skin_care**.

6. Insert named anchors to the left of the Body Treatments, Massages, and Packages headings using the following names: **body_treatments**, **massages**, and **packages**.

   Your screen should resemble Figure 9.

You created five named anchors on the activities page; one at top of the page, and four that will help viewers quickly access the Spa Services headings on the page.

Create an internal link to a named anchor

1. Select the words "skin care treatments" in the first paragraph, then drag the **Point to File icon** ⊕ from the Property inspector to the anchor named skin_care, as shown in Figure 10.

   The words "skin care treatments" are now linked to the skin_care named anchor. When viewers click the words "skin care treatments" the browser will display the Skin Care Treatments heading at the top of the browser window.

   TIP The name of a named anchor is always preceded by a pound (#) sign in the Link text box in the Property inspector.

2. Create internal links for body treatments, massages, and spa packages in the first paragraph by first selecting each of these words or phrases, then dragging the **Point to File icon** ⊕ to the appropriate named anchor icon.

   The words body "treatments," "massages," and "spa packages" are now links that connect to the Body Treatments, Massages, and Spa Packages headings.

   TIP Once you select the text you want to link, you might need to scroll down to view the named anchor on the screen. Once you see the named anchor on your screen, you can drag the Point to File icon on top of it.

   (continued)

FIGURE 10

Dragging the Point to File icon to a named anchor

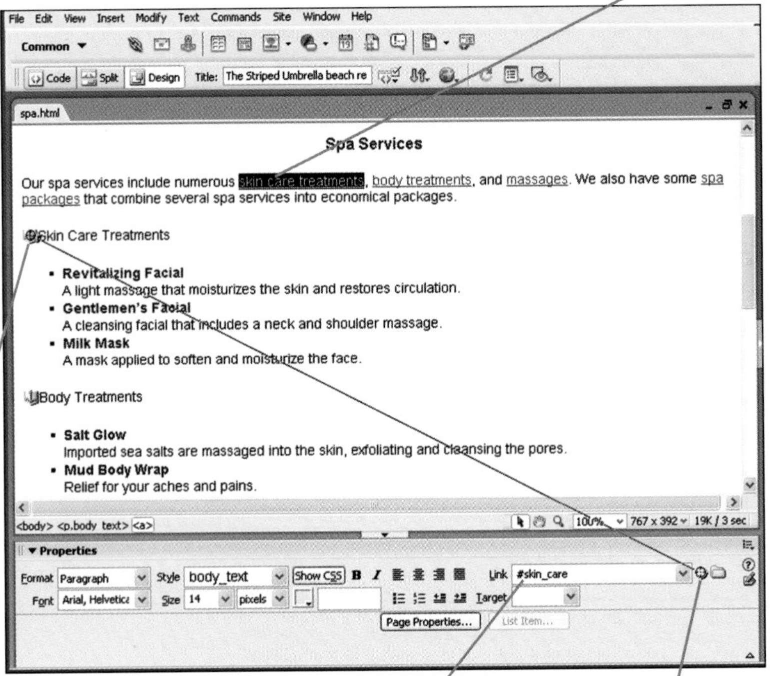

Selected text to link to named anchor

Point to File icon dragged to named anchor

Named anchor name preceded by # sign

Point to File icon

Working with Links

FIGURE 11

Spa page in Internet Explorer with internal links to named anchors

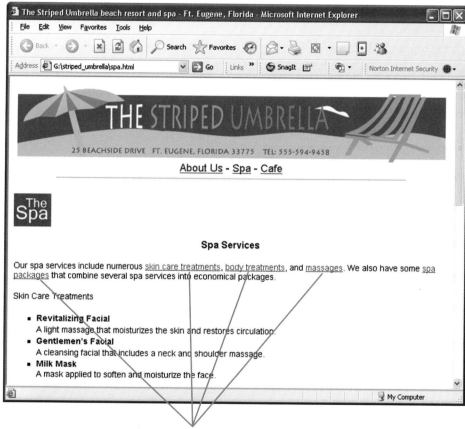

Internal links to named anchors

3. Save your work, preview the page in your browser, as shown in Figure 11, then test the links to each named anchor.

   Notice that when you click the spa packages link in the browser, the associated named anchor appears in the middle of the page instead of at the top. This happens because the spa page is not long enough to position this named anchor at the top of the page.

4. Close your browser.

You created internal links to the named anchors next to the Spa Services headings on the spa page. You then previewed the page in your browser and tested each link.

INSERT ROLLOVERS
WITH FLASH TEXT

What You'll Do

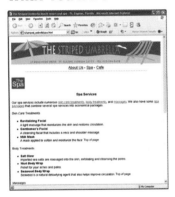

 In this lesson, you will use the Insert Flash Text dialog box to create a button that links to the top named anchor on the spa page. You will copy this button to several locations on the spa page, and then change the alignment of each button.

Understanding Flash Text

Flash is a Macromedia software program that you can use to create vector-based graphics and animations. **Vector-based graphics** are graphics that are based on mathematical formulas, as opposed to other types of graphic files such as JPG and BMP, which are based on pixels. Vector-based graphics have a smoother look and are smaller in file size than pixel-based graphics. Because they download quickly, vector-based graphics are ideal for Web sites. **Flash text** is a vector-based graphic file that contains text. You can insert Flash text to add visual interest to an otherwise dull Web page or to help deliver or reinforce a message. You can use Flash text to create internal or external links. Flash text files are saved with the .swf filename extension.

QUICK TIP

In order to view Flash animations, you must have the Flash player installed on your computer. The Flash player is free software that lets you view movies created with Macromedia software.

Inserting Flash Text on a Web Page

You can create Flash text in Dreamweaver without opening the Flash program. To insert Flash text on a Web page, you choose Common from the Insert bar, click the Media list arrow, then click Flash Text, as shown in Figure 12. Clicking this button opens the Insert Flash Text dialog box, which you use to specify the settings for the Flash text. You first need to specify the text you want to create as Flash text by typing it in the Text text box. You can then specify the font, size, and color of the Flash text, apply bold or italic styles to it, and align it using left, center, or right alignment options. You can also specify a **rollover color**, or the color in which the text will appear when the mouse pointer is placed on it. You also need to enter the path for the destination link in the Link text box. The destination link can be an internal link to another page in the site or to a named anchor on the same page, or an external link to a page on another Web site. You then use the Target list to specify how to open the destination page. The four options are described in Table 2.

QUICKTIP

Notice that the _parent option in the table specifies to display the page in the parent frameset. A **frameset** is a group of Web pages displayed using more than one **frame** or window.

Before you close the Insert Flash Text dialog box, you need to type a descriptive name for your Flash text file in the Save as text box. Flash text files must be saved in the same folder as the page that contains the Flash text. For this reason, you should save your Flash text files in the root folder of the Web site.

FIGURE 12
Media menu on the Insert bar

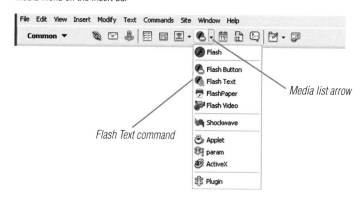

Flash Text command

Media list arrow

TABLE 2: Options in the Target list

target	result
_blank	Displays the destination page in a separate browser window
_parent	Displays the destination page in the parent frameset (replaces the frameset)
_self	Displays the destination page in the same frame or window
_top	Displays the destination page in the whole browser window

Create Flash text

1. Click after the last word on the spa page, then press **[Enter]** (Win) or **[return]** (Mac) twice to end the ordered list.

2. Click the **Insert bar list arrow**, click **Common**, click the **Media list arrow**, then click **Flash Text** to open the Insert Flash Text dialog box.

3. Type **Top of page** in the Text text box, set the Font to Arial, set the Size to 14, set the Color to #000066, set the Rollover color to #66CCFF, type **spa.html#top** in the Link text box, use the Target list arrow to set the Target to _top, type **top.swf** in the Save as text box, as shown in Figure 13, then click **OK**.

4. Type **Link to top of page** in the Flash Accessibility Attributes dialog box, then click **OK**.

   The Top of page Flash text now appears as a button at the bottom of the page. When a viewer clicks this button, the browser will display the top of the page.

5. Click **Assets** in the Files panel group to open the Assets panel, click the **Flash button** on the Assets panel, as shown in Figure 14, then click the **play button** ▷ to see the Flash text preview.

6. Drag **top.swf** from the Assets panel to the end of each of the spa services groups to insert four more links to the top of the page, adding the alternate text **Link to top of page** for each one.

   TIP Drag top.swf directly after the period in each section.

7. Click the **Files panel tab**, then refresh the Files panel (if necessary).

(continued)

FIGURE 13
Insert Flash Text dialog box

FIGURE 14
Flash category on the Assets panel

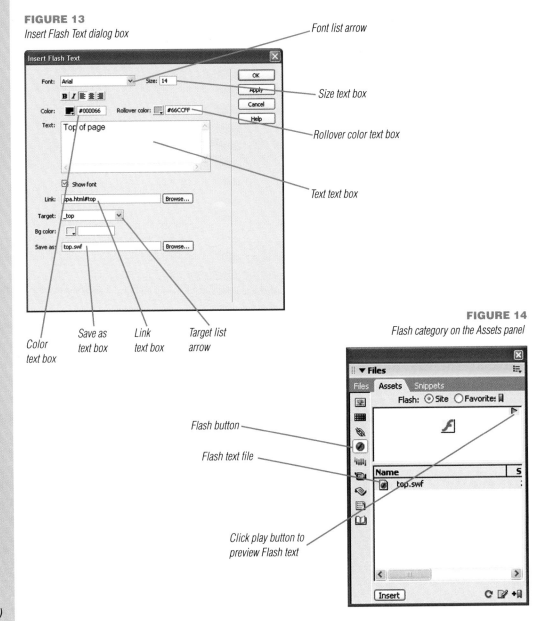

Font list arrow

Size text box

Rollover color text box

Text text box

Color text box

Save as text box

Link text box

Target list arrow

Flash button

Flash text file

Click play button to preview Flash text

Working with Links

FIGURE 15
Flash text aligned to top

Spa Services

Our spa services include numerous <u>skin care treatments</u>, <u>body treatments</u>, and <u>massages</u>. We also have some <u>spa packages</u> that combine several spa services into economical packages.

Skin Care Treatments

- **Revitalizing Facial**
  A light massage that moisturizes the skin and restores circulation.
- **Gentlemen's Facial**
  A cleansing facial that includes a neck and shoulder massage.
- **Milk Mask**
  A mask applied to soften and moisturize the face. Top of page

Body Treatments

*Flash text aligned with top of
paragraph text line*

Using Flash Player

To play Flash movies in Dreamweaver and in your browser, you must have the Flash Player installed on your computer. If the Flash Player is not installed, you can download it from the Macromedia Web site at (*www.macromedia.com*). In addition, you need to choose a specific setting in your browser. If you are using Internet Explorer, click Tools on the menu bar, click Internet Options, click the Advanced tab, click the Allow active content to run in files on my computer check box, then click OK. If you are using another browser, look for a similar setting in your Options or Preferences dialog boxes.

8. Save your work, preview the spa page in your browser, test each Top of page link, then close your browser.

> TIP If the top of the page is already displayed, the window will not move when you click the Flash text.

You used the Insert Flash Text dialog box to create a Top of page button that links to the top named anchor on the spa page. You also inserted the Top of page button at the end of each separate list of spa services, so viewers will be able to go quickly to the top of the page without scrolling.

Change the alignment of Flash text

1. Click the **Top of page button** at the end of the Skin Care Treatments section, expand the Property inspector, click the **Align list arrow** in the Property inspector, then click **Top**.

   The Top of page button is now aligned with the top of the line of text, as shown in Figure 15.

2. Apply the Top alignment setting to the Top of page button located at the end of the Body Treatments, Massages, and Spa Packages sections.

3. Collapse the Property inspector, turn off Invisible Elements, then save your work.

4. Preview the spa page in your browser, test each Top of page button, then close your browser.

You aligned the Flash text to improve its appearance on the page.

CREATE, MODIFY, AND COPY
A NAVIGATION BAR

What You'll Do

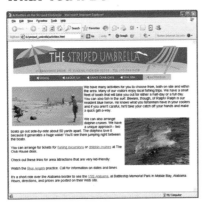

 *In this lesson, you will create a navi-
gation bar on the spa page that can
be used to link to each major page in
the Web site. The navigation bar will
have five elements: home, about us,
cafe, spa, and activities. You will also
copy the new navigation bar to other
pages in the Web site. On each page
you will modify the appropriate element state to reflect the current page.*

Creating a Navigation Bar Using Images

To make your Web site more visually appealing, you can create a navigation bar with
graphics rather than text. Any graphics
you use in a navigation bar must be created
in a graphics software program, such as
Macromedia Fireworks or Adobe Illustrator.
In order for a browser to display a navigation
bar correctly, all graphic links in the navigation bar must be exactly the same size. You
insert a navigation bar by clicking Insert
on the menu bar, pointing to Image Objects,
then clicking Navigation Bar. The Insert
Navigation Bar dialog box appears. You use
this dialog box to specify the appearance
of each graphic link, called an **element**, in
each of four possible states. A **state** is the
condition of the element in relation to the
mouse pointer. The four states are as follows: **Up image** (the state when the mouse
pointer is not on top of the element), **Over
image** (the state when the mouse pointer
is positioned on top of the element), **Down
image** (the state when you click the element), and **Over while down image**

(the state when you click the element and
continue pressing and holding the mouse
button). You can create a rollover effect by
using different colors or images to represent
each element state. You can add many special effects to navigation bars or to links on a
Web page. For instance, the Web site shown
in Figure 16 contains a navigation bar that
uses rollovers and also contains images that
link to featured items in the Web site.

QUICKTIP

You can place only one navigation bar on a Web page
using the Insert Navigation Bar dialog box. Another way
to insert a navigation bar is to choose Navigation Bar
from the Images menu when the Common category is
chosen on the Insert bar.

Copying and Modifying a Navigation Bar

After you create a navigation bar, you can
copy and paste it to the other main pages
in your site to save time. Make sure you
place the navigation bar in the same

position on each page. This practice ensures that the navigation bar will look the same on each page, making it much easier for viewers to navigate to all the pages in a Web site.

You can then use the Modify Navigation Bar dialog box to customize the appearance of the copied navigation bar on each page. For example, you can change the appearance of the spa navigation bar element on the spa page so that it appears in a different color. Highlighting the navigation element for the current page provides a visual reminder so that viewers can quickly tell which page they are viewing. This process ensures that the navigation bar will look consistent across all pages, but will be customized for each page.

FIGURE 16
Ohio Historical Society Web site

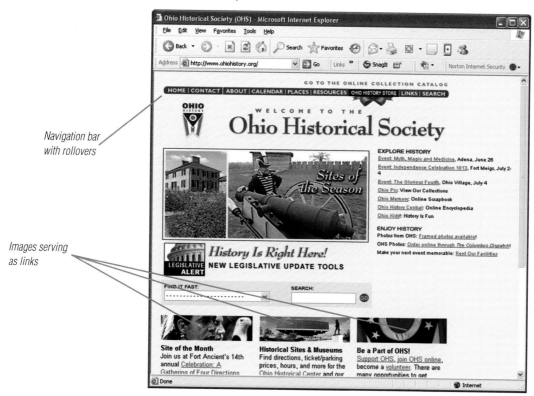

Navigation bar with rollovers

Images serving as links

Create a navigation bar using images

1. Select the navigation bar (About Us - Spa - Cafe) on the spa page, then delete it.

   The insertion point is now positioned between the banner and the horizontal rule.

2. Click the **Insert bar list arrow**, click **Common**, click the **Images list arrow**, then click **Navigation Bar**.

3. Type **home** in the Element name text box, click the **Insert list arrow** in the dialog box, click **Horizontally** (if necessary), to specify that the navigation bar be placed horizontally on the page, then remove the check mark in the Use tables check box.

4. Click **Browse** next to the Up image text box, navigate to the drive and folder where your Data Files are stored, double-click (Win) or click (Mac) the **chapter_4 folder**, double-click (Win) or click (Mac) the **assets folder**, then double-click **home_up.gif**.

   The path to the file home_up.gif appears in the Up image text box, as shown in Figure 17.

5. Click **Browse** next to the Over image text box to specify a path to the file home_down.gif located in the chapter_4 assets folder.

   (continued)

FIGURE 17
Insert Navigation Bar dialog box

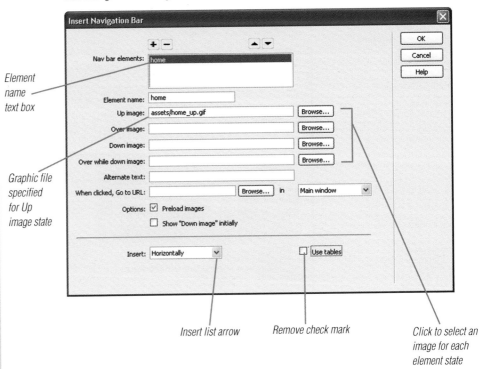

Element name text box

Graphic file specified for Up image state

Insert list arrow

Remove check mark

Click to select an image for each element state

Working with Links

FIGURE 18

Home element of the navigation bar

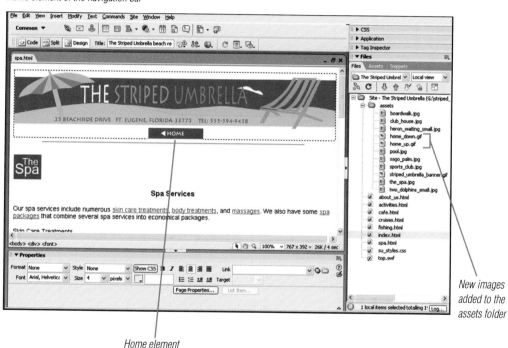

Home element

New images
added to the
assets folder

6. Click **Browse** next to the Down image text box to specify a path to the file home_down.gif located in the chapter_4 assets folder, overwriting the existing file.

> TIP Instead of clicking Browse in Steps 6 and 7, you could copy the path of the home_down.gif file in the Over image text box and paste it to the Down image and Over while down image text boxes. You could also reference the home_down.gif file in The Striped Umbrella assets folder once it is copied there in Step 5.

7. Click **Browse** next to the Over while down image text box to specify a path to the file home_down.gif located in the chapter_4 assets folder, overwriting the existing file.

   By specifying one graphic for the Up image state, and another graphic for the Over image, Down image, and Over while down image states, you will create a rollover effect.

8. Type **Navigation button linking to home page** in the Alternate text text box, click **Browse** next to the When clicked, Go to URL text box, then double-click **index.html** in the striped_umbrella root folder.

9. Click **OK**, refresh the Files panel to view the new images you added to The Striped Umbrella assets folder, deselect the button, place the insertion point in front of the button, press **[Backspace]** (Win) or **[delete]** (Mac), press **[Shift][Enter]** (Win) or **[Shift][return]** (Mac), compare your screen to Figure 18, then save your work.

You used the Insert Navigation Bar dialog box to create a navigation bar for the spa page and added the home element to it. You used two images for each state, one for the Up image state and one for the other three states.

Add elements to a navigation bar

1. Click **Modify** on the menu bar, then click **Navigation Bar**.

2. Click the **Add button** ⊞ in the Modify Navigation Bar dialog box, type **about_us** in the Element name text box, then compare your screen with Figure 19.

   TIP You use the Add button ⊞ to add a new navigation element to the navigation bar, and the Delete button ⊟ to delete a navigation element from the navigation bar.

3. Click **Browse** next to the Up image text box, navigate to the chapter_4 assets folder, click **about_us_up.gif**, then click **OK** (Win) or **Choose** (Mac).

   TIP If a dialog box appears asking if you would like to copy the file to the root folder, click Yes, then click Save (Mac).

4. Click **Browse** next to the Over image text box to specify a path to the file about_us_down.gif located in the chapter_4 assets folder.

5. Click **Browse** next to the Down image text box to specify a path to the file about_us_down.gif located in the chapter_4 assets folder, overwriting the existing file.

6. Click **Browse** next to the Over while down image text box to specify a path to the file about_us_down.gif located in the chapter_4 assets folder, overwriting the existing file.

(continued)

FIGURE 19

Add elements to a navigation bar

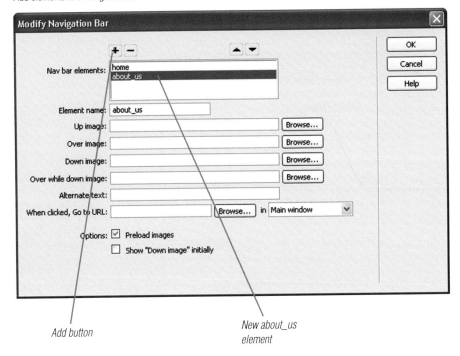

Add button

New about_us element

FIGURE 20

Navigation bar with all elements added

TABLE 3: Settings to use in the Modify Navigation Bar dialog box for each new element

dialog box item	cafe element	spa element	activities element
Up image file	cafe_up.gif	spa_up.gif	activities_up.gif
Over image file	cafe_down.gif	spa_down.gif	activities_down.gif
Down image file	cafe_down.gif	spa_down.gif	activities_down.gif
Over while down image file	cafe_down.gif	spa_down.gif	activities_down.gif
Alternate text	Navigation button linking to cafe page	Navigation button linking to spa page	Navigation button linking to activities page
When clicked, Go to URL	cafe.html	spa.html	activities.html

Lesson 4 Create, Modify, and Copy a Navigation Bar

7. Type **Navigation button linking to the about us page** in the Alternate text text box, click **Browse** next to the When clicked, Go to URL text box, then double-click **about_us.html**.

8. Using the information provided in Table 3, add three more navigation bar elements in the Modify Navigation Bar dialog box called **cafe**, **spa**, and **activities**.

   TIP   All files listed in the table are located in the assets folder of the chapter_4 folder where your Data Files are stored.

9. Click **OK** to close the Modify Navigation Bar dialog box.

10. Save your work, preview the page in your browser, compare your screen to Figure 20, check each link to verify that each element works correctly, then close your browser.

You completed The Striped Umbrella navigation bar by adding four more elements to it, each of which contain links to four pages in the site. All images added to the navigation bar are now stored in the assets folder of The Striped Umbrella Web site.

Copy and paste a navigation bar

1. Place the insertion point to the left of the navigation bar, press and hold **[Shift]**, then click to the right of the navigation bar.

2. Click **Edit** on the menu bar, then click **Copy**.

3. Double-click **activities.html** in the Files panel to open the activities page.

4. Select the original navigation bar on the page, click **Edit** on the menu bar, click **Paste**, then compare your screen to Figure 21.

5. Click in front of the navigation bar, then press **[Backspace]** (Win) or **[delete]** (Mac), then press **[Shift][Enter]** (Win) or **[Shift][return]** (Mac).

You copied the navigation bar from the spa page and pasted it on the activities page.

Customize a navigation bar

1. Click **Modify** on the menu bar, then click **Navigation Bar** to open the Modify Navigation Bar dialog box.

2. Click **activities** in the Nav bar elements text box, then click the **Show "Down image" initially check box**, as shown in Figure 22.

   An asterisk appears next to activities in the Nav bar elements text box, indicating that this element will be displayed in the Down image state initially. The sand-colored activities navigation element normally used for the Down image state of the activities navigation bar element will remind viewers that they are on the activities page.

(continued)

FIGURE 21
Navigation bar copied to the activities page

FIGURE 22
Changing settings for the activities element

Show "Down image" initially is selected

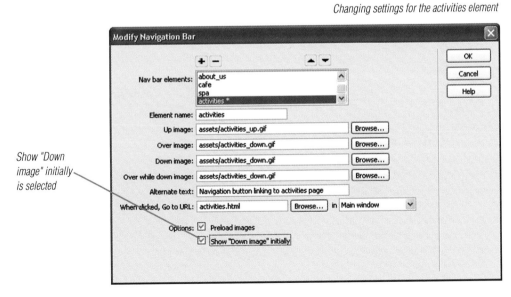

Working with Links

FIGURE 23

about us page with the modified navigation bar

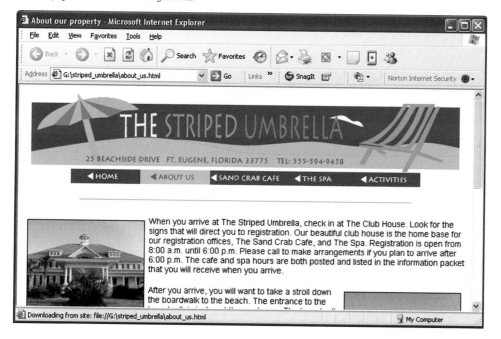

Creating an image map

Another way to create navigation links for Web pages is to create an image map. An **image map** is a graphic that has one or more hotspots placed on top of it. A **hotspot** is an area on a graphic that, when clicked, links to a different location on the page or to another Web page. For example, a map of the United States could have a hotspot placed on each state so that viewers could click a state to link to information about that state. To create a hotspot on an image, select the image on which you want to place the hotspot, then create the hotspot using one of the hotspot tools in the Property inspector.

3. Click **OK** to save the new settings and close the Modify Navigation Bar dialog box, then save and close the activities page.

4. Repeat Steps 1 through 3 to modify the navigation bar on the spa page to show the Down image initially for the spa element, then save and close the spa page.

   TIP The Show "Down image" initially check box should be checked only for the element that links to the current page.

5. Open the home page, paste the navigation bar on top of the original navigation bar, then modify the navigation bar to show the Down image initially for the home element.

6. Save and close the home page.

7. Open the about us page, paste the navigation bar on top of the original navigation bar, then use the Modify Navigation Bar dialog box to specify that the Down image be displayed initially for the about_us element, then compare your screen to Figure 23.

8. Save your work, preview the current page in your browser, test the navigation bar on the home, about us, spa, and activities pages, then close your browser.

You modified the navigation bar on the activities page to show the activities element in the Down state initially. You then copied the navigation bar to two additional pages in The Striped Umbrella Web site, modifying the navigation bar elements each time to show the Down image state initially.

MANAGE WEB
SITE LINKS

What You'll Do

 In this lesson, you will use some of Dreamweaver's reporting features to check The Striped Umbrella Web site for broken links and orphaned files.

Managing Web Site Links

Because the World Wide Web changes constantly, Web sites may be up one day and down the next. To avoid having broken links on your Web site, you need to check external links frequently. If a Web site changes server locations or goes down due to technical difficulties or a power failure, the links to it become broken. An external link can also become broken when an Internet connection fails to work properly. Broken links, like misspelled words on a Web page, indicate that a Web site is not being maintained diligently.

Checking links to make sure they work is an ongoing and crucial task you need to perform on a regular basis. You must check external links manually by reviewing your Web site in a browser and clicking each link to make sure it works correctly. The Check Links Sitewide feature is a helpful tool for managing your internal links. You can use it to check your entire Web site for the total number of links and the number of links that are okay, external, or broken, and then view the results in the Link Checker panel. The Link Checker panel also provides a list of all of the files used in a Web site, including those that are **orphaned files**, or files that are not linked to any pages in the Web site.

DESIGNTIP **Considering navigation design issues**

As you work on the navigation structure for a Web site, you should try to limit the number of links on each page to no more than is necessary. Too many links may confuse visitors to your Web site. You should also design links so that viewers can reach the information they want within three or four clicks. If finding information takes more than three or four clicks, the viewer may become discouraged or lost in the site. It's a good idea to provide visual clues on each page to let viewers know where they are, much like a "You are here" marker on a store directory at the mall.

FIGURE 24
Link Checker panel displaying external links

External links
displayed

Show list arrow

FIGURE 25
Link Checker panel displaying no orphaned files

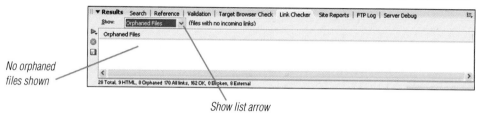

No orphaned
files shown

Show list arrow

FIGURE 26
Assets panel displaying links

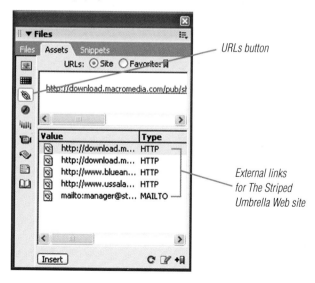

URLs button

External links
for The Striped
Umbrella Web site

Manage Web site links

1. Click **Site** on the menu bar, point to **Advanced**, then click **Recreate Site Cache**.

2. Click **Site** on the menu bar, then click **Check Links Sitewide**.

   The Results panel group opens with the Link Checker panel displayed. By default the Link Checker panel initially displays any broken internal links found in the Web site. The Striped Umbrella Web site has no broken links.

3. Click the **Show list arrow** in the Link Checker panel, click **External Links**, then compare your screen to Figure 24.

   Some external links are listed more than once because the Link Checker displays each instance of an external link.

4. Click the **Show list arrow**, then click **Orphaned Files** to view the orphaned files in the Link Checker panel, as shown in Figure 25.

   The Striped Umbrella Web site has no orphaned files.

5. Click the **Options button** 🏛 in the Results panel group title bar, then click **Close panel group**.

6. Display the Assets panel (if necessary), then click the **URLs button** 🖋 in the Assets panel to display the list of links in the Web site.

   The Assets panel displays the external links used in the Web site, as shown in Figure 26.

7. Close all open pages.

You used the Link Checker panel to check for broken links, external links, and orphaned files in The Striped Umbrella Web site.

Update a page

1. Open dw4_2.html from the chapter_4 folder where your Data Files are stored, then save it as **fishing.html** in the striped_umbrella root folder, overwriting the existing fishing page, but not updating the links.

2. Click the broken link graphic placeholder, click the **Browse for File icon** 📁 next to the Src text box on the Property inspector, then browse to the chapter_4 assets folder and select the file heron_small.jpg to copy the file to the striped_umbrella assets folder.

3. Deselect the image placeholder and the image will appear as shown in Figure 27.

   Notice that the text is automatically updated with the body text style. The code was already in place on the page linking the su_styles.css to the file.

4. Save and close the page.

FIGURE 27
Fishing page updated

FIGURE 28

Cruises page updated

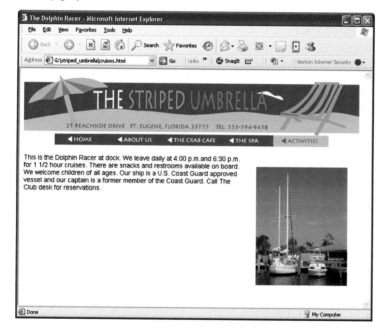

3. Open dw4_3.html from the chapter_4 folder where your Data Files are stored, then save it as **cruises.html** in the striped_umbrella root folder, overwriting the existing cruises page, but not updating the links.

4. Click the broken link graphic placeholder, click the **Browse for File icon** next to the Src text box on the Property inspector, then browse to the chapter_4 assets folder and select the file boats.jpg to copy the file to the striped_umbrella assets folder.

5. Deselect the image placeholder and the image will appear as shown in Figure 28.

   Notice that the text is automatically updated with the body text style. The code was already in place on the page linking the su_styles.css to the file.

6. Save and close the page.

Create external and internal links.

1. Open the blooms & bulbs Web site.
2. Open dw4_4.html from the chapter_4 Data Files folder, then save it as **newsletter.html** in the blooms & bulbs Web site, overwriting the existing file without updating the links.
3. Verify that the banner path is set correctly to the assets folder in the Web site and correct it, if it is not.
4. Scroll to the bottom of the page, then link the National Gardening Association text to *http://www.garden.org*.
5. Link the Better Homes and Gardens Gardening Home Page text to *http://bhg.com/gardening*.
6. Link the Southern Living text to *http://www.southernliving.com/southern*.
7. Save the file, then preview the page in your browser, verifying that each link works correctly.
8. Close your browser, then return to the newsletter page in Dreamweaver.
9. Scroll to the paragraph about gardening issues, select the gardening tips text in the last sentence, then link the selected text to the tips.html file in the blooms root folder.
10. Add a new rule to the blooms_styles.css file called **bodytext** using the following formatting choices: Font: Arial, Helvetica, sans-serif; Style: normal; Weight: normal; and Size: 14.

11. Apply the headings style to the text "Gardening Matters", the seasons style to the subheadings on the page, and the bodytext style to the descriptions under each subheading.
12. Center the "Gardening Matters" text.
13. Change the page title to **Gardening Matters**, save all open files, test the links in your browser, then close your browser.
14. Open the plants page and add the following sentence to the end of the last paragraph: **We have many annuals, perennials, and water plants that have just arrived**.
15. Link the "annuals" text to the annuals.html file, link the "perennials" text to the perennials.html file, and the "water plants" text to the water_plants.html file.
16. Save your work, test the links in your browser, then close your browser.

Create internal links to named anchors.

1. Show Invisible Elements (if necessary).
2. Click the Insert bar list arrow, then click Common.
3. Switch to the newsletter page, if necessary, then insert a named anchor in front of the Grass heading named **grass**.
4. Insert a named anchor in front of the Plants heading named **plants**.

5. Insert a named anchor in front of the Trees heading named **trees**.
6. Insert a named anchor at the top of the page named **top**.
7. Click the Point to File icon in the Property inspector to create a link from the word grass in the Gardening Issues paragraph to the grass named anchor.
8. Create a link from the word trees in the Gardening Issues paragraph to the trees named anchor.
9. Create a link from the word plants in the Gardening Issues paragraph to the plants named anchor.
10. Save your work, view the page in your browser, test all the links to make sure they work, then close your browser.

Insert Flash text.

1. Insert Flash text at the bottom of the page that will take you to the top of the page. Use the following settings: Font: Arial, Size: 16, Color: #000066, Rollover color: #3366FF, Text: Top of page, Link: newsletter.html#top, Target: _top.
2. Save the Flash text file as **top.swf** and enter the title **Link to top of page** in the Flash Accessibility Attributes dialog box.
3. Save all open files, view the page in your browser, test the Flash text link, then close your browser.

Create, modify, and copy a navigation bar.

1. Place your insertion point right under the banner, click the Images list arrow on the Insert bar, then click Navigation Bar to insert a horizontal navigation bar at the top of the newsletter page below the banner.

2. Type **home** as the first element name, then use the b_home_up.jpg file for the Up image state. This file is in the assets folder of the chapter_4 Data Files folder.

3. Specify the file b_home_down.jpg file for the three remaining states. This file (and all files for the remainder of this exercise) are in the assets folder of the chapter_4 Data Files folder.

4. Enter **Link to home page** as the alternate text, then set the index.html file as the link for the home element.

5. Create a new element named **plants** and use the b_plants_up.jpg file for the Up image state and the b_plants_down.jpg file for the remaining three states.

6. Enter **Link to plants page** as the alternate text, then set the plants.html file as the link for the plants element.

7. Create a new element named **tips** and use the b_tips_up.jpg file for the Up image state and the b_tips_down.jpg file for the remaining three states.

8. Enter **Link to tips page** as the alternate text, then set the tips.html file as the link for the tips element.

9. Create a new element named **classes** and use the b_classes_up.jpg file for the Up image state and the b_classes_down.jpg file for the remaining three states.

10. Enter **Link to classes page** as the alternate text, then set the classes.html file as the link for the classes element.

11. Create a new element named **newsletter**, then use the b_newsletter_up.jpg file for the Up image state and the b_newsletter_down.jpg file for the remaining three states.

12. Enter the alternate text **Link to newsletter page**, then set the newsletter.html file as the link for the newsletter element.

13. Center the navigation bar (if necessary), save the page and test the links in your browser, then close the browser.

14. Select and copy the navigation bar, then open the home page.

15. Delete the current navigation bar on the home page, then paste the new navigation bar under the banner. (*Hint*: Insert a line break after the banner before you paste so that the navigation bar is directly below the banner.)

16. Modify the home element on the navigation bar to show the Down image state initially.

17. Save the page, test the links in your browser, then close the browser and the page.

18. Modify the navigation bar on the newsletter page so the Down image is shown initially for the newsletter element, then save and close the newsletter page.

19. Paste the navigation bar on the plants page and the tips page, making the necessary modifications so that the Down image is shown initially for each element.

20. Save your work, preview all the pages in your browser, compare your newsletter page to Figure 29, test all the links, then close your browser.

Manage Web site links.

1. Use the Link Checker panel to view and fix broken links, external links, and orphaned files in the blooms & bulbs Web site.

2. Open dw4_5.html from the chapter_4 Data Files folder, then save it as **annuals.html**, replacing the original file. Do not update links, but save the file fuschia.jpg in the assets folder of the Web site.

3. Repeat Step 2 using dw4_6.html to replace perennials.html, saving the iris.jpg file in the assets folder and using dw4_7.html to replace water_plants.html, saving the water_hyacinth.jpg file in the assets folder.

4. Save your work, then close all open pages.

FIGURE 29
Completed Skills Review

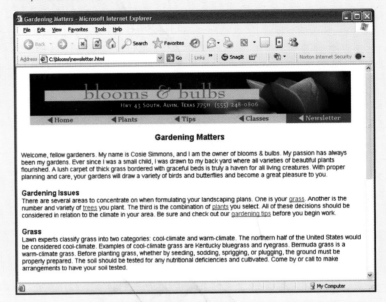

Working with Links

Use Figure 30 as a guide to continue your work on the TripSmart Web site that you began in Project Builder 1 in Chapter 1. You have been asked to create a new page for the Web site that lists helpful links for customers. You will also add content to the destinations, kenya, and amazon pages.

1. Open the TripSmart Web site.
2. Open dw4_8.html from the chapter_4 Data Files folder, then save it as **services.html** in the TripSmart Web site root folder, not updating links.
3. Verify that the TripSmart banner is in the assets folder of the root folder.
4. Apply the bodytext style to the paragraphs of text and the heading style to the paragraph headings.
5. Create named anchors named **reservations, outfitters, tours**, and **links** in front of the respective headings on the page, then link each named anchor to "Reservations", "Travel Outfitters", "Escorted Tours", and "Helpful Links in Travel Planning" in the first paragraph.
6. Link the text "on-line catalog" in the Travel Outfitters paragraph to the catalog.html page.
7. Link the text "CNN Travel Channel" under the heading Travel Information Sites to http://www.cnn.com/TRAVEL.
8. Repeat Step 7 to create links for the rest of the Web sites listed:
   US Department of State:
   http://travel.state.gov
   Yahoo! : http://yahoo.com/Recreation/Travel
   MapQuest:
   http://www.mapquest.com
   Rand McNally:
   http://www.randmcnally.com
   AccuWeather:
   http://www.accuweather.com
   The Weather Channel:
   http://www.weather.com
9. Reformat the navigation bar on the home page with a style of your choice, then place it on each completed page of the Web site. If you decide to use graphics for the navigation bar, you will have to create your own graphic files using a graphics program. There are no data files for you to use. (*Hint*: If you create your own graphic files, be sure to create two graphic files for each element: one for the Up image state and one for the Down image state.) To design a navigation bar using text, you simply type the text for each navigation bar element, format the text appropriately, and insert links to each text element as you did in Chapter 2. The navigation bar should contain the following elements: Home, Catalog, Services, Destinations, and Newsletter.

10. Save each page, then check for broken links and orphaned files. (*Hint*: The two orphaned files will be removed after completing the next steps.)

11. Open the destinations.html file in your root folder and save it as **kenya.html**, overwriting the existing file, then close the file.

12. Open dw4_9.html from the chapter_4 Data Files folder, then save it as **amazon.html**, overwriting the existing file. Do not update links, but save the water_lily.jpg and sloth.jpg files in the assets folder of the Web site, then save and close the file.

13. Open dw4_10.html from the chapter_4 Data Files folder, then save the file as **destinations.html**, overwriting the existing file. Do not update links, but save the parrot.jpg and giraffe.jpg files in the assets folder of the Web site.

14. Link the text "Amazon" in the second sentence of the first paragraph to the amazon.html file.

15. Link the text "Kenya" in the first sentence in the second paragraph to the kenya.html file.

16. Copy your customized navigation bar to the two new pages so they will match the other pages.

17. Save all files.

18. Test all links in your browser, close your browser, then close all open pages.

FIGURE 30
Sample Project Builder 1

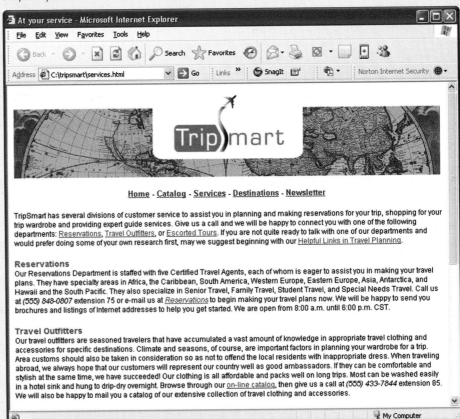

Working with Links

Use Figure 31 as a guide to continue your work on the emma's book bag Web site that you started in Project Builder 2 in Chapter 1. Emma Claire has asked you to create a page describing the upcoming book sale and a book signing event. You will create the content for that page and individual pages describing each event.

1. Open the emma's book bag Web site.
2. Open dw4_11.html from the chapter_4 Data Files folder, save it as **events.html** in the root folder of the emma's book bag Web site, overwriting the existing file and not updating the links.
3. Check the path of the book_bag banner to make sure it is linking to the banner in the assets folder of the Web site, then check the path for each link in the navigation bar to make sure each text link is linking to the files in the root folder.
4. Select the text "annual book sale" in the first paragraph, then link it to the seasonal.html page. (*Hint*: This page has not been developed yet.)
5. Select the text "book signing" in the second paragraph and link it to the signings.html page. (*Hint*: This page has not been developed yet.)
6. Add the page title **book bag happenings**.
7. Insert the file grif_stockley.jpg from the chapter_4 assets folder at the beginning of

the second paragraph, add appropriate alternate text, then choose your own alignment and formatting settings.
8. Save and close the file.
9. Open dw4_12.html from the chapter_4 Data Files folder, then save it as **seasonal.html**, overwriting the existing file and not updating links. Save the image books.jpg from the chapter_4 assets folder in the Web site assets folder.
10. Save and close the file.

11. Repeat Steps 9 and 10 to open the dw4_13.html file and save it as **signings.html**, overwriting the existing file and saving the salted_with_fire.jpg in the assets folder.
12. Save all the pages, then check for broken links and orphaned files.
13. Preview all the pages in your browser, check to make sure the links work correctly, close your browser, then close all open pages.

FIGURE 31
Completed Project Builder 2

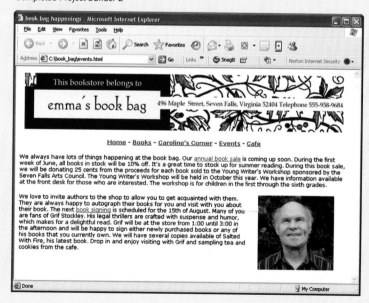

DESIGN PROJECT

Grace Keiko is a talented young water-color artist who specializes in botanical works. She wants to develop a Web site to advertise her work but isn't sure what she would like to include in a Web site or how to tie the pages together. She decides to spend several hours looking at other artists' Web sites to help her get started.

1. Connect to the Internet, navigate to the Online Companion, and review the links for this chapter. The Web site pictured in Figure 32 is *www.katenessler.com*.
2. Spend some time looking at several of the artist Web sites that you find to familiarize yourself with the types of content that each contains.
3. What categories of page content would you include on your Web site if you were Grace?
4. What external links would you consider including?
5. Describe how you would place external links on the pages and list examples of ones you would use.
6. Would you use text or graphics for your navigation bar?
7. Would you include rollover effects on the navigation bar elements? If so, describe how they might look.

8. How could you incorporate named anchors on any of the pages?
9. Sketch a Web site plan for Grace, including the pages that you would use as links from the home page.

10. Refer to your Web site sketch, then create a home page for Grace that includes a navigation bar, a short introductory paragraph about her art, and a few external links.

FIGURE 32
Design Project

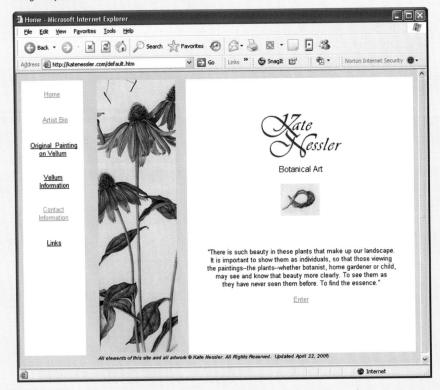

Working with Links

In this assignment, you will continue to work on the Web site that you started in Chapter 1 and developed in Chapters 2 and 3.

You will continue building your Web site by designing and completing a page with a navigation bar. After creating the navigation bar, you will copy it to each completed page in the Web site. In addition to the navigation bar, you will add several external links and several internal links to other pages as well as to named anchors. You will also link Flash text to a named anchor. After you complete this work, you will check for broken links and orphaned files.

1. Consult your storyboard to decide which page or pages you would like to develop in this chapter. Decide how to design and where to place the navigation bar, named anchors, Flash text, and any additional page elements you decide to use. Decide which reports should be run on the Web site to check for accuracy.
2. Research Web sites that could be included on one or more of your pages as external links of interest to your viewers. Create a list of the external links you want to use. Using your storyboard as a guide, decide where each external link should be placed in the site.

3. Add the external links to existing pages or create any additional pages that contain external links.
4. Create named anchors for key locations on the page, such as the top of the page, then link appropriate text on the page to them.
5. Insert at least one Flash text object that links to either a named anchor or an internal link.
6. Decide on a design for a navigation bar that will be used on all pages of the Web site.
7. Create the navigation bar and copy it to all finished pages on the Web site. If you decided to use graphics for the navigation bar, create the graphics that will be used.

8. Use the Link Checker panel to check for broken links and orphaned files.
9. Use the check list in Figure 33 to make sure your Web site is complete, save your work, then close all open pages.

FIGURE 33
Portfolio Project check list

Web Site Check List

1. Do all pages have a page title?
2. Does the home page have a description and keywords?
3. Does the home page contain contact information?
4. Does every page in the Web site have consistent navigation links?
5. Does the home page have a last updated statement that will automatically update when the page is saved?
6. Do all paths for links and images work correctly?
7. Do all images have alternate text?
8. Are all colors Websafe?
9. Are there any unnecessary files that you can delete from the assets folder?
10. Is there a style sheet with at least two styles?
11. Did you apply the style sheet to page content?
12. Does at least one page contain links to one or more named anchors?
13. Does at least one page contain Flash text that links to either a named anchor or an internal link?
14. Do all pages view well using at least two different browsers?

WORKING WITH
TABLES

1. Create a table.

2. Resize, split, and merge cells.

3. Insert and align graphics in table cells.

4. Insert text and format cell content.

5. Perform Web site maintenance.

Introduction

You have learned how to place and align elements on a page and enhance them using various formatting options. However, page layout options are fairly limited without the use of tables. Tables offer another solution for organizing text and graphics on a page. **Tables** are placeholders made up of small boxes called **cells**, into which you can insert text and graphics. Cells in a table are arranged horizontally in **rows** and vertically in **columns**. Using tables on a Web page gives you total control over the placement of each object on the page. In this chapter, you will learn how to create and format tables, work with table rows and columns, and format the contents of table cells. You will also learn how to select and format table cells using table tags on the tag selector. Clicking a table tag on the tag selector selects the table element associated with that tag.

Inserting Graphics and Text in Tables

Once you insert a table on a Web page, it becomes very easy to place text and graphics exactly where you want them on the page. You can use a table to control both the placement of elements in relation to each other and the amount of space between each page element. Before you insert a table, however, you should always plan how your table will look with all the text and graphics in it. Even a rough sketch before you begin will save you time as you add content to the page.

Maintaining a Web Site

You already know how to check for broken links and Non-Websafe colors in your Web site. Dreamweaver also provides many other management tools to help you identify other problems. For instance, you can run a report to check for pages that have no page titles, or to search for images that are missing alternate text. It's a good idea to set up a schedule to run these and other reports on a regular basis.

Tools You'll Use

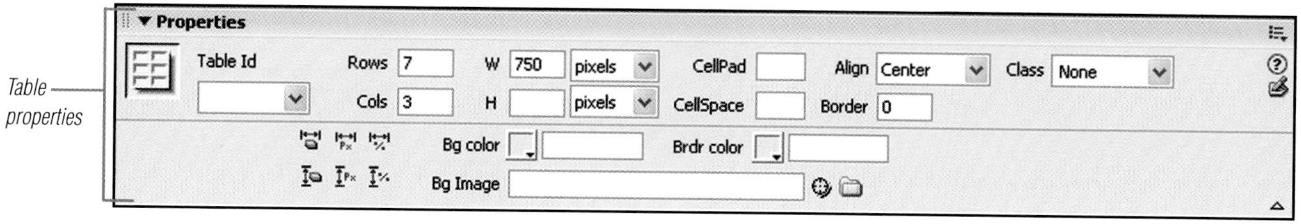

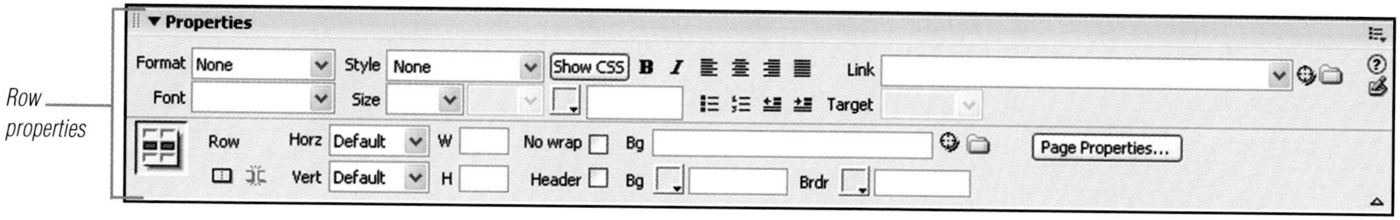

Table properties

▼ Properties

Table Id
Rows 7 W 750 pixels
Cols 3 H pixels
CellPad Align Center Class None
CellSpace Border 0
Bg color
Brdr color
Bg Image

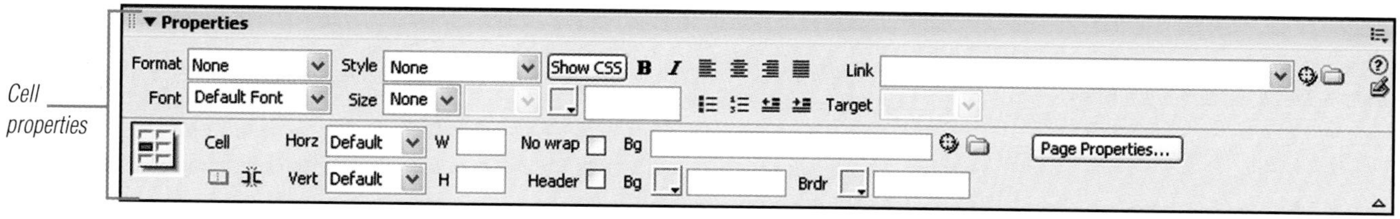

Cell properties

▼ Properties

Format None Style None Show CSS **B** *I* Link
Font Default Font Size None
Cell Horz Default W No wrap Bg Page Properties...
Vert Default H Header Bg Brdr
Target

Row properties

▼ Properties

Format None Style None Show CSS **B** *I* Link
Font Size
Row Horz Default W No wrap Bg Page Properties...
Vert Default H Header Bg Brdr
Target

CREATE A TABLE

What You'll Do

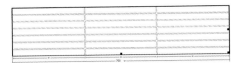

 In this lesson, you will create a table for the cafe page in The Striped Umbrella Web site to provide the framework for the page layout.

Understanding Table Modes

There are two ways to create a table in Dreamweaver. Each method requires working in Design view. The first method is to click the Table button on the Insert bar. The Table button is available in the Common category of the Insert bar and in the Layout category of the Insert bar, whenever the Standard mode button is enabled. The second method is to click the Insert bar list arrow, click Layout, click the Layout mode button on the Insert bar, then click the Layout Table button or the Draw Layout Cell button. You can choose Standard mode, Expanded Tables mode, or Layout mode by clicking the appropriate button on the Insert bar, when the Layout category of the Insert bar is displayed.

Creating a Table in Standard Mode

Creating a table in Standard mode is useful when you want to create a table with a specific number of columns and rows. To create a table in Standard mode, click the Table button on the Insert bar to open the Table dialog box. Enter values for the number of rows and columns, the border thickness, table width, cell padding, and cell spacing. The **border** is the outline or frame around the table and the individual cells and is measured in pixels. The table width, which can be specified in pixels or as a percentage, refers to the width of the table. When the table width is specified as a percentage, the table width will adjust to the width of the browser window. When the table width is specified in pixels, the table width stays the same, regardless of the size of the browser window. **Cell padding** is the distance between the cell content and the **cell walls**, the lines inside the cell borders. **Cell spacing** is the distance between cells.

Setting Table Accessibility Preferences for Tables

You can make a table more accessible to visually handicapped viewers by adding a table caption and a table summary that can be read by screen readers. The table caption appears on the screen. The table summary does not. These features are especially useful for tables that are used for tabular data. **Table headers** are another way to provide accessibility. Table headers can be placed at the top or sides of a table with data. They are automatically centered and bold and are used by screen readers to help viewers identify the table content. Table captions, summaries, and headers are all created in the Table dialog box.

Drawing a Table in Layout Mode

You use Layout mode when you want to draw your own table. Drawing a table is ideal when you want to place page elements on a Web page and have no need for a specific number of rows and columns. You can use the Draw Layout Cell button or the Layout Table button in the Layout category of the Insert bar to draw a cell or a table. After you draw the first cell, Dreamweaver plots a table for you automatically.

Planning a Table

Before you create a table, you should sketch a plan for it that shows its location on the Web page and the placement of text and graphics in its cells. You should also decide whether to include borders around the tables and cells. Setting the border value to 0 causes the table to appear invisible, so that viewers will not realize that you used a table for the page layout unless they look at the code. Figure 1 shows a sketch of the table you will create on The Striped Umbrella cafe page to organize graphics and text.

FIGURE 1

Sketch of table on cafe page

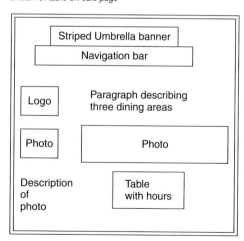

Create a table

1. Open The Striped Umbrella Web site that you completed in Chapter 4.

2. Double-click **cafe.html** in the Files panel to open the cafe page in Design view.

   The cafe page is blank.

3. Click the **Insert bar list arrow**, click **Layout**, click the **Standard mode button** Standard, then click the **Table button** .

4. Type **7** in the Rows text box, type **3** in the Columns text box, type **750** in the Table width text box, click the **Table width list arrow**, click **pixels**, then type **0** in the Border thickness text box, as shown in Figure 2.

   TIP   It is better to add more rows than you think you will need when you create your table. It is far easier to delete rows than to add rows if you decide later to split or merge cells in the table.

   (continued)

FIGURE 2
Table dialog box

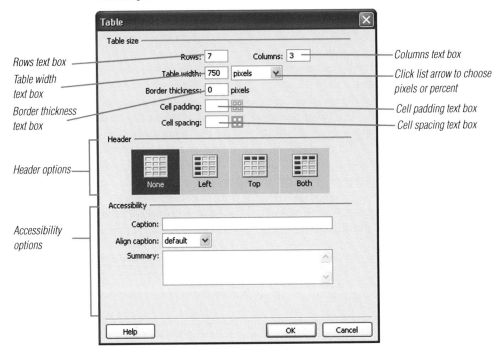

Rows text box
Table width text box
Border thickness text box
Header options
Accessibility options

Columns text box
Click list arrow to choose pixels or percent
Cell padding text box
Cell spacing text box

Expanded Tables mode

Expanded Tables mode is a feature that allows you to change to a table view with expanded table borders and temporary cell padding and cell spacing. This mode makes it much easier to actually see how many rows and columns you have in your table. Many times, especially after splitting empty cells, it is difficult to place the insertion point precisely in a table cell. The Expanded Tables mode allows you to see each cell clearly. However, most of the time you will want to work in Standard mode to maintain the WYSIWYG environment. **WYSIWYG** is the acronym for What You See Is What You Get. This means that your Web page should look the same in the browser as it does in the Web editor. You can toggle between Expanded Tables mode and Standard mode by pressing [F6]. You can access Layout mode by pressing and holding [Ctrl] [F6] (Win) or ⌘ [F6] (Mac).

FIGURE 3
Table dialog box

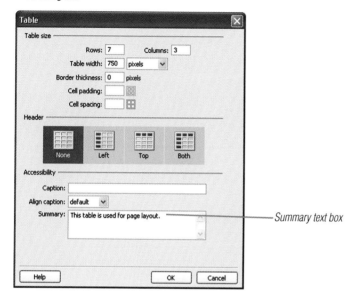

Summary text box

FIGURE 4
Expanded Tables mode

Click to exit
Expanded
Tables mode

Expanded Tables
mode displays more
space between cells
for easier editing

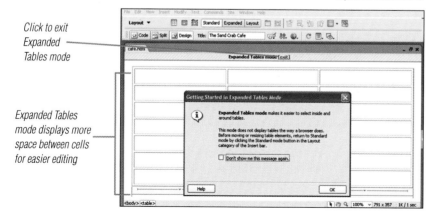

5. Type **This table is used for page layout.** in the Summary text box, then compare your screen to Figure 3.

6. Click **OK**.

   The table appears on the page, but the table summary is not visible. The summary will not appear in the browser but will be read by screen readers.

   TIP   To edit accessibility preferences for a table, switch to Code view to edit the code directly.

7. Click the **Expanded Tables mode button** Expanded , then click **OK** in the Getting Started in Expanded Tables Mode dialog box, as shown in Figure 4.

   The Expanded Tables mode makes it easier to select and edit tables.

8. Click the **Standard mode button** Standard to return to Standard mode.

   TIP   You can also return to Standard mode by clicking [exit] at the top of the table.

You opened the cafe page in The Striped Umbrella Web site. You then created a table containing seven rows and three columns and set the width to 750 pixels so it will appear in the same size regardless of the browser window size. Finally, you entered a table summary that will be read by screen readers.

Set table properties

1. Move the pointer slowly to the edge of the table until you see the pointer change to a table pointer ⛀, then click the table border to select the table.

   TIP You can also select a table by (1) clicking the insertion point in the table, then clicking Modify, Table, Select Table; (2) selecting a cell in the table, then clicking Edit, Select All; or (3) clicking the table tag <table> on the tag selector.

2. Expand the Property inspector (if necessary) to display the current properties of the new table.

   TIP The Property inspector will display information about the table only if the table is selected.

3. Click the **Align list arrow** on the Property inspector, then click **Center** to center the table on the page, as shown in Figure 5.

   The center alignment formatting ensures that the table will be centered in all browser windows, regardless of the screen size.

   You selected and center-aligned the table.

FIGURE 5

Property inspector showing properties of selected table

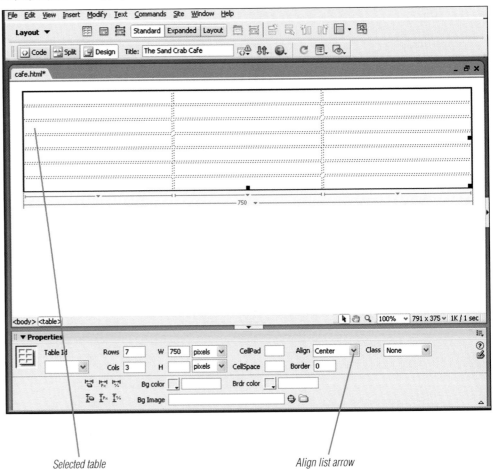

Selected table   Align list arrow

FIGURE 6

Table in Layout mode

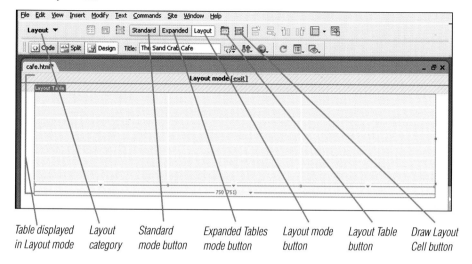

Table displayed in Layout mode   Layout category   Standard mode button   Expanded Tables mode button   Layout mode button   Layout Table button   Draw Layout Cell button

View the table in Layout mode

1. Click the **Layout mode button** Layout on the Insert bar.

   The table appears in Layout mode, as shown in Figure 6.

   > TIP The Getting Started in Layout Mode dialog box might open, providing instructions on creating and editing a table in Layout mode.

2. Click **OK** (if necessary) to close the Getting Started in Layout Mode dialog box.

3. Click the **Standard mode button** Standard to return to Standard mode.

4. Click the **Insert bar list arrow**, then click **Common**.

You viewed the table in Layout mode, then returned to Standard mode.

DESIGNTIP **Setting table and cell widths**

If you use a table to place all the text and graphics contained on a Web page, it is wise to set the width of the table in pixels. This ensures that the table will not resize itself proportionately if the browser window size is changed. If you set the width of a table using pixels, the table will remain one size, regardless of the browser window size. For instance, if the width of a table is set to slightly less than 800, the table will stretch across the whole width of a browser window set at a resolution of 800×600. The same table would be the same size on a screen set at 1024×768 and therefore would not stretch across the entire screen. Most designers use a resolution of 800×600. Be aware, however, that if you set the width of your table at 800 pixels, your table will be too wide to print the entire width of the page, and part of the right side of the page will be cut off. If you are designing a table layout for a page that is likely to be printed by the viewer, you should make your table narrower to fit on a printed page. If you set a table width as a percentage, however, the table would resize itself proportionately in any browser window, regardless of the resolution. You can also set each cell width as either a percentage of the table or as fixed pixels.

Lesson 1 Create a Table

RESIZE, SPLIT, AND
MERGE CELLS

What You'll Do

 In this lesson, you will set the width of the table cells to be split across the table in predetermined widths. You will then split one cell. You will also merge some cells to provide space for the banner.

Resizing Table Elements

You can resize the rows or columns of a table manually. To resize a table, row, or column, you must first select the table, then drag one of the table's three selection handles. To change all the columns in a table so that they are the same size, drag the middle-right selection handle. To resize the height of all rows simultaneously, drag the middle-bottom selection handle. To resize the entire table, drag the right-corner selection handle. To resize a row or column individually, drag the interior cell borders up, down, to the left, or to the right. You can also resize selected columns, rows, or individual cells by entering specific measurements in the W and H text boxes in the Property inspector specified either in pixels or as a percentage. Cells whose width or height is specified as a percentage will maintain that percentage in relation to the width or height of the entire table if the table is resized.

Resetting table widths and heights

After resizing columns and rows in a table, you might want to change the sizes of the columns and rows back to their previous sizes. To reset columns and rows to their previous widths and heights, click Modify on the menu bar, point to Table, then click Clear Cell Heights or Clear Cell Widths. Using the Clear Cell Heights command also forces the cell border to snap to the bottom of any inserted graphics, so you can also use this command to tighten up extra white space in a cell.

Splitting and Merging Cells

Using the Table button creates a new table with evenly spaced columns and rows. Sometimes you might want to adjust the cells in a table by splitting or merging them. To split a cell means to divide it into multiple rows or columns. To merge cells means to combine multiple cells into one cell. Using split and merged cells gives you more flexibility and control in placing page elements on a page and can help you create a more visually exciting layout. When you merge cells, the HTML tag used to describe the merged cell changes from a width size tag to a column span or row span tag. For example, <td colspan="2"> is the code for two cells that have been merged into one cell that spans two columns.

QUICKTIP

You can split merged cells and merge split cells.

DESIGNTIP   **Using nested tables**

A nested table is a table inside a table. To create a nested table, you place the insertion point in the cell where you want to insert the nested table, then click the Table button on the Insert bar. The nested table is a separate table that can be formatted differently from the table in which it is placed. Nested tables are useful when you want part of your table data to have visible borders and part to have invisible borders. For example, you can nest a table with red borders inside a table with invisible borders. You need to plan carefully when you insert nested tables. It is easy to get carried away and insert too many nested tables, which makes it more difficult to apply formatting and rearrange table elements. Before you insert a nested table, consider whether you could achieve the same result by adding rows and columns or by splitting cells.

Resize columns

1. Click inside the first cell in the bottom row, then click the **cell tag <td>** on the tag selector, as shown in Figure 7.

   Clicking the cell tag (the HTML tag for that cell) selects the corresponding cell in the table.

   TIP You can also click inside a cell to select it. To select the entire table, click the <table> tag on the tag selector.

2. Type **30%** in the W text box in the Property inspector, then press **[Enter]** (Win) or **[return]** (Mac) to change the width of the cell to 30 percent of the table width.

   Notice that the column width is displayed at the bottom of the first column in the table, along with the table width of 750 pixels.

   TIP You need to type the % sign next to the number you type in the W text box. Otherwise, the width will be expressed in pixels.

3. Repeat Steps 1 and 2 for the next two cells in the last row, using **30%** for the middle cell and **40%** for the last cell.

   The combined widths of the three cells add up to 100 percent. As you add content to the table, the columns will remain in this proportion unless you insert a graphic that is larger than the table cell. If a larger graphic is inserted, the cell width will expand to display it.

   TIP Changing the width of a single cell changes the width of the entire column.

You set the width of each of the three cells in the bottom row to set the column sizes for the table. This will keep the table from resizing when you add content.

FIGURE 7
Selecting a cell

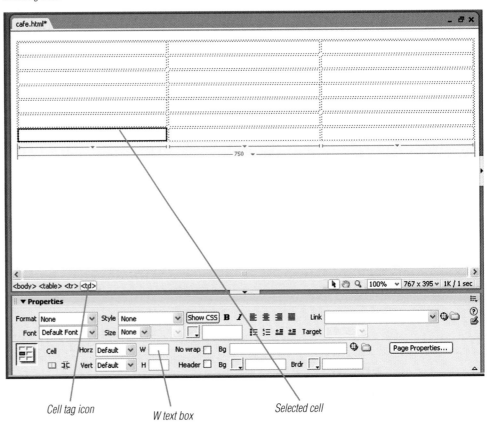

Cell tag icon   W text box   Selected cell

Working with Tables

FIGURE 8

Resizing the height of a row

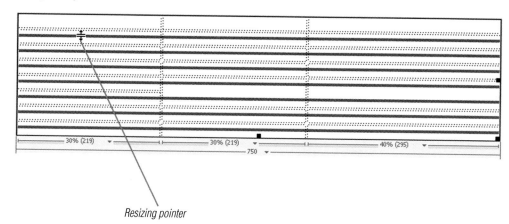

Resizing pointer

1. Place the pointer over the bottom border of the first row until it changes to a resizing pointer ⬍ , as shown in Figure 8, then click and drag down about ¼ of an inch to increase the height of the row.

   The border turns darker when you select and drag it.

2. Click **Window** on the menu bar, click **History**, then drag the **slider** in the History panel up one line to return the row to its original height.

3. Close the History panel group.

You changed the height of the top row, then used the History panel to change it back it to its original height.

HTML table tags

When formatting a table, it is important to understand the basic HTML table tags. The tags used for creating a table are <table> </table>. The tags used to create table rows are <tr></tr>. The tags used to create table cells are <td></td>. Dreamweaver places the   code into each empty table cell at the time it is created. The   code represents a nonbreaking space, or a space that a browser will display on the page. Some browsers will collapse an empty cell, which can ruin the look of a table. The nonbreaking space will hold the cell until content is placed in it, at which time it will be automatically removed.

Split cells

1. Click inside the first cell in the fifth row, then click the **cell tag <td>** in the tag selector.

2. Click the **Splits cell into rows or columns button** 〗〔 in the Property inspector.

3. Click the **Split cell into Rows option button** (if necessary), type **2** in the Number of rows text box (if necessary), as shown in Figure 9, then click **OK**.

   TIP To create a new row identical to the one above it, place the insertion point in the last cell of a table, then press [Tab].

You split a cell into two rows.

FIGURE 9
Splitting a cell into two rows

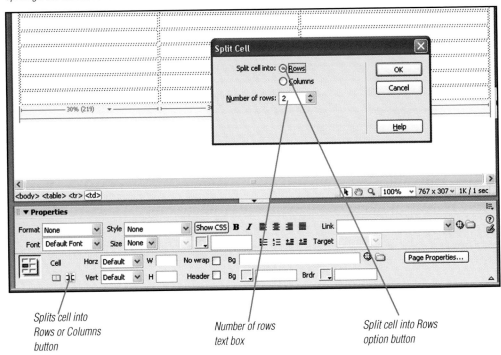

Splits cell into
Rows or Columns
button

Number of rows
text box

Split cell into Rows
option button

Adding or deleting a row

As you add new content to your table, you might find that you have too many or too few rows or columns. You can add or delete one row or column at a time or several at once. You use commands on the Modify menu to add and delete table rows and columns. When you add a new column or row, you must first select the existing column or row to which the new column or row will be adjacent. The Insert Rows or Columns dialog box lets you choose how many rows or columns you want to insert or delete, and where you want them placed in relationship to the selected row or column. The new column or row will have the same formatting and number of cells as the selected column or row.

Working with Tables

FIGURE 10
Merging selected cells into one cell

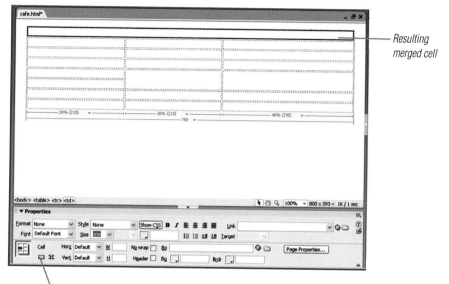

Resulting
merged cell

Merges selected cells
using spans button

1. Click the insertion point in the first cell in the top row, then click and drag to the right to select the second and third cells in the top row.

2. Click the **Merges selected cells using spans button** 🔲 in the Property inspector.

   The three cells are merged into one cell, as shown in Figure 10. Merged cells are good placeholders for banners or page headings.

   TIP   You can only merge cells that are adjacent to each other.

3. Click the **Show Code view button** 〈/〉 Code , then view the code for the merged cells, as shown in Figure 11.

   Notice the table tags denoting the column span (td colspan="3") and the nonbreaking spaces ( ) inserted in the empty cells.

4. Click the **Show Design view button** 🖥 Design , then save your work.

You merged three cells in the first row to make room for The Striped Umbrella banner.

FIGURE 11
Code view for merged cells

```
1   <!DOCTYPE html PUBLIC "-//W3C//DTD XHTML 1.0 Transitional//EN"
    "http://www.w3.org/TR/xhtml1/DTD/xhtml1-transitional.dtd">
2   <html xmlns="http://www.w3.org/1999/xhtml">
3   <head>
4   <meta http-equiv="Content-Type" content="text/html; charset=iso-8859-1" />
5   <title>The Sand Crab Cafe</title>
6   </head>
7
8   <body>
9   <table width="750" border="0" align="center" summary="This table is used for page layout.">
10    <tr>
11      <td colspan="3"> </td>
12    </tr>
13    <tr>
14      <td> </td>
15      <td> </td>
16      <td> </td>
17    </tr>
```

colspan tag

INSERT AND ALIGN
GRAPHICS IN TABLE CELLS

What You'll Do

 In this lesson, you will insert The Striped Umbrella banner in the top row of the table. You will then insert three graphics in three different cells. After placing the three graphics, you will align them within their cells.

Inserting Graphics in Table Cells

You can insert graphics in the cells of a table using the Image command in the Images menu on the Insert bar. If you already have graphics saved in your Web site that you would like to insert in a table, you can drag them from the Assets panel into the table cells. When you add a large graphic to a cell, the cell expands to accommodate the inserted graphic. If you select the Show attributes when inserting Images check box in the Accessibility category of the Preferences dialog box, the Image Tag Accessibility Attributes dialog box will open after you insert a graphic, prompting you to enter alternate text. Figure 12 shows the John Deere Web site, which uses a table for page layout and contains several images in its table cells. Notice that some images appear in cells by themselves, and some appear in cells containing text or other graphics. Some cells have a white background, and some have a green background.

Aligning Graphics in Table Cells

You can align graphics both horizontally and vertically within a cell. You can align a graphic horizontally using the Horz (horizontal) alignment options in the Property inspector. This option is used to align the entire contents of the cell, whether there is one object, or several. You can also align a graphic vertically by the top, middle, bottom, or baseline of a cell. To align a graphic vertically within a cell, use the Vert (vertical) Align list arrow in the Property inspector, then choose an alignment option, as shown in Figure 13. To control spacing between cells, you can use cell padding and cell spacing. **Cell padding** is the space between a cell's border and its contents. **Cell spacing** is the distance between adjacent cells.

FIGURE 12

John Deere Web site (courtesy of Deere & Company)

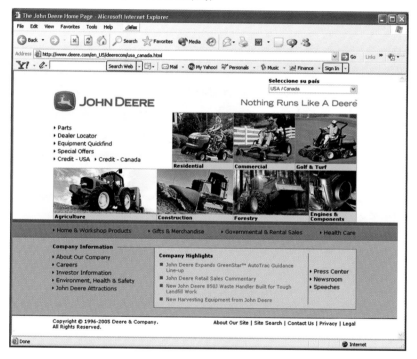

FIGURE 13

Vertical alignment options in the Property inspector

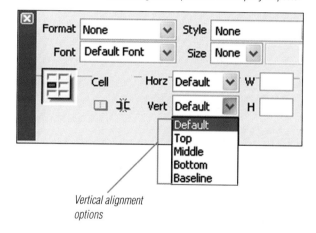

Vertical alignment options

Insert graphics in table cells

1. Open the index page, click the **banner** to select it, press and hold **[Shift]**, then click to the right of the navigation bar to select both the banner and the navigation bar.

2. Click **Edit** on the menu bar, click **Copy**, then close the index page.

3. Click in the top cell on the cafe page, click **Edit** on the menu bar, then click **Paste**.

   The Image Description (Alt Text) dialog box opens showing that alt text is missing from the banner graphic.

   > TIP If you are working on a Macintosh computer, the Image Description (Alt Text) dialog box may not appear.

4. Click the pointer in the blank space under the Description heading, as shown in Figure 14, type **Striped Umbrella banner**, then click **OK**.

   (continued)

FIGURE 14
Image Description (Alt Text) dialog box

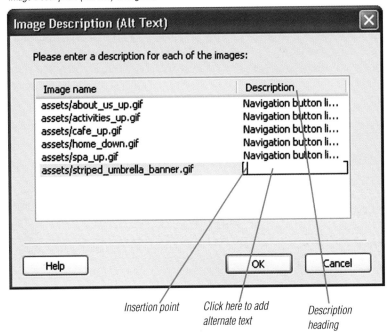

Insertion point

Click here to add alternate text

Description heading

Using visual aids

There is an option in Dreamweaver for turning on and off various borders that are displayed in Design view but are not displayed in the browser. This tool is called Visual Aids and can be accessed through the View menu or through the Visual Aids button on the Document toolbar. Most of the time these borders are very helpful while you are editing and formatting a page. However, turning them off is a quick way to see how the page will be viewed in the browser without having to open it in the browser window.

FIGURE 15

Sand Crab Cafe logo imported into table cell

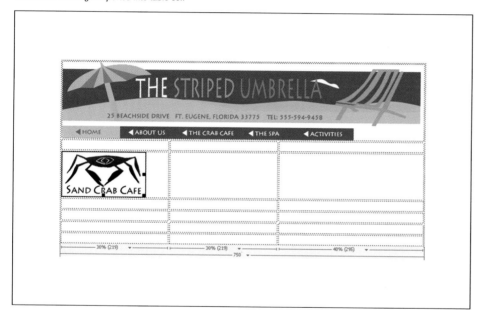

5. Click in the first cell in the third row and insert cafe_logo.gif from the chapter_5 assets folder, then type **Sand Crab Cafe logo** as the alternate text.

6. Compare your screen to Figure 15.

7. Repeat Step 5 to insert cheesecake.jpg in the first cell in the fifth row (the top row in the set of split cells), using **Banana Chocolate Cheesecake** for the alternate text.

(continued)

8. Merge the two cells to the right of the cheesecake graphic, repeat Step 5 to insert the cafe_photo.jpg in the newly merged cells, using **The Sand Crab Cafe** as the alternate text, then compare your screen to Figure 16.

   TIP   Press [Tab] to move the insertion point to the next cell in a row. Press [Shift][Tab] to move the insertion point to the previous cell.

9. Refresh the Assets panel to verify that the three new graphics were copied to The Striped Umbrella Web site assets folder.

10. Save your work, then preview the page in your browser.

   Notice that the page would look better if the new graphics had better placement on the page.

11. Close your browser.

You inserted images into four cells of the table on the cafe page.

FIGURE 16
Graphics inserted into table cells

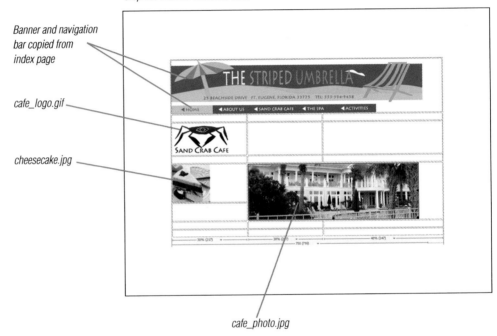

Banner and navigation bar copied from index page

cafe_logo.gif

cheesecake.jpg

cafe_photo.jpg

FIGURE 17
Aligning images in cells

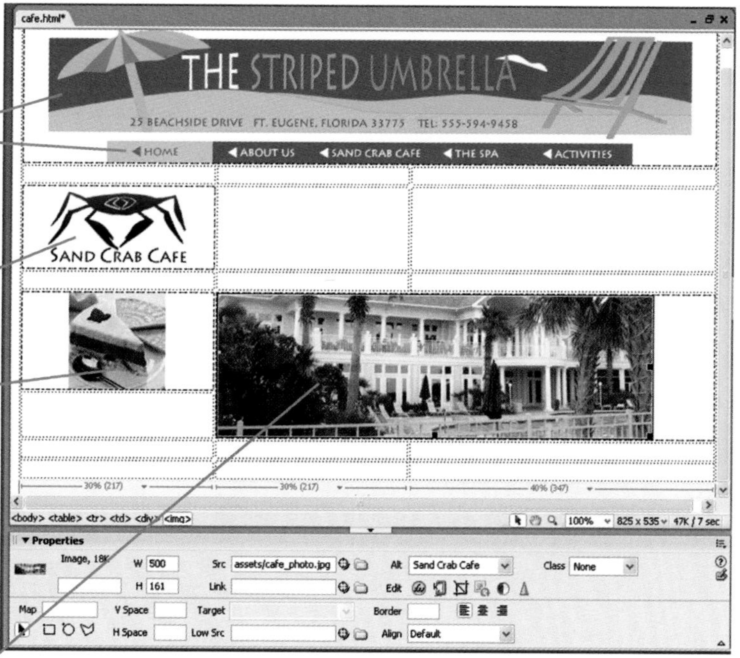

Centered banner
and navigation bar

Centered logo

Centered cheesecake
photo

Left-aligned cafe
photo

1. Click the **banner**, then click the **Align Center button** ≣ in the Property inspector.

   The banner and navigation bar move together to become centered in the cell. You may have copied the center alignment tag when you copied the banner and navigation bar from the index page. In that case, the banner and navigation bar will already be centered on the cafe page.

2. Center-align the logo and cheesecake images, then left-align the cafe photo, as shown in Figure 17.

   Notice the extra dotted lines surrounding the four images. Each one represents a div tag that was generated when the alignment button was applied to the graphic.

3. Save your work.

4. Preview the page in your browser, view the aligned images, then close your browser.

You center-aligned The Striped Umbrella banner and two other graphics within their respective cells. You left-aligned the fourth graphic.

INSERT TEXT AND FORMAT
CELL CONTENT

What You'll Do

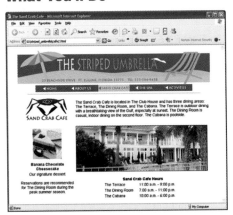

In this lesson, you will insert text that describes the restaurant in a cell, type text in two cells, and then type the cafe hours in a nested table. You will also format the text to enhance its appearance on the page. Last, you will add formatting to some of the cells and cell content.

Inserting Text in a Table

You can enter text in a table either by typing it in a cell, copying it from another source and pasting it into a cell, or importing it from another program. Once you place text in a table cell, you can format it to make it more readable and more visually appealing on the page.

Formatting Cell Content

Making modifications and formatting changes to a table and its contents is easier to do in Standard mode than in Layout mode. To format the contents of a cell in Standard mode, select the contents in the cell, then apply formatting to it. If a cell contains multiple objects of the same type, such as text, you can either format each item individually or select the entire cell and apply formatting that will be applied identically to all items. You can tell whether you have selected the cell contents or the cell by looking to see what options are showing in the Property inspector. Figure 18 shows a selected graphic in a cell. Notice that the Property inspector displays options for formatting the object, rather than options for formatting the cell.

Formatting Cells

Formatting cells is different than formatting cell contents. Formatting a cell can include setting properties that visually enhance the cell appearance, such as setting a cell width, assigning a background color, or setting global alignment properties for the cell content. To format a cell, you need to either select the cell or place the insertion point inside the cell you want to format, then choose the cell formatting options you want in the Property inspector. For example, to choose a fill color for a selected cell, click the Background Color button in the Property inspector, then choose a color from the color picker. In order to format a cell, you must expand the Property inspector to display the cell formatting options. In Figure 19, notice that the insertion point is positioned in the cafe logo cell, but the logo graphic is not selected. The Property inspector displays the formatting options for cells.

FIGURE 18

Property inspector showing options for formatting cell contents

FIGURE 19

Property inspector showing options for formatting a cell

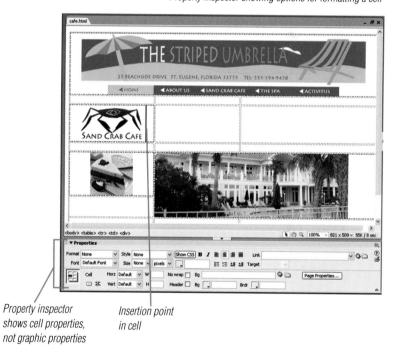

Property inspector shows properties for selected graphic

Graphic selected inside a cell

Property inspector shows cell properties, not graphic properties

Insertion point in cell

Insert text

1. Merge the two cells to the right of the cafe logo, click in the newly merged cell, then import the Word document, cafe.doc, from the chapter_5 assets folder.

2. Click in the cell under the cheesecake photo, then type **Banana Chocolate**, press **[Shift][Enter]** (Win) or **[Shift][return]** (Mac), type **Cheesecake**, press **[Shift][Enter]** (Win) or **[Shift][return]** (Mac), then type **Our signature dessert**.

3. Click in the next cell down and type **Reservations are recommended for The Dining Room during the peak summer season**, as shown in Figure 20.

You imported a Word document describing the restaurant into one cell and typed two descriptive paragraphs into two cells.

FIGURE 20
Importing and typing text into cells

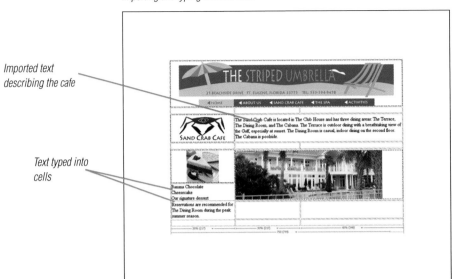

Imported text describing the cafe

Text typed into cells

Importing and exporting data from tables

You can import and export tabular data into and out of Dreamweaver. Tabular data is data that is arranged in columns and rows and separated by a **delimiter**: a comma, tab, colon, semicolon, or similar character. **Importing** means to bring data created in another software program into Dreamweaver, and **exporting** means to save data created in Dreamweaver in a special file format that can be inserted into other programs. Files that are imported into Dreamweaver must be saved as delimited files. **Delimited files** are database or spreadsheet files that have been saved as text files with delimiters such as tabs or commas separating the data. Programs such as Microsoft Access and Microsoft Excel offer many file formats for saving files. To import a delimited file, click File on the menu bar, point to Import, then click Tabular Data. The Import Tabular Data dialog box opens, offering you formatting options for the imported table. To export a table that you created in Dreamweaver, click File on the menu bar, point to Export, then click Table. The Export Table dialog box opens, letting you choose the type of delimiter you want for the delimited file.

Working with Tables

FIGURE 21
Table dialog box settings for nested table

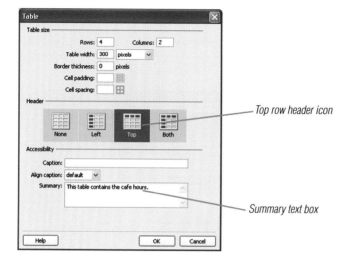

Top row header icon

Summary text box

FIGURE 22
Adding a nested table

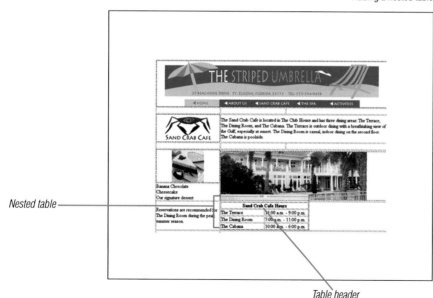

Nested table

Table header

Insert text using a nested table

1. Merge the two empty cells under the cafe photo.

2. Place the insertion point inside the newly merged cells, then click the **Table button** ▦.

3. Type **4** in the Rows text box, type **2** in the Columns text box, type **300** in the Table width text box, click the **Table width list arrow**, click **pixels**, type **0** in the Border thickness text box, click the **Top row header icon** in the Header section, type **This table contains the cafe hours**. in the Summary text box, compare your Table dialog box to Figure 21, then click **OK**.

   The Top header option will automatically center and bold the text that is typed into the top cells of the table. The header will be read by screen readers, providing more accessibility for the table.

4. Merge the top row of cells in the nested table, then type **Sand Crab Cafe Hours**.

5. Enter the cafe dining area names and their hours, as shown in Figure 22.

You inserted a nested table and entered a schedule for the cafe hours.

Format cell content

1. Expand the CSS panel group (if necessary).

2. Click the **Attach Style Sheet button** 🔘 to attach the su_styles.css file to the cafe page.

3. Select the paragraph next to the cafe logo, then use the Property inspector to apply the body_text style.

4. Select the text "Banana Chocolate Cheesecake", then apply the bullets style.

5. Select the text "Our Signature dessert" and the "Reservations information", then apply the body_text style.

6. Repeat Step 5 to apply the body_text style to the nested table text.

    Your screen should resemble Figure 23.

You formatted text in table cells using a Cascading Style Sheet.

FIGURE 23

Formatting text using a Cascading Style Sheet

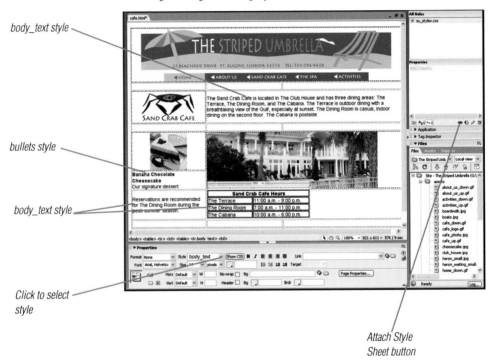

body_text style

bullets style

body_text style

Click to select style

Attach Style Sheet button

FIGURE 24

Formatting cells using horizontal alignment

Horz list arrow

Insertion
point inside
cell with no
elements
selected

Vert list arrow

Format cells

1. Click to place the insertion point in the cell with the cheesecake name.

2. Click the **Horz list arrow**, then click **Center** to center the cell contents.

   You do not need to select the text because you are setting the alignment for all contents in the cell.

3. Repeat Steps 1 and 2 for the cell with the reservations paragraph as well as the cell with the nested table.

4. Click in the cell with the Reservations text, click the **Vert list arrow**, then click **Middle**, as shown in Figure 24.

5. Save your work.

You formatted table cells by adding horizontal and vertical alignment.

Modify cell content

1. Click **Modify** on the menu bar, then click **Navigation Bar** to open the Modify Navigation Bar dialog box.

2. Click the **Show "Down image" initially check box** to remove the check mark for the home button.

3. Click **cafe** in the Nav bar elements box, click the **Show "Down image" initially check box** to add a check mark, then click **OK**.

   The button now shows viewers that they are on the cafe page by displaying the down state when the page is open, as shown in Figure 25.

4. Save your work.

You edited the navigation bar to show the correct down state intially.

FIGURE 25
Edited navigation bar on the cafe page

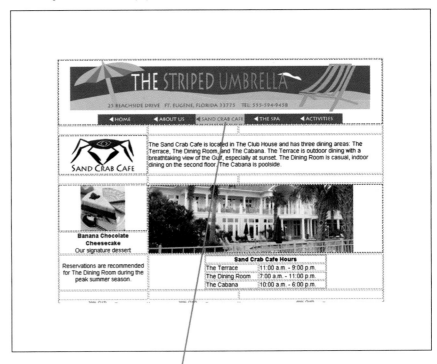

Correct button is shown in
the down state

Working with Tables

FIGURE 26
Hiding visual aids

Visual Aids button

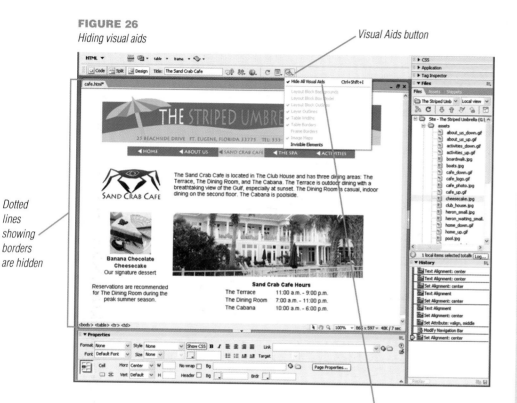

Dotted
lines
showing
borders
are hidden

Hide All Visual Aids
menu item

1. Click the **Visual Aids button** on the Document toolbar, then click **Hide All Visual Aids**, as shown in Figure 26.

    The borders around the table, table cells, and div tags (where you used alignment options) are all hidden, allowing you to see more clearly how the page will look in the browser.

2. Repeat Step 1 to show the visual aids again.

3. Save your work, preview the cafe page in the browser, then close the browser.

You used the Hide All Visual Aids command to hide the table borders and layout block outlines, then showed them again.

PERFORM WEB SITE
MAINTENANCE

What You'll Do

 In this lesson, you will use some of Dreamweaver's site maintenance tools to check for broken links, orphaned files, and missing alternate text. You will also verify that all colors are Websafe. You will then correct any problems that you find.

Maintaining a Web Site

As you add pages, links, and content to a Web site, it can quickly become difficult to manage. It's important to perform maintenance tasks frequently to make sure your Web site operates smoothly. To keep a Web site "clean," you should use Dreamweaver's site maintenance tools frequently. You have already learned about some of the tools described in the paragraphs below. Although it is important to use them as you create and modify your pages, it is also important to run them at periodic intervals after publishing your Web site to make sure your Web site is always error-free.

Checking Links Sitewide

Before and after you publish your Web site, you should use the Link Checker panel to make sure all internal links are working. If the Link Checker panel displays any broken links, you should repair them. If the Link Checker panel displays any orphaned files, you should evaluate whether to delete them or link them to existing pages.

Using the Assets Panel

You should also use the Assets panel to check the list of images and colors used in your Web site. If you see images listed that are not being used, you should move them to a storage folder outside the Web site until you need them. If you are concerned about using only Websafe colors, you should also check the Colors list to make sure that all colors in the site are Websafe. If there are non-Websafe colors in the list, locate the elements to which these colors are applied and apply Websafe colors to them.

Using Site Reports

You can use the Reports command in the Site menu to generate six different HTML reports that can help you maintain your Web site. You choose the type of report you want to run in the Reports dialog box, shown in Figure 27. You can specify whether to generate the report for the entire current local site, selected files in the site, or a selected folder. You can also generate Workflow reports to see files that have been checked out by others or recently modified or to view the Design Notes attached to files.

Using the Site Map

You can use the site map to check your navigation structure. Does the site map show that you have followed the file hierarchy in the storyboard and flow chart? Does the navigation structure shown in the site map reflect a logically organized flowchart? Is each page three or four clicks from the home page? If the answer is no to any of these questions, make adjustments to improve the navigation structure.

Testing Pages

Finally, you should test your Web site using many different types and versions of browsers, platforms, and screen resolutions. You should test all links to make sure they connect to valid, active Web sites. Pages that download slowly should be trimmed in size to improve performance. You should analyze all feedback on the Web site objectively, saving both positive and negative comments for future reference to help you make improvements to the site.

FIGURE 27
Reports dialog box

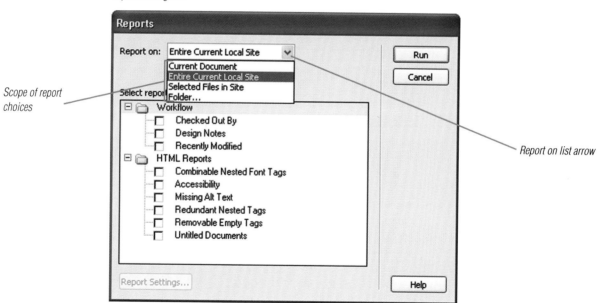

Scope of report choices

Report on list arrow

Check for broken links

1. Show the Files panel (if necessary).

2. Click **Site** on the menu bar, point to **Advanced**, then click **Recreate Site Cache**.

3. Click **Site** on the menu bar, then click **Check Links Sitewide**.

   No broken links are listed in the Link Checker, as shown in Figure 28.

You verified that there are no broken links in the Web site.

Check for orphaned files

1. Click the **Show list arrow**, then click **Orphaned Files**.

   As Figure 29 shows, there are no orphaned files.

2. Close the Results panel group.

You verified that there are no orphaned files in the Web site.

FIGURE 28

Link Checker panel displaying no broken links

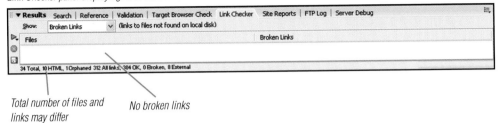

Total number of files and links may differ

No broken links

FIGURE 29

Link Checker panel displaying no orphaned files

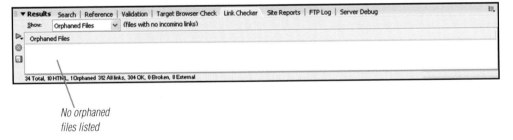

No orphaned files listed

FIGURE 30

Assets panel displaying Websafe colors

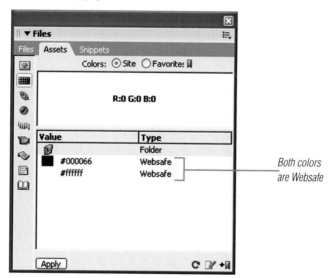

Both colors
are Websafe

1. Click the **Colors button** 🔳 on the Assets panel to view the Web site colors, as shown in Figure 30.

    The Assets panel shows that all colors used in the Web site are Websafe.

You verified that the Web site contains all Websafe colors.

Check for untitled documents

1. Click **Site** on the menu bar, then click **Reports** to open the Reports dialog box.

2. Click the **Untitled Documents check box**, click the **Report on list arrow**, click **Entire Current Local Site**, as shown in Figure 31, then click **Run**.

   The Site Reports panel opens and shows no files, indicating that all documents in the Web site contain titles.

3. Close the Results panel group.

You verified that the Web site contains no untitled documents.

FIGURE 31

Reports dialog box with Untitled Documents option selected

Report on
list arrow

Untitled
Documents
check box

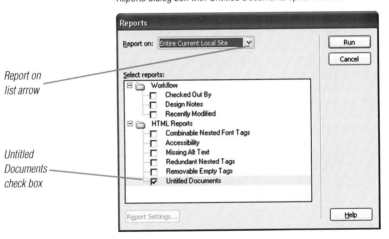

FIGURE 32

Reports dialog box with Missing Alt Text option selected

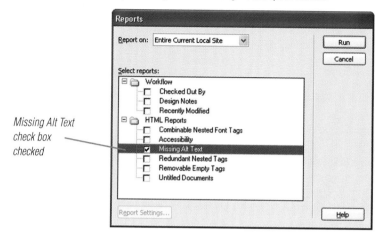

Missing Alt Text check box checked

Check for missing alternate text

1. Using Figure 32 as a guide, run another report that checks the entire current local site for missing alternate text.

   Two pages contain images that are missing alternate text, as shown in Figure 33.

2. Open the home page, then find the image that is missing alternate text.

   TIP The Reports panel documents the code line numbers where the missing alt tags occur. Sometimes it is faster to locate the errors in Code view, rather than in Design view.

3. Add appropriate alternate text to the image.

4. Repeat Steps 2 and 3 to locate the images on the spa page that are missing alternate text, then add alternate text to them.

5. Save your work, then run the report again to check the entire site for missing alternate text.

   No files should appear in the Site Reports panel.

6. Close the Results panel group, then close all open pages.

You ran a report to check for missing alternate text in the entire site. You then added alternate text to three images and ran the report again.

FIGURE 33

Site Reports panel displaying missing "alt" tags

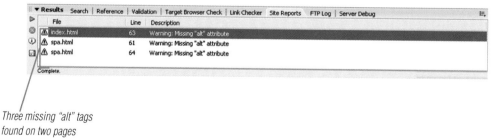

Three missing "alt" tags found on two pages

Create a table.

1. Open the blooms & bulbs Web site.
2. Open classes.html from the Web site.
3. Insert a table on the page with the following settings: Rows: 5, Columns: 3, Table width: 750 pixels, Border thickness: 0, Cell padding: 5, and Cell spacing: 5.
4. Enter the text **This table is used for page layout.** in the Summary text box.
5. Left-align the table on the page, then use Figure 34 as a guide for completing this exercise.
6. Title the page **Master Gardener classes begin soon!**, then save your work.

Resize, split, and merge cells.

1. Select the first cell in the first row, then set the cell width to 25%.
2. Select the second cell in the first row, then set the cell width to 40%.
3. Select the third cell in the first row, then set the cell width to 35%.
4. Merge the three cells in the first row.
5. Merge the first two cells in the second row.
6. Merge the third cell in the third row with the third cell in the fourth row.
7. Split the first cell in the fourth row into two columns.
8. Merge the three cells in the last row.
9. Save your work.

Insert and align graphics in table cells.

1. Copy the banner and the navigation bar together from the home page and paste them into the first row of the table.
2. Center the banner and the navigation bar.
3. Modify the navigation bar to show the classes element in the Down image state and the home element in the Up image state.
4. Use the Insert bar to insert flower_bed.jpg in the last row. You can find the flower_bed.jpg file in the chapter_5 assets folder where your Data Files are stored. Add the alternate text **Flower bed in downtown Alvin** to the flower_bed.jpg image when prompted, then center the image in the cell.
5. Use the tag selector to select the cell containing the flower_bed.jpg image, then set the vertical alignment to Top.
6. Save your work.

Insert text and format cell content.

1. Type **Master Gardener Classes Beginning Soon!** in the first cell in the second row.
2. Type **Who are Master Gardeners?** in the second cell in the second row.
3. Type **Schedule** in the first cell in the third row.
4. Type **Registration** in the second cell in the third row.
5. Type the dates and times for the classes from Figure 34 in the first and second cells in the fourth row.
6. Use Import Word Document command (File menu) to import the file registration.doc into the third cell in the fourth row, then use the Clean up Word HTML command (Commands menu) to remove any unnecessary code.
7. Repeat Step 6 to place the text from the gardeners.doc file into the next empty cell.
8. Attach the blooms_styles.css file, then apply the bodytext style to the dates, times, and two paragraphs of text describing the program.
9. Create a new style in the blooms_styles.css style sheet named **subheadings** with the following settings: Font: Arial, Helvetica, sans-serif; Size: 14; Style: normal; Weight: bold; Color: #003366.
10. Create another new style in the blooms_styles.css style sheet named **reverse_text** with the following settings: Font: Arial, Helvetica, sans-serif; Size: 14; Style: normal; Weight: bold; Color: #FFFFFF.
11. Select each cell that contains text and set the vertical alignment to Top.
12. Center-align the four headings (Master Gardener Classes Beginning Soon!, Who are Master Gardeners?, Schedule, and Registration).

13. Set the horizontal alignment for the cell with the dates to Center.

14. Set the horizontal alignment for the cell with the times and the cells describing registration and Master Gardeners to Left.

15. Select the cell with the word "Registration" in it, then change the cell background color to #000099.

16. Apply the subheadings style to the text "Schedule" and "Who are Master Gardeners".

17. Apply the reverse_text style to the heading "Registration," then apply the seasons style to the text "Master Gardener Classes Beginning Soon!"

18. Save your work, preview the page in your browser, then close your browser.

Perform Web site maintenance.

1. Use the Link Checker panel to check for broken links, then fix any broken links that appear.

2. Use the Link Checker panel to check for orphaned files. If any orphaned files appear in the report, take steps to link them to appropriate pages or remove them.

3. Use the Assets panel to check for Non-Websafe colors.

4. Run an Untitled Documents report for the entire local site. If the report lists any pages that have no titles, add page titles to the untitled pages. Run the report again to verify that all pages have page titles.

5. Run a report to look for missing alternate text. Add alternate text to any graphics that need it, then run the report again to verify that all images contain alternate text.

6. Save your work, then close all open pages.

FIGURE 34
Completed Skills Review

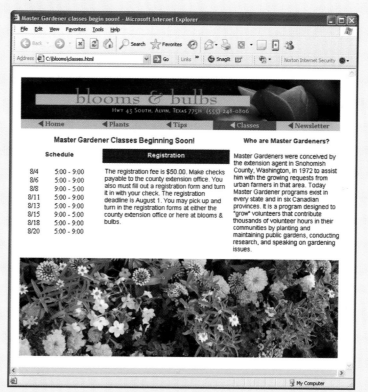

In this exercise you will continue your work on the TripSmart Web site that you began in Project Builder 1 in Chapter 1 and developed in Chapters 2 through 4. You are ready to begin work on a page that will feature catalog items. You plan to use a table for page layout.

1. Open the TripSmart Web site.
2. Open catalog.html from the Web site.
3. Insert a table with the following settings: Rows: 6, Columns: 3, Table width: 750 pixels, Border thickness: 0. Enter an appropriate table summary, then center-align the table.
4. Set the cell widths in the bottom row to 33%, 33%, and 34%.
5. Merge the cells in the top row, copy the TripSmart banner and navigation bar from the home page, paste them into the resulting merged cell, then center the banner if necessary. Add the following alternate text to the image: **TripSmart banner**, then center the banner.
6. Center the navigation bar, if necessary.
7. Merge the three cells in the second row, type **Our products are backed by a 100% guarantee**, then center the text.
8. Type **Protection from harmful UV rays, Cool, light-weight, versatile**, and **Pockets for everything** in the three cells in the third row.
9. Place the files hat.jpg, pants.jpg, and vest.jpg files from the chapter_5 assets folder in the three cells in the fourth row, add the following alternate text to the images: **Safari hat, Kenya convertible pants**, and **Photographer's vest**, then center the three images.
10. Type **Safari Hat, Kenya Convertible Pants**, and **Photographer's Vest** in the three cells in the fifth row, then center each label.
11. Type **Item number 50501** and **$29.00** with a line break between them in the first cell in the sixth row.
12. Repeat Step 11 to type **Item number 62495** and **$39.50** in the second cell in the sixth row.
13. Repeat Step 11 to type **Item number 52301** and **$54.95** in the third cell in the sixth row.
14. Attach the tripsmart_styles.css file to the page, apply the bodytext style to the three descriptions in the third row, then center each description.
15. Create a new style in the tripsmart_styles.css style sheet named **reverse_text** with the following settings: Font, Verdana, Arial, Helvetica, sans-serif; Size, 14 px; Style, normal; Weight, bold; Color, #FFFFFF.
16. Apply the reverse_text style to the text "Our products are backed by a 100% guarantee.", then change the cell background color to #666666.

17. Apply the reverse_text style to the three item names under the images, then change the background color to #999999 for the three cells containing the images.

18. Create a new style called **item_numbers** with the following settings: Font: Verdana, Arial, Helvetica, sans-serif; Size: 10 px; Style: normal; Weight: bold.

19. Apply the item_numbers style to the three items' numbers and prices.

20. Save your work, view the page in your browser, compare your screen with Figure 35, then close the browser.

21. Run reports for broken links, orphaned files, missing alternate text, and untitled documents. Make corrections as necessary.

22. Save your work, then close all open pages.

FIGURE 35
Completed Project Builder 1

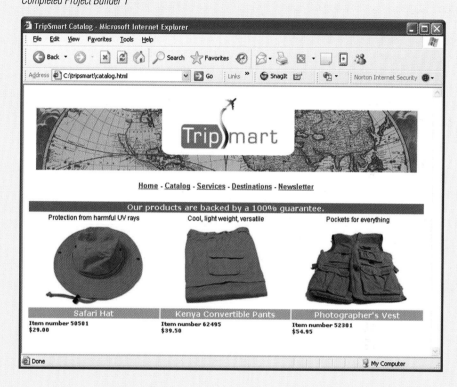

PROJECT BUILDER 2

Use Figure 36 as a guide to continue your work on the emma's book bag Web site that you started in Project Builder 2 in Chapter 1 and developed in Chapters 2 through 4. You are now ready to begin work on a page that will showcase the small cafe in the bookstore. You decide to use a table to lay out the page.

1. Open the emma's book bag Web site, then open cafe.html.
2. Type **Cafe** for the page title, replacing the original title.
3. Create a table on the page with the following settings: Rows: 5, Columns: 3, Table width: 750 pixels, Border thickness: 0, adding an appropriate table summary.

4. Center-align the table and set the width of the three cells in the bottom row to 35%, 35%, and 30%.
5. Merge the cells in the first row, then insert the banner and navigation bar. (*Hint*: Copy the banner and navigation bar from the home page.) Enter appropriate alternate text for the banner, then center-align the banner and navigation bar, if necessary.
6. Merge the first two cells in the second row, then type **The Cafe is the perfect place to relax for a few minutes while you browse through a book or two or wait for a friend**.
7. Attach the book_bag_styles.css file to the page, then apply the bodytext style to the sentence you typed in Step 6.

8. Insert a horizontal rule in the first cell in the third row that is 200 pixels wide.
9. Type **Cafe hours:**, **Monday through Saturday, 10:30 - 2:00** in the second cell in the third row, using a line break between each line.
10. Import book club.doc in the first cell in the fourth row, then apply the bodytext style to the paragraph.
11. Type **Scones, cookies, and muffins are delivered fresh daily from an award winning local bakery. We proudly serve Starbucks Coffee and Republic of Tea tea**. in the second cell of the fourth row, then apply the bodytext style to the paragraph.

Working with Tables

12. Create a new style in the book_bag_styles.css file called **subheading** with the following settings: Font: Verdana, Arial, Helvetica, sans-serif; Size: 12 px; Weight: bold; Color: #000066; apply it to the Cafe hours text, then center the text.

13. Merge the last cells in the second, third, fourth, and fifth rows, then insert muffins.jpg from the chapter_5 assets folder, adding appropriate alternate text.

14. Merge the first and second cells in the last row, then copy the two lines of text from the home page listing the name and hours of the bookstore into the newly merged cell.

15. Use horizontal and vertical cell alignment to balance the placement of the text in the cells.

16. Save your work, then preview the page in your browser.

17. Run reports for broken links, orphaned files, missing alternate text, and untitled documents. Make corrections as necessary, then close all open pages.

FIGURE 36
Completed Project Builder 2

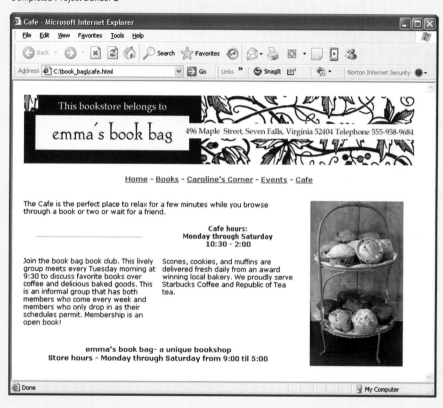

Vesta Everitt has opened a new shop called Needles and Thread that carries needle-point, cross-stitching, and smocking supplies. She is considering creating a Web site to promote her services and products and would like to gather some ideas before she hires a Web designer. She decides to visit retail Web sites to look for design ideas, as shown in Figures 37 and 38.

1. Connect to the Internet, navigate to the Online Companion, then select a link for this chapter. The Web sites shown in the figures are Teva and L.L. Bean.
2. Click View on your browser's menu bar, then click the Source command to view the source code for the Web site you selected.
3. Search the code for table tags. Note the number that you find.

4. Select another link from the Online Companion, and repeat Steps 2 and 3.
5. Using a word processor or scrap paper, list five design ideas that you like from either of these pages. Be sure to specify which page was the source of each idea.

FIGURE 37
Design Project

FIGURE 38
Design Project

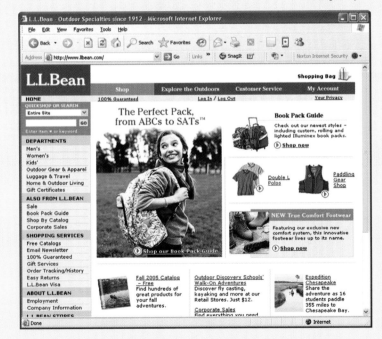

In this assignment, you will continue to work on the Web site that you started in Chapter 1 and developed in Chapters 2 through 4. There will be no data files supplied. You are building this Web site from chapter to chapter, so you must do each Portfolio Project assignment in each chapter to complete your Web site.

You will continue building your Web site by designing and completing a page that contains a table used for page layout. After completing your page, you will run several reports to test the Web site.

1. Take a few minutes to evaluate your storyboard. Choose a page or pages to develop in which you will use a table for page layout.
2. Plan the content for the new page (or pages) by making a sketch of the table that shows where the content will be placed in the table cells. Split and merge cells and align each element as necessary to create a visually attractive layout.
3. Create the table and place the content in the cells using the sketch for guidance.

4. After you complete the pages, run a report that checks for broken links in the Web site. Correct any broken links that appear in the report.
5. Run a report on the Web site for orphaned files and correct any if found.
6. Run a report on pages that are missing alternate text. Add alternate text to elements that need it.
7. Run a report on any pages that do not have page titles and add titles to any pages, as needed.

8. Check for any Non-Websafe colors in the Web site. If any are found, replace them with Websafe colors.
9. Preview all the pages in your browser and test all links. Evaluate the pages for both content and layout, then use the check list in Figure 39 to make sure your Web site is completed.
10. Make any modifications necessary to improve the pages.

FIGURE 39
Portfolio Project check list

Web Site Check List
1. Title any pages that have no page titles.
2. Check to see that all pages have consistent navigation links.
3. Check to see that all links work correctly.
4. Check to see that all images have alternate text.
5. Remove any Non-Websafe colors.
6. Delete any unnecessary files.
7. Remove any orphaned files.
8. Use tables for layout when possible.
9. View all pages using at least two different browsers.
10. Verify that the home page has keywords, a description, and a point of contact.

chapter

6 COLLECTING DATA
WITH FORMS

1. Plan and create a form.

2. Edit and format a form.

3. Work with form objects.

4. Test a form.

Introduction

Many Web sites have pages designed to collect information from viewers. You've likely seen such pages when ordering books online from Barnes & Noble or purchasing airline tickets from an airline Web site. Adding a form to a Web page provides interactivity between your viewers and your business. To collect information from viewers, you add forms for them to fill out and send to a Web server to be processed. Forms on a Web page are no different from forms in everyday life. Your checks are simple forms that ask for information: the date, the amount of the check, the name of the check's recipient, and your signature. A form on a Web page consists of **form objects** such as text boxes or radio buttons into which viewers type information or from which they make selections.

In this chapter you will import a redesigned Striped Umbrella Web site. Each page has been redesigned using tables for page layout to provide better consistency when the pages are viewed in a browser. You will replace your current Web site with this new one. You will add a form to a page that provides a way for interested viewers to ask for more information about the resort.

It will also give them the opportunity to comment on the Web site and make helpful suggestions. Feedback is a vital part of a Web site and must be made easy for a viewer to submit.

Using Forms to Collect Information

Forms are just one of the many different tools that Web developers use to collect information from viewers. A simple form can consist of one form object and a button that submits information to a Web server, for example, a search text box that you fill out, and a button that you click to start the search. More complex forms can collect contact information, or even allow students to take exams online and receive grades after a short wait. You can use forms to insert information into databases, or to find a specific record in a database. The range of uses for forms is limited only by your imagination.

All forms need to be connected to an application that will process the information that the form collects. This application can store the form data in a database, or simply send it to you in an e-mail message. You need to specify how you want the information used, stored, and processed.

Tools You'll Use

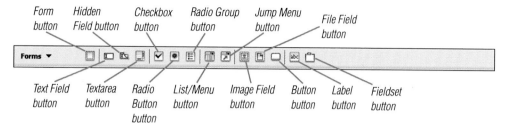

Form button — Hidden Field button — Checkbox button — Radio Group button — Jump Menu button — File Field button

Text Field button — Textarea button — Radio Button button — List/Menu button — Image Field button — Button button — Label button — Fieldset button

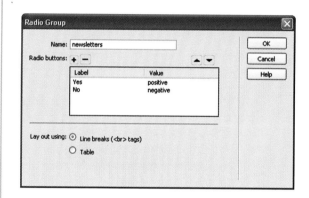

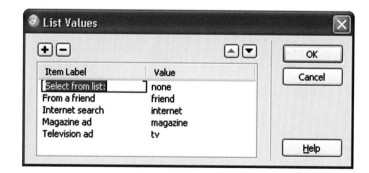

PLAN AND
CREATE A FORM

What You'll Do

 In this lesson, you will replace your Striped Umbrella files by importing a revised Web site. You will then add a new form to the feedback page in The Striped Umbrella Web site.

Planning a Form

Before you use Dreamweaver to create a form, it's a good idea to write down the information you want to collect and the order in which you want to collect it. It's also a good idea to make a sketch of the form. Planning your form content at the beginning saves you from spending time organizing the information when you create the form in Dreamweaver. The form you will create for The Striped Umbrella Web site will contain a form for viewers to request more information, sign up for an electronic newsletter, and submit their comments about the Web site. Figure 1 shows a sketch of the form that you will create in this chapter.

When planning your form content, you should organize the information in a logical order that will make sense to viewers. For instance, no one will expect to fill in their address before their name, simply because it isn't typically done that way. Almost all forms, from your birth certificate to your IRS tax forms, request your name before your address, so you should follow this stan-

dard. Placing information in an unusual order will only confuse your viewers.

QUICKTIP

People on the Internet are notoriously hurried and will often provide only information that is required or that is located on the top half of the form. Therefore, it's a good idea to put the most important information at the top of your form.

Creating Forms

Once you have finished planning your form content, you are ready to create the form in Dreamweaver. To create a form on a Web page, you use the Form button in the Forms category of the Insert bar. Clicking the Form button will insert a dashed red outline around the area of the form. In order to make your form function correctly, you then need to configure the form so that it "talks" to the scripts or e-mail server and processes the information submitted by the viewer. By itself, a form can do nothing. It has to have some type of script or program running behind it that will process the information to be used in a certain way.

There are two methods used to process the information your form collects: server-side scripting and client-side scripting. **Server-side scripting** uses applications that reside on your Web server and interact with the information collected in the form. The most common types of server-side applications are **Common Gateway Interface (CGI)** scripts, **Cold Fusion** programs, and **Active Server Pages (ASP)** applications. **Client-side scripting** means that the form is processed on the user's computer. The script resides on the Web page, rather than on the server. An example of this is a mortgage calculator that allows you to estimate mortgage payments. The data is processed on the user's computer. The most common types of scripts stored on a Web page are created with a scripting language called **JavaScript**, or **Jscript** if you are using a Microsoft Web browser. Server-side applications and scripts collect the information from the form, process the information, and react to the information the form contains.

You can process form information in a variety of ways. The easiest and most common way is to collect the information from the form and e-mail it to the owner of the Web site. You can also specify that form data be stored in a database for the Web site owner to use at a later date. You can even specify that the application do both: collect the form data in a database, as well as send it in an e-mail message. You can also specify that the form data be processed instead of stored. For instance, you can create a form that totals the various prices and provides a total price to the site viewer on the order page, without recording any subtotals in a database or e-mail message. In this example, only the final total of the order would be stored in the database or sent in an e-mail message.

FIGURE 1

Sketch of Web form you will add to survey page

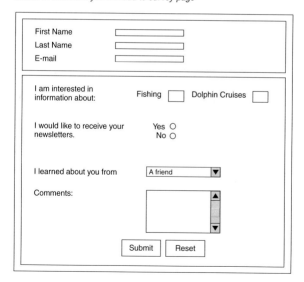

You can also create forms that make changes to your Web page based on information entered by viewers. For example, you could create a form that asks viewers to select a background color for a Web page. In this type of form, the information could be collected and sent to the processor. The processor could then compare the selected background color to the current background color and change the color if it is different from the viewer's selection.

Setting Form Properties

After you insert a form, use the Property inspector to specify the application that will process the form information and to specify how the information will be sent to the processing application. The **Action property** in the Property inspector specifies the application or script that will process the form data. Most of the time the Action property is the name and location of a CGI script, such as /cgi-bin/myscript.

cgi; a Cold Fusion page, such as mypage.cfm; or an Active Server Page, such as mypage.asp. Figure 2 shows the properties of a selected form.

FIGURE 2
Form controls in the Property inspector

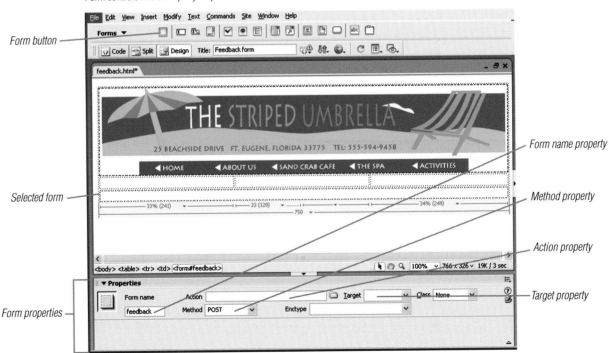

The **Method property** specifies the HyperText Transfer Protocol (HTTP) method used to send the form data to the Web server. The **GET method** specifies that ASCII data collected in the form will be sent to the server appended to the URL or file included in the Action property. For instance, if the Action property is set to /cgi-bin/myscript.cgi, then the data will be sent as a string of characters after the address, as follows: /cgi-bin/ myscript.cgi?a+collection+of+data+ collected+by+the+form. Data sent with the GET method is usually limited to 8K or less, depending on the Web browser. The **POST method** specifies that the form data be sent to the processing script as a binary or encrypted file, allowing you to send data securely. When you specify the POST method, there is no limit to the amount of information that can be collected in the form, and the information is secure.

The **Form name property** specifies a unique name for the form. The name can be a string of any alphanumeric characters and cannot include spaces. The **Target property** lets you specify the window in which you want the form data to be processed.

Understanding CGI Scripts

CGI is one of the most popular tools used to collect form data. CGI allows a Web browser to work directly with the programs that are running on the server and also makes it possible for a Web site to change in response to user input. CGI programs can be written in Perl or in C, depending

on the type of server that is hosting your Web site. When a CGI script collects data from a Web form, it passes the data to a program running on a Web server, which in turn passes the data back to your Web browser, which then makes changes to the Web site in response to the form data. The

resulting data is then stored in a database or sent to an e-mail server, which then sends the information in an e-mail message to a designated recipient. Figure 3 illustrates how a CGI script processes information collected by a form.

FIGURE 3
Illustration of CGI process on Web server

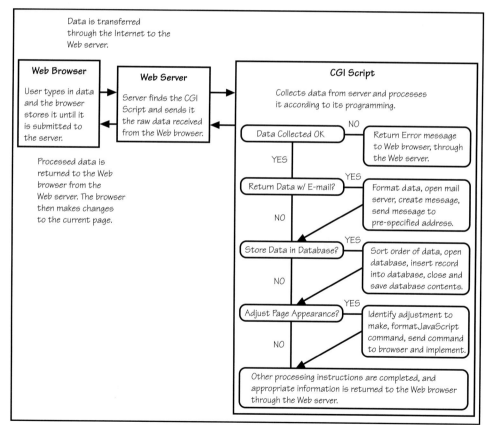

Import the revised Striped Umbrella Web site (Win)

1. Open Windows Explorer, then navigate to the chapter_6 Data Files folder, so that the contents of the chapter_6 Data Files folder appear in the right pane.

2. Press and hold **[Ctrl]**, then drag the **striped_umbrella folder** from the chapter_6 Data Files folder in the right pane on top of the parent folder to the original striped_umbrella root folder, as shown in Figure 4, then click **Yes to All** to replace all files.

   The redesigned pages replace the existing pages in the striped_umbrella root folder.

3. Close Windows Explorer, then start Dreamweaver.

4. Click **Site** on the menu bar, click **Manage Sites**, verify that The Striped Umbrella Web site is selected, click **Remove,** then click **Yes** in the warning dialog box.

   It is better to remove the previous site, because the site you will be importing has the same name. Remember that deleting a Web site in the Manage Sites dialog box does not actually delete the files. It just deletes the site definition.

5. Click **Import**.

   The Import Site dialog box opens.

6. Click the **Look in list arrow** to navigate to the chapter_6 Data Files folder, click **The Striped Umbrella.ste**, as shown in Figure 5, then click **Open**.

   (continued)

FIGURE 4
Dragging the striped_umbrella folder to another folder or drive

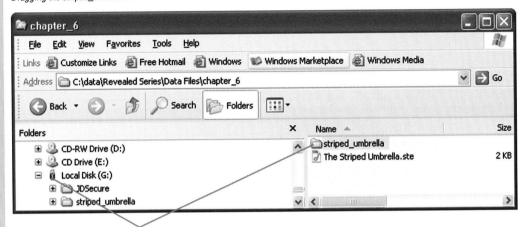

Drag the striped_umbrella folder from the right pane (Data Files folder) on top of the parent folder (or drive) to the original striped_umbrella root folder overwriting the existing striped_umbrella folder

FIGURE 5
Import Site dialog box

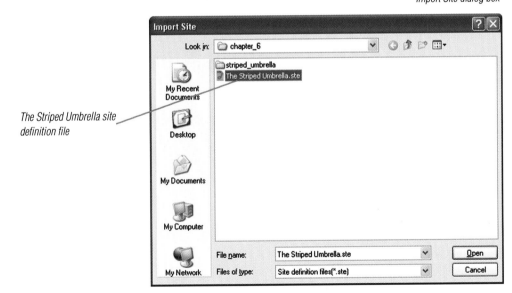

The Striped Umbrella site definition file

Collecting Data with Forms

FIGURE 6

Site Definition for The Striped Umbrella dialog box (Win)

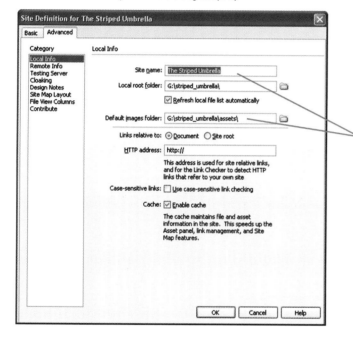

Your paths will be different depending on the location you chose for the striped_umbrella folder and will probably be the same locations you chose for the original files

The ste file is an XML file that contains information about the Web site including any information entered in the Manage Sites dialog box.

7. Click the **striped_umbrella folder** in the Choose local root folder for site The Striped Umbrella dialog box (not the one in your Data Files folder—the one in your root folder for the site), click **Open**, click the **assets folder** in the Choose local root folder for site The Striped Umbrella dialog box, click **Open**, then click **Select**.

8. Verify that The Striped Umbrella site is selected in the Manage Sites dialog box, then click **Edit**.

9. Verify that the striped_umbrella folder is the root folder for the Web site and the assets folder under the striped_umbrella folder is the default location for images, as shown in Figure 6.

   TIP If you receive a warning that the selected folder does not contain the current site's home page, click Edit again to return to the Site Definition dialog box, click Site Map Layout in the Category column, click the Browse for File icon 🗀 next to the Home page text box, then double-click index.html in the striped_umbrella root folder.

10. Click **OK**, then click **Done**.

   TIP If you do not see the files listed in the Files panel, click the plus sign next to the root folder.

You copied the striped_umbrella folder from the chapter_6 Data Files folder to a different folder on your computer or external drive. You then imported the revised Striped Umbrella site and verified that the root folder was set to the striped_umbrella folder that you copied. You also verified that the default images folder is still the assets folder of the striped_umbrella folder.

Import the revised Striped Umbrella Web site (Mac)

1. Open Finder, then navigate to the folder on your computer or external drive where you want to store the revised Striped Umbrella Web site.

2. Click **File** on the menu bar, then click **New Finder Window** to open another version of Finder, then open the chapter_6 Data Files folder.

3. Drag the striped_umbrella folder from the chapter_6 folder to the drive and folder where you want to store The Striped Umbrella Web site, as shown in Figure 7.

4. Close the Finder windows, start Dreamweaver (if necessary), click **Site** on the menu bar, click **Manage Sites**, verify that The Striped Umbrella Web site is selected, click **Remove**, then click **Yes** in the Warning dialog box.

    It is better to remove the previous site, since the site you will be importing has the same name. Remember that deleting a Web site in the Manage Sites dialog box does not actually delete the files. It just deletes the site definition.

5. Click **Import**.

    The Import Site dialog box opens.

6. Click **The Striped Umbrella.ste** in the chapter_6 folder that you moved in Step 3, then click **Open**.

    The Choose Local Root Folder for Site The Striped Umbrella opens.

    (continued)

FIGURE 7

Dragging the striped_umbrella folder to a new location (Mac)

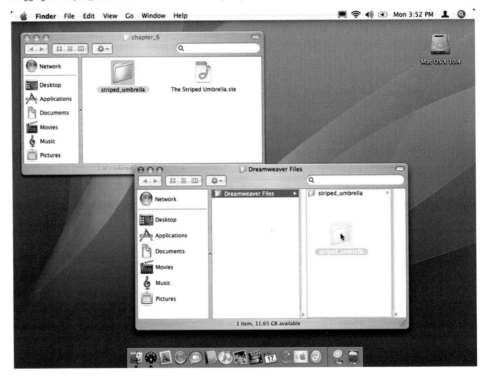

FIGURE 8

Site Definition for The Striped Umbrella dialog box (Mac)

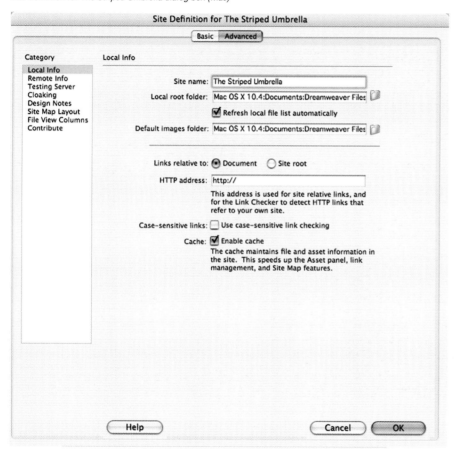

7. Navigate to the striped_umbrella folder that you moved in Step 3, then click **Choose**.

   The Choose local images folder for site The Striped Umbrella dialog box opens.

8. Click the **assets folder** in the striped_umbrella folder, then click **Choose**.

   This sets the Default Images Folder path to the assets folder located in the striped_umbrella folder.

9. Verify that The Striped Umbrella site is selected in the Manage Sites dialog box, then click **Edit**.

10. Click the **Advanced tab** (if necessary), then click the **Local Info category** (if necessary).

11. Compare your screen with Figure 8, click **OK**, then click **Done**.

You copied the striped_umbrella folder from the chapter_6 Data Files folder to a different folder on your computer or external drive. You then imported The Striped Umbrella site and verified that the default images folder is still the assets folder of the striped_umbrella folder.

Insert a form

1. Open the feedback page in the Web site.

2. Merge the three cells in the bottom row, then click inside the merged cell.

   This is the space on the page where you will place your form.

3. Click the **Insert bar list arrow**, click **Forms**, then click the **Form button** ☐ to insert a new form on the page.

   A dashed red rectangular outline appears on the page, as shown in Figure 9.

   TIP   You will be able to see the form only if Invisible Elements are turned on. To turn on Invisible Elements, click View on the menu bar, point to Visual Aids, then click Invisible Elements.

You inserted a new form on the feedback page of The Striped Umbrella Web site.

FIGURE 9
New form in Design view

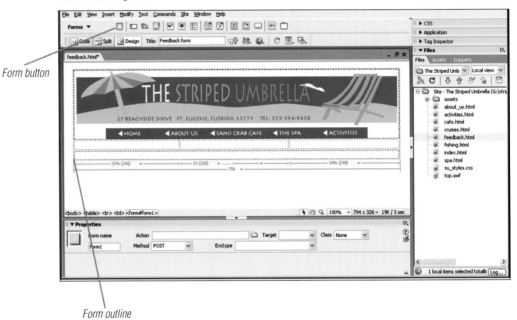

Form button

Form outline

Collecting Data with Forms

FIGURE 10
Property inspector showing properties of selected form

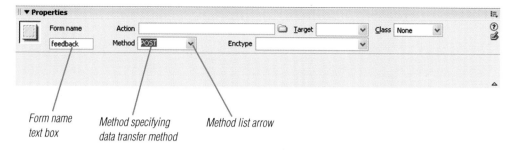

Form name
text box

Method specifying
data transfer method

Method list arrow

Set form properties

1. Click the **Form tag (<form#form1>)** in the tag selector located on the status bar to select the form and display the form properties in the Property inspector.

2. Select **form1** in the Form name text box in the Property inspector, then type **feedback**.

3. Click the **Method list arrow** in the Property inspector, then click **POST** (if necessary), as shown in Figure 10.

   TIP Leave the Action and Target text boxes blank unless you have the information necessary to process the form.

4. Save your work.

You configured the form on the feedback page.

Using CGI scripts

You can use CGI scripts to start and stop external programs or to specify that a page update automatically based on viewer input. You can use CGI scripts to create surveys, site search tools, and games. You can even use CGI to do basic tasks such as record entries to a guest book or count the number of people who have accessed a specific page of your site. CGI also lets you create dynamic Web documents "on the fly" so that pages can be generated in response to preferences specified by the viewer. Unless you have a specific application that you want your script applied to, you can probably find a low-priced script by searching on Google. Instructions for creating and modifying CGI scripts are not covered in this text.

EDIT AND FORMAT A FORM

What You'll Do

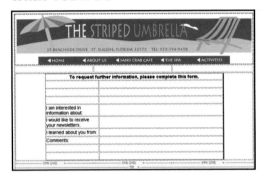

 In this lesson, you will insert a table to create a basic structure for the form on the feedback page. You will also add and format form labels.

Using Tables to Lay Out a Form

Just as you can use a table to help place page elements on a Web page, you can also use tables to help lay out a form. To make sure that your labels and form objects appear in the exact positions you want on a Web page, you can place them in table cells. When you use a table to lay out a form, you usually place labels in the first column and place form objects in the second column, as shown in Figure 11. Although there are different ways to lay out form elements, this two-column approach is probably the cleanest and simplest.

Using Fieldsets to Group Form Objects

If you are creating a long form on a Web page, you might want to organize your form elements in sections to make it easier for viewers to fill out the form. You can use fieldsets to group similar form elements together. A **fieldset** is an HTML tag used to group related form elements together. You can have as many fieldsets on a page as you want. To create a fieldset, use the Fieldset button on the Insert bar.

Adding Labels to Form Objects

When you create a form, you need to include form field labels so that viewers know what information you want them to enter in each field of the form. Because labels play such an important part in identifying the information that the form collects, you need to make sure to use labels that make sense to your viewers. For example, First Name and Last Name are good form field labels, because viewers understand clearly what information they should enter. However, a label such as Top 6 Directory Names might confuse viewers and cause them to leave the field blank or enter incorrect information. When you create a form field label, you should use a simple name that makes it obvious what information viewers should enter in the form field. If creating a simple and obvious label is not possible, then include a short paragraph that describes the information that should be entered into the form field. Figure 12 shows very clearly marked labels for both the form fields and the groups of related information.

You can add labels to a form using one of two methods. You can simply type a label in the appropriate table cell of your form or use the Label button on the Forms group of the Insert bar to link the label to the form object.

FIGURE 11

Web site that uses a table to lay out a form

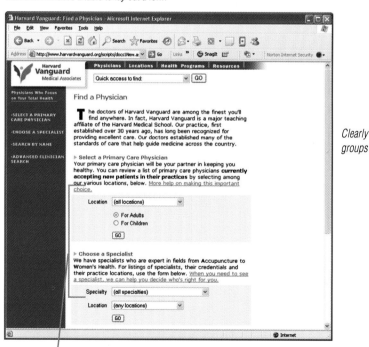

Form objects in columns

FIGURE 12

Web site that uses clearly marked labels for form fields and groups of related information

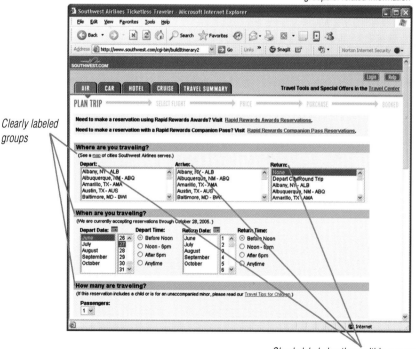

Clearly labeled groups

Clearly labeled options within groups

Add a table to a form

1. Click to place the insertion point inside the form, as shown in Figure 13.

2. Click the **Insert bar list arrow**, click **Common**, then click the **Table button**.

3. In the Table dialog box, set the Rows to **10**, Columns to **2**, Table width to **75 percent**, Border thickness to **0**, Cell padding to **2**, Cell spacing to **1**, then click the **Top row header icon** in the Header section.

4. Type **Table used for form layout.** in the Summary text box, compare your screen to Figure 14, then click **OK**.

   TIP The table may look like it is creeping over the bottom edge of the form. If it does, click the form tag on the Property inspector.

5. Center the table in the form, set the bottom-left cell width to 30%, set the bottom-right cell width to 70%, then save your work.

You added a table to the form on the feedback page.

FIGURE 13
Placing the insertion point inside the form

Insertion point
placed inside form

FIGURE 14
Table dialog box

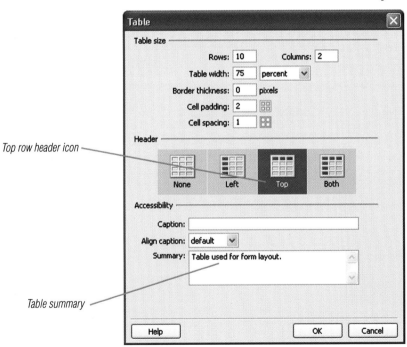

Top row header icon

Table summary

Collecting Data with Forms

FIGURE 15

Typing and formatting labels in table cells

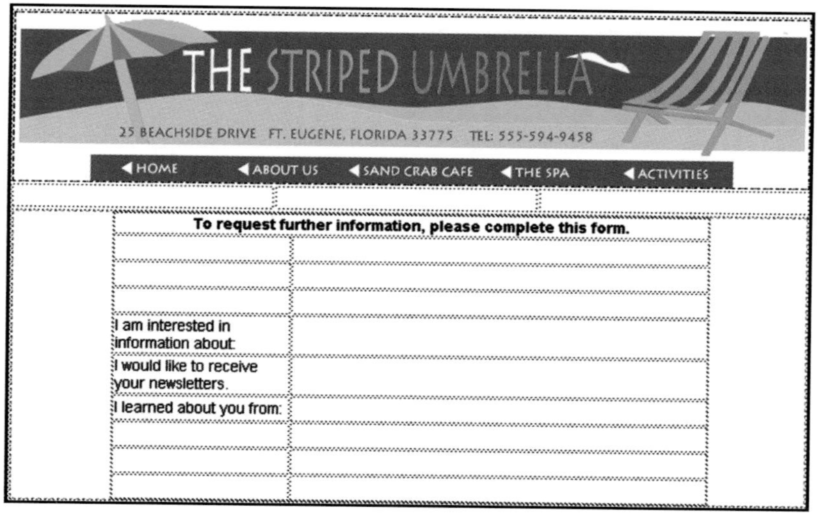

Add form labels to table cells

1. Merge the top two cells in the first row of the table, then type **To request further information**, **please complete this form.**, then apply the body_text style to the sentence.

   Because you designated a header for this table, the top row text is automatically centered and bolded. The header will be used by screen readers to assist visually impaired viewers to identify the table.

2. Click in the first cell in the fifth row, then type **I am interested in information about:**.

3. Press [↓], then type **I would like to receive your newsletters.**

4. Click [↓], type **I learned about you from:**, then press [↓].

5. Format each of the labels you entered with the body_text style, then compare your screen to Figure 15.

You added a header and three form labels to table cells in the form and formatted them with the body_text style.

Add form labels using the Label button

1. Click in the cell below the cell that contains the text "I learned about you from:".

2. Click the **Insert bar list arrow**, click **Forms**, then click the **Label button** 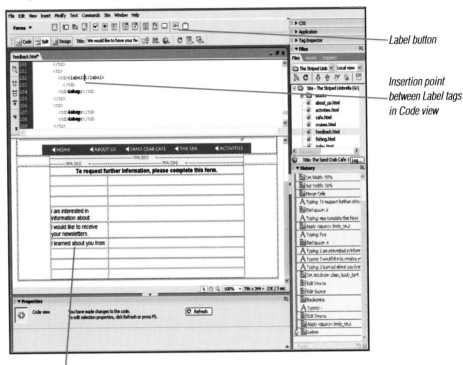.

> TIP You may need to scroll down in the Design pane to see the cell.

The view changes to Code and Design view, as shown in Figure 16. The insertion point is positioned in the Code view pane between the tags <label> and </label>, which were added when you clicked the Label button.

(continued)

FIGURE 16

Adding a label to a form using the Label button

Label button

Insertion point between Label tags in Code view

Insertion point in cell in Design view

Collecting Data with Forms

FIGURE 17

New label added using the Label button

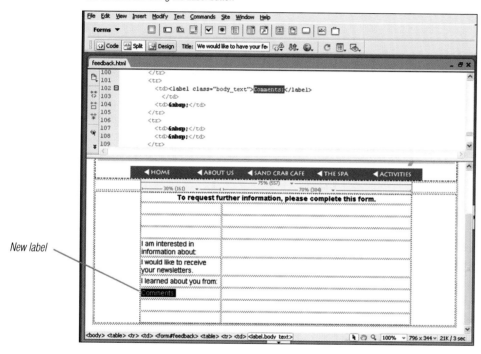

New label

3. Type **Comments:**, then click anywhere in the Design view pane.

The label appears in the table cell in the Design view pane.

TIP You can also click Refresh in the Property inspector or press [F5] to refresh the page in Design view.

4. Format the new label as body_text, then compare your screen to Figure 17.

5. Click the **Show Design view button**
   Design, then save your work.

You added a new label to the form on the feedback page using the Label button, then formatted it with the body_text style.

WORK WITH FORM OBJECTS

What You'll Do

In this lesson, you will add form objects to the form on the feedback page.

Understanding Form Objects

A form provides a structure in which you can place form objects. Form objects—which are also called **form elements**, **form controls**, or **fields**—are the components of a form such as checkboxes, text boxes, and radio buttons that allow viewers to provide information and interact with the Web site. You can use form objects in any combination to collect the information you require. Figure 18 shows a form that contains a wide range of form objects.

Text fields are the most common type of form object and are used for collecting a string of characters, such as a name, address, password, or e-mail address. For some text fields, such as those collecting dollar amounts, you might want to set an initial value of 0. Use the Text Field button on the Insert bar to insert a text field.

A **text area field** is a text field that can store several lines of text. You can use text area fields to collect descriptions of problems, answers to long questions, comments, or even a résumé. Use the Textarea button on the Insert bar to insert a text area.

You can use **checkboxes** to create a list of options from which a viewer can make multiple selections. For instance, you could add a series of checkboxes listing hobbies and ask the viewer to select the ones that interest him/her. You could also use a checkbox to answer a yes or no question.

You can use **radio buttons** to provide a list of options from which only one selection can be made. A group of radio buttons is called a **radio group**. Each radio group you create allows only one selection from within that group. You could use radio groups to ask viewers to select their annual salary range, their age group, or the t-shirt color they want to order. Use the Radio Group button on the Insert bar to insert a radio group.

You can insert a **menu** or **list** on a form using the List/Menu button on the Insert bar. You use menus when you want a viewer to select a single option from a list of choices. You use lists when you want a viewer to select one or more options from a list of choices. Menus are often used to provide navigation on a Web site, while lists are commonly used in order forms to let viewers choose from a list of possibilities. Menus must be opened to see all of the options they contain, whereas lists display some of their options all of the time. When you create a list, you need to specify the number of lines that will be visible on the screen by setting a value for the Height property in the Property inspector.

Using **hidden fields** makes it possible to provide information to the Web server and form processing script without the viewer knowing that the information is being sent. For instance, you could add a hidden field that tells the server who should receive an e-mail message and what the subject of the message should be. You can also use hidden fields to collect information from a viewer without his/her knowledge. For instance, you can use a hidden field to send you the viewer's browser type or her IP address.

You can insert an **image field** into a form using the Image Field button on the Insert bar. You can use the Image Field button to create buttons that contain custom graphics.

FIGURE 18
Web site displaying several form objects

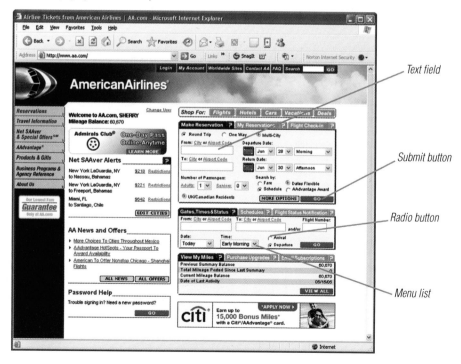

Text field

Submit button

Radio button

Menu list

If you want your viewers to upload files to your Web server, you can insert a **file field**. You could insert a file field to let your viewers upload sample files to your Web site or to post photos to your Web site's photo gallery.

All forms must include a Submit button, which a viewer clicks to transfer his form data to the Web server. You can also insert a Reset button, which lets viewers clear data from a form and reset it to its default values. You can also insert a plain button to trigger an action that you specify on the page. You can insert a Submit, Reset, or plain button using the Button button on the Insert bar.

Jump menus are navigational menus that let viewers go quickly to different pages in your site or to different sites on the Internet. You can create jump menus quickly and easily by using the Jump Menu button.

Figure 19 shows the Insert bar with all of the form object buttons labeled. When you insert a form object in a form, you use the Property inspector to specify a unique name for it. You can also use the Property inspector to set other appropriate properties for the object, such as the number of lines or characters you wish the object to display.

QUICKTIP

To obtain form controls designed for creating specific types of forms, such as online tests and surveys, you can visit the Macromedia Dreamweaver Exchange and search available extensions (*www.m2cromedia.com/exchange/dreamweaver*).

FIGURE 19
Insert bar showing form object buttons

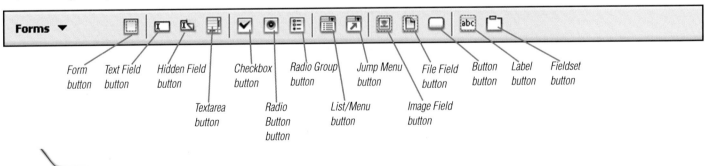

FIGURE 20
Input Tag Accessibility Attributes dialog box

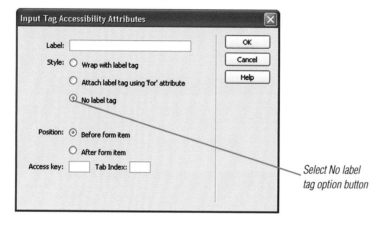

Select No label
tag option button

Insert single-line text fields

1. Place the insertion point in the first cell under the header, then type **First Name**.

2. Press **[Tab]**, then click the **Text Field button** on the Insert bar.

3. Click the **No label tag option button**, as shown in Figure 20, then click **OK**.

4. Select textfield in the TextField text box in the Property inspector, then type **first_name**.

5. Click the **Single line option button** in the Property inspector (if necessary).

6. Type **40** in the Char width text box in the Property inspector.

   This specifies that 40 characters will be visible inside this text field when displayed in a browser.

7. Type **100** in the Max Chars text box in the Property inspector, then compare your screen to Figure 21.

   This specifies that a user can type no more than 100 characters in this field.

(continued)

FIGURE 21
Property inspector showing properties of selected text field

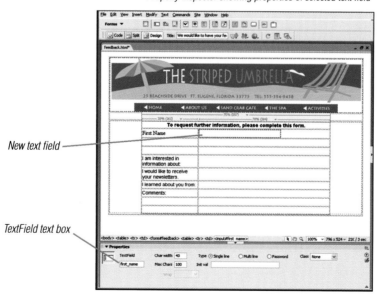

New text field

TextField text box

8. Repeat Steps 1 through 7 to create another label and single-line text field under the First Name label and text field, using **Last Name** for the label, **last_name** for the text field, and specifying **40** for Char width and **100** for Max Chars.

9. Repeat Steps 1 through 7 to create another label and single-line text field under the Last Name label and text field, using **E-mail** for the label, **email** for the TextField name, and specifying **40** for Char width and **100** for Max Chars.

10. Apply the body_text style to the three new labels.

11. Save your changes, preview the page in your browser, compare your screen to Figure 22, then close your browser.

You added three single-line text fields to the form and previewed the page in your browser.

FIGURE 22
Form with single-line text fields added

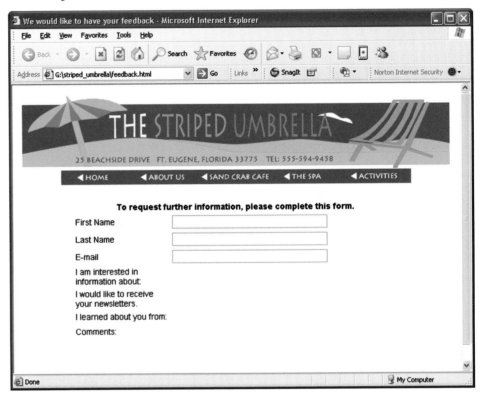

Collecting Data with Forms

FIGURE 23

Property inspector with properties of selected text area displayed

Textarea
button

New multiple-line
text field

Char width
text box

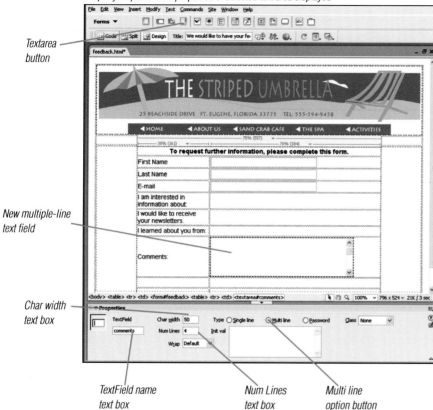

TextField name
text box

Num Lines
text box

Multi line
option button

Insert a multiple-line text field

1. Click in the cell to the right of the Comments: label.

2. Click the **Textarea button** 🖳 on the Insert bar, click the **No label tag option button** on the Input Tag Accessibility Attributes dialog box, then click **OK**.

3. Select **textarea** in the TextField text box in the Property inspector, then type **comments**.

4. Click the **Multi line option button** in the Property inspector (if necessary).

5. Type **50** in the Char width text box in the Property inspector.

   This specifies that 50 characters will be visible inside this text field when the page is displayed in a browser.

6. Type **4** in the Num Lines text box in the Property inspector, as shown in Figure 23.

   This specifies that the text box will display four lines of text.

You added a multiple-line text field to the form.

Insert checkboxes

1. Place the insertion point in the empty table cell to the right of "I am interested in information about:".
2. Click the **Checkbox button** ☑ on the Insert bar to insert a checkbox in the form.
3. Type **Fishing** in the Label text box, click the **Wrap with label tag option button** in the Style section, click the **After form item option button** in the Position section, as shown in Figure 24, then click **OK**.
4. Select the checkbox, then type **fishing** in the Checkbox name text box in the Property inspector.
5. Type **fish** in the Checked value text box in the Property inspector.
   This is the value that will be sent to your script or program when the form is processed.
6. Click the **Unchecked option button** in the Property inspector (if necessary), as shown in Figure 25.
   Selecting the Checked option button would make a check mark appear in the checkbox by default.

(continued)

(continued)

FIGURE 24
Input Tag Accessibility Attributes dialog box for Fishing label

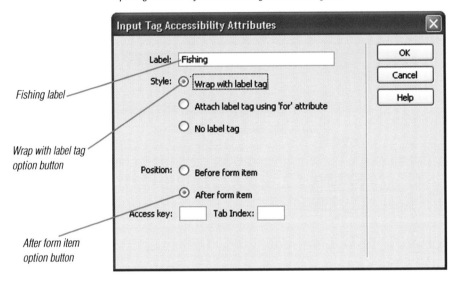

Fishing label

Wrap with label tag
option button

After form item
option button

FIGURE 25
Property inspector with checkbox properties displayed

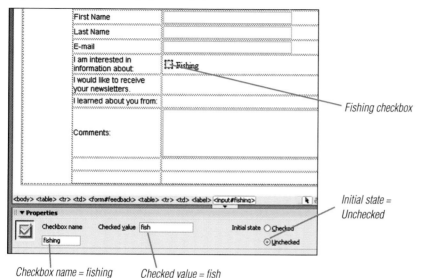

First Name

Last Name

E-mail

I am interested in
information about: ☐ Fishing

I would like to receive
your newsletters.

I learned about you from:

Comments:

`<body> <table> <tr> <td> <form#feedback> <table> <tr> <td> <label> <input#fishing>`

▼ Properties

Checkbox name   Checked value `fish`   Initial state ○ Checked
`fishing`   ⊙ Unchecked

Fishing checkbox

Initial state = Unchecked

Checkbox name = fishing   *Checked value = fish*

FIGURE 26
Feedback page in browser with checkboxes added to the form

7. Format the Fishing text label with the body_text style.

8. Insert a space after the Fishing label, then repeat Steps 2 through 6 to place a checkbox to the left of the Fishing text box with the label **Cruises**, the Checkbox name **cruises**, a Checked value of **cruise**, and the Initial state of **Unchecked**.

9. Format the Cruises label with the body_text style, save your changes, preview the page in your Web browser, compare your screen to Figure 26, then close your browser.

You added two checkboxes to the form that will let viewers request more information about fishing and dolphin cruises.

Add radio groups to a form

1. Click in the empty table cell to the right of "I would like to receive your newsletters."

2. Click the **Radio Group button** 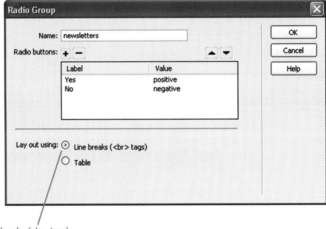 on the Insert bar to open the Radio Group dialog box.

3. Type **newsletters** in the Name text box.

4. Click the first instance of Radio in the Label column of the Radio Group dialog box to select it, then type **Yes**.

5. Click the first instance of radio in the Value column to select it, then type **positive**.

   You specified that the first radio button will be named Yes and set positive as the value that will be sent to your script or program when the form is processed.

6. Click the **Line breaks (
 tags) option button**, if necessary.

   TIP   If the Table option button is selected, then the radio buttons will appear in a separate table within the currently selected table.

7. Repeat Steps 4 and 5 to add another radio button named **No** with a value of **negative**.

8. Compare your screen with Figure 27, then click **OK** to close the Radio Group dialog box.

   (continued)

FIGURE 27
Radio Group dialog box

*Line breaks (
 tags) option button*

FIGURE 28

Feedback page showing new radio group

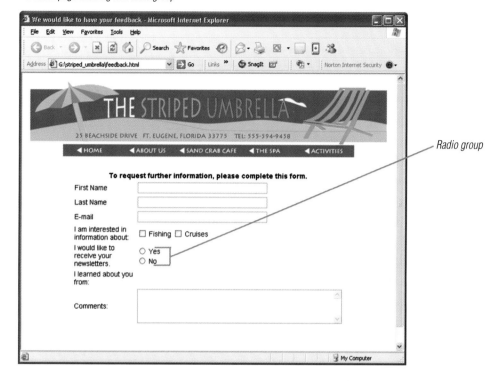

Radio group

9. Format the radio button labels using the body_text style.

10. Save your work, preview the page in your browser, compare your screen to Figure 28, then close your browser.

   TIP To create radio buttons that are not part of a radio button group, click the Radio Button button 🔘 on the Insert bar.

You added a radio button group that will let viewers answer whether they would like to receive The Striped Umbrella newsletters.

Add a menu

1. Click in the cell to the right of the text "I learned about you from:".

2. Click the **List/Menu button** 🔳 on the Insert bar, click the **No label tag option button** in the Input Tag Accessibility Attributes dialog box, then click **OK**.

3. Type **reference** in the List/Menu text box in the Property inspector.

4. Verify that the **Menu option button** in the Type section is selected in the Property inspector, as shown in Figure 29, then click **List Values** to open the List Values dialog box.

5. Click below the Item Label column heading (if necessary), type **Select from list:**, then press **[Tab]**.

6. Type **none** below the Value column heading.

   This value will be sent to the processing program when a viewer accidentally skips this menu. If one of the real choices was in the top position, it might return false positives when viewers really did not select it, but just skipped it.

7. Press **[Tab]**, then add **From a friend** as a new Item Label with the Value **friend**.

(continued)

FIGURE 29

Property inspector showing properties of selected List/Menu

Menu option button   List Values button

Collecting Data with Forms

FIGURE 30

List Values dialog box

Add button

New item labels

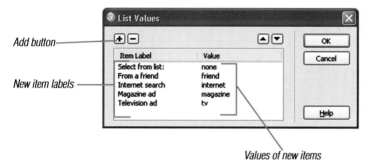

Values of new items

FIGURE 31

Feedback page in browser with menu option

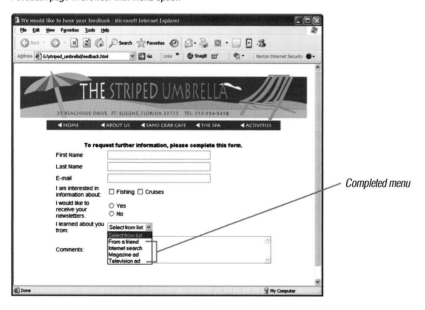

Completed menu

8. Add the following three Item Labels: **Internet search**, **Magazine ad**, and **Television ad**, setting the Values as **internet**, **magazine**, and **tv**.

9. Compare your screen to Figure 30, then click **OK**.

10. Save your work, preview the page in your browser, click the **list arrow** to view the menu, compare your screen to Figure 31, then close your browser.

You added a menu to the form on the feedback page.

Insert a hidden field

1. Click to the left of the First Name label at the top of the form to place the insertion point.

2. Click the **Hidden Field button** 🖼 on the Insert bar.

   A Hidden Field icon appears at the insertion point.

   TIP   If you do not see the Hidden Field icon, click View on the menu bar, point to Visual Aids, then click Invisible Elements.

3. Type **required** in the HiddenField text box, then type **first_name**, **last_name**, **email** in the Value text box in the Property inspector, as shown in Figure 32.

   Typing first_name, last_name, email in the Value text box specifies that viewers must enter text in the First Name, Last Name, and E-mail fields before the script can process the form. These names must match the names of other fields in your form exactly.

You added a hidden field to the form.

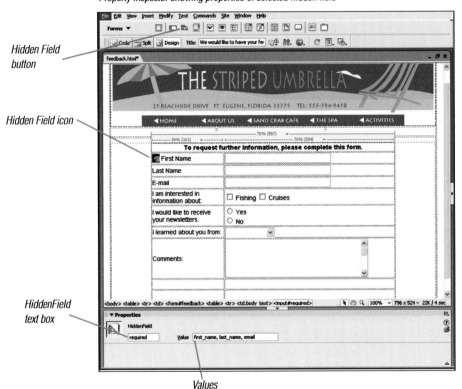

FIGURE 32
Property inspector showing properties of selected hidden field

Hidden Field button

Hidden Field icon

HiddenField text box

Values

FIGURE 33

New Submit and Reset buttons added to form

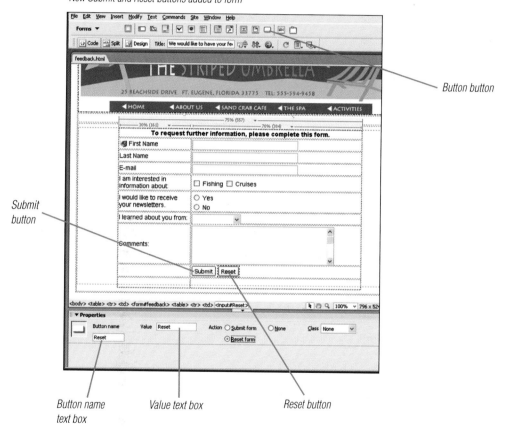

Button button

Submit button

Button name text box

Value text box

Reset button

1. Click in the second cell of the second to last row of the table.

2. Click the **Button button** 🔲 on the Insert bar, click the **No label tag option button** in the Input Tag Accessiblity Attributes dialog box, then click **OK**.

3. Verify that the Submit form option button is selected in the Property inspector.

   When a viewer clicks this Submit button, the information in the form will be sent to the processing script.

4. Verify that "Submit" is entered in the Button name text box and the Value text box in the Property inspector.

   The name Submit is automatically set when you select the Submit form option in the Property inspector.

5. Click the **Button button** 🔲 on the Insert bar, click the **No label tag option button** in the Input Tag Accessibility Attributes dialog box, click **OK**, click the **Reset form option button** in the Property inspector, name the new button **Reset**, verify that the Value text box is set to **Reset**, then compare your screen to Figure 33.

   When a viewer clicks this Reset button, the form will remove any information typed by the viewer.

6. Save your work.

You added a Submit button and a Reset button to the form.

TEST A
FORM

What You'll Do

In this lesson, you will check the spelling on the feedback page, create a link to the feedback page on the about us page, then open the about us page in your browser, click the feedback link, then test the form and reset it.

Creating User Friendly Forms

After you create a form, you will want to test it to make sure that it works correctly and is easy to use.

When a form contains several required fields, fields that must be filled out before the form can be processed, it is a good idea to provide visual clues that label these fields as required fields. Many times you see an asterisk next to a required field with a corresponding note at either the top or the bottom of the form explaining that all fields marked with asterisks are required fields. This will encourage viewers to initially complete these fields rather than attempting to submit the form and then receiving an error message asking them to complete required fields that have been left blank. Using a different font color for the asterisks and notes is an easy way to call attention to them to make them stand out on the page.

As is true with all pages, your forms should have good contrast between the color of the text and the color of the table background. There should be a logical flow for the data fields, so the viewer is not confused about where to go next when completing the form. The Submit and Reset buttons should be at the end of the form. You should always have several people test your form before you publish it.

Understanding jump menus

If your Web site contains a large number of pages, you can add a jump menu to make it easier for viewers to navigate through the site. Jump menus are menus that let viewers go directly from the current Web page to another page in the site with a single click. You can also use jump menus to provide links to other Web sites. You can create jump menus using the Jump Menu button on the Insert bar to open the Insert Jump Menu dialog box.

FIGURE 34
Creating a required field

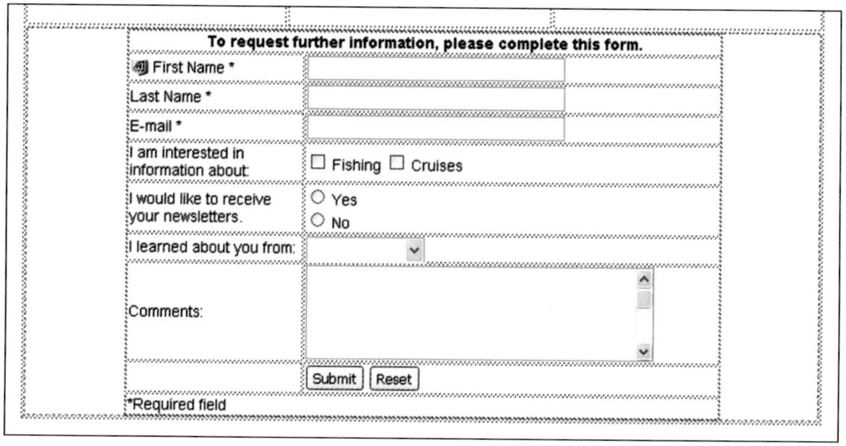

Creating required fields

1. Click **Text** on the menu bar, then click **Check Spelling**, to check the spelling on the form.

2. Correct any spelling errors you find using the Check Spelling dialog box.

3. Click after the text First Name, then type an **asterisk**.

   The asterisk will give viewers a clue that this is a required field.

4. Repeat Step 3 after the words "Last Name" and "E-mail".

5. Merge the two cells in the last row, type *** Required field**, as shown in Figure 34, then apply the body_text style to it.

6. Save and close the feedback page.

7. Open the about us page and add a row to the bottom of the page.

> TIP Click in the cell with the text beginning "If you would like to play tennis . . ." in the bottom row, then press [Tab].

8. Merge the cells in the new row, type **Please give us your feedback so that we may make your next stay the best vacation ever**.

9. Select the text you typed in Step 8, format it with the body_text style, then center-align the text in the newly merged cells.

10. Select the word "feedback", then use the **Point to File icon** ⊕ to link the feedback text to the feedback page.

11. Compare your screen with Figure 35, save your work, then preview the page in the browser.

FIGURE 35
Viewing the feedback link

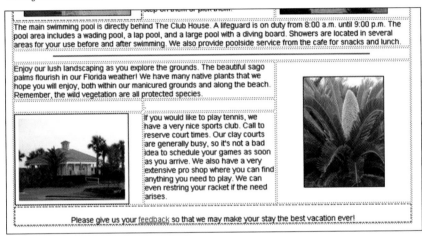

The main swimming pool is directly behind The Club House. A lifeguard is on duty from 8:00 a.m. until 9:00 p.m. The pool area includes a wading pool, a lap pool, and a large pool with a diving board. Showers are located in several areas for your use before and after swimming. We also provide poolside service from the cafe for snacks and lunch.

Enjoy our lush landscaping as you explore the grounds. The beautiful sago palms flourish in our Florida weather! We have many native plants that we hope you will enjoy, both within our manicured grounds and along the beach. Remember, the wild vegetation are all protected species.

If you would like to play tennis, we have a very nice sports club. Call to reserve court times. Our clay courts are generally busy, so it's not a bad idea to schedule your games as soon as you arrive. We also have a very extensive pro shop where you can find anything you need to play. We can even restring your racket if the need arises.

Please give us your feedback so that we may make your stay the best vacation ever!

Collecting Data with Forms

FIGURE 36

Feedback page in Internet Explorer

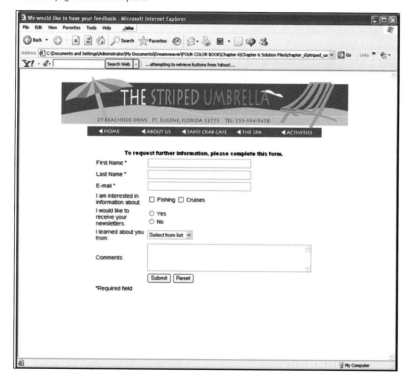

12. Click the **feedback link** to test it.

    The feedback page opens in a new window, as shown in Figure 36.

13. Test the form by filling it out, then clicking the Reset button.

    The Reset button will clear the form, but the Submit button will not work because this form has not been set up to send information to a database. Linking to a database is beyond the scope of this book. Refer to the information on page 6-13 to learn more about CGI scripts.

You checked the spelling on the feedback page, then added asterisks to the required fields on the page. Next, you typed text explaining what the asterisks mean and formatted the text with the body_text style. Last, you created a link on the about us page to link to the feedback form, and tested it in your browser.

Plan and create a form.

1. Copy the blooms folder from the chapter_6 Data Files folder and replace your blooms folder with it. The new files are all designed with tables for continuity.
2. Open the tips page.
3. Scroll to the bottom of the page, insert two paragraph breaks to end the ordered list after the last line of text, then insert a form.
4. Set the Method to POST in the Property inspector.
5. Name the form **submit_tips**.
6. Set the Target to _self.
7. Save your work.

Format a form.

1. Insert a table within the form that contains 9 rows and 2 columns. Set the Table width to 75%, set the Border thickness to 0, the Cell padding to 2, and the Cell spacing to 1.
2. Choose the top row header icon, then include an appropriate table summary that indicates that the table will be used for form layout purposes.
3. Merge the cells in the top row and type **Submit Your Favorite Gardening Tip** in the newly merged cell, then left-align the text.
4. Format the text you typed in Step 3 with the **seasons** style.
5. Type **E-mail** in the first cell in the second row.
6. Type **Category** in the first cell in the third row.

7. Type **Subject** in the first cell in the fourth row.
8. Type **Description** in the first cell in the fifth row.
9. Apply the bodytext style to the labels you typed in Steps 5 through 8.
10. Merge both cells in the sixth row of the table, then insert the label **How long have you been gardening?** in the resulting merged cell.
11. Merge both cells in the seventh row of the table, then insert the label **Receive notification when new tips are submitted?** in the resulting merged cell.
12. Apply the bodytext style to the text you typed in Steps 10 and 11, then save your work.

Work with form objects.

1. Click in the second cell of the second row. Insert a text field, click OK to close the Image Tag Accessibility Attributes dialog box, then name the new text field **email**. Set the Char width property to 30 and the Max Chars property to 150. (*Hint*: The Image Tag Accessibility Attributes dialog box will not appear if you do not have the accessibility preference set for adding form objects.)
2. Select the second cell of the fourth row, then insert a text field with the name **subject**. (*Hint*: Each time the Image Tag Accessibility Attributes dialog box opens, click OK to close it.) Set Char width to 30 and Max Chars to 150.

3. Select the second cell of the fifth row, then insert a textarea with the name **description**. Set Char width to 40 and Num Lines to 5.
4. Insert a check box to the right of the "Receive notification when new tips are submitted" label. Set the name of the check box to **receivetips**, then type **yes** in the Checked value text box.
5. Insert a radio group named **duration_gardener** to the right of How long have you been gardening? that contains the following labels: **1 - 5 years, 5 - 10 years, Over 10 years**. Use the following corresponding values for each label: **1-5, 5-10,** and **10+**.
6. Insert a list/menu named **category** in the empty cell to the right of Category. Set the Type to List and the Height to 3. Use the List Values dialog box to add the following item labels: **Weed control, General growth,** and **Pest control**, and set the corresponding values for each to **weeds, growth,** and **pests**.
7. Insert a hidden field named **required** in the first cell of the eighth row that has the value **email**.
8. Insert a Submit button named **Submit** in the second cell of the eighth row.
9. With your insertion point to the right of the Submit button, insert a Reset button named **Reset** with the Reset form action.
10. Save your work.

Test a form.

1. Check the spelling on the form and correct any errors you find.

2. Type an asterisk after the label E-mail.

3. Merge the cells in the last row, then type ***Required field** in the last row.

4. Apply the subheadings style to the text you typed in Steps 2 and 3.

5. Insert a horizontal rule that is 700 pixels wide and centered both before and after the form.

6. Center the table in the form.

7. Save your work.

8. Preview the page in your browser, compare your form to Figure 37, then test the form by filling it out and using the Reset button.

9. Close your browser, then close all open pages.

FIGURE 37
Completed Skills Review

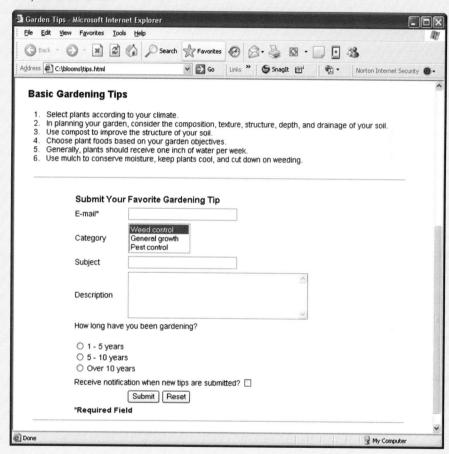

In this exercise you will continue your work on the TripSmart Web site you created in Chapters 1 through 5. The owner, Thomas Howard, wants you to create a form to collect information from viewers who are interested in receiving more information on one or more of the featured trips.

1. Replace your tripsmart folder with the tripsmart folder in the chapter_6 Data Files.
2. Open the destinations page.
3. Insert a form named **information** in the bottom row of the table.
4. Specify the Method as POST.
5. Insert a table in the form that contains 11 rows, 2 columns, a Table width of 75%, a Border thickness of 0, Cell padding of 1, Cell spacing of 1, and add an appropriate table summary.
6. Merge the cells in the top row, type **Please complete this form for additional information on these tours.**, apply the reverse_text style, then change the cell background color to #666666.
7. Beginning in the second row, type the following labels in the cells in the first column: **First Name**, **Last Name**, **Street**, **City**, **State**, **Zip Code**, **Phone**, **E-mail**, and **I am interested in:**, then right-align them and apply the bodytext style to all of them.
8. Insert single-line text fields in the eight cells in the second column and assign the following names: **first_name**, **last_name**, **street**, **city**, **state**, **zip**, **phone**, and **email**.
9. Set the Char width to 30 and the Max Chars to 100 for each of these text fields.
10. In the second cell of the tenth row, insert a checkbox with the label **The Amazon**, the name **amazon**, and a Checked value of **yes**.

11. Repeat Step 10 to add another checkbox under the Amazon checkbox with the label **Kenya**, the name **kenya**, and a Checked Value of **yes**.

12. Apply the bodytext style to the Amazon and Kenya labels.

13. Left-align the cells with the text boxes and checkboxes, then set each cell's vertical alignment to Top.

14. Insert a Submit button and a Reset button in the second cell of the eleventh row.

15. Insert a horizontal rule that is 550 pixels wide below the form.

16. Save your work, preview the page in your browser, test the form, compare your screen to Figure 38, close your browser, then close the destinations page.

FIGURE 38
Completed Project Builder 1

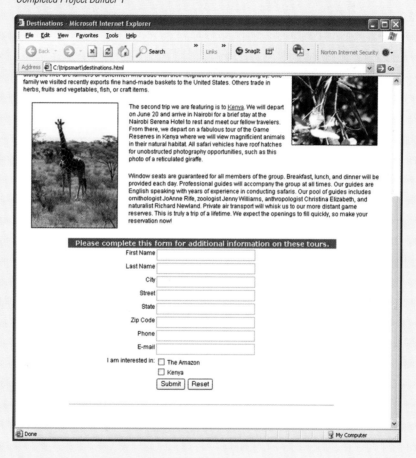

Use Figure 38 as a guide to continue your work on the emma's book bag Web site you created in Project Builder 2 in Chapters 1 through 5. Emma Claire asked you to place a simple form on the events page that will allow customers to add their names to the e-mail list for future events.

1. Replace your book_bag folder with the book_bag folder from the chapter_5 Data Files folder.

2. Open the events page.
3. Insert a form called **mailing_list** in the last row of the table at the bottom of the page.
4. Insert a table in the form that contains 5 rows, 2 columns, and your choice of table width, border thickness, cell padding, and cell spacing. Specify an appropriate table summary.
5. Merge the cells in the top row and type **Please complete and submit to be added to our e-mail list for future events**.

6. In the first column of cells, type the following labels under the table header: **First Name**, **Last Name**, and **E-mail address**.
7. In the second cell of the second, third, and fourth rows, insert text fields with the following names: **first_name**, **last_name**, and **email**. Set the Char width to 30 and the Max Chars to 100 for each of these text fields.

8. In the first cell of the last row, insert a hidden field named **recipient** with the value **mailbox@bookbag.com**.

9. Insert a Submit button and a Reset button in the second cell of the last row.

10. Format the form using your CSS styles, then add a horizontal rule above the form and format it attractively.

11. Save your work, preview the page in a browser, test the form, compare your screen to Figure 39, close your browser, then close the events page.

FIGURE 39
Completed Project Builder 2

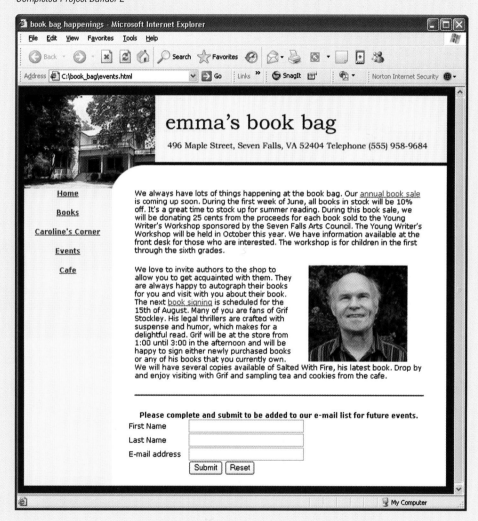

Web sites use many form objects to collect donations from viewers. The form, shown in Figure 40, is well organized and requests information that most people are comfortable giving over the Internet, such as name, address, and phone number. The form also contains text fields where viewers can specify a donation amount and pay using a credit card. Because the form is secure, viewers should feel comfortable providing their credit card numbers.

1. Connect to the Internet, navigate to the Online Companion, then select a link to review for this chapter. The Web site pictured in Figure 40 is *www.girlsandboystown.org*.

2. Does this site use forms to collect information? If so, identify each of the form objects used to create the form.

3. Is the form organized logically? Explain why or why not.

4. What CGI script is being used to process the form? And where is that script located? Remember the name of the processing CGI script is included in the Action attribute of your form tag. (*Hint:* To view the code of a page in a browser, click View on the menu bar of your browser, then click Source.)

5. What types of hidden information are being sent to the CGI script?

6. Is this form secure?

7. Could the information in this form be collected with different types of form objects? If so, which form objects would you use?

8. Does the form use tables for page layout?

9. Does the form use fieldsets? If so, identify the fieldset labels used.

10. Does the form use labels for its fields? If so, were the labels created using the <label> element or with text labels in table cells?

FIGURE 40
Source for Design Project

In this project, you will continue to work on the Web site that you have been developing since Chapter 1.

You will continue building your Web site by designing and completing a page that contains a form to collect visitor information as it relates to the topic of your site.

1. Review your storyboard. Choose a page to develop that will use a form to collect information. Choose another page that you already developed on which you will place a jump menu.

2. Plan the content for the new page by making a list of the information that you will collect and the types of form objects you will use to collect that information. Plan to include at least one of every type of form object you learned about in the chapter. Be sure to specify whether you will organize the form into fieldsets and how you will use a table to structure the form.

3. Create the form and its contents.

4. Create the jump menu.

5. Run a report that checks for broken links in the Web site. Correct any broken links that appear in the report.

6. Test the form by previewing it in a browser, entering information into it, and submitting it. Check to make sure the information gets to its specified location, whether that is a database or an e-mail address.

7. Preview all the pages in a browser, then test all menus and links. Evaluate the pages for both content and layout.

8. Review the check list shown in Figure 41. Make any modifications necessary to improve the form, the jump menu, or the page containing the form.

9. Close all open pages.

FIGURE 41
Portfolio Project check list

Web Site Check List
1. Do all navigation links work?
2. Do all images appear?
3. Are all colors Websafe?
4. Do all form objects align correctly with their labels?
5. Do any extra items appear on the form that need to be removed?
6. Does the order of form fields make sense?
7. Does the most important information appear at the top of the form?
8. Did you test the pages in at least two different browsers?
9. Do your pages look good in at least two different screen resolutions?

Collecting Data with Forms

chapter

7
USING STYLES AND
STYLE SHEETS

1. Create and use embedded styles.

2. Work with external CSS style sheets.

3. Work with conflicting styles.

USING STYLES AND
STYLE SHEETS

Introduction

In Chapter 3, you learned how to create, apply, and edit Cascading Style Sheets (CSS styles). Using CSS styles is the best and most powerful way to ensure that all elements in a Web site are formatted consistently. The advantage of using CSS styles is that all of your formatting rules are kept in a separate or **external** style sheet file, so that you can change the appearance of every page to which the style sheet is attached by modifying the style sheet file. For instance, suppose your external style sheet contains a style called headings that is applied to all top-level headings in your Web site. If you decide that you want the headings to be blue to make them more prominent, you could simply change the color attribute to blue in the style sheet file, and all headings in the Web site would change instantly to blue. You would not need to format the content of the Web site at all.

You can also create **embedded** CSS styles, which are styles whose code is located within the head section of the HTML code of a Web page. The advantage of embedded styles is that you can use them to override an external style. For instance, if all headings in your Web site are blue because the external style applied to them specifies blue as the color attribute, you could change the color of one of those headings to purple by creating and applying an embedded style that specifies purple as the color attribute. However, in general, you should avoid using embedded styles to format all the pages of a Web site; it is a better practice to keep formatting rules in a separate file from the content. Another advantage of using CSS styles is that you reduce the overall file sizes of your pages, since most of the formatting code can be stored in a single file, rather than in each individual page file.

Most people today use browsers that can read style sheets. When a browser that cannot read a style sheet is used, the styles are ignored.

In this chapter, you will create and apply embedded styles and work with external CSS style sheets to format The Striped Umbrella Web site.

Tools You'll Use

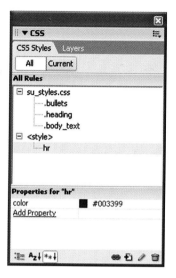

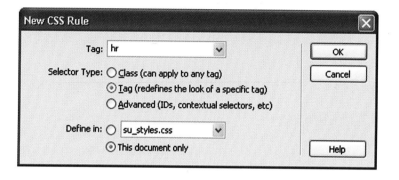

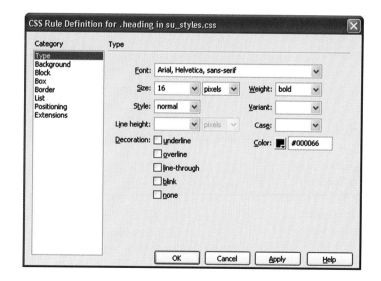

CREATE AND USE
EMBEDDED STYLES

What You'll Do

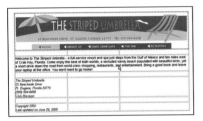

In this lesson, you will create, apply, and modify an embedded style on the home page. You will also redefine the hr and body HTML tags. You will then edit the hr style and see those edits automatically applied to the horizontal rules. Finally, you will delete a style.

Understanding Embedded Styles

In Chapter 3 you learned how to create and use an external style sheet to apply consistent formatting to the elements of a Web site. An external style sheet is a separate file with a .css extension that contains a collection of rules for formatting elements of a Web site. External style sheets can be applied to multiple pages, and are therefore great tools to help ensure formatting consistency across all pages of a Web site. Sometimes, however, you might want to create a style that is used only on a single page of your Web site. You can do this using **embedded styles**, or styles whose code is embedded in the code of a particular page. Embedded styles are handy when you want a particular page in your Web site to contain formatting that is different from the rules specified in an external style sheet. If both an external style and embedded style are applied to a single element, the embedded style overrides the external style. There is also a type of style similar to an embedded style called an inline style. Like an embedded style, the **inline style** is part of the individual page code, but

it is written in the body section, rather than the head section. Inline styles refer to a specific instance of a tag, rather than a global tag style on a page.

Creating, Applying, and Modifying a Custom Style

To create an embedded style, you use the New CSS Rule button in the CSS Styles panel to open the New CSS Rule dialog box, as shown in Figure 1. You use this dialog box to create both embedded styles as well as styles that are added to external style sheets. To specify the new style as an embedded style, click the This document only option button in the Define in section. If you click the New Style Sheet File option button, you will need to name and save a new CSS style sheet using the Save Style Sheet File As dialog box. You also have the choice of creating a new style in an existing CSS style sheet, such as the one you have already created for The Striped Umbrella Web site.

You use the New CSS Rule dialog box to create a **custom style** (also known as a **class style**), which contains a combination of

Using Styles and Style Sheets

formatting attributes that can be applied to a block of text or other page elements. When you name a custom style, you begin the name with a period (.).

QUICKTIP

If you don't type a period at the beginning of a custom style name, it will automatically be added for you.

After you name the style and click OK, the CSS Rule Definition dialog box will open with settings for the Type category displayed, as shown in Figure 2. This dialog box contains eight different categories whose settings can be defined. To specify the settings for a category, click the category, then enter the settings. When you finish specifying settings for all of the desired categories, click OK.

Once you create a custom style, it appears in the CSS Styles panel and as a choice in the list of Styles in the Property inspector. To apply a custom style to an element on a Web page, select the element, then click the style from the Style list in the Property inspector.

To edit a custom style, click the style you want to edit, click the Edit Style button in the CSS Styles panel, then use the CSS Rule Definition dialog box to change the settings as you wish, or simply enter the new settings in the CSS properties panel. Any changes that you make to the style are automatically reflected on the page; all elements to which the style is attached will update to reflect the change.

Redefining HTML Tags

When you use the Property inspector to format a Web page element, a predefined HTML tag is added to that element. Sometimes, you might want to change the definition of an HTML tag to add more "pizzazz" to elements that have that tag. For instance, perhaps you want all text that has

FIGURE 1
New CSS Rule dialog box

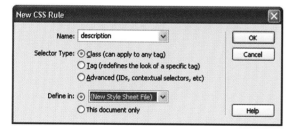

FIGURE 2
CSS Rule Definition for .heading in su_styles.css dialog box

Choose a category to see property options for that category

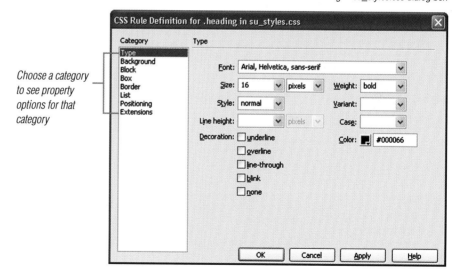

the <em> tag, which is the tag used for italic formatting, to appear in purple bold. To change the definition of an HTML tag, click the Tag option button in the New CSS Rule dialog box, click the Tag list arrow to view all available HTML tags, click the tag you want to redefine, then click OK to open the CSS Rule Definition dialog box, where you specify the desired formatting settings. Once you save the style and apply that tag, selected text will be formatted according to the altered settings you specified. To edit a setting, click the setting in the CSS Styles panel, as shown in Figure 3, to display the list of customized HTML tags. Select the HTML tag you want

to change, then click the Edit Style button to open the CSS Rule Definition dialog box where you can make any changes you want, or use the CSS properties panel to quickly enter the changes. There are two modes in the CSS Styles panel: All (document mode) and Current (selection mode). When All is selected, you will see style sheet rules listed in the top half of the panel, which is called the All Rules pane. When you click one of the rules, the bottom half, which is called the Properties pane, lists that rule's properties, as shown in Figure 3.

When Current mode is selected, the top half of the panel is called the Summary for

Selection pane. When an object with a style is selected on an open Web page, the Summary for Selection pane will display the properties for that style. If the object is not associated with a style, the Summary for Selection pane will show other formatting properties, as shown in Figure 4. The bottom half of the CSS Styles panel is called the Properties pane in either mode.

QUICKTIP

To delete an embedded style, click the style you wish to delete, then click the Delete CSS Rule button in the CSS Styles panel.

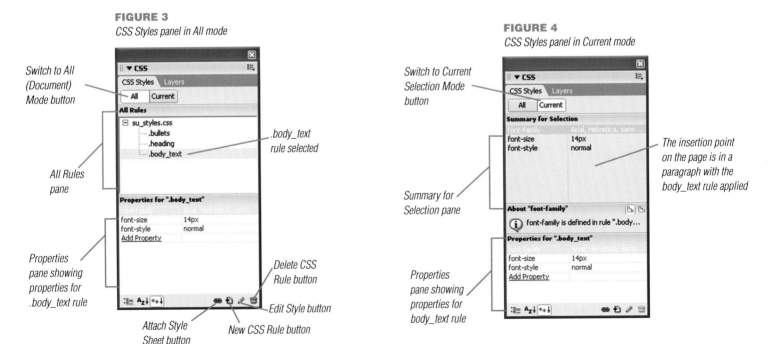

FIGURE 3
CSS Styles panel in All mode

Switch to All (Document) Mode button

All Rules pane

Properties pane showing properties for .body_text rule

.body_text rule selected

Delete CSS Rule button

Edit Style button

New CSS Rule button

Attach Style Sheet button

FIGURE 4
CSS Styles panel in Current mode

Switch to Current Selection Mode button

Summary for Selection pane

Properties pane showing properties for body_text rule

The insertion point on the page is in a paragraph with the body_text rule applied

FIGURE 5
New CSS Rule dialog box with settings for contact_info style

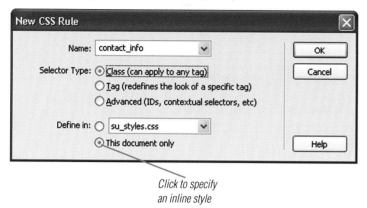

Click to specify
an inline style

FIGURE 6
CSS Rule definition for .contact_info dialog box with Type category selected

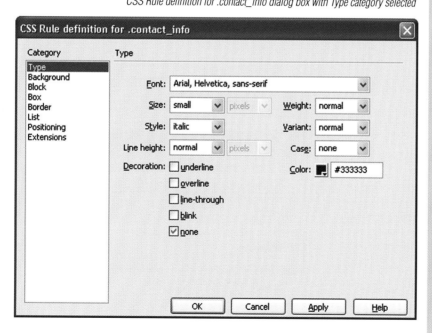

1. Open the home page in The Striped Umbrella Web site, expand the CSS Styles panel, then click the **Switch to All (Document) Mode button** .

2. Click the **New CSS Rule button** in the CSS Styles panel to open the New CSS Rule dialog box.

3. Type **contact_info** in the Name text box, verify that the Class option button is selected, click the **This document only option button**, then compare your screen to Figure 5.

4. Click **OK** to open the CSS Rule definition for .contact_info dialog box, which has the Type category selected.

5. Set the Font to **Arial, Helvetica, sans-serif**; set the Size to **small**; set the Style to **italic**; set the Line height to **normal**; set the Decoration to **none**; set the Weight to **normal**; set the Variant to **normal**; set the Case to **none**; set the Color to **#333333**, then compare your screen to Figure 6.

6. Click **OK**.

    The contact_info style appears in the CSS Styles panel.

    TIP   Click the plus sign (Win) or the triangle (Mac) next to <style> in the CSS Styles panel if you do not see the contact_info style.

You created a new custom style named contact_info and defined the formatting for it.

Apply a custom style

1. Select the paragraph with The Striped Umbrella contact information.

2. Use the Property inspector to change the Font to Default Font and the Size to None, then click the **Italic button** *I* to remove the italic formatting.

   You must remove manual formatting before applying a CSS style.

3. Click the **Style list arrow** in the Property inspector, click **contact_info** as shown in Figure 7, then deselect the text.

   The selected text now appears in dark gray and has the contact_info style applied to it.

4. Select the copyright and last updated statements, then repeat Step 2 to remove any prior formatting.

5. Apply the contact_info style to the copyright and last updated statements, then compare your screen to Figure 8.

   Notice how the contact_info style is displayed in the CSS Styles panel, but not as a part of the su_styles.css style sheet. The contact_info style is an embedded style. The rest of the styles are external styles that reside in the su_styles.css file.

You used the Property inspector to apply the contact_info style to selected text.

FIGURE 7

Applying the contact_info style using the Property inspector

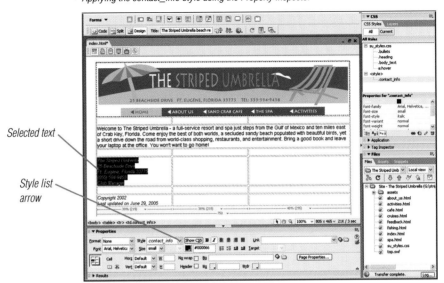

Selected text

Style list arrow

FIGURE 8

Copyright and date with contact_info style applied

External styles

Inline style

Copyright and date with contact_info style applied

Using Styles and Style Sheets

FIGURE 9

CSS Rule definition for .contact_info dialog box with modified type settings

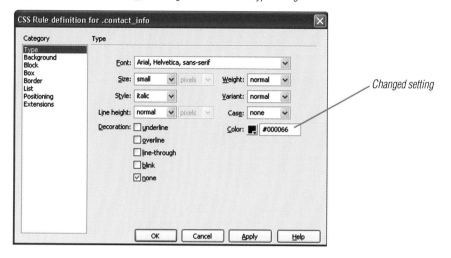

Changed setting

FIGURE 10

Text with the contact_info style applied

Text with contact_info style now appears in blue

Redefine an HTML tag

1. Open the about us page, then click the **New CSS Rule button** ⊞ in the CSS Styles panel to open the New CSS Rule dialog box.

2. Click the **Tag option button**, click the **Tag list arrow**, scroll down, click **hr**, then click the **This document only option button**.

   The hr tag is the tag that creates a horizontal rule.

   TIP To scroll quickly to the tags that begin with the letter h, type h after you click the Tag list arrow.

3. Click **OK** to open the CSS Rule definition for hr dialog box, set the Color to **blue (#000066)**, compare your screen to Figure 11, then click **OK**.

   Notice that the two horizontal rules on the page changed to blue because the rule has changed the way a horizontal rule is rendered.

4. Using Steps 1 through 3 as a guide, create a new CSS style that redefines the body HTML tag, by using the Background category rather than the Type category to set the Background color to **#FFFFCC**, as shown in Figure 12, then click **OK**.

   Notice that the page now has a yellow background.

   (continued)

FIGURE 11
Redefining the hr HTML tag

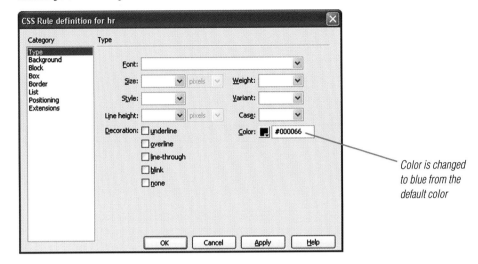

Color is changed to blue from the default color

FIGURE 12
Redefining the body HTML tag

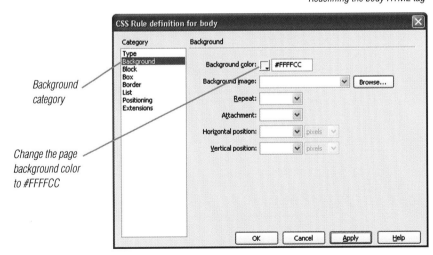

Background category

Change the page background color to #FFFFCC

Using Styles and Style Sheets

FIGURE 13

Viewing the code for embedded styles

Code redefining the hr and body HTML tags

The code is part of the head section

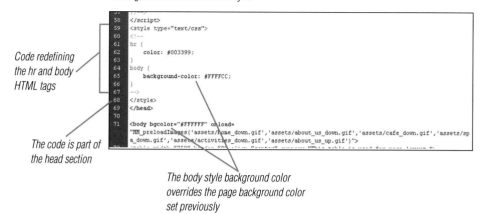

The body style background color overrides the page background color set previously

FIGURE 14

Viewing the code linking an external style sheet file

The code linking the file resides in the head section of the code

Code linking the su_styles.css file to the about us page

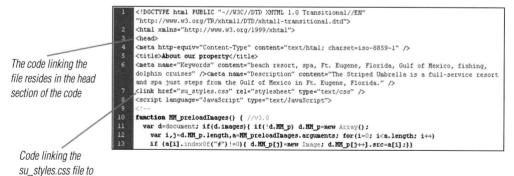

5. Switch to Code view to view the code changing the properties for the horizontal rule, as shown in Figure 13.

   Because these are embedded styles, the code for the styles is embedded into the page in the head section of the code. Notice that the style changing the background page color to yellow overrode the white page background color that was defined by using the Page Properties dialog box earlier.

6. Scroll up in the code, if necessary, to find the code that links the external style sheet file, as shown in Figure 14.

   You cannot see the individual rule properties, because the file is linked, not embedded. If you open the su_styles.css file, however, you will see the rules and properties listed.

   TIP   You can tell which tag takes precedence by its position in the tag selector. Tags with greater precedence are positioned to the right of other tags in the tag selector.

You used the New CSS Rule dialog box to redefine the hr and body HTML tags. You also viewed the code for the new embedded styles and the code that links the external style sheet file.

Edit an embedded style

1. Switch to Design view, then view the styles for the about us page in the CSS Styles panel.

2. Click the **hr style** in the CSS Styles panel.

   The properties of the hr rule are displayed in the Properties pane.

3. Click the **color picker** in the Properties pane, click color **#003399** to change the horizontal rule to a lighter blue, then compare your screen to Figure 15.

You used the CSS Styles panel to change the color settings for the hr embedded style.

FIGURE 15
Changing the color property of the hr HTML tag

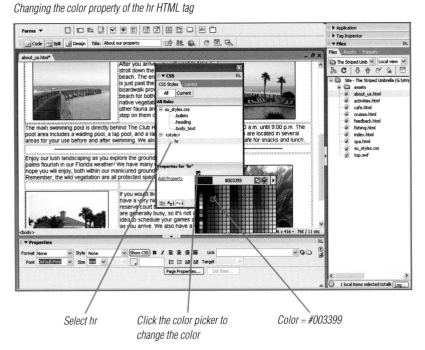

Select hr   Click the color picker to   Color = #003399
                   change the color

Using Styles and Style Sheets

1. Click the **body style** in the CSS Styles panel to select it.

2. Click the **Delete CSS Rule button** 🗑, then compare your screen to Figure 16.

   The body style is removed from the CSS Styles panel. The page background changes back to white.

   TIP   You can also delete an embedded style by right-clicking (Win) or [control]-clicking (Mac) the style in the CSS Styles panel, then clicking Delete.

3. Save your changes, then close the about us page.

You used the CSS Styles panel to delete the body style.

FIGURE 16
CSS Styles panel after deleting body style

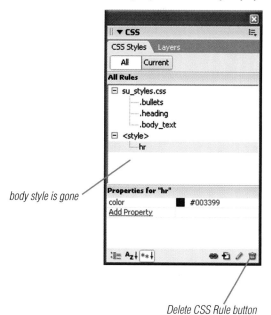

body style is gone

Delete CSS Rule button

WORK WITH EXTERNAL
CSS STYLE SHEETS

What You'll Do

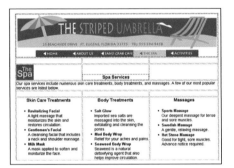

 In this lesson, you will make formatting changes in the style sheet and see those changes reflected on pages. You will also add hyperlink styles and custom code to the su_styles style sheet. Finally, you will delete a style from the su_styles style sheet.

Using External CSS Style Sheets

If you want to ensure consistent formatting across all elements of a Web site, it's a good idea to use external CSS style sheets instead of HTML styles or embedded styles. Most Web developers prefer to use external CSS style sheets so they can make changes to the appearance of a Web site without opening each page. Using embedded styles requires you to make changes to the styles on each page, which takes more time and leaves room for error and inconsistency.

Attaching an External CSS Style Sheet to a Page or Template

One of the big advantages of using external CSS style sheets is that you can attach them to pages that you've already created. When you do this, all of the rules specified in the style sheet are applied to the HTML tags on the page. So for instance, if your external style sheet specifies that all first-level headings are formatted in Arial 14-point red bold, then all text in your Web page that has the <h1> tag will change to reflect these settings when you attach the style sheet to the page. To attach an external style sheet to a page, open the page, then use the Attach Style Sheet button in the CSS Styles panel to open the Attach External Style Sheet dialog box, as shown in Figure 17. Use this dialog box to browse for the external style sheet file you want to attach and to specify whether to link or import the file. In most cases, you should choose to link the file so that the content of the page is kept separate from the style sheet file.

If all the pages in your site are based on a template, you can save an enormous amount of time and development effort by attaching an external style sheet to the template. Doing this saves you from having to attach the style sheet to every page in the site; you have to attach it only to the template file. Then, when you make changes to the style sheet, those changes will be reflected in the template and will be updated in every page based on the template, when you save the template.

Adding Hyperlink Styles to a CSS Style Sheet

You can use an external style sheet to create styles for all links in a Web site. To do this, open the style sheet so it appears in the document window, then click the New CSS Rule button to open the New CSS Rule dialog box. Click the Advanced option button, then choose one of the selectors from the Selector list, as shown and described in Figure 18. After you choose a selector and click OK, the CSS Rule Definition dialog box opens, which you can use to specify the formatting of the selected link. However, not all browsers recognize link styles.

Adding Custom Code to a CSS Style Sheet

You can make changes to a style sheet by changing its code or adding code directly into the style sheet file. To do this, open the style sheet file so that it appears in the document window, click where you want to add code, then type the code you want. For instance, you can add code to the body tag of the style sheet that changes the colors of a viewer's scroll bar to match the colors of your Web site.

FIGURE 17
Attach External Style Sheet dialog box

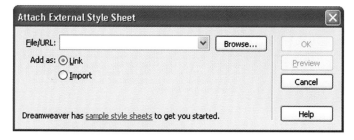

FIGURE 18
New CSS Rule dialog box with Advanced Selector Types displayed

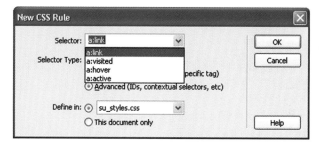

Modify an external CSS style sheet

1. Open the activities page.

2. Double-click the **su_styles.css file** in the root folder in the Files panel.

   The su_styles.css file opens in the document window.

3. Switch back to the activities page, then click the **New CSS Rule button** ➕ in the CSS Styles panel to open the New CSS Rule dialog box.

4. Click the **Advanced option button**, then click the **Define in su_styles.css option button**.

5. Click the **Selector list arrow**, click **a:link**, then click **OK** to open the CSS Rule Definition for a:link in su_styles.css dialog box.

6. Set the Font to **Arial, Helvetica, sans-serif**; set the Size to **small**; set the Weight to **bold**; set the Color to **#003366**; compare your screen to Figure 19; then click **OK**.

   The su_styles.css page now contains new code that reflects the type settings you specified for the a:link style.

7. Save your changes, switch to the activities page, scroll down the page, then compare your screen to Figure 20.

   The fishing excursions and dolphin cruises page links in the paragraph text now appear in another shade of blue, reflecting the formatting changes that you made to the a:link style.

You opened the su_styles.css file and made modifications to the a:link style using the CSS Rule Definition dialog box.

FIGURE 19
Modifying the a:link style

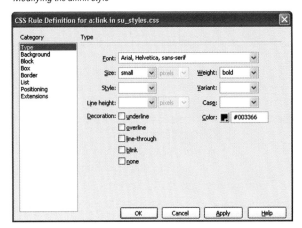

FIGURE 20
Activities page after modifying a:link style

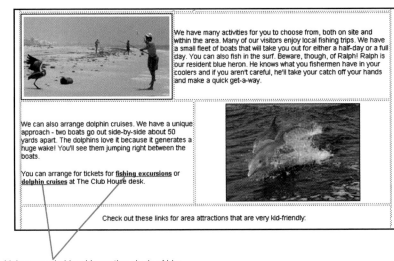

Links appear bold and in another shade of blue

FIGURE 21
Activities page after modifying a:hover style

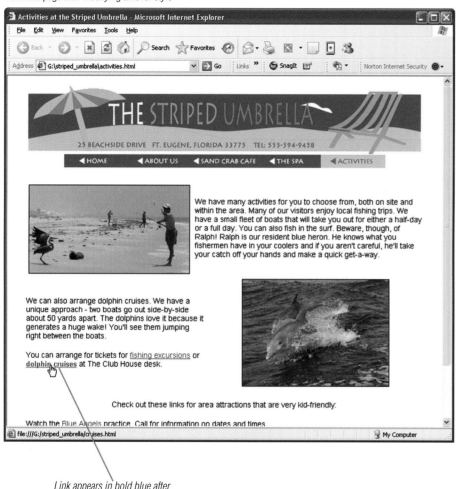

Link appears in bold blue after
changing a:hover style

1. Switch to the su_styles.css file.

2. Click the **New CSS Rule button** in the CSS Styles panel to open the New CSS Rule dialog box.

3. Click the **Advanced option button**, then click the **This document only option button**, if necessary.

4. Click the **Selector list arrow**, click **a:hover**, then click **OK** to open the CSS Rule definition for a:hover dialog box.

5. Set the Font to **Arial, Helvetica, sans-serif**; set the Size to **small**; set the Weight to **bold**; set the Color to **#0066CC**; then click **OK**.

   The su_styles.css page now contains new code that reflects the font specifications you set for the a:hover style.

6. Click **File** on the menu bar, then click **Save All** to save both pages, switch to the activities page, preview the page in your browser, position the mouse pointer over the dolphin cruises link, then compare your screen to Figure 21.

   The fishing excursions and dolphin cruises links in the paragraph text appear in bold blue when the mouse pointer rolls over them, reflecting the formatting changes that you made to the a:hover style.

7. Close your browser, then close the activities page.

You opened the su_styles.css file and then made modifications to the a:hover style using the CSS Rule definition dialog box.

Add custom code to a style sheet

1. Open the spa page, then switch to the su_styles.css file.

2. Locate the bullets tag code on the page, then replace the font size with **small** as shown in Figure 22.

3. Click **Refresh** on the CSS Styles panel to display the change you made in the code.

4. Switch to the spa page, then compare your screen to Figure 23.

   The text with the bullets style is smaller now and looks better on the page.

5. Close the spa page.

You opened the su_styles.css file and made changes to the bullets style directly in the code.

FIGURE 22
Changing the bullets style font size to small

```
1   .bullets {
2       font-family: Arial, Helvetica, sans-serif;
3       font-size: small;
4       font-style: normal;
5       font-weight: bold;
6       color: #000066;
7   }
8   .heading {
9       font-family: Arial, Helvetica, sans-serif;
10      font-size: 16px;
11      font-style: normal;
12      font-weight: bold;
13      color: #000066;
14      text-align: center;
15  }
16  .body_text {
17      font-family: Arial, Helvetica, sans-serif;
```

Font size changed to small

FIGURE 23
Viewing the modified bullets style applied to text on the spa page

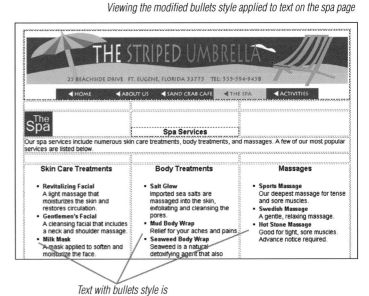

Text with bullets style is smaller now

FIGURE 24

Selected a:link code in su_styles.css file

```
1    .bullets {
2        font-family: Arial, Helvetica, sans-serif;
3        font-size: small;
4        font-style: normal;
5        font-weight: bold;
6        color: #000066;
7    }
8    .heading {
9        font-family: Arial, Helvetica, sans-serif;
10       font-size: 16px;
11       font-style: normal;
12       font-weight: bold;
13       color: #000066;
14       text-align: center;
15   }
16   .body_text {
17       font-family: Arial, Helvetica, sans-serif;
18       font-size: 14px;
19       font-style: normal;
20   }
21   a:link {
22       font-family: Arial, Helvetica, sans-serif;
23       font-size: small;
24       font-weight: normal;
25       color: #003366;
26   }
27   a:hover {
28       font-family: Arial, Helvetica, sans-serif;
29       font-size: small;
30       font-weight: bold;
31       color: #0066CC;
32   }
```

Selected a:link code

Delete external styles from a style sheet

1. Select the **a:link tag** and the five lines of code below it, then compare your screen to Figure 24.

2. Press **[Delete]** (Win) or **[delete]** (Mac), save your changes, then click **Refresh** on the CSS Styles panel.

   Notice that the a:link style no longer appears in the CSS Styles panel.

3. Open the activities page, then preview it in your browser.

   Notice that the activities page text links no longer appear as bold, indicating that the a:link style has been deleted from the style sheet.

   TIP You can detach a style sheet from a template or Web page by clicking the style sheet file in the CSS Styles panel, then clicking the Delete CSS Rule button. When you do this, the file is no longer linked to the Web page, but it is not actually deleted; it remains in its original location on your hard drive.

4. Save and close all open files.

You deleted the a:link style from the su_styles.css file and then saved your changes.

WORK WITH
CONFLICTING STYLES

What You'll Do

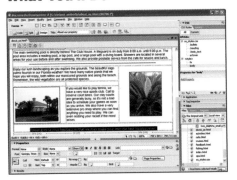

 In this lesson, you will discover that embedded styles have precedence over styles redefining HTML tags.

When you have a mixture of embedded styles, external styles, and styles redefining HTML tags, you need to understand what happens when the styles conflict. In general, embedded styles override external styles and also override styles redefining HTML tags. Styles can also conflict with formatting applied using the Property inspector. If you try to use the Property inspector to format text that already has a style applied to it,

Dreamweaver will automatically create an additional style based on the first style using the default naming convention (Style 1, Style 2, etc.). It is always better to use styles to format text than to use the Property inspector for better consistency, cleaner code, and work efficiency. While you are just beginning to understand Cascading Style Sheets, it might be wise to stick to external style sheets until you build your confidence.

Using Styles and Style Sheets

FIGURE 25

Text with style applied from redefined body tag

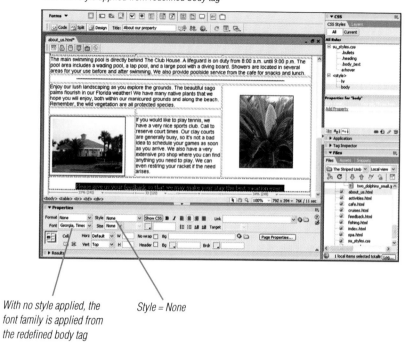

With no style applied, the
font family is applied from
the redefined body tag

Style = None

1. Open the about us page.

2. Click the **New CSS Rule button** ⊞ on the CSS Styles panel, click the **Tag option button** in the Selector Type section, click the **This document only option button**, click the **Tag list arrow**, click **body**, then click **OK**.

3. Click the **Font list arrow**, click **Georgia, Times New Roman, Times, serif**, then click **OK**.

   The body style is listed in the CSS Styles panel as an embedded style, specifying that all text in the body of the page be displayed using the Georgia, Times New Roman, Times, serif font family. However, the text on the page did not change because the body_text style from the su_styles.css file takes precedence over the style that changed the body tag.

4. Select the last sentence on the page, click the **Style list arrow**, then click **None**.

   When the body_text style is removed, the style from the body tag is applied, as shown in Figure 25.

5. Click **Edit** on the menu bar, then click **Undo** to apply the body_text style again.

6. Delete the body style from the CSS Styles panel.

7. Save and close the about us page.

You found that an embedded style has precedence over a style redefining an HTML tag.

Create and use embedded styles.

1. Open the blooms & bulbs Web site that you created and developed in Chapters 1 through 6.

2. Open the plants page.

3. Position the cursor to the right of the petunias image, then enter a line break to place the insertion point under the image.

4. Type **Moonlight White Petunia (Mini-Spreading)**.

5. Create a new embedded style using the Class selector type and name it **flower_names**.

6. Choose the following type settings: Font: Arial, Helvetica, sans-serif, Size: 12 pixels, Style: italic, Weight: bold, and Color: #003399.

7. Apply the flower_names style to the text you typed in Step 4.

8. Repeat Steps 3 and 4 to label the verbena image **Silver Blue Verbena**.

9. Apply the flower_names style to the verbena label.

10. Type **Golden Dream Lantana** under the lantana image, then apply the flower_names style to the label.

11. Modify the flower_names style to change the text size to small.

12. Save your changes, preview the plants page in your browser, compare your screen to Figure 26, close your browser, and close the page.

Work with external CSS style sheets.

1. Open the newsletter page.

2. Use the New CSS Rule dialog box to add the a:link style to the blooms_styles.css file. Set the Font to Arial, Helvetica, sans-serif; set the Size to 14 pixels; set the Weight to normal; then set the Color to #003399.

3. Save your changes, then make sure that the text links on the page now appear in a different shade of blue.

4. Use the New CSS Rule dialog box to add the a:hover style to the blooms_styles.css file. Set the Font to Arial, Helvetica, sans-serif; set the Size to 14 pixels; set the Weight to bold; then set the Color to #0066FF.

5. Save your work, then preview the newsletter page in your browser and make sure that the links appear according to the settings you specified. (*Hint*: Visited links will remain a purple color.)

6. Edit the headings style to change the weight to normal.

7. Close the newsletter page.

Work with Conflicting Styles

1. Open the index page.

2. Create a new CSS rule to redefine the body tag in this document only.

3. Choose the Georgia, Times New Roman, Times, serif font.

4. Select the paragraph of text and remove the bodytext style.

5. Reapply the bodytext style and delete the body style from the CSS Styles panel.

6. Save and close all open pages.

FIGURE 26
Completed Skills Review

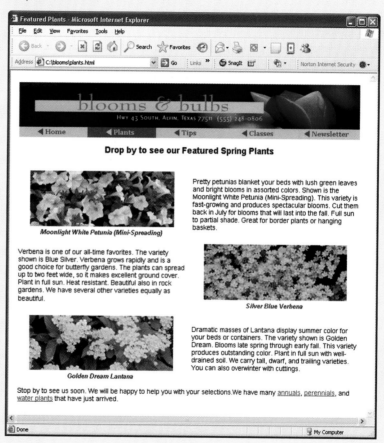

In this Project Builder you will continue your work on the TripSmart Web site. You have decided to add a few more styles to the style sheet to improve some of the page formatting.

1. Open the TripSmart Web site.
2. Open the newsletter page.
3. Create a new embedded style named **.bullets** with the following settings: Font: Arial, Helvetica, sans-serif, Size: 12 pixels, Weight: bold, and Color: #000033.
4. Apply the .bullets custom style to the items listed at the beginning of each bullet, using Figure 27 as a guide.
5. Edit the heading style to change the color to #000033.
6. Add a horizontal rule under the list of items. (*Hint*: Remember to enter two paragraph breaks to end the unordered list. If you have difficulty ending the unordered list, click the Unordered List button.)
7. Create a new custom style in the tripsmart_styles.css file that redefines the hr tag as centered and with the color #000033. Notice how the horizontal rule on the page changes color slightly.

8. Change the horizontal rule width to 500 pixels.
9. Save all files.

10. Preview the newsletter page in your browser, then compare your screen to Figure 27.
11. Close your browser, then close all open files.

FIGURE 27
Sample Project Builder 1

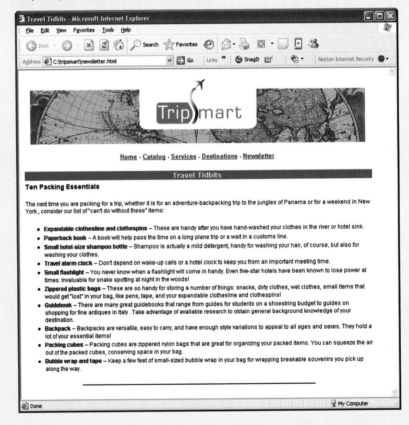

In this Project Builder, you will continue your work on the emma's book bag Web site that you started in Project Builder 2 in Chapter 1. You will continue to work on the page formatting to include as much formatting as you can with the use of CSS styles.

1. Open the emma's book bag Web site that you created in Chapters 1 through 6.
2. Open the books page.
3. Create a new custom style in the book_bag_styles.css file called **books**.
4. Refer to Figure 28, then select the settings of your choice for the books style to format the names of the books in the list on the page.
5. Select each book title and apply the books style.
6. Save and close the books page, then open the events page.
7. Create a new style for this page only, named **form**, that redefines the form tag.
8. In the CSS Rule definition for form dialog box, click the Box category, then set the Padding to 5 and the Margin to 10 for all sides of the form.(*Hint*: If you click the Same for all check box, you need to type only values in the Top text box.)
9. Click the Border category, click the first list arrow next to Top, click solid, click the second list arrow next to Top, click thin, change the Color to #000099. Verify that the Same for all check box is checked under the Style, Width, and Color columns, then click OK.
10. Delete the horizontal rule on the page above the form.
11. Save your work, preview the events page in your browser, then compare your screen to Figure 29.
12. Close your browser, then close all open files.

FIGURE 28
Completed Project Builder 2, Part 1

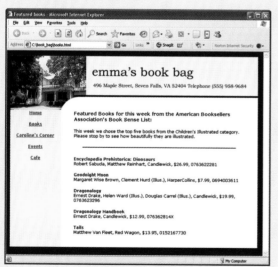

FIGURE 29
Completed Project Builder 2, Part 2

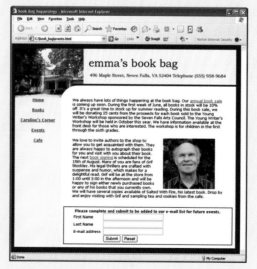

Using Styles and Style Sheets

Many of today's leading Web sites use CSS style sheets to ensure consistent formatting and positioning of text and other elements. For instance, the United States Department of Justice Web site uses them. Figure 30 shows the Department of Justice home page.

1. Connect to the Internet, navigate to the Online Companion, then select a link for this chapter.

2. Spend some time exploring the many pages of this site.

3. When you finish exploring all of the different pages, return to the home page. Click View on your browser's menu bar, then click Source to view the code for the page.

4. Look in the head content area for code relating to the CSS style sheet used. Note whether any styles are defined for a:link or a:hover and write down the specified formatting for those styles. Write down any other code you see that relates to styles.

5. Close the Source window, then look at the home page. Make a list of all the different text elements that you see on the page that you think should have CSS styles applied to them.

6. Review the other link for this chapter. Use the Source command on the View menu of your browser window to determine whether the site uses CSS styles.

7. Print out the home page of this site, along with the source code that contains CSS styles.

FIGURE 30
Design Project

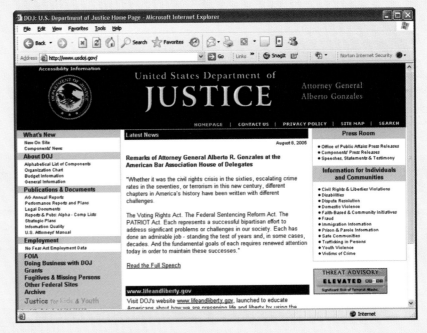

Using Styles and Style Sheets

In this assignment, you will continue to work on the Web site that you created in Chapters 1 through 6.

You will continue refining your Web site by using CSS style sheets and embedded styles to format the text in your Web site consistently.

1. Write a plan in which you define styles for all of the text elements in your site. Your plan should include how you will use an external style sheet as well as embedded styles. You can use either the external style sheet you created in Chapter 3 or create a new one. Your plan should include at least one custom style, one style that redefines an HTML tag, and one style that uses a selector.

2. Attach the completed style sheet to all individual pages in the site.

3. Create and apply the embedded styles you identified in your plan.

4. Create and apply the styles that will be added to the external style sheet.

5. Review the pages and make sure that all text elements appear as they should and look appropriate. Use the check list in Figure 31 to make sure you have completed everything according to the assignment.

6. Make any necessary changes.

7. Save your work, then close all open pages.

FIGURE 31
Portfolio Project check list

Web Site Check List

1. Do all text elements in the site have a style applied to them?
2. Does your site have at least one embedded style?
3. Is the external style sheet attached to each page in the site?
4. Did you define and apply at least one custom style and one style that redefines an HTML tag?
5. Are you happy with the overall appearance of each page?

chapter

8 POSITIONING OBJECTS
WITH LAYERS

1. Create a layer.

2. Set the position and size of a layer.

3. Add content to a layer.

4. Use the Layers panel.

5. Configure layer preferences.

6. Convert layers to tables and tables to layers.

Introduction

If you want to control the position of text and graphic elements with precision on your Web pages, another option you can use is layers. **Layers** are containers in which you place text and graphics and use to position elements on a Web page according to specific pixel coordinates. Using layers, you can position elements next to each other as well as on top of each other in a stack. In this chapter you will use layers to place text and graphics on a page.

Using Layers versus Tables for Page Layout

Like tables, layers let you control the appearance of your Web page. But unlike tables, layers allow you to stack your information in a vertical pile, allowing for just one piece of information to be visible at a time. Tables are static, which makes it difficult to change them on the fly. Layers, on the other hand, are treated as their own documents, so that you can easily change their contents. Dreamweaver even includes the JavaScript behavior to do so. **Behaviors** in Dreamweaver are simple action scripts that allow you to perform common tasks quickly, either on a Web page while it is being viewed in a browser, or to a Web page while you are creating it in Dreamweaver.

The biggest factor you should consider when deciding between layers or tables for page layout is the browsers that will be used to view the pages. If you think a high percentage of Netscape Navigator 4.0 users will view your site, then you should use tables for laying out your pages. Netscape Navigator 4.0 and earlier versions do not support all of the formatting and options available with layers in Dreamweaver. All versions of Internet Explorer 4 and later fully support Dreamweaver's layers.

Tools You'll Use

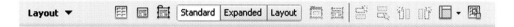

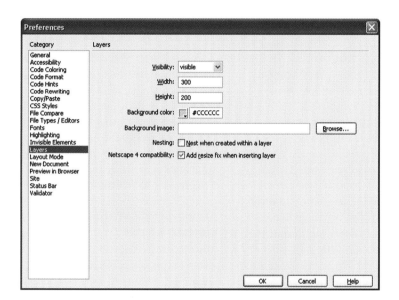

CREATE A
LAYER

What You'll Do

 In this lesson, you will draw a layer on The Striped Umbrella home page and set its properties using the Property inspector.

Understanding Layers

Layers are one of the newer developments in the world of Web page layout and design. Using layers, you can stack elements on top of each other and specify that only certain elements be visible at certain times or in specified conditions. Layers can be used to create special effects on a Web page. For instance, you can use layers to build a whole image from individual pieces. You can also use them to create a jigsaw puzzle that allows you to slide the pieces into their positions one at a time. You can also use layers to create dynamic pages that contain moving parts or objects that become visible or invisible based on a selection made by the Web site viewer.

Using layers to lay out a Web page is like working with a stack of transparency sheets that you can stack on top of each other. Figure 1 illustrates how to use layers to stack graphical elements on top of each other to create the single image of a flower.

To insert a layer, you can use the Draw Layer button on the Insert bar and drag a rectangular-shaped layer anywhere on your page, as shown in Figure 2. You can also insert a layer using the Insert Layer command. Specify the exact dimensions, color, and other attributes of a new layer by changing the layer settings in the Preferences dialog box.

Using HTML Tags to Create Layers

You can create layers in Dreamweaver using one of two HTML tags: <div> or <span>. Both tags support all types of images, backgrounds, and advanced formatting options for layers. The default tag in Dreamweaver is the <div> tag because it is supported by all browsers, including the early versions of Netscape Navigator. Netscape Navigator browsers prior to version 4.5 do not support the <span> tag.

Understanding Layer Content

A layer is like a separate document within a Web page. It can contain the same types of elements that a page can, such as background colors, images, links, tables, and text. You can also make the contents of a layer work directly with a specified Dreamweaver behavior to make the page interact with a viewer in a certain way.

Using Advanced Layer Formatting

You should be careful not to add too much content to a layer. If a layer contains more information than it can readily display, you will need to use the advanced layer formatting controls to format the content so that it appears the way you want it to. You can control the appearance of a selected layer

by making changes to the Clip, Visibility, and Overflow properties in the Property inspector.

The **Clip property** identifies the portion of a layer's content that is visible when displayed in a Web browser. By default, the clipping region matches the outside borders of the layer, but you can change the amount that is visible by clipping one or all sides of the layer. For instance, if you set the L (left) Clip property to 10 pixels, then everything from the eleventh pixel to the right will be displayed in the browser. If you clip off 10 pixels from the right side, you will need to subtract 10 from the total width of the layer and then type this value in the Clip R text box in the Property inspector. The clip setting can be applied

only to layers that have an Overflow attribute set to a value other than visible.

The **Vis (visible) property** lets you control whether the selected layer is visible. You can set the Vis property to default, visible, hidden, or **inherit**, which means that the visibility of the layer is automatically inherited from its parent layer or page.

The **Overflow property** specifies how to treat excess content that does not fit inside a layer. You can choose to make the content visible, specify that scroll bars appear on the layer, hide the content, or let the current layer automatically deal with the extra content in the same manner as its parent layer or page.

FIGURE 1

Using layers to create a single image

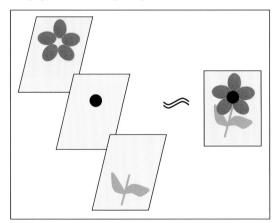

FIGURE 2

Inserting a layer using the Draw Layer button

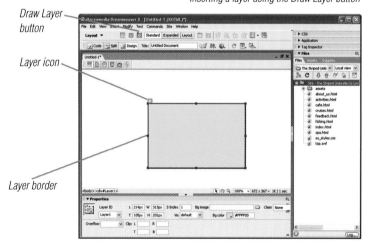

Draw a layer

1. Open The Striped Umbrella home page.

2. Click the **Insert bar list arrow**, click **Layout**, then click the **Draw Layer button** 📇.

3. Using Figure 3 as a guide, drag a rectangle in the middle of the home page that is approximately 4 inches wide and 2 inches tall.

   A new layer appears on the page, but it is not selected. A layer icon appears above the upper-left corner of the layer.

   | TIP   You can also insert a layer by clicking Insert on the menu bar, pointing to Layout Objects, then clicking Layer.

4. Click the **layer icon** ⬚ above the layer to select it.

   | TIP   You can also select a layer by clicking one of its borders.

You drew a layer on the home page, then selected it.

FIGURE 3

New layer added to the home page

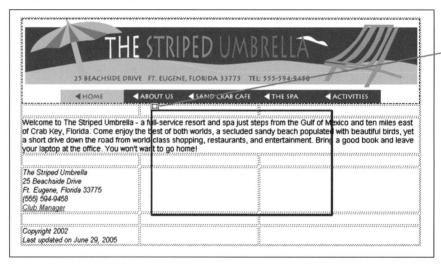

Layer icon

Positioning Objects with Layers

FIGURE 4

Property inspector showing properties of selected layer

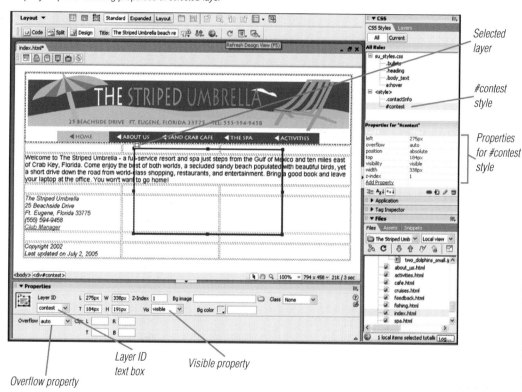

Selected layer

#contest style

Properties for #contest style

Overflow property

Layer ID text box

Visible property

1. With the layer selected, select **Layer1** in the Layer ID text box in the Property inspector, type **contest**, then press **[Enter]** (Win) or **[return]** (Mac).

2. Verify that <div#contest> is selected in the Tag selector.

3. Click the **Overflow list arrow** in the Property inspector, then click **auto**.

4. Click the **Vis list arrow**, then click **visible**.

5. Compare your screen to Figure 4.

   The L, T, W, and H settings in the Property inspector specify the position and size of the layer. Your settings will probably differ from those shown in the figure because you probably drew your layer with slightly different measurements.

   Notice that a new style has been defined in the CSS Styles panel called #contest. The properties for this style are listed in the Properties pane. When you draw a layer, Dreamweaver automatically creates a style for the layer. As you make changes to the layer properties, they are displayed in the Properties pane, when the style is selected.

You specified a name and other properties for the selected layer. You viewed the properties in the CSS Styles panel.

SET THE POSITION AND SIZE
OF A LAYER

What You'll Do

In this lesson, you will use the Property inspector to position and size layers on the home page of The Striped Umbrella Web site.

Understanding Absolute Positioning

One of the greatest benefits of using layers to lay out a page is that you can position them precisely using a practice called **absolute positioning**. A layer is positioned absolutely by specifying the distance between the upper-left corner of the layer and the upper-left corner of the page or layer in which it is contained. Figure 5 illustrates how an absolutely positioned layer keeps its relative position on a page when the page is scrolled. Because Dreamweaver treats layers as if they are separate documents contained within a page, layers do not interrupt the flow of content on the page or layer in which they are contained. This means that layers placed on top of a page will hide the contents of the page.

Absolute-positioned layers have no impact on the location of other layers. In other words, if you position a layer using absolute positioning, the remaining page elements that follow it within the code will continue along with the flow of the page, ignoring the presence of the

absolute-positioned layer. This means you can create overlapping layers. You can create dynamic effects with overlapping layers on a Web page by using JavaScript or CGI programs to change the attributes associated with each layer in response to actions by the viewer. For instance, a layer could move or change its size when a viewer clicks or moves the mouse over a link on the page or in the layer.

Setting Positioning Attributes

You can control the absolute positioning of layers by setting five primary attributes, four of which are available in the Property inspector. These attributes work together to create a layer that will hold its position on a page.

The **Position property** plays the most important role in turning a standard <div> or <span> tag into your positioned layer. Use this property to define how an object is positioned on the page. Standard HTML allows for fixed, absolute, relative, or static. When configuring your layers in Dreamweaver, you do not need to set this property. It is automatically set to absolute when you create a layer.

The **Left property (L)** in the Property inspector specifies the distance between the left edge of your layer and the left edge of the page or layer that contains it. The **Top property (T)** in the Property inspector specifies the distance between the top edge of your layer and the top edge of the page or layer that contains it.

The **Width (W)** and **Height (H) properties** specify the dimensions of the layer, most often in pixels, although it can be specified as a percentage of your screen dimension. For instance, you can specify that your layer be 250 pixels by 250 pixels, or you can set it to 25% by 25%, which will create a layer that is roughly 200 by 150 on a fully expanded Web browser in an 800×600 resolution monitor.

Use the **Z-Index property** in the Property inspector to specify the vertical stacking order of layers on a page. If you think of the page itself as layer 0, then any number higher than that will appear on top of the page. For instance, if you have three layers with the Z-Index values of 1, 2, and 3, then 1 will appear below 2 and 3, while 3 will always appear above 1 and 2. You can create a dynamic Web site by adjusting the Z-Index settings on the fly using Dreamweaver's built-in JavaScript behaviors within the Web page you are creating.

QUICK TIP

You cannot set Z-Index values below 0.

FIGURE 5

Scrolling a page containing an absolutely positioned layer

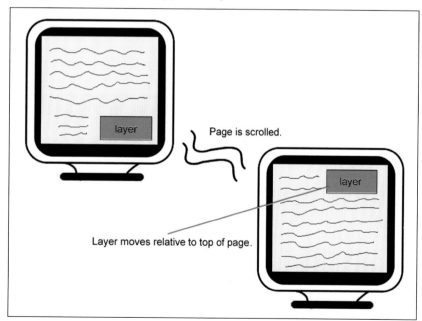

Set the left and top position of a layer

1. Click the **layer border** to select the layer (if necessary).

2. Type **420px** in the L text box in the Layer ID section of the Properties inspector, then press **[Enter]** (Win) or **[return]** (Mac).

   The layer moves automatically to the position you specified.

3. Type **260px** in the T text box, then press **[Enter]** (Win) or **[return]** (Mac).

4. Save your work, then compare your screen to Figure 6.

You adjusted the upper-left corner position of the layer.

Set layer height and width

1. Click the **layer border** to select the layer (if necessary).

2. Type **200px** in the W text box, then press **[Tab]**.

   The layer automatically adjusts its width to the dimension you specified.

3. Type **175px** in the H text box, then press **[Tab]**.

   The layer automatically adjusts to the height you specified. Notice that the upper-left corner stays in the same position.

4. Save your work, then compare your screen to Figure 7.

You adjusted the height and width of the layer.

FIGURE 6

Layer moved down and to the right on the page

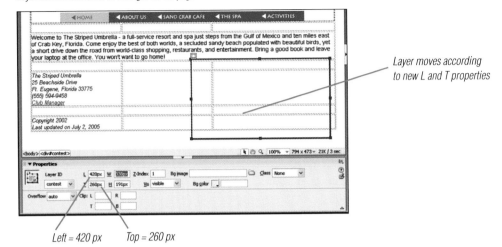

Layer moves according to new L and T properties

Left = 420 px   Top = 260 px

FIGURE 7

Layer with width and height adjusted

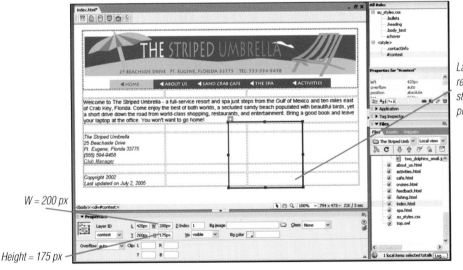

Layer is resized, but stays in same position

W = 200 px

Height = 175 px

FIGURE 8
New background layer on top of contest layer

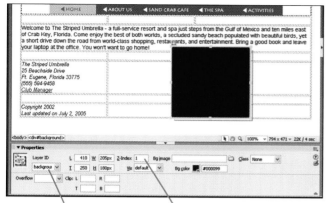

New layer name = background   Z-Index = 1

FIGURE 9
Contest layer moved on top of background layer

Contest layer positioned on top
of images layer with Z-Index
value changed to 2

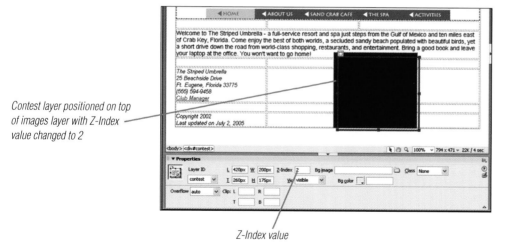

Z-Index value

Set a layer's Z-Index value

1. Create another layer anywhere on the page, select it, then name it **background**.

2. Select the **background layer** (if necessary), then adjust its size and position by setting the following properties in the Property inspector: L: **410px**, T: **250px**, W: **205px**, and H: **180px**.

   The new layer is now positioned on top of the contest layer.

3. Click the **Color picker button** next to the Bg color text box, then change the background color of the background layer to dark blue, **#000099**.

4. Change the Z-Index value of the background layer to **1** in the Property inspector, as shown in Figure 8.

5. Click the **contest layer** to select it.

   TIP Be careful to click the border of the contest layer, not the background layer.

6. Change the Z-Index value of the contest layer to **2** in the Property inspector.

   The background layer is now positioned behind the contest layer to act as an outline, as shown in Figure 9.

   The contest layer has no content yet, so you can see the background layer behind it.

7. Save your work.

You added a new layer named background to the home page, and specified its dimensions and position on the page using the Property inspector. You set the background color of the background layer, then adjusted the vertical stacking order of the two layers.

ADD CONTENT
TO A LAYER

What You'll Do

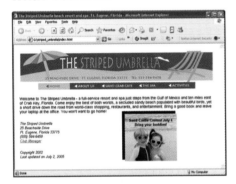

 In this lesson, you will add an image to a layer and use an another image as the layer background. You'll also add and format text on a layer.

Understanding Layer Content

As you learned in Lesson 1, a layer is like a separate document within a Web page. It can contain the same types of elements that a page can, such as background colors, images, links, tables, and text. If you just want to include an image as part of the layer content, but not the background, insert the image just as you would insert one on a page using the Property inspector. Figure 10 shows a layer with a blue background color and an image with a transparent background inserted at the bottom of the cell. If you have an image you would like to be able to type over, insert the image as the layer background, as shown in Figure 11.

If you add more content than the preset image size, the layer will enlarge to display the content on your page in Dreamweaver. However, when you preview the page in the browser, the amount displayed will depend on how you set your Overflow settings.

Like a Web page, if you specify both a background color and a background image, the background image will override the background color. As the page is loading, the layer background color may display until the layer background image finishes loading.

Also, as with formatting text on a Web page, you should use CSS styles to format your text on a layer. You can also add all other layer properties such as text indent, padding, margins, and background color using CSS styles.

FIGURE 10

Layer with a background color and an inserted image

FIGURE 11

Layer with an image inserted as a background image

Set a background color

1. With the contest layer selected, click in the Bg color text box in the Property inspector.

2. Type the hex value **#FFFFFF**.

   The layer is now filled with white, as shown in Figure 12.

You added a background color to the layer.

FIGURE 12
White background color applied to layer

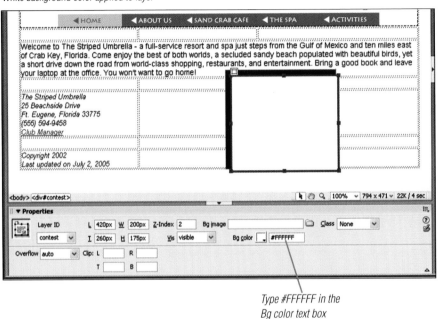

Type #FFFFFF in the Bg color text box

FIGURE 13

Image added to layer

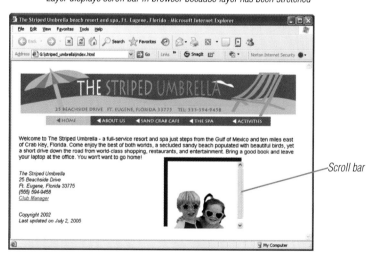

FIGURE 14

Layer displays scroll bar in browser because layer has been stretched

Scroll bar

1. Deselect the layer, then click in the layer to set the insertion point.

2. Click the **Insert bar list arrow**, click **Common**, click the **Images list arrow**, then click **Image**.

3. Navigate to the chapter_8 assets folder, then double-click **contestants.gif**.

4. Type **Two young contestants** in the Image Tag Accessibility Attributes dialog box, then click **OK**.

   TIP If the Image Tag Accessibility Attributes dialog box does not appear, type appropriate alternate text in the Alt text box in the Property inspector.

5. Click [←] to place the insertion point in front of the image, insert three line breaks by pressing **[Shift][Enter]** (Win) or **[Shift][return]** (Mac) three times, then compare your screen to Figure 13.

6. Save your work, preview the page in your Web browser, then compare your screen to Figure 14.

   Notice the scroll bar in the layer. The layer had to stretch to fit in the three page breaks and the image. Because the Overflow is set to Auto, the scroll bar automatically appears when there is more content than can fit in the layer dimensions.

You added an image to the layer, then added alternate text to it.

Set a background image

1. Remove both the background color and the image from the layer.

2. Press **[Backspace]** three times to delete the line breaks.

3. Select the layer, click the **Browse for File icon** 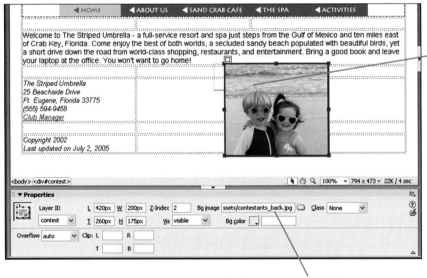 next to the Bg image text box in the Property inspector to open the Select Image Source dialog box.

4. Navigate to the chapter_8 assets folder, then click **contestants_bak.jpg**.

5. Click **OK** (Win) or **Choose** (Mac), then compare your screen to Figure 15.

6. Refresh the Files panel to verify that contestants_bak.jpg was copied to the assets folder of the Web site.

You added a background image to the contest layer.

FIGURE 15
Layer containing a background image

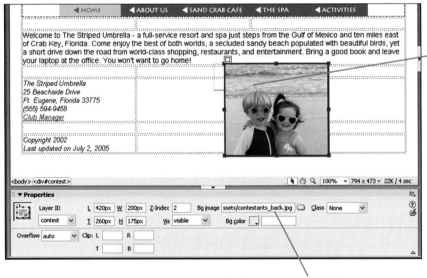

Image serves as layer background

Bg image = contestants_bak.jpg

FIGURE 16

Editing the #contest style

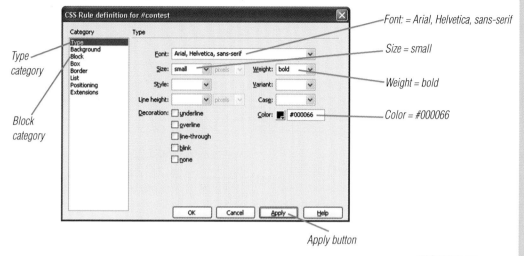

Type category

Block category

Font: = Arial, Helvetica, sans-serif

Size = small

Weight = bold

Color = #000066

Apply button

FIGURE 17

Index page shown in Internet Explorer with the formatted layer

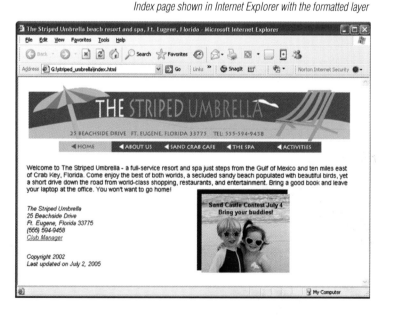

Add and format text on a layer

1. Click inside the layer to set the insertion point, then enter a line break.

2. Type **Sand Castle Contest July 4**, press **[Shift][Enter]** (Win) or **[Shift][return]** (Mac), then type **Bring your buddies!**.

3. Select the contest style in the CSS Styles panel, then click the **Edit CSS style button** .

4. Click the **Type category**, as shown in Figure 16, then change Font to **Arial, Helvetica, sans-serif**; Size to **small**; Weight to **bold**; Color to **#000066**; then click the **Apply button**.

5. Click the **Block category,** change the Text align setting to **Center**, then click **OK**.

   The text changes to reflect the properties you have added to the contest style. It is blue and centered on the layer. When you have text on a layer, it is strongly recommended that you edit the text using the layer style in the CSS Styles panel, rather than the Property inspector.

6. Save your work, preview the page in your Web browser, compare your screen with Figure 17, then close your browser.

You added text to the layer and formatted it using the CSS Styles panel.

USE THE
LAYERS PANEL

What You'll Do

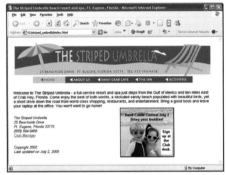

 In this lesson, you will use the Layers panel to change the name of a layer, view and hide a layer, and work with nested layers.

Controlling Layers

You can use the **Layers panel** to control the visibility, name, and Z-Index order of all the layers on a Web page. You can also use the Layers panel to see how a layer is nested within the page structure and to change the nesting status of a layer. **Nested layers** are layers whose HTML code is included within another layer's code. A nested layer does not affect the way a layer appears to the page viewer; it establishes a relationship of how it appears in relation to its parent layer. To change the nesting status of a layer, drag the nested layer to a new location in the Layers panel. Figure 18 shows the Layers panel with a nested layer.

You can open the Layers panel using the Window menu. The Layers panel is very handy when you are trying to select a layer on the bottom of a stack of layers. Clicking the layer name selects the layer on the page. You can access the same information that is available in the Layers panel by selecting the layer and viewing its settings in the Property inspector.

Using the Layers panel is the easiest way to change a series of layer names, control layer visibility while testing a site, and control the visible stacking order of layers. The Layers panel also keeps track of all the layers on a page, making it easy to review the settings for each.

FIGURE 18
Layers panel

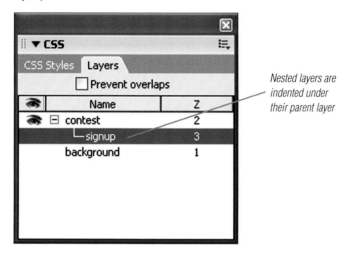

Nested layers are
indented under
their parent layer

FIGURE 19
Using the Layers panel to change a layer name

Layer names

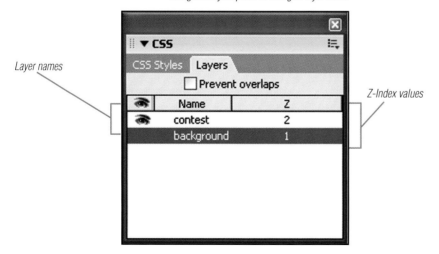

Z-Index values

Change the name of a layer

1. Click **Window** on the menu bar, then click **Layers,** or click **Layers** in the CSS Styles panel group.

   The CSS panel group opens with the Layers panel displayed, as shown in Figure 19.

2. Click **background** on the Layers panel to select the background layer.

3. Double-click **background** on the Layers panel to edit its name.

4. Type **outline**, then press **[Enter]** (Win) or **[return]** (Mac).

   The name of the layer is now outline.

5. With the outline layer selected, press [→] and [↓] each about eight times to reposition the outline layer so it is centered behind the contest layer, serving as an outline for the contest layer.

You used the Layers panel to change the name of one of the layers on the home page.

Controlling layer visibility

1. Click the **Eye icon column** twice for the contest layer in the Layers panel, then compare your screen with Figure 20.

   The Closed eye icon appears indicating that the contest layer no longer appears in the document window.

2. Click the **Closed eye icon** 🗨 on the contest layer.

   Clicking the Closed eye icon makes the layer visible, as shown in Figure 21. The Eye icon appears in the Layers panel.

3. Click the **Eye icon** 👁 on the contest layer.

   Clicking the Eye icon makes the layer inherit the visibility status of its parent objects. In this case, the parent object of the contest layer is the home page. Because the home page is visible, the images layer is visible too.

You used the Layers panel to change the visibility status of the contest layer.

FIGURE 20
Using the Layers panel to hide the contest layer

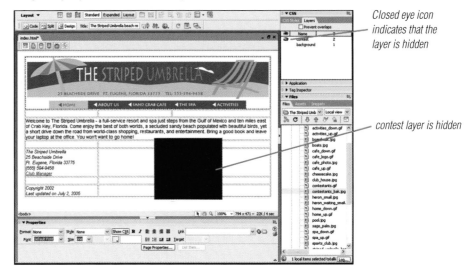

Closed eye icon indicates that the layer is hidden

contest layer is hidden

FIGURE 21
Using the Layers panel to make the contest layer visible

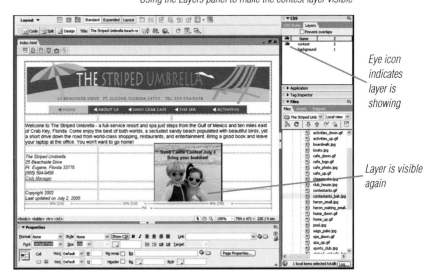

Eye icon indicates layer is showing

Layer is visible again

Positioning Objects with Layers

FIGURE 22

Nested layer shown with parent layer properties

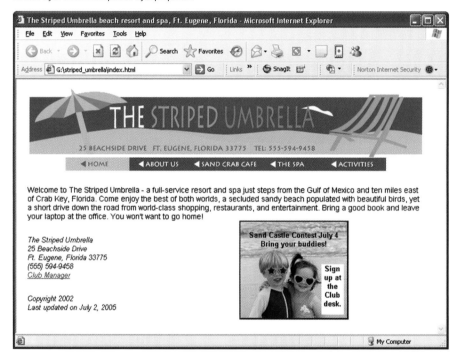

1. Click the **contest layer** in the Layers panel, then click in the contest layer in the document window after the word "buddies!" to place the insertion point.

2. Click **Insert** on the menu bar, point to **Layout Objects**, then click **Layer**.

   A new layer is inserted as a nested layer of the contest layer.

3. Use the Layers panel to select this new nested layer, then name this new layer **signup**.

4. Type **152px** in the L text box, then type **77px** in the T text box.

5. Type **42px** in the W text box, then type **92px** in the H text box.

   These dimensions specify the position and size of the nested layer in relation to the upper-left corner of the contest layer.

6. Set the background color to **#FFFFFF**.

7. Click in the **sign up layer** to place the insertion point, then type **Sign up at the Club desk**.

   Notice that the text is automatically formatted using the properties for the contest layer, the parent layer for the nested layer.

8. Save your work, preview the page in your browser, then compare your screen to Figure 22.

You created a nested layer within the contest layer.

CONFIGURE LAYER
PREFERENCES

What You'll Do

In this lesson, you will configure the default preferences for layers.

Setting Layer Preferences

If you know that you want all new layers to have a consistent appearance, you can save time by using the Preferences dialog box to set default specifications for new layers. Once you set layer preferences, you can then use the Insert Layer command to insert a layer that has the size and color settings you specified. When you draw a new layer using the Draw Layer button, the background color and image options specified in the Preferences dialog box are applied to the new layer. Figure 23 shows an example of a page that contains four different layers. One of the layers was inserted based on settings in the Preferences dialog box. The other three were customized with different colors and dimensions.

Fixing the Netscape Resize Problem

Netscape Navigator 4 was one of the first browsers that had support for layers, but it had a problem. It did not adjust the position of layers based on changes in the screen size. As you can imagine, this created oddly formatted pages after the screen size was altered or whenever adjustments were made to the page appearance during the processing of any scripts contained on the page.

Although Netscape 4 is used by a relatively small number of people today, it is easy to provide code to fix the problem. To fix this problem, you can use the Preferences dialog box to specify that a special JavaScript function automatically be added to the code of any page that contains layers. This code is shown in Figure 24.

QUICKTIP

If you convert tables to layers on a Web page, the code for the Netscape Resize Fix is not automatically added to the code for your page. To add the code, you need to add one additional layer to the page, which can be removed after adding the code. Before you remove the layer, however, switch to Code view and make sure that the code has been added.

FIGURE 23

Page containing default layer and customized layers

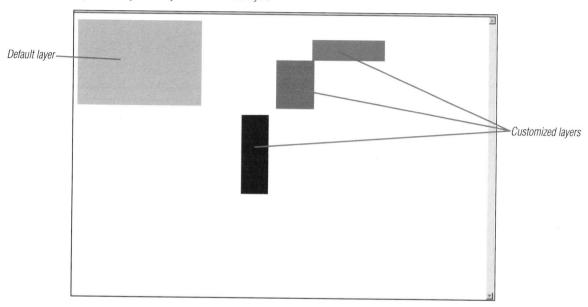

Default layer

Customized layers

FIGURE 24

JavaScript function added to page containing layers in Code view

New code to handle
Netscape resize problem

```
108  -->
109  </style>
110  <script language="JavaScript" type="text/JavaScript">
111  <!--
112  function MM_reloadPage(init) {  //reloads the window if Nav4 resized
113    if (init==true) with (navigator) {if ((appName=="Netscape")&&(parseInt(appVersion)==4)) {
114      document.MM_pgW=innerWidth; document.MM_pgH=innerHeight; onresize=MM_reloadPage; }}
115    else if (innerWidth!=document.MM_pgW || innerHeight!=document.MM_pgH) location.reload();
116  }
117  MM_reloadPage(true);
118  //-->
119  </script>
120  </head>
121
```

Control the appearance of a layer

1. Click **Edit** (Win) or **Dreamweaver** (Mac) on the menu bar, then click **Preferences** to open the Preferences dialog box.

2. Click **Layers** in the Category list.

3. Click the **Visibility list arrow**, then click **visible**.

4. Type **300** in the Width text box, then type **200** in the Height text box.

5. Set the Background color to **#CCCCCC**.

   TIP   If you want all layers to have a default background image, you can specify an image file in the Background image text box.

6. Compare your settings to Figure 25, then click **OK**.

7. Click the **page** to place the insertion point, click **Insert** on the menu bar, point to **Layout Objects**, click **Layer**, then compare your screen with Figure 26.

   A new layer appears on the page that has a gray background and is 300px wide by 200px high, as you specified in your preferences.

8. Click **Edit** on the menu bar, then click **Undo Insert** (Win) or **Undo** (Mac) to remove this layer.

You used the Preferences dialog box to adjust the default appearance of new layers.

FIGURE 25
Preferences dialog box with new default settings for layers

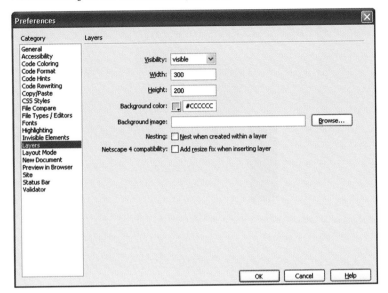

FIGURE 26
New layer with new default layer settings applied

New layer with modified default settings (yours may appear in a different location)

Positioning Objects with Layers

FIGURE 27

Reload page function for the Netscape Resize Fix error

```
108  -->
109  </style>
110  <script language="JavaScript" type="text/JavaScript">
111  <!--
112  function MM_reloadPage(init) {  //reloads the window if Nav4 resized
113    if (init==true) with (navigator) {if ((appName=="Netscape")&&(parseInt(appVersion)==4)) {
114      document.MM_pgW=innerWidth; document.MM_pgH=innerHeight; onresize=MM_reloadPage; }}
115    else if (innerWidth!=document.MM_pgW || innerHeight!=document.MM_pgH) location.reload();
116  }
117  MM_reloadPage(true);
118  //-->
119  </script>
120  </head>
```

*New code added
to deal with
Netscape resize
problem*

1. Click **Edit** (Win) or **Dreamweaver** (Mac) on the menu bar, then click **Preferences**.

2. Click **Layers** in the Category list (if necessary).

3. Verify that the Netscape 4 compatibility check box is checked, then click **OK**.

4. Click the **Show Code view button** [⟨⟩ Code] on the Document toolbar.

5. Scroll to the head area of the page, just before the closing head tag.

6. Verify that the MM_reloadPage function has been added to the code for the page, as shown in Figure 27.

7. Click the **Show Design view button** [Design] on the Document toolbar.

8. Save your work, then close all open pages.

You set up Dreamweaver to deal with the Netscape layer resize problem.

CONVERT LAYERS TO TABLES
AND TABLES TO LAYERS

What You'll Do

In this lesson, you will learn about converting tables to layers and layers to a table.

Using Layers and Tables for Page Layout

Layers and tables are the two most common formats that Web designers use to lay out Web pages. Figure 28 shows a Web page using layers for page layout, and Figure 29 shows a Web page that uses tables for page layout. The ability to convert easily between these two different layout styles is one of Dreamweaver's most powerful features.

Of course, like anything else, there are pros and cons to using each type of layout. The primary reason to use tables over layers is that all versions of Web browsers prior to Internet Explorer 4.0 and Netscape Navigator 4.5 are unable to read layers. All versions of browsers, however, are able to read tables.

For this reason, you will probably find the Convert Layers to Tables command a useful tool. Pages designed with layers can be converted to allow all browsers to display the information properly. These commands are designed to work with pages that are designed either entirely in tables or entirely in layers.

Converting Layers to Tables

When you convert layers to tables, you need to keep a few important rules in mind. First, you cannot convert overlapping layers. Therefore, you must adjust the positioning of overlapping layers prior to converting them to a table. This sometimes forces you to make changes to the layout of your page. Second, you cannot convert nested layers into tables, which means that you need to remove any code related to nested layers. This might require you to change the nesting of your layers in the Layers pane by dragging your layer to a new location. You can convert the layers on a page to a table by clicking Modify on the menu bar, pointing to Convert, then clicking Layers to Table.

Converting Tables to Layers

To convert tables on a Web page to layers, click Modify on the menu bar, point to Convert, then click Tables to Layers. Unlike converting layers to a table, nested tables do not create a problem for the conversion program. Any nested tables contained on a page will be properly converted into layers, but you will probably lose the formatting information contained in the table cell holding the nested table. Also, because tables cannot overlap, you don't need to worry about changing your page layout before converting to layers.

FIGURE 28

Web page that uses layers for page layout

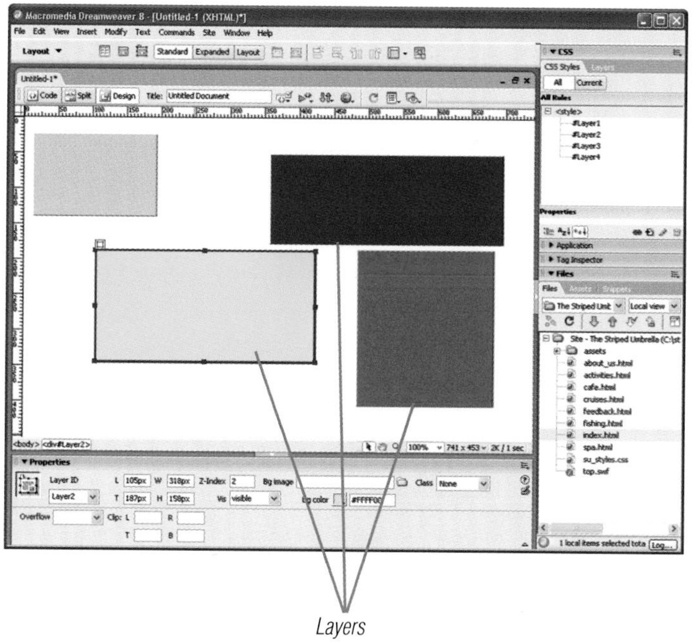

FIGURE 29

Web page that uses tables for page layout

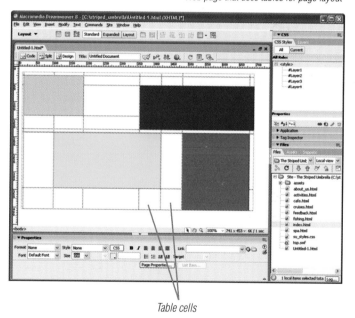

Layers

Table cells

Create a layer.

1. Open the blooms & bulbs Web site that you created in Chapters 1 through 7, then open the home page.
2. Use the Draw Layer button to draw a long thin rectangle, about 2 inches tall by 1 inch wide on the bottom half of your page. Name this layer **organic**.
3. Select the organic layer, remove the background color, if necessary, then insert the background image peaches_small.jpg from the chapter_8 assets folder.
4. Set the Vis property to default.
5. Set the Overflow property to visible.
6. Place the insertion point in the organic layer, then type **Organic Gardening**.
7. Insert a line break, then type **Class begins soon!**.
8. Center the text, then apply the subheadings style. Notice the style that has been created in the Styles panel for your new layer.
9. Save your work.

Set the position and size of a layer.

1. Select the organic layer, the set the Left property to 400 pixels.
2. Set the Top property to 230 pixels.
3. Set the Width property to 175 pixels.
4. Set the Height property to 219 pixels.
5. Set the Z-Index property to 1.
6. Save your work.

Use the Layers panel.

1. Open the Layers panel (if necessary).
2. Use the Property inspector to change the organic layer's name to **organic_class**.
3. Set the Vis property to visible.
4. Save your work.

Configure layer preferences.

1. Use the Preferences dialog box to change the settings for default layers using the following settings: Bg Color: #FFCC33, Visibility: visible, Width: 200, Height: 100.
2. Insert a new layer using the appropriate menu command, then name this layer **contact**.

3. Select the contact layer, then change the background color to #FFCC99.
4. Set the Vis property to default and the Overflow property to visible.
5. Place the insertion point in the layer, then type **Call 248-0806 to sign up**.

6. Apply the subheadings style to the text.
7. Select the contact layer, then set the Left property to 480 pixels.
8. Set the Top property to 435 pixels.
9. Set the Width property to 180 pixels.
10. Set the Height property to 20 pixels.
11. Set the Z-Index property to 2 (if necessary).
12. Save your work.
13. Preview the page in your browser, compare your screen to Figure 30, close your browser, adjust the layer position if necessary, then save and close the home page.

FIGURE 30
Completed Skills Review

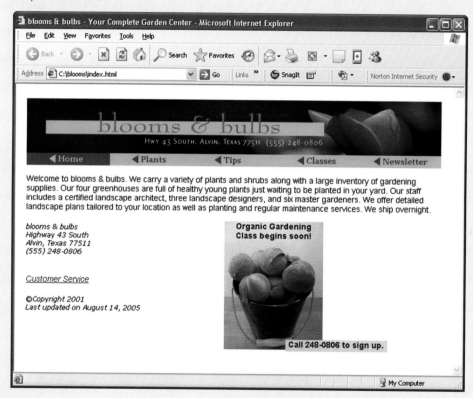

In this exercise you will continue your work on the TripSmart Web site you created in Project Builder 1 in Chapters 1 through 7. The owner, Thomas Howard, wants you to create a layer on the catalog page that advertises a special price on Packing Cubes.

1. Open the TripSmart Web site that you completed in Chapter 7, then open the catalog page.
2. Draw a layer that is approximately 1 inch tall and 3 inches wide in the middle of the page, then name it **special**.
3. Set the background color of the layer to transparent by clicking the Strikethrough button on the color picker toolbar.
4. Insert packing_cube.jpg from the chapter_8 Data Files folder into the layer adding appropriate alternate text, then set the Align option to Left.
5. Set the Left property to 195 pixels and the Top property to 475 pixels.
6. Set the width to 350 pixels, the height to 80 pixels, and the Z-Index property to 1.
7. Add the following text to the right of the image **Packing Cubes on sale this week!**.
8. Format the Packing Cubes on sale this week text using the heading style.
9. Enter a line break, type **Large: $15.00; Medium: $10.00; Small: $5.00**; then format this text with the item_numbers style.

10. Enter a paragraph break, type **Call (555) 848-0807**, enter a line break, type **to order**, then apply the bodytext style.
11. Bold and center the text typed in Step 10.
12. Edit the #special style in the CSS Styles panel to add a solid border around the layer with the color #666666 and a margin of 10 pixels.

13. Set the Overflow property to visible.
14. Save your work, preview the page in your browser, compare your screen to Figure 31, close your browser, make any spacing adjustments necessary for the layer size or position, then close the catalog page.

FIGURE 31
Completed Project Builder 1

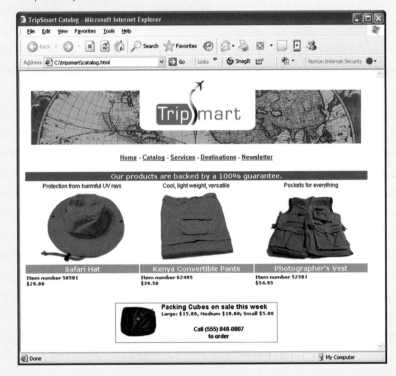

Use Figure 32 as a guide to continue your work on the emma's book bag Web site you created in Project Builder 2 in Chapters 1 through 7. Emma Claire would like you to add a picture of two children during the craft part of story hour. You decide to use a layer to insert the picture into.

1. Open the emma's book bag Web site that you completed in Chapter 7, then open the corner page.
2. Use the Preferences dialog box to specify the following settings for new layers: Visibility: visible, Width: 150, Height: 150, Background color: #FFFFFF. Verify that the Add resize fix when inserting layer check box is selected.
3. Use the Insert Layer command to insert a new layer on the page, then adjust its location to a location that you choose. You can either match the figure or choose a different location.
4. Name the layer **craft_time**.

5. Place the insertion point in the layer, then insert two_girls.jpg from the chapter_8 Data Files folder, adding appropriate alternate text.
6. If necessary, reposition the craft_time layer so that it looks balanced on the page and doesn't cover any of the page text, resizing the layer if necessary.

7. Save your work, preview the page in your browser, close your browser, then close the corner page.

FIGURE 32
Completed Project Builder 2

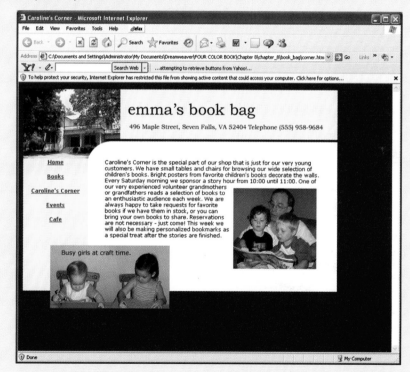

Sharon Woods has recently been asked to redesign a Web site for a small college. She has decided to use tables for her basic design structure, but would like to use layers for additional information that will appear on the page when a mouse is rolled over text links. Because she has never developed a Web site with these features before, she decides to look at some other college Web sites for ideas and inspiration.

1. Connect to the Internet, navigate to the Online Companion link, then select one of the links for this chapter.

2. How are layers used in this site?

3. How are layers used to prevent an overload of information in one area of the screen?

4. View the source code for the page and locate the html tags that control the layers on the page.

5. Use the Reference panel in Dreamweaver to look up the code used in this site to place the layers on the page.

6. Select two other sites from the Online Companion and compare the use of layers on these pages to your original selection.

FIGURE 33
Design Project

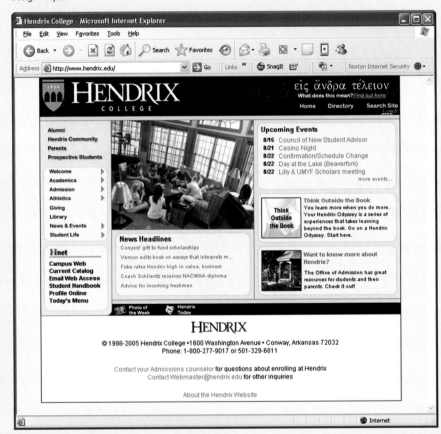

For this assignment, you will continue to work on the portfolio project that you have been developing since Chapter 1. There will be no data files supplied. You are building this Web site from chapter to chapter, so you must do each Portfolio Project assignment in each chapter to complete your Web site.

You will continue building your Web site by designing and completing a page that uses layers rather than tables to control the layout of information.

1. Consult your storyboard to decide which page to create and develop for this chapter. Draw a sketch of the page to show how you will use layers to lay out the content.
2. Create the new page for the site and set the default preferences for layers. Add the appropriate number of layers to the new page and configure them appropriately, making sure to name them and set the properties for each.
3. Add text, background images, and background colors to the layers.

4. Create the navigation links that will allow you to add this page to your site.
5. Update the other pages of your site so that each page includes a link to this new page.
6. Add images in the layers (where appropriate), making sure to align them with text so they look good.

7. Check to ensure that all layers are properly stacked using the Z-Index property.
8. Review the check list in Figure 34 and make any necessary modifications.
9. Save your work, preview the page in your browser, make any necessary modifications to make the page look good, close your browser, then close all open pages.

FIGURE 34
Portfolio Project check list

Web Site Check List

1. Are all layers properly stacked with Z-Index values assigned correctly?
2. Do all pages have titles?
3. Do all navigation links still work?
4. Are all colors in your layers Websafe?
5. Does the use of layers in your Web site improve the site navigation?
6. Do any extra layers appear that need to be removed?
7. Do your pages look acceptable in at least the two major browsers?
8. Do layers hide any information on your pages?
9. Do all images in your layers appear correctly?

9

ADDING MULTIMEDIA
ELEMENTS

1. Add and modify Macromedia Flash objects.

2. Add rollover images.

3. Add sounds.

4. Create an image map.

Introduction

You can use Dreamweaver to add multimedia files created in other programs to the pages of your Web site. Some of the external multimedia file types that Dreamweaver allows you to insert include Macromedia Fireworks navigation bars, rollover images, and buttons; Macromedia Flash buttons, video, sound, and animation; Macromedia Director and Shockwave movies and presentations; Java applets; ActiveX controls; server-side controls; and a variety of plug-ins. This means you can create complex, interactive Web sites with multimedia effects that can be viewed within the pages themselves, rather than loading an external document player such as Windows Media Player or RealPlayer by Real Networks. In this chapter, you will use Dreamweaver to add Flash and Fireworks objects to The Striped Umbrella Web site.

Understanding Multimedia

The term "multimedia" has different meanings, depending on who you are talking to, and the industry in which they work. For our purposes, **multimedia** is the combination of visual and audio effects and text to create a fully engaging experience with a Web site. Although this might be an open-ended definition, it is the experience you are striving for when you add video and audio elements to a Web page. Think about the experience of watching a movie. You are engaged not just by the actors, but also by the sounds and special effects you experience. You want to create this same type of experience for your Web site viewers by adding multimedia elements to your pages.

You can use Dreamweaver to insert a wide variety of multimedia effects on your Web pages, including Flash buttons, movies, and text; Flash video; and a series of built-in JavaScript behaviors such as sounds, rollover images, pop-up messages, and menus.

Tools You'll Use

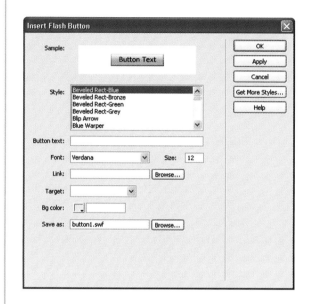

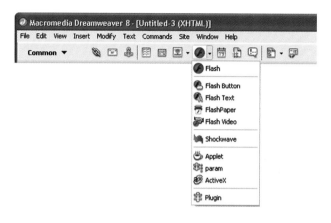

ADD AND MODIFY MACROMEDIA
FLASH OBJECTS

What You'll Do

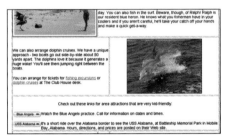

In this lesson, you will insert and edit two Flash buttons on the activities page of The Striped Umbrella Web site. You will also insert and modify a Flash movie on the cafe page, and then play the movie both in Dreamweaver and in a browser.

Understanding Macromedia Flash

Macromedia Flash is a software program that allows you to create low-bandwidth animations and interactive elements that can be placed on your Web pages. These animations use a series of vector-based graphics that load quickly and merge with other graphics and sounds to create short movies. Figure 1 shows a Web page that contains several Flash objects. Figure 2 shows the Macromedia Flash program used to create Flash objects.

Once these short movies are created, you can place them directly on your Web

pages. In order to view Flash movies, you need the Macromedia Flash Player, a software program that is included in the latest versions of both Internet Explorer and Netscape Navigator. If you are using an older browser that does not support the version of Flash used to create your movie, you can download the latest Flash player from the Macromedia Web site, located at *www.macromedia.com*. Today more than 98 percent of Internet-enabled desktops worldwide are using the Flash player. In addition, other tools such as hand-held devices, also use the Flash player.

Collecting Flash objects

Macromedia and their devoted product users provide you with a variety of download-able Flash buttons that are available on the Macromedia Exchange Web site, located at *www.macromedia.com/exchange/*. At this site you can find collections of different buttons, such as space and planet theme sets, and just about anything else you might want. If you can't find a movie or button that interests you, you can download a demo version of Macromedia Flash to create your own Flash objects.

Inserting Flash Buttons and Movies

A **Flash button** is a button made from a small, predefined Flash movie that can be inserted on a Web page to provide navigation on your Web site. Like all Flash objects, Flash buttons are saved with the .swf file extension. Using Dreamweaver, you can insert customized Flash buttons on your Web pages without having Macromedia Flash installed. To do this, use the Flash Button command in the Media menu on the Insert bar when the Common category is displayed. This will open the Insert Flash Button dialog box, where you can choose from 44 different styles of buttons. You also use this dialog box to specify the button text, formatting, an internal or external page to which to link the button, a background color, and a filename for the button.

Using Macromedia Flash, you can create Flash movies that include a variety of multimedia elements, such as audio files (both music and voice-overs), animated objects, scripted objects, clickable links, and just about any other animated or clickable object imaginable. Flash movies can be used to add presentations to your existing Web site or to create an entire Web site. To add a Flash movie to a Web page, click Flash from the Media menu on the Insert bar to open the Select File dialog box, then choose the Flash movie you want to insert.

FIGURE 1
Web site based on Flash

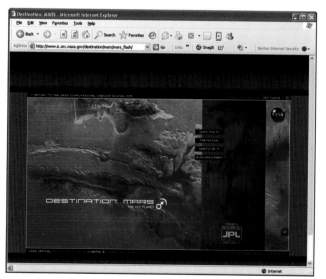

FIGURE 2
Macromedia Flash 8 window

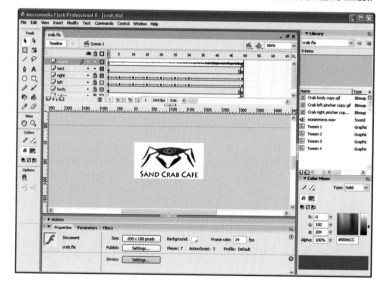

Insert Flash buttons

1. Open The Striped Umbrella Web site, then open the activities page.

2. Click at the beginning of the sentence that begins "Watch the Blue Angels practice" to set the insertion point.

3. Click the **Insert bar list arrow**, click **Common**, click the **Media list arrow**, then click **Flash Button** to open the Insert Flash Button dialog box, as shown in Figure 3.

4. Select **Chrome Bar** from the Style list.

5. Type **Blue Angels** in the Button text text box.

6. Click the **Font list arrow**, click **Verdana,** then type **14** in the Size text box.

7. Type *http://www.blueangels.navy.mil* in the Link text box.

8. Set the Target to _blank.

   The _blank setting ensures that the Blue Angels Web site will open in a new window, keeping The Striped Umbrella Web site open also.

9. Type **angels.swf** in the Save as text box, then click **OK**.

   This is a step that is easily overlooked. Be sure to name your new Flash file or it will use the default "button1.swf" name, which is not very descriptive.

   (continued)

FIGURE 3
Insert Flash button dialog box

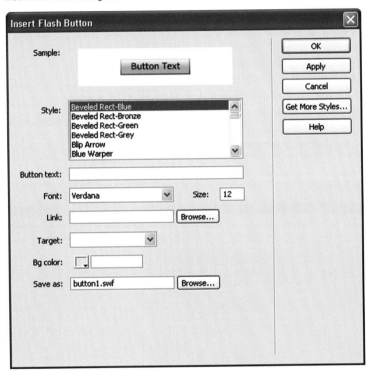

FIGURE 4
Flash button added to the activities page

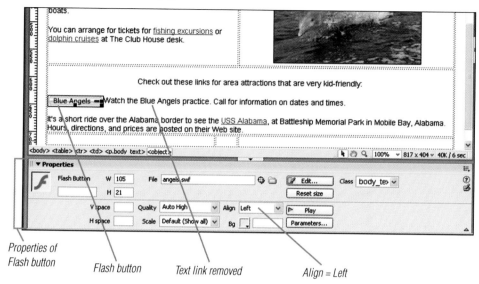

boats.

You can arrange for tickets for fishing excursions or dolphin cruises at The Club House desk.

Check out these links for area attractions that are very kid-friendly:

Blue Angels — Watch the Blue Angels practice. Call for information on dates and times.

It's a short ride over the Alabama border to see the USS Alabama, at Battleship Memorial Park in Mobile Bay, Alabama. Hours, directions, and prices are posted on their Web site.

`<body> <table> <tr> <td> <p.body text> <object>`

▼ Properties

Flash Button | W 105 | File angels.swf | Edit... | Class body_te
| H 21 | | Reset size
| V space | Quality Auto High | Align Left | ▷ Play
| H space | Scale Default (Show all) | Bg | Parameters...

Properties of Flash button

Flash button

Text link removed

Align = Left

FIGURE 5
Viewing the activities page with new Flash buttons added

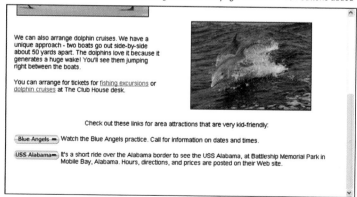

We can also arrange dolphin cruises. We have a unique approach - two boats go out side-by-side about 50 yards apart. The dolphins love it because it generates a huge wake! You'll see them jumping right between the boats.

You can arrange for tickets for fishing excursions or dolphin cruises at The Club House desk.

Check out these links for area attractions that are very kid-friendly:

Blue Angels — Watch the Blue Angels practice. Call for information on dates and times.

USS Alabama — It's a short ride over the Alabama border to see the USS Alabama, at Battleship Memorial Park in Mobile Bay, Alabama. Hours, directions, and prices are posted on their Web site.

10. Type **Link to Blue Angels Web site** in the Title text box in the Flash Accessibility Attributes dialog box, then click **OK**.

11. With the Flash button selected, click the **Align list arrow** in the Property inspector, then click **Left**.

   The Flash button is aligned to the left of the line of text beside it.

12. Select the text link to the Blue Angels Web site, then delete the link in the Property inspector.

   Because you now have a Flash button to serve as the link, you no longer need the text link.

13. Repeat Steps 2 through 12 to create a Flash button that links to the USS Alabama site, using **USS Alabama** as the button text, **Link to USS Alabama** as the title in the Flash Accessibility Attributes dialog box, and **alabama.swf** as the filename.

   TIP If the text on your Flash buttons appears too large, you can choose a smaller font size or a different font.

14. Save your work, preview the page in your browser, test the Flash buttons, compare your screen to Figure 5, then close the browser.

   Notice that both Web sites opened in new windows, leaving The Striped Umbrella Web site window open.

   TIP If a dialog box opens warning you about Flash Player security issues, click the Settings button and set the security options.

You added two Flash buttons to the activities page of The Striped Umbrella Web site.

Edit a Flash button

1. Click the **Blue Angels Flash button**, then click **Edit** in the Property inspector.

2. Change the Font to Arial, click **OK**, then click **OK** again to close the Flash Accessibility Attributes dialog box.

3. Repeat Steps 1 and 2 to change the font on the USS Alabama button.

4. Click the **Refresh button** 🔄 on the Files panel to view the two new Flash button files, as shown in Figure 6.

   To work properly, the Flash buttons should be saved in the root folder.

5. Close the activities page.

You changed the font of the two Flash buttons to Arial.

FIGURE 6
Viewing the two Flash button files in the Files panel

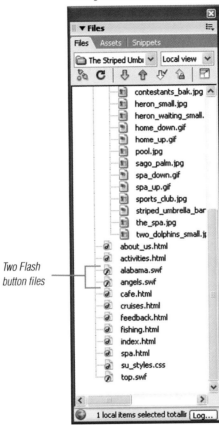

Two Flash button files

FIGURE 7
Flash movie placeholder on the cafe page

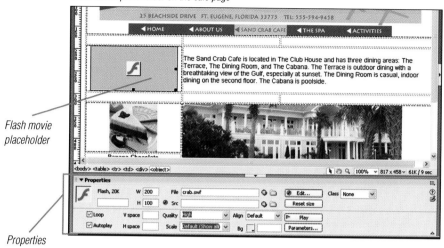

Flash movie
placeholder

Properties
of selected
Flash movie

FIGURE 8
Flash movie playing in Dreamweaver

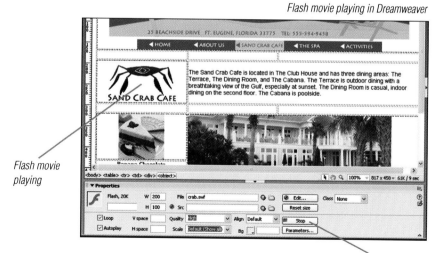

Flash movie
playing

Click to stop movie

Insert Flash movies

1. Open the cafe page in The Striped Umbrella Web site.

2. Select the **cafe logo** in the top-left corner of the page, then click **[Delete]** (Win) or **[delete]** (Mac).

3. Click the **Media list arrow** on the Insert bar, then click **Flash**.

4. Navigate to the chapter_9 data files folder, click **crab.swf**, click **OK** (Win) or **Choose** (Mac), save the movie in the root folder of the Web site, type **Flash Movie of crab logo** in the Object Tag Accessibility Attributes text box, then click **OK**.

   A Flash movie placeholder appears on the page, as shown in Figure 7.

   TIP If you already have the Flash file in your root folder, you can drag and drop it from the Assets panel rather than use the Insert bar or Insert menu.

You inserted a Flash movie on the cafe page of The Striped Umbrella Web site.

Play a Flash movie in Dreamweaver and in a browser

1. With the placeholder selected, click **Play** in the Property inspector to view the crab.swf movie, as shown in Figure 8, then click **Stop**.

2. Save your work, preview the page in your browser, compare your screen to Figure 9, then close your browser.

(continued)

TIP To play Flash movies in Dreamweaver and in your browser, you must have the Flash Player installed on your computer. If the Flash Player is not installed, you can download it at the Macromedia Web site (*www.macromedia.com*).

3. If the movie did not play in Internet Explorer, click **Tools** on the menu bar, click **Internet Options**, click the **Advanced tab**, then click the **Allow active content to run in files on my computer check box**.

TIP If you are using a different browser or a version of Internet Explorer that is earlier than 6.0, look for a similar setting.

You played a Flash movie on the cafe page in The Striped Umbrella Web site in Dreamweaver and in your browser.

Modify a Flash file from Dreamweaver

1. If you have Macromedia Flash installed on your computer, go to Step 2. If you do not have it installed, skip to Lesson 2 on page 9-12.

2. Use Explorer (Win) or Finder (Mac) to copy the file crab.fla from the chapter_9 Data Files folder to the root folder of The Striped Umbrella Web site.

   To use this source file, you must copy it to your root folder to be able to make changes to it.

3. Close Explorer (Win) or Finder (Mac), then return to Dreamweaver.

4. With the Flash placeholder selected, click **Edit** in the Property inspector.

5. Click **crab.fla** in the striped_umbrella root folder in the Locate Macromedia Flash Document File dialog box, then click **Open**.

(continued)

FIGURE 9
Flash movie playing in Internet Explorer

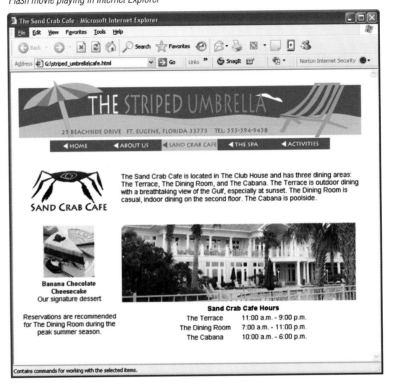

Adding Multimedia Elements

FIGURE 10
Closing Flash and returning to Dreamweaver

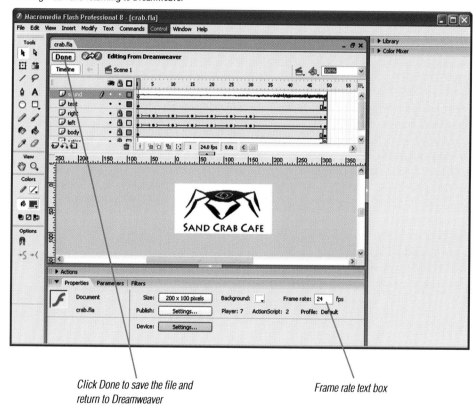

Click Done to save the file and
return to Dreamweaver

Frame rate text box

The .swf file is a Flash player file and cannot
be edited. The .fla file is the editable Flash file.
You must have this source file to edit the
movie. After you select the .fla file, the file
opens in Flash.

> TIP   If you receive a warning that one or
> more fonts used for this movie are not
> available, click Choose Substitute, then
> choose another font.

6. Click in the **Frame rate text box** on the
Property inspector, then change the frame
rate from 12 to 24 fps (frames per second),
as shown in Figure 10, then click **Done**.

   Flash automatically saves both the crab.fla
   file and the crab.swf file, then closes.

7. Save and preview the page in your browser,
then close the browser and close the cafe
page.

   Notice that the movie plays a little faster
   now. You changed the frames per second to
   a larger number, which had the effect of the
   movie playing faster. The sound, however,
   plays out after the animation stops. A sound
   will continue playing until it is finished
   regardless of how long the Flash movie is.

*You used the Edit button on the Property inspector
to find and modify the Flash movie in Flash, then
returned to Dreamweaver.*

ADD ROLLOVER IMAGES

What You'll Do

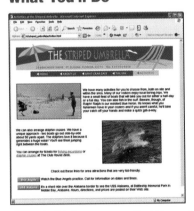

In this lesson, you will add two rollover images to the activities page of The Striped Umbrella Web site.

Understanding Rollover Images

A **rollover image** is an image that changes its appearance when the mouse pointer is placed over it in a browser. A rollover image actually consists of two images. The first image is the one that appears when the mouse pointer is not positioned over it, and the second image is the one that appears when the mouse pointer is positioned over it. Rollover images are often used to help create a feeling of action and excitement on a Web page. For instance, suppose you are creating a Web site that promotes a series of dance classes. You could create a rollover image using two images of a dancer in two different poses. When a viewer places the mouse pointer over the image of the dancer in the first pose, the image would change to show the dancer in a different pose, creating a feeling of movement and action.

QUICKTIP

You can also add a link to a rollover image, so that the image will change only when the image is clicked.

Adding Shockwave movies

Macromedia Shockwave is part of the Macromedia Director Shockwave Studio, a software suite used to create full-blown interactive, multimedia presentations that combine text, graphics, video, animations, and sound. Adding Shockwave files to your Web pages can add excitement, sizzle, and interactivity to engage your users. To add a Shockwave movie to a Web page in Dreamweaver, select Shockwave from the Media menu on the Insert bar, select the file you want in the Select File dialog box, then click OK. Shockwave files have a .dcr file extension.

Adding Rollover Images

You add rollover images to a Web page using the Rollover Image command in the Images menu on the Insert bar shown in Figure 11. You specify both the original image and the rollover image in the Insert Rollover Image dialog box. The rollover image is the image that is swapped when the mouse rolls over the original image. Another way to create a rollover image, button, or navigation bar is to insert it as a Fireworks HTML file. The code for the rollover is inserted in the file when it is created and exported from Fireworks. The Fireworks HTML command is also in the Images menu, as shown in Figure 11.

QUICKTIP

It's a good idea to click the Preload rollover image check box in the Insert Rollover Image dialog box to ensure that the rollover image appears without a delay.

Rollover images can also be used to display an image associated with a text link. For instance, suppose you are creating a Web site for an upcoming election. You could create a Web page that contains a list of candidates for the election and add a rollover image for each candidate's name that would cause a photograph of the candidate to appear when the mouse is placed over his or her name. You can also use this effect to make appropriate images appear when you point to different menu options. For instance, Figure 12 shows the North Arkansas College Web site, which uses rollover images to highlight each menu option on its home page.

FIGURE 11
Images menu on the Insert bar

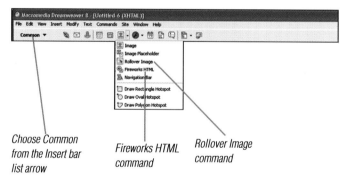

Choose Common from the Insert bar list arrow

Fireworks HTML command

Rollover Image command

FIGURE 12
North Arkansas College Web site with rollover image

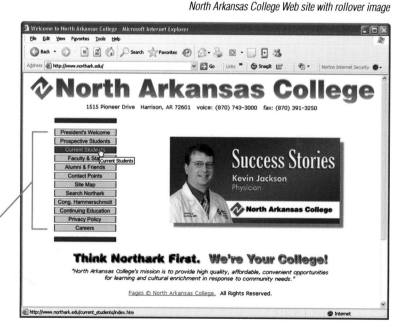

Rollover images change when mouse is positioned over new menu item

Add a rollover image

1. Open the activities page of The Striped Umbrella Web site.

2. Scroll down to find the Flash button linking to the Blue Angels Web site, then delete it.

3. Click the **Images list arrow** on the Insert bar, then click **Fireworks HTML**.

4. Click **Browse** in the Insert Fireworks HTML dialog box, browse to the chapter_9 Data Files folder, click **blue_angels.html**, click **Open**, compare your Insert Fireworks HTML dialog box to Figure 13, then click **OK**.

5. Click **OK** in the dialog box asking you if you want to copy images to your Web site, then double-click the **assets folder**, then click **Select** (Win) or **Choose** (Mac) to select your assets folder to store them in.

6. Select the # in the Link text box, then replace it with **http://www.blueangels.navy.mil**, as shown in Figure 14.

7. With the button selected, click the **Align list arrow** on the Property inspector, then click **Left**.

8. Type **Link to Blue Angels Web site** as the alternate text for the button in the Alt text box in the Property inspector.

(continued)

FIGURE 13
Browsing to find the source file for the rollover created in Fireworks

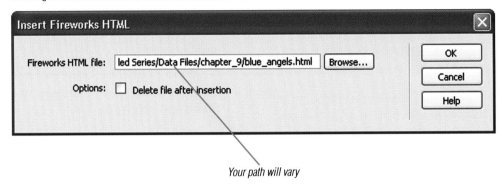

Your path will vary

FIGURE 14
Link added to rollover image

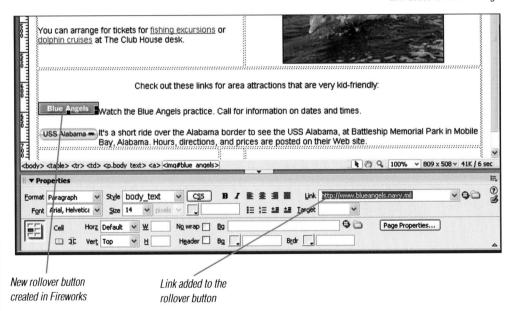

New rollover button created in Fireworks

Link added to the rollover button

Adding Multimedia Elements

FIGURE 15

Activities page with rollover images created in Fireworks

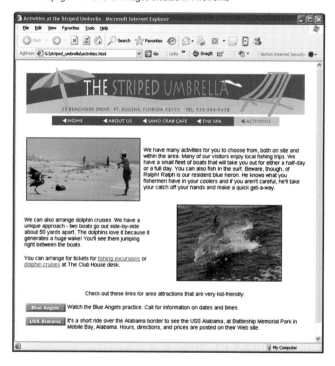

9. Repeat Steps 2 through 8 to insert another button that links to the USS Alabama Web site using the file **uss_alabama.html** for the source file, **http://www.ussalabama.com** for the link, and **Link to USS Alabama Web site** for the alternate text.

10. Select each button, then type **5** in the H text box in the Property inspector to insert some space around each button.

11. Save your work, preview the page in your browser, place the mouse pointer over the images to see the rollover effect, test the links to make sure they work correctly, compare your screen to Figure 15, then close your browser.

You added two rollover images that were created in Macromedia Fireworks to the activities page of The Striped Umbrella Web site.

ADD SOUNDS

What You'll Do

In this lesson, you will add an action that plays a sound effect to the activities page of The Striped Umbrella Web site. You will then change the event for that action.

Adding Interactive Elements

You can make your Web pages come alive by adding interactive elements such as sounds to them. For instance, if you are creating a Web page about your favorite animals, you could attach the sound of a dog barking to a photograph of a dog so that the barking sound would play when the viewer clicked the photograph. You can add sound and other multimedia actions to elements by attaching behaviors to them. **Behaviors** are sets of instructions that you can attach to page elements that tell the page element to respond in a specific way when an event occurs, such as when the mouse pointer is positioned over the element. When you attach a behavior to an element, JavaScript code for the behavior is automatically generated and inserted into the code for your page.

Using the Behaviors Panel

You can use the Behaviors panel located in the Tag panel group to insert a variety of

JavaScript-based behaviors on a page. For instance, using the Behaviors panel you can automate tasks, respond to visitor selections and mouse movements, add sounds, create games, or add automatic dynamic effects to a Web page. To insert a behavior, click the Add behavior button on the Behaviors panel to open the Actions menu, as shown in Figure 16, then click a behavior from the menu.

Inserting Sound Effects

Sound effects can add a new dimension to any Web site. You can use sounds to enhance the effect of positioning the mouse on a rollover image, clicking a link, or even loading or closing a page. By adding sounds, you can make your pages cheep, chirp, click, or squawk.

To apply a sound effect, select the link or object to which you want the sound effect added, and then select the Play Sound behavior located in the Actions

Adding Multimedia Elements

menu of the Behaviors panel. Sound effects should be used very sparingly, and only if they add to the overall good design for the page. Sound effects that loop, or repeat continuously, may be annoying to viewers.

Understanding Actions and Events

Actions are triggered by events. For instance, if you want your viewer to hear a sound when an image is clicked, you would attach the Play Sound action using the onClick event to trigger the action. Other examples of events are onMouseOver and onLoad. The onMouseOver event will trigger an action when the mouse is placed over an object. The onLoad event will trigger an action when the page is first loaded in the browser window.

FIGURE 16
Behaviors panel with the Actions menu displayed

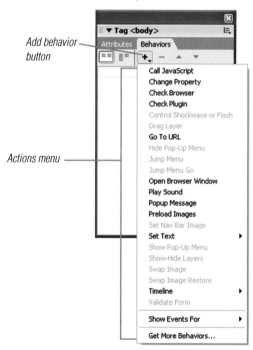

Add behavior button

Actions menu

Add sound effects

1. Select the **dolphin image** on the activities page, click **Window** on the menu bar, then click **Behaviors** to open the Behaviors panel.

2. Click the **Add behavior button** ⊞▾ on the Behaviors panel toolbar to open the Actions menu, then click **Play Sound** to open the Play Sound dialog box, as shown in Figure 17.

3. Click **Browse**, navigate to the chapter_9, Data Files folder, click **dolphin.wav**, then click **OK** (Win) or **Choose** (Mac).

   TIP If a dialog box opens asking if you want to copy the dolphin.wav file to the Web site, click Yes, navigate to the assets folder of the Web site, then click Save.

4. Click **OK** to close the Play Sound dialog box.

   Notice that Play Sound appears as an action in the Behaviors panel. The left column shows onClick as the event. This means that the Play Sound behavior will be triggered when the image is clicked.

5. Save your work, preview the page in your browser, test the sound effect by clicking the dolphin image, then close your browser.

You added a sound effect to an image on the activities page of The Striped Umbrella Web site.

FIGURE 17
Play Sound dialog box

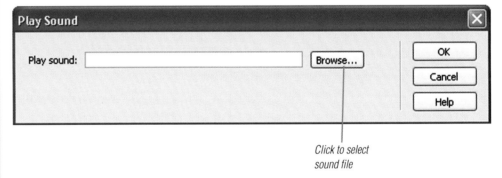

Click to select sound file

FIGURE 18

Changing the event for the Play Sound action

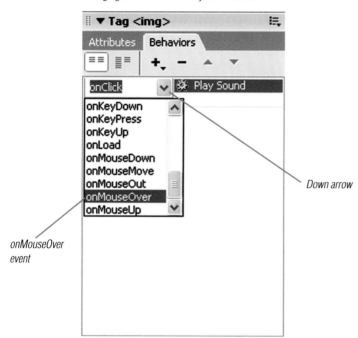

onMouseOver
event

Down arrow

1. Click the left column of the Play Sound action in the Behaviors panel to display the events list arrow, click the **down arrow**, then click **onMouseOver**, as shown in Figure 18.

2. Save your changes, preview the page in your browser, then move the pointer over the dolphin image.

   The sound plays without clicking the image.

3. Close the browser.

You changed the event for the Play Sound action by editing the behavior in the Behaviors panel.

CREATE AN
IMAGE MAP

What You'll Do

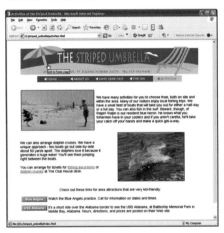

In this lesson, you will create an image map by placing a hotspot on The Striped Umbrella banner that will link to the home page.

Another way to create links for Web pages is to combine them with images by creating an image map. An **image map** is an image that has one or more hotspots placed on top of it. A **hotspot** is a clickable area on an image that, when clicked, links to a different location on the page or to another Web page. For example, a map of the United States could have a hotspot placed on each individual state so that viewers could click a state to link to information about that state. The National Park Service Web site is shown in Figure 19. As you place your mouse over a state, the state name is displayed using alternate text. When you click on a state, you will be linked to information about national parks in that state. You can create hotspots by

first selecting the image on which you want to place a hotspot, then using one of the hotspot tools in the Property inspector.

There are several ways to create image maps to make them more user-friendly and accessible. One way is to be sure to include alternate text for each hotspot. Another is to draw the hotspot boundaries a little larger than they need to be to cover the area you want to set as a link. This allows viewers a little leeway when they place their mouse over the hotspot by creating a larger target area for them.

The hotspot tools in Dreamweaver make creating image maps a snap. In addition to the Rectangular Hotspot Tool, there is an Oval Hotspot Tool and a Polygon Hotspot Tool for different shapes of areas. These tools can be used to create any shape hotspot that you need. For instance, on a map of the United States, you can draw an outline around each state with the Polygon Hotspot Tool. You can then make each state "clickable." Hotspots can be easily changed and rearranged on the image. Use the Pointer Hotspot Tool to select the hotspot you would like to edit. You can drag one of the hotspot selector handles to change the size or shape of a hotspot. You can also move the hotspot by dragging it to a new position on the image. It is a good idea to limit the number of complex hotspots in an image because the code can become too lengthy for the page to download in a reasonable length of time.

FIGURE 19

Viewing an image map on the National Park Service Web site

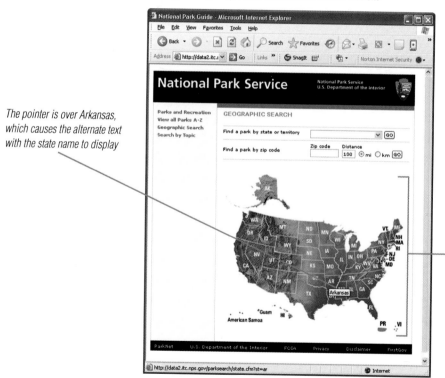

The pointer is over Arkansas, which causes the alternate text with the state name to display

Clicking on an individual state will link to parks in that state

Create an image map

1. Select the banner on the activities page, then click the **Rectangular Hotspot Tool** ⬚ in the Property inspector.

2. Click **OK** to close the dialog box that reminds you to supply alternate text for the hotspot, then drag the **pointer** to create a rectangle over the left side of the banner, as shown in Figure 20.

3. Use the **Point to File icon** 💠 in the Property inspector to link the index page to the hotspot.

4. Type **home** in the Map text box in the Property inspector to give the image map a unique name.

5. Click the **Target list arrow** in the Property inspector, then click **_self**.

   When the hotspot is clicked, the home page will open in the same window.

   (continued)

FIGURE 20

Drawing a rectangular hotspot on the banner

Outline of hotspot

Rectangular Hotspot Tool

Adding Multimedia Elements

FIGURE 21
Properties of the hotspot

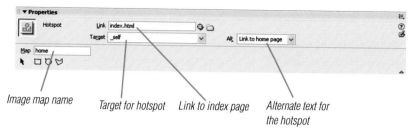

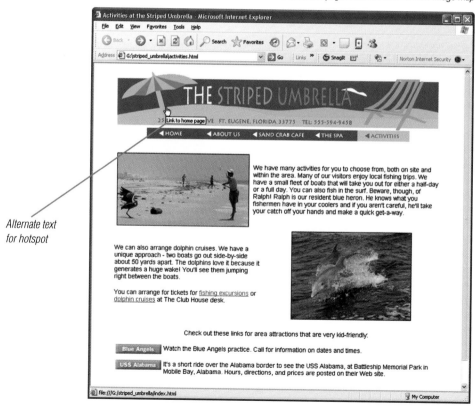

Image map name   Target for hotspot   Link to index page   Alternate text for
                                                            the hotspot

FIGURE 22
The activities page in the browser with an image map

Alternate text
for hotspot

6. Type **Link to home page** in the Alt text box in the Property inspector, as shown in Figure 21. then press **[Enter]** (Win) or **[return]** (Mac).

7. Save your work, then preview the page in your browser to test the link on the image map.

   As you place the pointer over the hotspot, you see the alternate text displayed and the pointer indicates the link, as shown in Figure 22.

8. Close the browser, then close all open pages.

You created an image map using the banner on the activities page. You then linked the hotspot to the home page.

Add and modify Macromedia Flash objects.

1. Open the blooms & bulbs Web site that you created in Chapters 1 through 8, then open the classes page.
2. Click after the paragraph about Master Gardeners, then insert a Flash button with the following settings: Style: Glass-Purple, Button Text: Master Gardeners, Font: Comic Sans MS, Size: 11 pixels, Link: http://aggie-horticulture.tamu.edu/mastergd/mg.html, Target: _blank, Save as: **m_gardeners.swf**, then click OK.
3. Enter **Link to Texas Master Gardeners** in the Flash Accessiblity Attributes dialog box.
4. Set the alignment to Top and add H space of 10.

5. Insert the garden_quote.swf Flash movie located in the chapter_9 Data Files folder directly below the paragraph about registration, then enter **Garden quote** in the Object Tag Accessibility Attributes dialog box.
6. Play the garden_quote.swf movie in Dreamweaver, save your work, preview the page in your browser, compare your screen to Figure 23, then close your browser.
7. Close the classes page.

Add rollover images.

1. Open the tips page, then delete the tips graphic text at the top of the page.
2. Verify that your insertion point is still where you just deleted the tips graphic.
3. Insert garden_tips.html from the chapter_9 Data Files folder, by clicking Insert on the menu bar, pointing to Image Objects, then clicking

Fireworks HTML. (*Hint*: Use the Browse button in the Insert Fireworks HTML dialog box to navigate to the Data Files folder, then click OK in the Insert Fireworks HTML dialog box when you are done.) garden_tips.html is a rollover image. Save the associated images in the assets folder of the Web site when prompted.
4. Save your work, preview the page in the browser to test the rollover, then close the tips page.

Add sounds.

1. Open the water_plants page.
2. Select the water plants image, then use the Behaviors panel to add the sound water.wav from the chapter_9 Data Files folder that will play when the image is clicked. Save the water.wav file in the assets folder of the Web site when prompted.

3. Edit the behavior to play the sound when the mouse rolls over the image.

4. Save your work, then preview the page in the browser. (*Hint*: Place the mouse over the image to test the water sound.)

5. Close the browser.

Create an image map.

1. Use the Rectangular Hotspot Tool to create an image map over the blooms & bulbs text portion of the banner on the water_plants page.

2. Use the Property inspector to link the hotspot to the index page, then add **Link to home page** as the alternate text.

3. Save your work, then preview the page in your browser to test the image map.

4. Close the browser, then close all open pages.

FIGURE 23
Completed Skills Review

In this exercise you will continue your work on the TripSmart Web site that you began in Project Builder 1 in Chapter 1. The owner of TripSmart would like you to work on the amazon page. He gives you a Flash file that shows the route of the ship that will take visitors down the Amazon river. You will also insert a sound of a lion roaring that will play when the mouse is placed over the lion image on the Kenya page.

1. Open the TripSmart Web site that you created in Chapter 1, then open the amazon page.
2. Place the insertion point at the end of the second paragraph, then split that cell into two rows.
3. Insert the amazon_map.swf file in the new row, then add the text **Amazon map animation** in the Object Tag Accessibly Attributes dialog box.
4. Center the Flash object in the cell, then save the file.
5. Preview the amazon page in the browser, then compare your screen to Figure 24.
6. Close the browser, then close the amazon page.

7. Open the kenya page, then select the lion image.
8. Use the Behaviors panel to add the sound lion.wav from the chapter_9 Data Files folder to the Web site so it will play when the mouse is rolled over the lion image on the page.

9. Save the page, then preview it in the browser to test the rollover sound.
10. Close the browser, then close all open pages.

FIGURE 24

Sample Project Builder 1

Use Figure 25 as a guide to continue your work on the emma's book bag Web site that you started in Project Builder 2 in Chapter 1. You have decided to use Flash buttons for the navigation links on the home page and to place an image map on the books page that will link to the home page.

1. Open the emma's book bag Web site.
2. Open the index page.
3. Replace the Home link on the side of the page with a Flash button. Choose a style, background color, and font that will work well with the existing color scheme and design of the emma's book bag Web site.
4. Link the button to index.html, then save it as **home.swf**.
5. Replace each of the other links in the navigation bar with Flash buttons, using the same formatting and fonts that you used for the Home button. Save the files using the filenames **books.swf**, **corner.swf**, **events.swf**, and **cafe.swf**.
6. Adjust the position of the buttons on the page to determine the most attractive layout, then copy the navigation buttons to the rest of the pages in the Web site, replacing the old navigation links. (*Hint*: You may want to reposition the layer on the corner.html page.)

7. Edit the buttons on the page to set each target to _top.
8. Save and preview the page in your browser, then close the browser and close the index page.
9. Open the books page, then use the Rectangular Hotspot Tool on the Property inspector to create an image map above the navigation bar and to the left of the banner that links to the index page.
10. Save the file, then preview the page in your browser to test the link.
11. Close the browser, then close all open pages.

FIGURE 25
Completed Project Builder 2

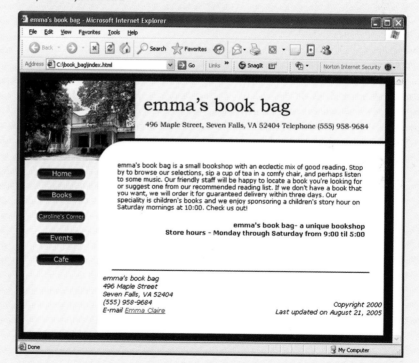

Henry Fisher is an astronomer. He would like to design a Web site about planets, like the example shown in Figure 26. He would like his Web site to incorporate Flash elements, rollovers, and sounds and would like to use Dreamweaver to build his site.

1. Connect to the Internet, go to *www.course.com*, navigate to the page for this book, click the Online Companion link, and then click the link for this chapter.
2. Which elements in the site are Flash objects?
3. Which objects in the site are made with rollover images?
4. How has adding the Flash effects improved the appearance of this site?
5. Go through the site and locate any popup message boxes.
6. Make a list of sounds that you noticed on the site. How did they contribute to the feel of the site?
7. Create a sketch of Henry's site that contains at least five pages. Indicate in your sketch what multimedia elements you plan to insert in the site, including where you would add Flash objects, rollover images, and sounds.

FIGURE 26
Design Project

Adding Multimedia Elements

PORTFOLIO PROJECT

In this assignment you will continue to work on the group Web site that you started in Chapter 1. There will be no data files supplied. You are building this Web site from chapter to chapter, so you must do each Portfolio Project assignment in each chapter to complete your Web site.

You will continue building your Web site by designing and completing a page that contains multimedia content or by adding multimedia content to existing pages. After completing your Web site, be sure to run appropriate reports to test the site.

1. Evaluate your storyboard, then choose a page, or series of pages, to develop in which you will include Flash objects as well as other multimedia content, such as rollover images, sounds, and popup messages.
2. Plan the content for your new page so that the layout works well with both the new and old pages in your site. Sketch a plan for the multimedia content you wish to add, showing which multimedia elements you will use and where you will place them.

3. Create the Flash buttons and Flash text you identified in your sketch, choosing appropriate formatting.
4. Add the rollover images to the page.
5. Either find a sound or record a sound to add to the page.
6. Run a report on your new page(s) to ensure that all links work correctly.

7. Preview the new page (or pages) in your browser and test all links. Evaluate your pages for content and layout. Use the check list in Figure 27 to make sure your Web site is complete.
8. Make any modifications that are necessary to improve the page.

FIGURE 27
Portfolio Project check list

Web Site Check List
1. Do all Flash buttons load correctly?
2. Do all Flash movies play properly in your browser?
3. Do all links work?
4. Do all sounds play correctly?
5. Are there any missing images or links on the pages?
6. Do all pages have a title?
7. Do all rollover images display properly?

Adding Multimedia Elements

10

CREATING AND
USING TEMPLATES

1. Create templates with editable regions.

2. Use templates to create pages.

3. Use templates to update a site.

4. Use advanced template options.

10 CREATING AND
USING TEMPLATES

Introduction

When you create a Web site, it's important to make sure that each page has a unified look so that viewers know they are in your site no matter what page they are viewing. For instance, you should make sure that common elements such as the navigation bar and company banner appear in the same place on every page and that every page has the same background color. One way to make sure that every page in your site has a consistent appearance is through the use of templates. A **template** is a special kind of page that contains both **locked regions**, which are areas on the page that cannot be modified by users of the template, as well as other types of regions that users can change or edit. For instance, an **optional region** is an area in the template that users can choose to show or hide, and an **editable region** is an area where users can add or change content.

Using templates not only ensures a consistent appearance throughout a Web site, but

also saves considerable development time. Templates are especially helpful if different people will be creating pages in your site. In this chapter, you will create a template from an existing page in The Striped Umbrella Web site and define editable regions in it.

Understanding How to Use Templates

The ideal process for using templates is for one person (the template author) to create a template that has a locked region containing the design elements common to every page in the site, as well as regions where content can be added or changed. Once the template is fully developed, other team members can use it to create each page of the site, adding appropriate content to the editable regions of each page. If the template author makes changes to the template, all pages to which the template is attached can be automatically updated to reflect those changes.

Tools You'll Use

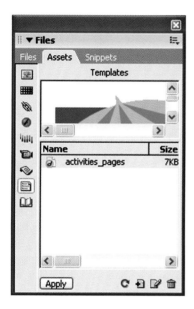

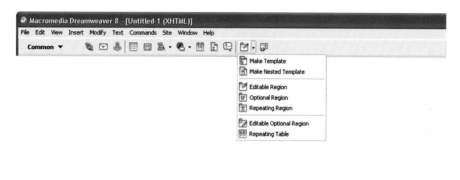

CREATE TEMPLATES WITH
EDITABLE REGIONS

What You'll Do

 In this lesson, you will create a template based on the cruises page of The Striped Umbrella Web site. You will then define editable regions in the template, rearrange some of the cell content, change the cell alignment of several cells, and add two Flash buttons to link to the cruises and fishing pages. Finally, you will delete the template page title.

Creating a Template from an Existing Page

If you have already created and designed a page that you think looks great, and you want to use the layout and design for other pages in your site, you can save the page as a template using the Save as Template command. Templates are saved with a .dwt extension and are stored in the Templates folder in the root folder of your Web site. If your site does not have a Templates folder, one will automatically be created for you the first time you save a template. To view a list of templates in your site, open the Templates folder in the Files panel. To preview a template before opening it, open the Assets panel, click the Templates button on the Assets panel toolbar, then click a template in the list. The template appears in the preview window above the templates list, as shown in Figure 1.

Defining Editable Regions

By default, when you save a template, all content on the page will be locked, which

means that no one else will be able to add content or modify any part of the template to create new pages. If your template is going to be used effectively, you need to have at least one editable region in it so that other users can add content. You can specify a name for the region using the New Editable Region dialog box. Editable regions are outlined in blue on the template page, and the names of the editable regions appear in blue shaded boxes, as shown in Figure 2.

Defining Optional Regions

In addition to editable regions, you can also add optional regions to a template. An optional region is an area in a template that users can choose to either show or hide. For instance, you could place a graphic in an optional region, so that users of the template can decide whether or not to show it on the page they are creating. An optional region's visibility is controlled by the conditional statement **if**. You can specify a page element as an optional region using the New Optional Region dialog box. You can name the region and specify whether to show or hide it by default. The Editable and Optional Region dialog boxes are both accessed by clicking the Templates list arrow on the Insert bar when the Common category is displayed.

Defining Editable Optional Regions

If you want to give users the ability to show or hide a page element, as well as make modifications to it, then you can define the element as an **editable optional region**. For instance, you might want to make an advertisement an editable optional region so that users of the template could change its text and specify whether to show or hide it. Using the New Optional Region dialog box, you can name the region and specify whether to show or hide it by default.

FIGURE 1
Template in the Assets panel

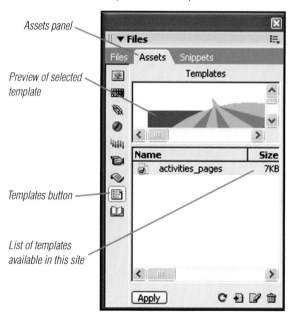

Assets panel

Preview of selected template

Templates button

List of templates available in this site

FIGURE 2
Template with locked and editable regions

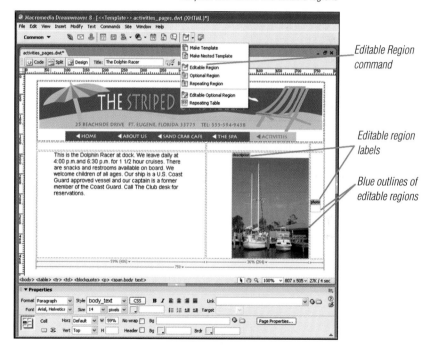

Editable Region command

Editable region labels

Blue outlines of editable regions

Create a template from an existing page

1. Open the cruises page.

2. Click **File** on the menu bar, then click **Save as Template** to open the Save As Template dialog box.

3. Type **activities_pages** in the Save as text box, compare your screen to Figure 3, click **Save**, update the links, then click the **Refresh button** 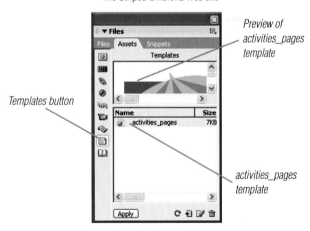 on the Files panel toolbar.

   Notice that the Templates folder, which contains the activities_pages template, appears in the Files panel.

4. Display the Assets panel, click the **Templates button** to view the list of templates in the site, click the **activities_pages template** in the list (if necessary), then compare your Assets panel to Figure 4.

   TIP To create a template from scratch, click File on the menu bar, click New to open the New Document dialog box, click the General tab, click Template page in the Category list, then click Create.

You created a template from the cruises page of The Striped Umbrella Web site.

FIGURE 3
Save As Template dialog box

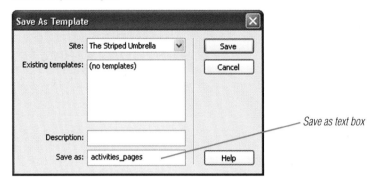

Save as text box

FIGURE 4
Assets panel showing saved template in The Striped Umbrella Web site

Templates button

Preview of activities_pages template

activities_pages template

Creating and Using Templates

FIGURE 5

New Editable Region dialog box

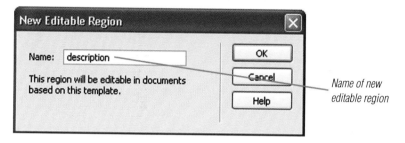

Name of new
editable region

Create an editable region

1. Click to place the insertion point in the cell with the boat graphic, then click the **<td> tag** in the tag selector to select all of the content in that cell.

2. Click the **Insert bar list arrow**, then click **Common**.

3. Click the **Templates list arrow** on the Insert bar, then click **Editable Region** to open the New Editable Region dialog box.

   TIP You can also press [Ctrl][Alt][V] (Win) or ⌘ [option][V] (Mac) to open the New Editable Region dialog box.

4. Type **description** in the Name text box, as shown in Figure 5, click **OK**, then press [→] to deselect the graphic.

   A blue shaded box containing "description" appears above the picture of the boat.

5. Press **[Tab]**, then repeat Steps 3 and 4 to create an editable region in the next empty cell to the right of the boat, name it **photo**, press **[Delete]** (Win) or **[delete]** (Mac) to remove the word "Photo" below the photo label, then compare your screen to Figure 6.

   TIP To remove an editable region from a template, select the editable region in the document window, click Modify on the menu bar, point to Templates, then click Remove Template Markup.

You created two editable regions in the activities_pages template.

FIGURE 6

activities_pages template with two editable regions added

Templates
list arrow

Editable
region label

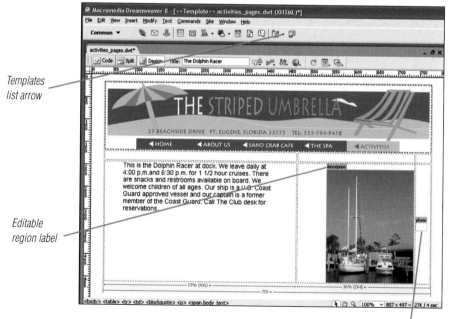

Editable region is marked
by blue outline

Modify a template

1. Select the boats graphic, then drag it into the photo editable area.

   You must drop the graphic inside the blue rectangle to be included in the editable area.

2. Select the paragraph of text, then drag it into the description editable area.

3. Place the insertion point in the empty cell to the left of the cell with the description and set the column width to 20%.

4. Repeat Step 3 to set the widths of the next two cells to 40% each, then compare your screen to Figure 7.

   TIP You may have to select the cell tag to be able to enter the width setting. Make sure no other cells have a width setting. If you find any, delete them.

5. Select the cell with the boats graphic, then change the vertical alignment (Vert) for the cell to Top and the horizontal alignment (Horz) to Center.

6. Select the cell with the description editable region, then change the horizontal alignment (Horz) to Left.

(continued)

FIGURE 7

Editing the activities_pages template

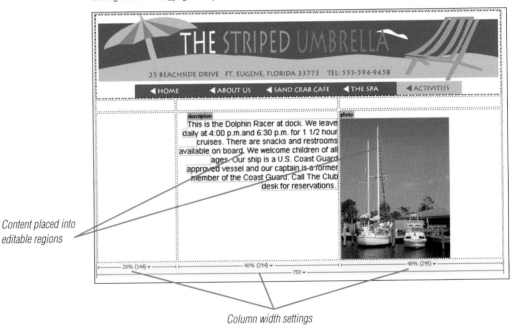

Content placed into editable regions

Column width settings

FIGURE 8

Links added to the activities_pages template

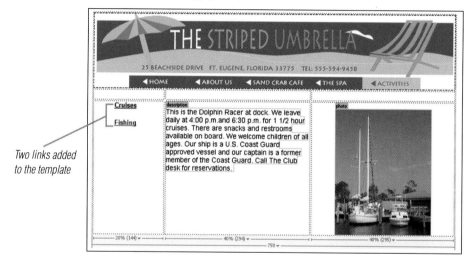

Two links added
to the template

7. Place the insertion point in the cell to the left of the cell with the description editable region, then type **Cruises**.

8. Press **[Enter]** (Win) or **[return]** (Mac), type **Fishing**, then apply the bullets style to the two words.

9. Link the Cruises text to cruises.html, then link the Fishing text to fishing.html.

10. Delete the page title from the Title text box, click **File** on the menu bar, click **Save as Template**, click **Save**, click **Yes** to overwrite the existing template, then compare your screen to Figure 8.

11. Close the activities_pages template.

You rearranged some of the content on the activities_pages template, changed the alignment of some cells, then added links to the cruises and fishing pages. Last, you deleted the page title from the template.

USE TEMPLATES
TO CREATE PAGES

What You'll Do

In this lesson, you will use the activities_pages template to create a new page in The Striped Umbrella Web site. You will add content to the editable regions, then apply the template to two existing pages in the Web site. You will also create a new page based on the template.

Creating Pages with Templates

There are many advantages to using a template to create a page. First, it saves a lot of time, because part of the content and format of your page is already set. Second, it ensures that the page you create matches the look and format of other pages in the site. You can create a page based on a template using many different methods. One way is to click File on the menu bar, click New to open the New Document dialog box, click the Templates tab, select the template you want to use, then click Create. Templates can be used only in the Web site that contains them.

> **QUICK**TIP
>
> You can also create a new page based on a template by right-clicking (Win) or [control]-clicking (Mac) a template in the Assets panel, then clicking New from Template.

Modifying Editable Regions

When you create a new page that is based on a template, certain areas of the new page will be locked. You can tell which areas are locked by the appearance of the mouse pointer. When positioned over a locked region, the mouse pointer will appear in the shape of a circle with a line cutting through it, as shown in Figure 9. Editable regions are outlined in blue and marked with a blue, shaded label.

Editing, deleting, or adding content in editable regions of a template-based page works just like it does on any other page. Simply select the element you want to modify and make your changes, or click in the editable region and insert the new content.

Creating Links in Template-based Pages

When you add a link to a page that is based on a template, it is important to use document-relative links. If you use links that are not document-relative, they will not work. The path to a link actually goes from the template file (not from the template-based page) to the linked page. To ensure that all of your links are document-relative, select the page element to which you want to add a link, then drag the Point to File icon from the Property inspector to the page you

FIGURE 9
Working with a template-based page

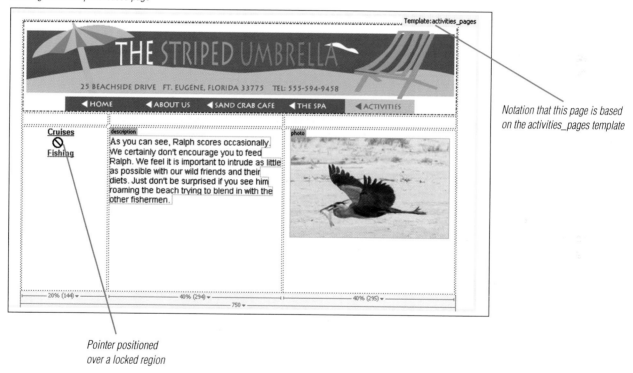

Notation that this page is based on the activities_pages template

Pointer positioned over a locked region

want to link to in the Files panel, as shown in Figure 10.

Attaching a Template to an Existing Page

Sometimes you might need to apply a template to a page that you have already created. For example, suppose you create a page for your department in your company's Web site, then your manager tells you that it must be based on the template created by the marketing department.

Before you attach a template to an existing page, you should delete any elements from your page that also appear in the template. For instance, if both your page and the template have a company logo, you should delete the logo on your page. If you don't delete it, the logo will appear twice. Once you delete all the duplicate content on your page, attach the template by opening your page, selecting the template in the Assets panel, and clicking Apply in the Assets panel. When you do this, the Inconsistent

Region Names dialog box opens, allowing you to specify in which regions of the template to place the document head and body content from your page.

QUICKTIP

You can also attach a template to an open page by dragging the template from the Assets panel to the document window.

FIGURE 10
Using the Point to File icon to specify a document-relative link

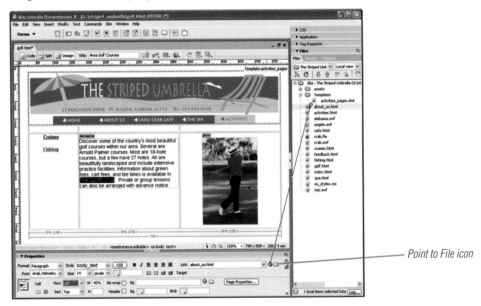

Point to File icon

Creating and Using Templates

FIGURE 11

New from Template dialog box

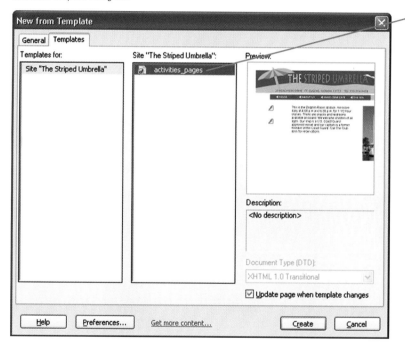

Click to create new page based on the activities_pages template

Create a new page based on a template

1. Click **File** on the menu bar, click **New**, then click the **Templates tab** (if necessary) to open the New from Template dialog box.

2. Click **Site "The Striped Umbrella"** in the Templates for list box, click **activities_pages** in the Site "The Striped Umbrella" list box (if necessary), compare your screen to Figure 11, then click **Create**.

   A new untitled page opens with the activities_pages template applied to it.

3. Click **File** on the menu bar, click **Save As** to open the Save As dialog box, type **golf.html** in the File name text box, then click **Save**.

   TIP Another way to create a new page based on a template is to open a new untitled page, click the Templates list arrow on the Insert bar, click Make Template to open the Save As Template dialog box, select a template in the Existing templates text box, then click Save.

You created a new page in The Striped Umbrella Web site that has the activities_pages template applied to it. You then saved this page as golf.html.

Modify editable regions in a template

1. Type **Area Golf Courses** in the Title text box.

2. Select the boats graphic, delete it, then insert golfer.jpg from the chapter_10 Data Files assets folder in the photo editable region, adding **Golfer swinging a club** as the alternate text.

3. Place the insertion point in the description editable region, select and delete the existing text, then use the Import Word Document command to import golf.doc.

   TIP If you are using a Macintosh, you'll need to copy and paste the text into Dreamweaver.

4. Select all of the new text, then apply the body_text style to it.

5. Compare your screen to Figure 12.

You deleted content from the editable region of a new golf page based on the activities_pages template. You then replaced the image in the photo editable region and imported text to replace the text in the description editable region.

Add links to template-based pages

1. Select the text "The Sports Club" in the paragraph, then use the **Point to File icon** ⊕ in the Property inspector to link the file about_us.html to the selected text, as shown in Figure 13.

2. Save and close the golf.html page.

You used the Point to File icon to link a file to the selected text.

FIGURE 12
Golf page with revised content in editable regions

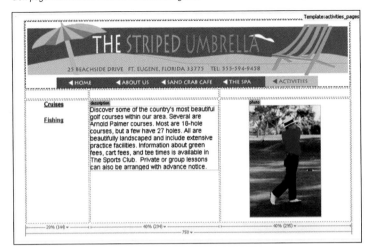

FIGURE 13
Dragging the Point to File icon to about_us.html in the Files panel

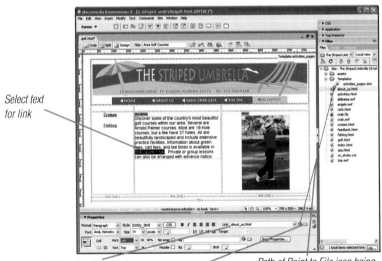

Select text for link

Link to about_us.html page

Point to File icon

Path of Point to File icon being dragged to about_us.html

Creating and Using Templates

FIGURE 14
Copying information from the original fishing.html page to the new fishing.html page based on a template

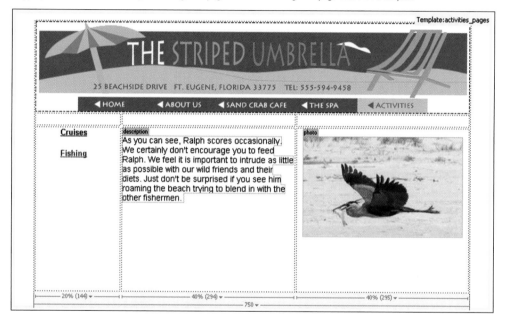

Convert existing pages to template-based pages

1. Open the fishing page.

2. Copy the paragraph text on the right side of the page, then close the fishing page.

3. Create a new HTML page based on the activities_pages template.

4. Replace the paragraph in the template with the paragraph you copied from the fishing page, as shown in Figure 14.

5. Delete the boat image and replace it with the heron_small.jpg image by dragging it from the assets folder into the photo editable region, adding **Ralph and his "catch"** for the alternate text.

6. Title the page **Fishing at The Striped Umbrella**, save the file as **fishing.html**, overwriting the existing file, compare your screen with Figure 14, then close the page.

7. Repeat Step 3 to create a new cruises page based on the activities_pages template. You will not have to replace any of the content because this is the page that was used for the template.

8. Enter **The Dolphin Racer** as the page title, then save and close the file.

You created a new HTML page based on a template and replaced text and images in the page. You then made an existing page into a template-based page.

USE TEMPLATES TO
UPDATE A SITE

What You'll Do

 In this lesson, you will make a change to the activities_pages template, then update the site so that all pages based on the template reflect the change.

Making Changes to a Template

If you create a successful site that draws large numbers of faithful viewers, your site will probably enjoy a long life. However, like everything else, Web sites need to change with the times. Your company might decide to make new products or offer new services. It might get purchased in a leveraged buy-out by a multi-million-dollar conglomerate. When changes occur in your company, on a large or small scale, you will need to make changes to your Web site's appearance and functionality. If your Web site pages are based on a template or group of templates, you will have a much easier time making those changes.

You use the same skills to make changes to a template as you would when creating a template. Start by opening the template from the Files panel or Assets panel, then

Using Macromedia templates

If you are a licensed Dreamweaver user, you can take advantage of the large collection of beautiful templates that Macromedia creates for the exclusive use of its customers. The wide-ranging templates are a great starting point for many different types of Web sites—from weddings, to clubs, to professions, and even to special events. To preview and download the templates, go to *www.macromedia.com/software/dreamweaver/download/templates/*. You can also find other Web sites that offer templates for downloading. Go to *www.google.com* and type templates in the Search text box. Some of these sites will have a fee for downloading a template.

add, delete, or edit content as you would on any non-template-based page. You can turn locked regions into editable regions using the New Editable Region command. To change an editable region back into a locked region, select the region, click Modify on the menu bar, point to Templates, then click Remove Template Markup.

Updating All Pages Based on a Template

One of the greatest benefits of working with templates is that any change you make to a template can be made automatically to all nested templates and pages that are based on the template. When you save a template that you have made modifications to, the Update Template Files dialog box opens, asking if you want to update all the files in your site that are based on that template, as shown in Figure 15. When you click Update, the Update Pages dialog box opens and provides a summary of all the files that were updated.

FIGURE 15
Update Template Files dialog box

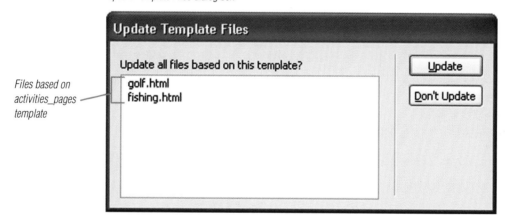

Files based on activities_pages template

Make changes to a template

1. Open the activities_pages template.

2. Click the insertion point after the second link, then press **[Enter]** (Win) **or [return]** (Mac).

3. Create a third link using the word **Golfing** that will link to the golf page, then compare your screen to Figure 16.

4. Open the fishing page.

   The new link does not appear because you have not yet saved the template and updated the site.

5. Close the fishing page.

You opened the activities_pages template and added a new link.

FIGURE 16

activities_pages template with new link added

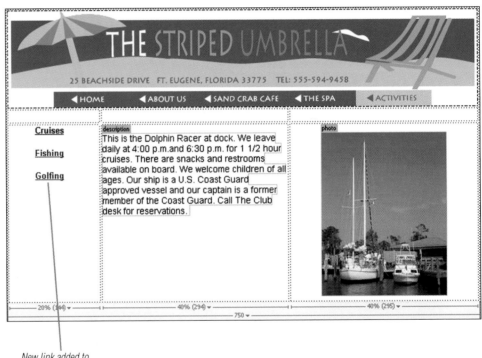

New link added to link to template

Creating and Using Templates

FIGURE 17
Update Pages dialog box

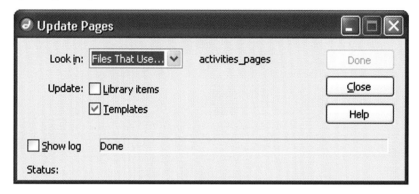

Update all template-based pages in a site

1. Return to the activities_pages template (if necessary), click **File** on the menu bar, then click **Save All**.

    The Update Template Files dialog box opens.

2. Click **Update** to open the Update Pages dialog box, as shown in Figure 17.

3. Close the Update Pages dialog box when it is finished.

4. Open the fishing page, then compare your screen to Figure 18.

    The fishing page, the cruises page, and the golf page in the Web site now show the new link.

5. Close the fishing page and the activities_pages template.

6. Open the activities page, then type **We can also arrange tee times for you at area golf courses**. at the end of the paragraph with the links to the cruises and fishing pages.

7. Link the text **tee times** to golf.html, then save and close the activities page.

You saved the activities_pages template and used the Update Template Files dialog box and the Update Pages dialog box to specify that all pages in the site based on the template be updated to reflect the template modifications.

FIGURE 18
Fishing page with template changes incorporated

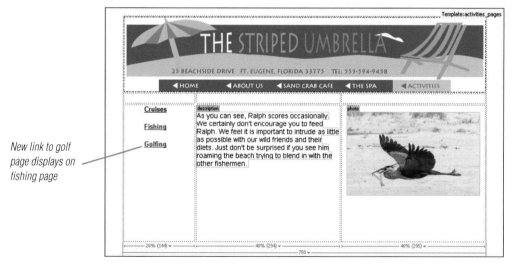

New link to golf page displays on fishing page

USE ADVANCED TEMPLATE
OPTIONS

What You'll Do

 In this lesson, you will learn about advanced template settings that can be used for more complex templates.

Setting Parameters for Optional Regions

If your template will be used by many people, it might be a good idea to include several optional regions in it so that users of the template can pick and choose from a wide range of content elements. You might also want to set parameters for optional regions, specifying that they are displayed or hidden based on specific conditions. For instance, let's say you have two optional regions named red and blue, respectively. You could set the blue optional region parameter to red so that the blue optional region would appear only when the red optional region is showing, and would be hidden only when the red optional region is hidden. Use the Advanced settings in the New Optional Region dialog box to set the parameters of an optional region. You can also write a conditional expression based on JavaScript. For instance, you could write the expression *red == false* to specify that the blue optional region appear only when the red optional region is hidden.

Nesting Templates

If you are working on a complex Web site that has many different pages used by different people or departments, you might need to create **nested templates**, which are templates that are based on another template. Nested templates are helpful when you want to define a page or parts of a page in greater detail. An advantage of using nested templates is that any changes made to the original template can be automatically updated in the nested template.

To create a nested template, create a new page based on the original template, then use the Save as Template command to save the page as a nested template. You can then make changes to the nested template by adding or deleting content and defining new editable regions. Note that editable regions in the original template are passed on as editable regions to the nested template. However, if you add a new editable or optional region to an editable region that was passed on from the original template, the original editable region changes to a locked region in the nested template.

Creating Editable Attributes

There might be times when you want users of your template to be able to change certain attributes of an element in a locked region. For instance, perhaps you want to give users the ability to change the cell background color of the top row in a repeating table, or change the source file for an image in a locked area of the template. You can use the Editable Tag Attributes dialog box, shown in Figure 19, to specify that certain attributes of locked regions be editable.

To do this, choose an attribute of a selected element, specify to make it editable, assign it a label, and specify its type and its default setting. When you define editable attributes of elements in locked regions, template users can make changes to the element's attributes using the Template Properties dialog box.

FIGURE 19
Editable Tag Attributes dialog box

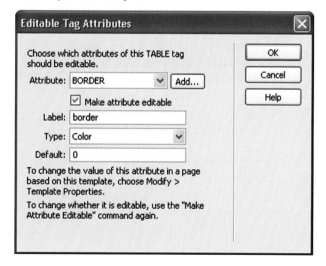

Create templates with editable and optional regions.

1. Open the blooms & bulbs Web site that you created and developed in Chapters 1 through 9, then open the plants page.
2. Save the plants page as a template called **plant_categories** and update the links.
3. Delete the bottom three rows in the table, then delete the content from the next two rows. You should have only the banner, navigation bar, and two empty rows left.
4. Type **Annuals - Perennials - Water Plants** in the top row (make sure there is a space before and after each dash), then set the cell horizontal alignment to Center.
5. Link the Annuals text to the annuals.html page, the Perennials text to the perennials.html page, and the Water Plants text to the water_plants.html page.

6. Insert an editable region named **image** in the first cell in the last row and an editable region named **description** in the second cell in the last row.
7. Set the horizontal alignment of the first cell in the bottom row to Center, and then set the vertical alignment to Top.
8. Set the horizontal alignment of the second cell in the bottom row to Left, and then set the vertical alignment to Top.
9. Save and close the plant_categories template.

Use templates to create pages.

1. Create a new page from the plant_categories template, then save it as **annuals.html**, overwriting the existing file.
2. Replace the placeholder text in the image editable area with the fuchsia.jpg file from

the Web site assets folder and type **Fuchsia** as the alternate text.
3. Open annuals.doc from the chapter_10 Data Files folder, then copy and paste the text from the file into the description editable area.
4. Apply the seasons style to the Annuals heading and the bodytext style to the paragraph text, then save and close the page.
5. Repeat Steps 1 through 4 to create a new perennials page based on the plant_categories template, using the iris.jpg image, and the perennials.doc text.
6. Repeat Steps 1 through 4 to create a new water_plants page based on the plant_categories template, using the water_hyacinth.jpg image and the water_plants.doc text.

Use templates to update a site.

1. Open the plant_categories template, then insert a horizontal rule that is 80% long and left-aligned in the right cell in the second row.
2. Create a style that defines the hr tag in the blooms_styles.css file as color #000066.
3. Change the width of the first cell in the last row to 45% and the width of the second cell in the last row to 55%.
4. Apply the subheading style to the three links.
5. Save the template and the style sheet file, then update all files in the site that are based on the template.
6. Preview all pages in your browser, compare your annuals page to Figure 20, close the browser, then close all open pages.

FIGURE 20

Completed Skills Review

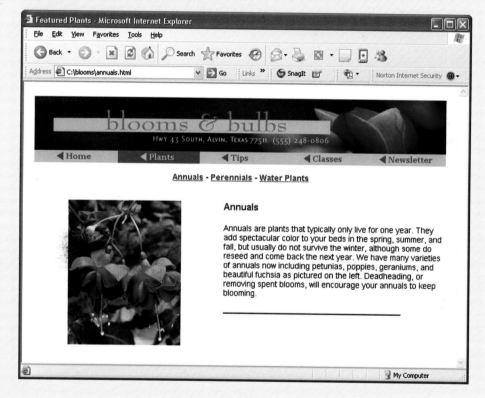

In this Project Builder, you will use a template to enhance the TripSmart Web site that you began in Project Builder 1 in Chapter 1. Use Figure 21 as a guide as you work with the template.

1. Open the TripSmart Web site that you created in Chapters 1 through 9.
2. Open the catalog page, save it as a template named **catalog_pages**, update the links, then delete the catalog.html page.
3. Open the services page, select the text link "on-line catalog", then break the link to the catalog page, because it has been deleted, then close the page.
4. Switch back to the template, then select the text label "Protection from harmful UV rays" and use it to create an editable region named **description1**.
5. Select the text label "Cool, lightweight, versatile" and use it to create an editable region named **description2**.
6. Select the text label "Pockets for everything" and use it to create an editable region named **description3**.

7. Select the hat and use it to create an editable region named **image1**.
8. Repeat Step 6 to make editable regions called **image2** from the pants image and **image3** from the vest image.
9. Create editable regions called **name1**, **name2**, and **name3** using the text Safari Hat, Kenya Convertible Pants, and Photographer's Vest.
10. Select each item number and create editable regions called **item_number1**, **item_number2**, and **item_number3**.
11. Select each price and make editable regions named **price1**, **price2**, and **price3**. (*Hint*: You may need to reposition the layer.)
12. Save and close the template.
13. Create a new page based on the catalog_pages template and save it as **clothing.html**. Because all the information is intact from the template, you do not need to alter it.
14. Save and close the clothing.html page.
15. Create a new page based on the catalog_pages template and save it as **accessories.html**.
16. Use Figure 21 as a guide to replace the images in the editable regions with the

images **packing_cube_large.jpg**, **headphones.jpg**, and **passport_holder.jpg** from the chapter_10 Data Files assets folder, then add appropriate alternate text.
17. Refer to Figure 21 and the following text to replace the text in the rest of the editable regions:

description1	**Makes packing a snap**
description2	**Block out annoying noises**
description3	**Organize your documents**
name1	**Packing Cube**
name2	**Headphones**
name3	**Passport Holder**
item_number1	**74983**
item_number2	**29857**
item_number3	**87432**
price1	**$20, $15, $10**
price2	**$40.00**
price3	**$22.50**

18. Save and close the accessories page.
19. Open the catalog_pages template and replace the catalog navigation bar link with two links: **Clothing** and **Accessories**.

Creating and Using Templates

20. Link the Clothing text to the clothing.html file and link the Accessories text to the accessories.html file.

21. Save the template and update the pages based on the template.

22. Open each page in the Web site and replace the catalog link with the two new links. (*Hint*: You can copy the new links and paste them in place on each page as long as you do not copy them from the template page. Because the template is in the Templates folder, the links are slightly different.)

23. Save all pages and preview them in the browser, testing each link.

FIGURE 21
Sample Project Builder 1

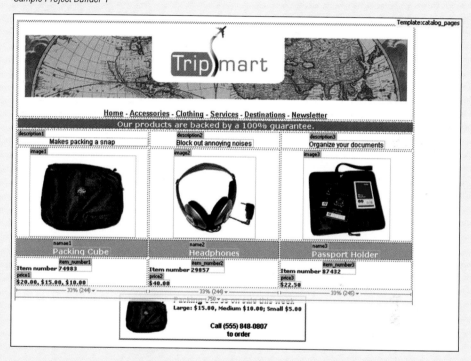

In this Project Builder, you will continue your work on the emma's book bag Web site that you started in Project Builder 2 in Chapter 1. Emma Claire would like to make sure that the pages of the Web site have a consistent appearance. She has asked you to create a template based on the home page that contains a large editable region for the main content for each page.

1. Open the emma's book bag Web site, then create a new template from the index page named **main_pages.dwt** and update the links. Click OK to close the warning message.

2. Select the text above the horizontal rule and create an editable region from it named **main_content**.

3. Save and close the template.

4. Create a new file based on the main_pages template and name it **index.html**, overwriting the existing index page.

5. Save and close the new index page.

6. Create another new page based on the main_pages template, then open the books page.

7. Copy the content from the books page, close the books page, then paste the content you copied into the editable area in the new unsaved file, replacing the original placeholder content.

8. Save the file as **books.html**, overwriting the existing file.

9. Repeat Steps 6 through 8 to create another page based on the main_pages template

that will replace the cafe page. This time you will need to insert a table in the editable region to hold the content that you copy from the original cafe page. Use Figure 22 as a guide.

10. Repeat Steps 6 through 8 to create another page based on the main_pages template that will replace the corner page.

11. Repeat Steps 6 through 8 to create another page based on the main_pages template that will replace the events page.

12. Repeat Steps 6 through 8 to create two new pages based on the main_pages template that will replace the seasonal and signings pages.

13. Save all files, preview the pages in the browser, testing all links, then close the browser and make any spacing adjustments as needed.

14. Close and save all open files.

FIGURE 22
Completed Project Builder 2

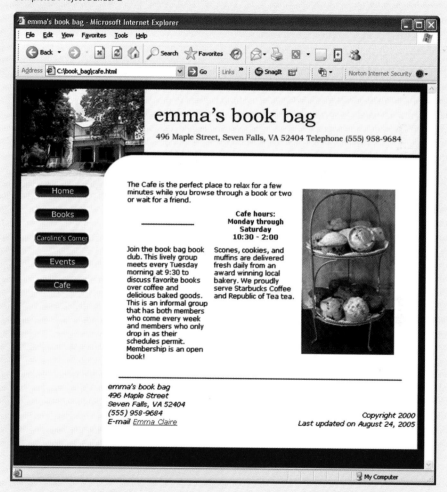

Macromedia offers registered users of Dreamweaver the benefit of downloading and using professionally designed templates from their Web site. There are a wide range of templates that are appropriate for different kinds of organizations and events. Figure 23 shows the Macromedia Web site with several templates available as free downloads for licensed Dreamweaver customers.

1. Connect to the Internet, then go to *www.course.com*. Navigate to the page for this book, click the Online Companion, then click the link for this chapter.

2. Spend some time exploring the templates on this site by previewing each one and opening each page.

3. Think of an idea for a new site that you would like to create. The site can be for a club, organization, event, or any topic or person that interests you. Draw an outline and a sketch of the site, including the content that will be on each page.

4. After you have completed your sketch, look through the Macromedia templates available at the Online Companion, then choose an appropriate template for your site. (*Note*: Skip to Step 9 if downloading files is not permitted.)

5. Download the template and copy the folder that contains the template files to a folder on your computer or external drive.

6. Use Dreamweaver to define a new site with an appropriate name that uses the site folder you downloaded as the root directory. Specify the Images folder as the default folder for images.

7. Open the site, then modify the pages of the sample site to match your site sketch. Replace any placeholder graphics, text, and other elements with content that is appropriate for your site's subject.

8. Save all pages in your site, preview them in a browser, print out each page, then close your browser and close all open pages.

9. If you are unable to download files, choose an appropriate template from the site and print out each page. Mark up each printed page, indicating how you would modify the template elements or replace particular elements with content appropriate for your site.

FIGURE 23
Design Project

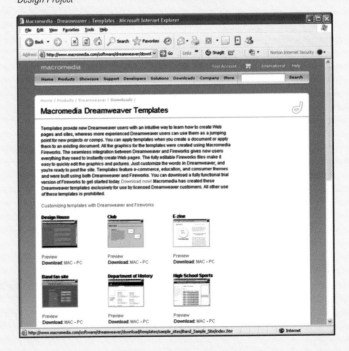

Creating and Using Templates

In this assignment, you will continue to work on the Web site that you created in Chapters 1 through 9.

You will continue to enhance your Web site by using templates. You will first create a template from one of your existing pages and define editable and optional regions in it. You will also insert a repeating table and set editable attributes for specific elements. You will then apply the template to a page and add content to the editable regions.

1. Consult your storyboard and decide which page you would like to save as a template. You will use the template to create at least one other page in your site.
2. Create a sketch of the template page you will create. Mark the page elements that will be in locked regions. Identify and mark at least one area that will be an editable region.
3. Create a new template, then define the editable regions in the template.

4. Make any necessary formatting adjustments to make sure it looks attractive, and then save the template. Create a new page based on the template, using the same name as the page on which the template is based, so that the earlier version of the page is overwritten.
5. Apply the template to another existing page of the site, making sure to delete all repeating elements contained in the template.

6. Review the template(s) and the template-based pages, and decide if you need to make improvements. Use the check list in Figure 24 to make sure you completed everything according to the assignment.
7. Make any necessary changes.
8. Save your work, then close all open pages.

FIGURE 24
Portfolio Project check list

Web Site Check List
1. Does your template include at least one editable region?
2. Are all links on templates-based pages document-relative?
3. Do all editable regions have appropriate names?
4. Do all links work correctly?
5. Do all pages view well using at least two different browsers?

11

WORKING WITH LIBRARY
ITEMS AND SNIPPETS

1. Create and modify library items.

2. Add library items to pages.

3. Add and modify snippets.

WORKING WITH LIBRARY
ITEMS AND SNIPPETS

Introduction

When creating a Web site, chances are good that you will want certain graphics or text blocks to appear in more than one place in the site. For instance, you might want the company tag line in several different places, or a footer containing links to the main pages of the site at the bottom of every page. Library items and snippets can help you work with these repeating elements more efficiently.

Understanding Library Items

If you want an element to appear repeatedly, then it's a good idea to save it as a library item. A **library item** is content that can contain text or graphics and is saved in a separate file in the Library folder of your Web site. The advantage of using library items is that when you make a change to the library item and then update the site, all instances of that item will be updated to reflect the change.

Understanding Snippets

Another way to use the same content repeatedly throughout a site is to insert code snippets. **Code snippets** are reusable pieces of code that can be inserted on a page. Dreamweaver provides a wide variety of ready-made code snippets you can use to create footers, drop-down menus, headers, and other elements.

In this chapter, you will work with library items and code snippets to enhance The Striped Umbrella Web site.

Tools You'll Use

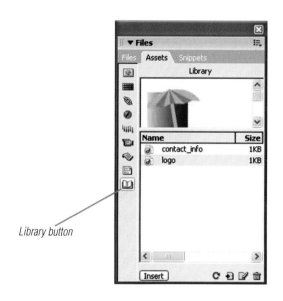

Library button

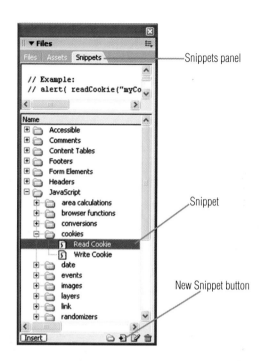

Snippets panel

Snippet

New Snippet button

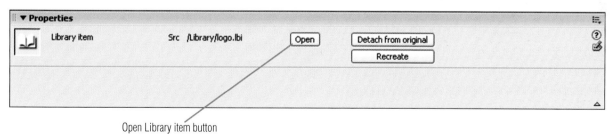

Open Library item button

CREATE AND MODIFY
LIBRARY ITEMS

What You'll Do

In this lesson, you will create a text-based library item. You will also create a library item that contains a graphic in the activities_pages template. You will then edit both library items and update the site to reflect those edits.

Understanding the Benefits of Library Items

Using library items for repetitive elements—especially those that need to be updated frequently—can save you considerable time. For instance, suppose you want to feature an employee of the month photograph on every page in your site. You could create a library item named employee_photo and add it to every page. Then, when you need to update the site to show a new employee photo, you could simply replace the photo contained in the library item, and the photo would be updated throughout the site. Library items can contain a wide range of content, including text, images, tables, and sounds.

Viewing and Creating Library Items

To view library items, show the Assets panel, then click the Library button. The library items appear in a list, and a preview of the selected library item appears above the list,

as shown in Figure 1. To save text or an image as a library item, select the item in the document window, then drag it to the Assets panel. You can also click Modify on the menu bar, point to Library, then click Add Object to Library. The item that you dragged will appear in the preview window in the Assets panel and in the library item list with the temporary name Untitled assigned to it. Type a new name, then press [Enter] (Win) or [return] (Mac) to give the library item a permanent name. Library items on a Web page appear in shaded yellow in the document window. When you click a library item in the document window, the entire item is selected and the Property inspector changes to display three buttons that you can use to work with the library item, as shown in Figure 2.

> QUICKTIP
>
> You can also view a list of available library items by expanding the Library folder in the Files panel.

Modifying Library Items

You cannot edit library items on the Web pages in which they appear. In order to make changes to a library item, you have to open it. To open a library item, select the item in the document window, then click Open in the Property inspector. The library item will appear in the document window, where you can make edits or add content to it. When you are satisfied with your edits, save the library item using the Save command on the File menu. When you do this, the Update Library Items dialog box will appear, asking if you want to update all instances of the library item throughout the site.

FIGURE 1
Library items in Assets panel

FIGURE 2
Web page containing library item

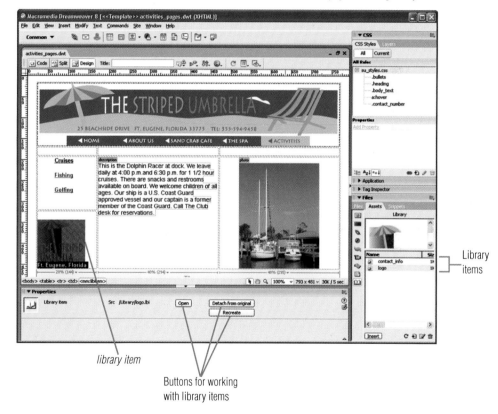

Preview of selected library item

Library items

Library button

library item

Buttons for working with library items

Library items

Create a text-based library item

1. Open The Striped Umbrella Web site, then open the index page.

2. Create a new rule in the su_styles.css file called **contact_number** with the following settings: Font = **Arial, Helvetica, sans-serif**, Size = **small**, Color = **#000099**, Weight = **bold**, Text align = **center**.

3. Insert two new rows at the bottom of the table in the index page, merge the cells in the last row, then type **The Striped Umbrella 1-555-594-9458**.

4. Apply the contact_number style to the text you typed in Step 3.

5. With the insertion point in the cell with the telephone number, click the **Background Color button (Bg)** ☐ on the Property inspector, then click **#66CCFF** to set the cell background color, as shown in Figure 3.

   The cell background is now a light blue, setting off the new text.

   (continued)

FIGURE 3
Changing row properties

Newly merged cells with blue background

Change cell background color to #66CCFF

FIGURE 4

Assets panel showing new contact_info library item

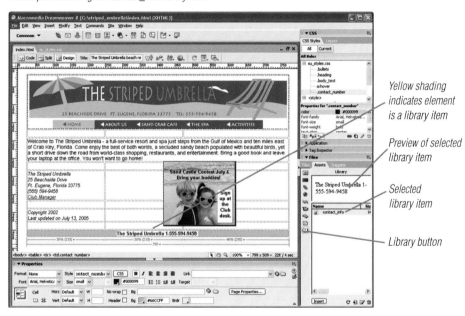

Yellow shading
indicates element
is a library item

Preview of selected
library item

Selected
library item

Library button

6. Display the Assets panel, then click the **Library button** 📖.

7. Select the line of text with the telephone number, then drag it to the Assets panel.

   The text that you dragged is now an unnamed library item in the Assets panel.

8. Type **contact_info**, press **[Enter]** (Win) or **[return]** (Mac) to name the library item, deselect the library item, then compare your screen to Figure 4.

   Notice that the contact information now has a very lightly shaded yellow background, indicating it is a library item.

9. Save and close all open files.

You created a text-based library item from text on the index page.

Create an image-based library item

1. Click the **Templates button** 🗏 on the Assets panel, then double-click the **activities_pages template** to open it.

2. Click the **Library button** 📖 on the Assets panel to display the library item in the Web site.

3. Split the cell with the three text links into two rows, then insert the su_logo.jpg from the chapter_11 Data Files folder in the bottom cell of the newly split cells.

4. Type **The Striped Umbrella logo** as the alternate text.

5. Click to the right of the logo, press **[Shift] [Enter]** (Win) or **[Shift][return]** (Mac) to insert a line break, then type **Ft. Eugene, Florida**, then apply the bullets style, as shown in Figure 5.

6. Click the **Vert list arrow** on the Property inspector, then click **Bottom** to set the cell's vertical alignment.

(continued)

FIGURE 5
Adding text below The Striped Umbrella logo on the activities_pages template

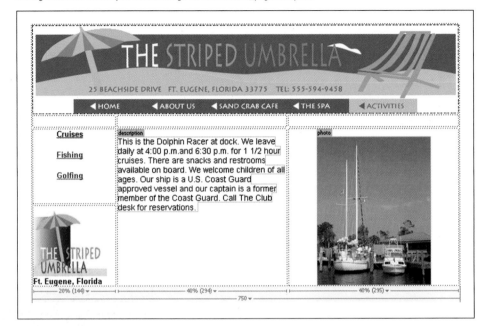

FIGURE 6
logo library item added to Assets panel

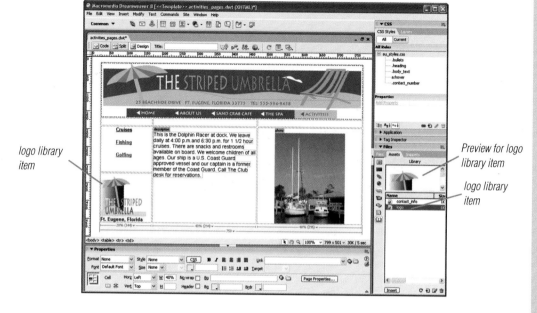

logo library item

Preview for logo library item

logo library item

7. Select the logo and address, drag the selection to the Library in the Assets panel, then click **OK** to close the dialog box warning you that the style was not copied (if necessary).

   The image and text are stored as one library item and appear in the preview window at the top of the Assets panel. A new untitled library item appears selected in the library item list.

8. Type **logo**, press **[Enter]** (Win) or **[return]** (Mac) to name the library item in the Assets panel, then compare your screen to Figure 6.

9. Save your changes, then click **Update** to open the Update Pages dialog box.

10. Click the **Look in list arrow**, click **Entire Site**, check the **Library items** and **Templates** check boxes, as shown in Figure 7, then click **Start**.

    Dreamweaver updates your files based on the changes made to the library item.

11. Click **Close**, open the golf page to view the library item on the page, then close the golf page.

You created a library item named logo that contains an image and text in the activities_pages template. You then saved the template and updated all pages in the site.

FIGURE 7
Update Pages dialog box with Library items and Templates check boxes checked

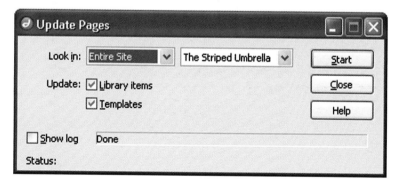

Edit an image-based library item

1. Click the **su_logo.jpg** image at the bottom of the activities_pages template.

2. Click **Open** in the Property inspector to open the logo library item.

    The image and text appear in the document window. The title bar displays the filename logo.lbi. The file extension .lbi denotes a library file.

    | TIP You can also open a library item by double-clicking it in the Assets panel.

3. Click the image in the document window, then click the **Crop button** ☒ in the Property inspector.

4. Click **OK** to the message warning "This operation will change the original image file."

    An outline surrounds the image, as shown in Figure 8. The outline is used to crop the image.

    (continued)

FIGURE 8
Preparing to crop the logo

Drag the right edge slightly to crop the image

The border and handles indicate you can crop the image

Ft. Eugene, Florida

FIGURE 9
Viewing the cropped logo

Ft. Eugene, Florida

5. Drag the right edge toward the center of the image to crop the right edge of the graphic, lining it up with the line of text underneath it.

6. When you are satisfied with the crop, double-click the middle of the image, then compare your screen to Figure 9.

You opened the logo library item, then cropped the image.

Update library items

1. Click **File** on the menu bar, then click **Save** to open the Update Library Items dialog box.

   The dialog box asks if you want to update the library item on the pages shown.

2. Click **Update** to open the Update Pages dialog box.

3. Click the **Look in list arrow**, click **Entire Site**, check the **Library items** and **Templates** check boxes, then click **Start**.

   Dreamweaver updates your files based on the changes made to the library item.

4. Click **Close**, close the logo.lbi file, then switch to the activities_pages template.

   Notice that the page reflects the change you made to the logo library item.

5. Compare your screen to Figure 10.

6. Close the activities_pages template.

You saved the logo library item and updated all pages in the site to incorporate the changes you made.

FIGURE 10

activities_pages template showing the updated logo library item

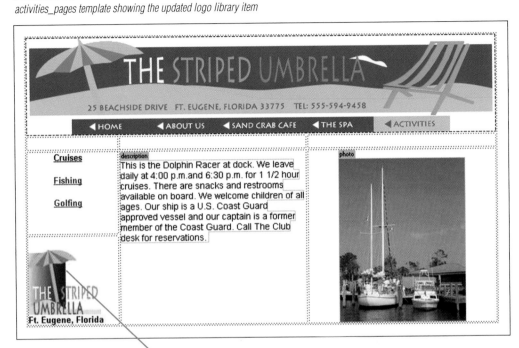

Logo is slightly
cropped

Working with Library Items and Snippets

FIGURE 11

contact_info library item after editing

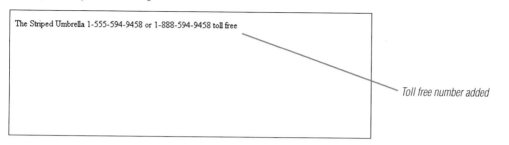

The Striped Umbrella 1-555-594-9458 or 1-888-594-9458 toll free

— Toll free number added

FIGURE 12

Page reflects edits made to contact_info library item

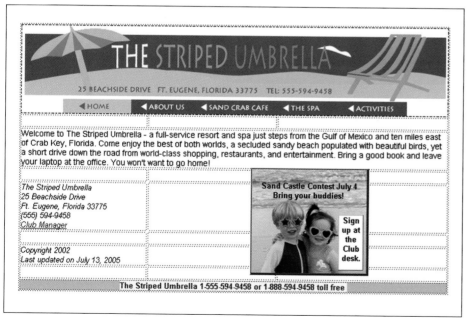

1. Open the index page (if necessary), then click the **telephone text** to select the contact_info library item.

2. Click **Open** in the Property inspector to open the contact_info library item.

3. Type **or 1-888-594-9458 toll free**, then compare your screen to Figure 11.

4. Save your changes, update the site, then close the contact_info library item.

5. Switch to the index page, then compare your screen to Figure 12.

   The text reflects the edits you made to the contact_info library item.

You edited the text in the contact_info library item, then saved the changes and updated the site.

ADD LIBRARY ITEMS
TO PAGES

What You'll Do

 In this lesson, you will add a text-based library item you created to the about us, activities, cafe, feedback, and spa pages. You will detach the library item on the index page and edit it. You will then delete one of the library items and restore the deleted item using the Recreate command.

Adding Library Items to a Page

Once you create a library item, it's easy to add it to any page in a Web site. All you need to do is drag the library item from the Assets panel to the desired location on the page. When you insert a library item, the actual content and a reference to the library item are copied into the code. The inserted library item is shaded in yellow in the document window and will be automatically updated to reflect any changes you make to the library item.

> QUICKTIP
>
> You can also insert a library item on a page by selecting the item in the Assets panel, then clicking Insert.

There may be times when you don't want content to be updated when you update the library item. For instance, suppose you want one of your pages to include photos of all past employees of the month. You would insert content from the current library item, but you do not want the photo to change when the library item is

updated to reflect next month's employee photo. To achieve this, you would insert the content of a library item on a page without inserting the reference to the library item. To do this, press and hold [Alt] (Win) or [option] (Mac) as you drag the library item from the Assets panel to the document window. The content from the library item will be inserted on the page, but it will not be linked to the library item.

Making Library Items Editable on a Page

There may be times when you would like to make changes to a particular instance of a library item on one page, without making those changes to other instances of the library item in the site. You can make a library item editable on a page by breaking its link to the library item. To do this, select the library item, then click Detach from original in the Property inspector. Once you have detached the library item, you can edit the content like you would any other element on the page.

Keep in mind, though, that this edited content will not be updated when you make changes to the library item.

Deleting and Recreating Library Items

If you know that you will never need to update a library item again, you might want to delete it. To delete a library item, select it in the Assets panel, then click the Delete button. Deleting a library item removes it from only the Library folder; it does not change the contents of the pages that contain that library item. All instances of the deleted library item will still appear in shaded yellow in the site unless you detach them from the original. Be aware that you cannot use the Undo command to bring back a library item. However, you can undelete a library item by selecting any instance of the item in the site and clicking Recreate in the Property inspector. After you recreate a library item, it reappears in the Assets panel and you can make changes to it and update all pages in the site again. Figure 13 shows the Property inspector with Library item settings.

FIGURE 13
Property inspector with Library item settings

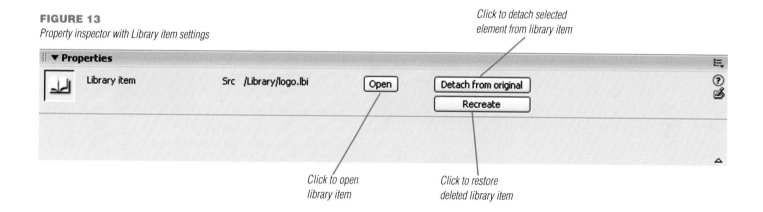

Click to detach selected
element from library item

Click to open
library item

Click to restore
deleted library item

Add a library item to a page

1. Open the about us page.

2. Insert a new row at the bottom of the table.

3. Open the Assets panel (if necessary), then drag the **contact_info library item** from the Assets panel to the new row.

   The contact_info heading now appears where you dragged it. Notice that it is shaded in yellow, indicating it is a library item.

4. Click to the right of the library item on the page, then use the Property inspector to apply the bullets style.

5. Center the cell contents, set the background color of the cell to **#66CCFF**, then compare your screen to Figure 14.

(continued)

FIGURE 14
about us page with library item added

beach for both our guests and the native vegetation. The sea oats and other fauna are tender. Please do not step on them or pick them.

The main swimming pool is directly behind The Club House. A lifeguard is on duty from 8:00 a.m. until 9:00 p.m. The pool area includes a wading pool, a lap pool, and a large pool with a diving board. Showers are located in several areas for your use before and after swimming. We also provide poolside service from the cafe for snacks and lunch.

Enjoy our lush landscaping as you explore the grounds. The beautiful sago palms flourish in our Florida weather! We have many native plants that we hope you will enjoy, both within our manicured grounds and along the beach. Remember, the wild vegetation are all protected species.

If you would like to play tennis, we have a very nice sports club. Call to reserve court times. Our clay courts are generally busy, so it's not a bad idea to schedule your games as soon as you arrive. We also have a very extensive pro shop where you can find anything you need to play. We can even restring your racket if the need arises.

Please give us your feedback so that we may make your stay the best vacation ever!

The Striped Umbrella 1-555-594-9458 or 1-888-594-9458 toll free

33% (241)   33 (120)   34% (249)

Library item

6. Save and close the about us page.

7. Repeat Steps 2 through 5 to add the contact_info library item to the activities page, as shown in Figure 15, then continue with the cafe, feedback, and spa pages.

   If the page already has an empty row, there is no need to add a new row.

8. Preview all of the edited pages in the browser, then close the browser.

9. Close and save all open pages.

You added the contact_info library item to the about us, activities, cafe, feedback, and spa pages.

FIGURE 15

activities page with library item added

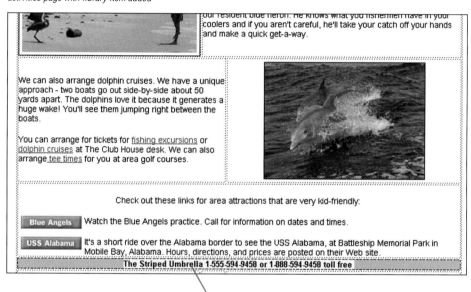

Library item

Creating library items

Although you can create library items with graphics, text, or a combination of the two, you can use only items that contain body elements. For instance, when editing a library item, the CSS Styles panel will be unavailable because style sheet code is embedded in the head section, rather than just the body section. Likewise, the Page Properties dialog box will be unavailable because library items cannot include a body tag attribute such as text color. You can apply a style after you have placed the library item on the page.

Make a library item editable on a page

1. Open the index page, then click the **contact_info library footer** on the index page.

   The Property inspector displays three buttons relating to library items.

2. Click **Detach from original** in the Property inspector.

   A dialog box opens, warning you that the item will no longer be automatically updated when the original library item changes.

3. Click **OK**.

   Notice that the contact information no longer appears in shaded yellow, indicating it is no longer a library item.

4. Type **in Florida** after the first telephone number, then compare your screen to Figure 16.

   The contact information is edited on the page.

5. Save and close the index page.

You detached the contact information from the contact_info library item to make the text editable on the index page. You then added two words to the contact information.

FIGURE 16

Editing a library item on a page

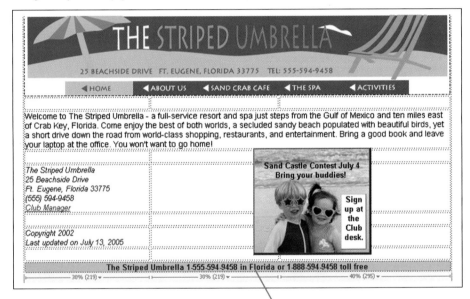

"in Florida" added to text

FIGURE 17

Assets panel after deleting the logo library item

Logo no longer appears

Delete button

FIGURE 18

Assets panel after recreating the logo library item

Recreated logo library item

Delete a library item

1. Select the **logo library item** in the Assets panel.

2. Click the **Delete button** 🗑 in the Assets panel.

   A dialog box opens, asking if you are sure you want to delete the library item.

3. Click **Yes**, then compare your screen to Figure 17.

   The logo library item no longer appears in the Assets panel.

You deleted the logo library item in the Assets panel.

Recreate a library item

1. Open the activities_pages template.

   The logo still appears in shaded yellow, indicating it is still a library item, even though you deleted the library item to which it is attached.

2. Click the **logo** to select it.

3. Click **Recreate** in the Property inspector, then compare your screen to Figure 18.

   The logo library item is added to the Assets panel.

   If you do not see the logo library item, recreate the site cache, then refresh the Assets panel.

4. Save and close the activities_pages template.

You recreated the logo library item that you deleted in the previous set of steps.

ADD AND MODIFY
SNIPPETS

What You'll Do

 In this lesson, you will add a predefined snippet from the Snippets panel to create a new footer for the index page. You will then replace the placeholder text and links in the snippet with appropriate text and links. Finally, you will save the modified snippet as a new snippet and add it to other pages.

Using the Snippets Panel

Creating a Web site is a huge task, so it's nice to know that you can save time by using ready-made code snippets to create various elements of your site. The Snippets panel, located in the Files panel group, contains a large collection of reusable code snippets organized in folders named by element type. The Snippets panel contains two panes, as shown in Figure 19. The lower pane contains folders that can be expanded to view the snippets. The upper pane displays a preview of the selected snippet. Use the buttons at the bottom of the Snippets panel to insert a snippet, create a new folder in the

Snippets panel, create a new snippet, edit a snippet, or remove a snippet.

Inserting and Modifying Snippets

Adding a snippet to a page is an easy task; simply drag the snippet from the Snippets panel to the desired location on the page. Once you position a snippet, you will need to replace the placeholder text, links, and images with appropriate content.

> **QUICK**TIP
>
> You can also add a snippet to a page by selecting the snippet in the Snippets panel, then clicking Insert.

Creating New Snippets

Once you've modified a snippet so that it contains text and graphics appropriate for your site, you might want to save it with a new name. Doing this will save time when using this snippet on other pages. To save a modified snippet as a new snippet, select the snippet content in the document window, then click the New Snippet button in the Snippets panel to open the Snippet dialog box. Use this dialog box to name the snippet and give it a description. Because the Snippet dialog box displays the snippet code, you can make edits to the code here if you wish. Any new snippets you create will appear in the Snippets panel.

FIGURE 19
Snippets panel

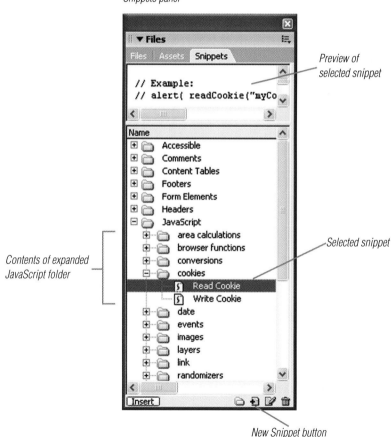

Preview of selected snippet

Selected snippet

Contents of expanded JavaScript folder

New Snippet button

Add a predefined snippet to a page

1. Open the index page.
2. Scroll to the bottom of the page, click to the right of the contact telephone numbers in the last cell, then press **[Shift] [Enter]** (Win) or **[Shift] [return]** (Mac) to add a line break.
3. Display the Files panel group, then click the **Snippets tab** to open the Snippets panel.

   TIP If the Files panel group is not open, click Window on the menu bar, then click Snippets.

4. Click the **plus sign (+)** (Win) or the **triangle** (Mac) next to the Navigation folder in the Snippets panel to display the contents of the Navigation folder, then click the **plus sign (+)** (Win) or **triangle** (Mac) next to the Horizontal folder to display the contents of the Horizontal folder.
5. Drag the **Bullet as separator** in the Horizontal folder to the bottom of the index page, under the contact telephone numbers in the last cell, as shown in Figure 20.

   This text will serve as placeholder text until you replace it with the appropriate links for The Striped Umbrella Web site.

   TIP It is always a good idea to have a navigation bar with plain text links on each main page of a Web site for accessibility purposes.

6. Save your changes.

You added a predefined navigation from the Snippets panel.

FIGURE 20
index page after editing snippet

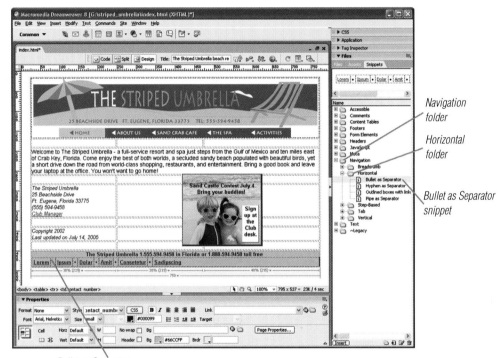

Navigation folder

Horizontal folder

Bullet as Separator snippet

Bullet as Separator snippet dragged from the Snippets panel

FIGURE 21

index page after editing snippet placeholder text

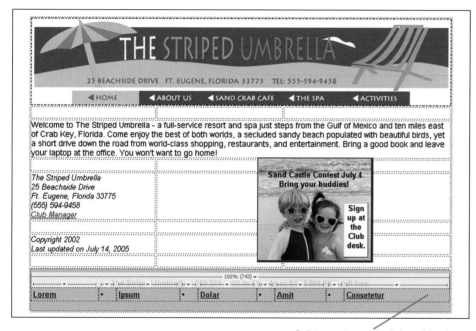

Bullet separator and last link are deleted

1. Click in the last cell of the navigation snippet with the text placeholder **"Sadipscing"**, click the **<td> tag** in the tag selector, then press **[Delete]**.

   The last link and the cell it was in are deleted.

2. Repeat Step 1 to delete the next cell to the left with the bullet.

   The bullet and cell are deleted.

3. Save your changes, then compare your screen to Figure 21.

You edited the placeholder text contained in the navigation snippet on the index page.

Modify snippet links

1. Select the **Lorem** placeholder link in the bottom row of the table, then type **Home**.

2. Replace the Ipsum placeholder link with **About Us**, replace the Dolar placeholder link with **Sand Crab Cafe**, replace the Amit placeholder link with **The Spa**, then replace the Consetetur placeholder link with Activities.

3. Select the **second table tag** in the tag selector, then change the width for the table with the navigation snippet to **60%**.

   The links are now spaced closer together.

4. Display the Files panel, select the **Home link text** at the bottom of the home page, then use the Point to File icon ⊙ in the Property inspector to set the Link property to the index page, as shown in Figure 22.

5. Use the Point to File icon ⊙ to set the Link property for the About Us, Sand Crab Cafe, The Spa, and Activities links.

6. Save your changes.

7. Preview the index page in your browser, test all the new navigation links, then close your browser.

You changed the names of the placeholder links and used the Point to File icon to create links to the five main pages in The Striped Umbrella Web site.

FIGURE 22
Using the Point to File icon to create document-relative links

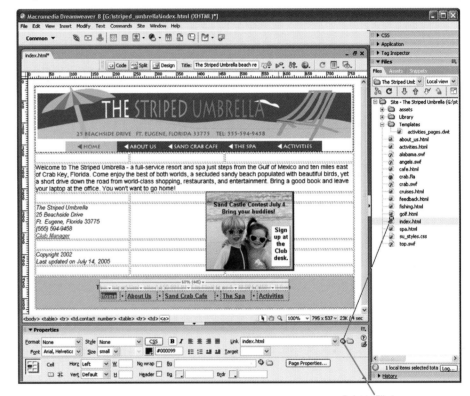

Point to File icon

Create a new snippet

1. Select the **navigation footer** on the index page.
2. Click the **New Snippet button** ➕ in the Snippets panel to open the Snippet dialog box.
3. Type **su_footer** in the Name text box.
4. Type **This is a text-based navigation bar.** in the Description text box, then compare your screen to Figure 23.
5. Click **OK**.

   The su_footer snippet now appears in the Snippets panel. You can insert it on any page by dragging it to the desired location in the document window.

6. Open the about us page, place the insertion point to the right of the telephone contact information, press **[Shift][Enter]** (Win) or **[Shift][return]** (Mac), then drag the **su_footer** from the Snippets panel to the page.
7. Repeat Step 6 to insert the su_footer snippet on the cafe, spa, and activities pages.
8. Save and preview all open pages in the browser, close each page, close the browser, then close Dreamweaver.

You copied the footer from the index page and saved it as a snippet called su_footer. You then copied it to the rest of the main pages in the Web site.

FIGURE 23
Snippet dialog box

Name text box

Description text box

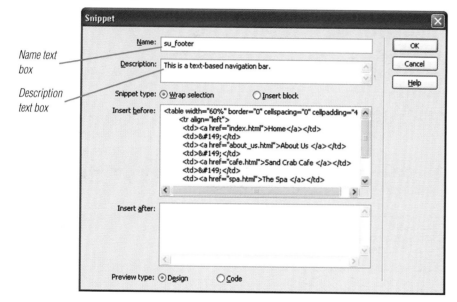

Create and modify library items.

1. Open the blooms & bulbs Web site, then open the index page.
2. Create a new style in the blooms_styles.css file called **telephone** with the following settings: Font: Verdana, Arial, Helvetica, sans-serif; Size: 14 pixels; Weight: bold; Style: normal; Color: #FFCC00.
3. Insert a new row in the table on the index page, type **blooms & bulbs (555) 248-0806** in the new row, then apply the telephone style to the text.
4. Select the text you typed in Step 3, drag it to the Assets panel with the Library category displayed to create a new library item, then name it **telephone**.
5. Set the background color of the new cell (row) to #003399, center the cell contents, then save the page.
6. Edit the library item to read 1-555-248-0806, then save the library item and update all pages with the library item.

7. Open the newsletter page, insert blooms_logo.jpg from the chaper_11 Data Files assets folder right after the e-mail link near the bottom of the page, then type **blooms & bulbs logo** as the alternate text.
8. Right-align the logo, then drag it to the Assets panel to create a new library item, then name it **logo**.
9. Save and close the newsletter page.

Add library items to pages.

1. Open the classes page, then add a new row to the bottom of the table.
2. Insert the telephone library item in the new row, apply the telephone style to the cell contents, center the telephone number, apply the telephone style to the cell contents, then set the cell background color to #003399.
3. Repeat Steps 1 and 2 to add the telephone number to the newsletter, plants, and tips pages, then save all pages.
4. Delete the telephone library item from the Assets panel.

5. Switch to the index page, select the telephone library item on the page, then re-create it.
6. Preview all pages in the browser, adjust the spacing on the page to prevent overlap, then compare your screen to Figure 24.

Add and modify snippets.

1. Scroll to the bottom of the index page and insert a new row.
2. Set the cell background color to default.
3. Insert the Bullet as Separator Horizontal Navigation snippet in the new row.

4. Delete the last link and separator, then delete the last two empty cells.
5. Replace the placeholder links in the footer with links to the home, plants, tips, classes, and newsletter pages.
6. Set the width of the table with the snippet to 50% and center the table in the row.
7. Create a new snippet from the footer you just inserted. Name the snippet **blooms_footer**, give it an appropriate description, then compare your screen with Figure 24 .
8. Insert the new footer at the bottom of the classes, newsletter, plants, and tips pages.
9. Save all pages, then preview each in the browser to test the links in the footer to make sure they work.
10. Close the browser, then close all open pages.

FIGURE 24
Completed Skills Review

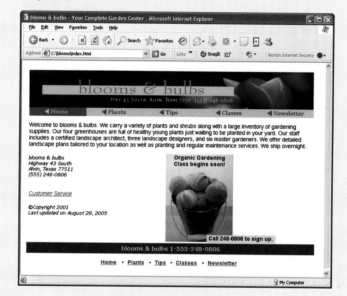

In this Project Builder you will continue your work on the TripSmart Web site that you began in Project Builder 1 in Chapter 1. You have been given the TripSmart logo to use in the Web site and decide to create a library item from the logo combined with the copyright statement.

1. Open the TripSmart Web site, then open the index page.
2. Insert a new row at the bottom of the table, then split the row into two columns.
3. Drag the address and last updated statement into the first cell in the new row, then delete the old copyright statement.
4. Insert the file tripsmart_logo.jpg from the chapter_11 Data Files assets folder into the second cell in the new row, adding **TripSmart logo** for the alternate text.
5. Type © **Copyright 2002** under the logo, then apply the item_numbers style. (*Hint*: The copyright symbol can be found under the Insert, HTML, Special Characters menu.)
6. Select both the logo and copyright statement, then use them to create a new library item called **logo**.
7. Set the first cell alignment to Left and Bottom.
8. Set the second cell alignment to Right and Bottom.

9. Save the file, preview the page in the browser, then compare your screen to Figure 25.
10. Close the browser, then make any spacing adjustments necessary to improve the page appearance.
11. Open the services page, then draw a layer in the bottom right corner of the table.

12. Drag the logo library item into the layer, then click to the right of the logo library item and apply the item_number style to it.
13. Save the file, then preview the page in the browser.
14. Close the browser, then make any necessary adjustments to improve the page appearance.
15. Close all files.

FIGURE 25
Completed Project Builder 1

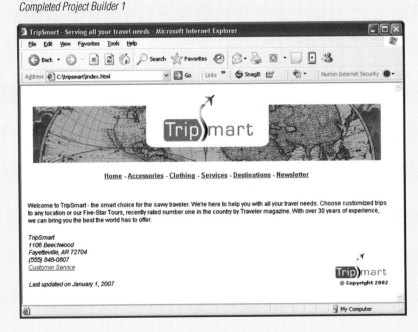

In this Project Builder, you will continue your work on the emma's book bag Web site that you started in Project Builder 2 in Chapter 1. Emma Claire has asked you to add some plain text links at the bottom of each page to provide viewers with more accessible links that do not depend on Flash. This will be easy, because all pages in the Web site are based on one template.

1. Open the emma's book bag Web site.
2. Open the main_pages.dwt template.
3. Merge the middle and last cells in the last row.
4. Insert the Pipe as Separator snippet in the merged cells. (*Hint*: This snippet is located in the Snippets panel. Open the Accessible folder, then the Navigation folder, and finally the Horizontal folder.)
5. Delete the two cells with the last text placeholder and pipe, then replace each placeholder with links to the main pages, using Figure 26 as a guide.
6. Apply the subheading style to the navigation bar, set the table width to 65%, then center it.
7. Merge the two cells above the new navigation bar, then insert a horizontal rule that matches the current one on the page.
8. Save the template, then update the pages based on the template.

9. Preview each page in the browser, then close the browser.
10. Make any adjustments to the template that will improve the page appearance, then save your work and close all open pages.

FIGURE 26
Completed Project Builder 2

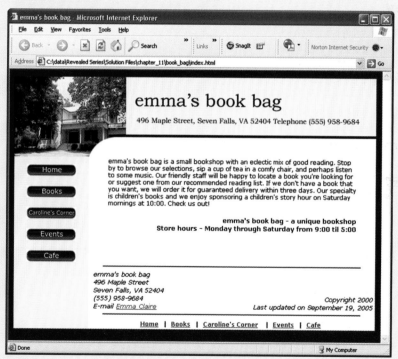

Library items and snippets are commonly used in Web sites to ensure that repetitive information is updated quickly and accurately.

1. Connect to the Internet, navigate to the page for the Online Companion, then select a link for this chapter. Figure 27 shows the www.bostonchefs.com Web site.
2. Spend some time exploring the pages of this site to become familiar with its elements. Do you see many repeating elements?
3. If you were developing this site, which images or text would you convert into library items? Print out two pages from this Web site and write a list of all the text and visual elements from these pages that you would make into library items.
4. Review a second link for this chapter, then print out two pages from the site.
5. Write a list of all the elements shown on the printed pages that you think should be made into library items.

FIGURE 27
Design Project

In this project, you will continue to work on the Web site that you created in Chapter 1.

You will continue to enhance your Web site by using library items and snippets.

1. Consult your storyboard and decide which text and graphic elements in the site should be converted into library items. Write a list of these items.
2. Discuss what content to include in a footer that you will add to each page of the site using a snippet.
3. Convert all the text elements you identified in your list into library items.
4. Insert the library items that were created in Step 3 in appropriate places in the Web site.
5. Convert all the graphic elements you identified in Step 1 into library items.
6. Insert the graphic library items that were created in Step 5 in appropriate places in the Web site.

7. Edit two of the library items that were created, then save and update all instances of the library item in the site.
8. Add a footer to the Web site using one of the snippets in the Footers folder of the Snippets panel. Replace all placeholder links with appropriate links to each major page in the site and replace placeholder text with text that is suitable for your site.

9. Create a new snippet from the footer that was created in Step 8. Insert this snippet on the other pages of the site.
10. Save your work, preview all pages in a browser, then test all the links. Use the check list in Figure 28 to make sure your Web site is complete.
11. Make any necessary changes, then save and close all open pages.

FIGURE 28
Portfolio Project check list

Web Site Check List

1. Have you converted all repeating text elements into library items?
2. Have you converted all repeating graphic elements, such as logos, into library items?
3. Did you save and update the library items after making edits to them?
4. Do all links work?
5. Did you add the footer to all pages in the Web site?

12

MANAGING A WEB
SERVER AND FILES

1. Publish a Web site and transfer files.

2. Check files out and in.

3. Cloak files.

4. Import and export a site definition.

5. Evaluate Web content for legal use.

Introduction

Once you have created all the pages of
your Web site, finalized all the content,
and performed site maintenance to ensure
that all links work, all colors are Websafe,
and all orphaned pages are eliminated, you
are ready to publish your site to a remote
server so the rest of the world can access it.
In this chapter, you will start by defining
the remote site for The Striped Umbrella
Web site. You will then transfer files to the
remote site and learn how to keep them up
to date. You will also check out a file so
that it is not available to other team members while you are editing it and learn
how to cloak files. When a file is **cloaked**
it is excluded from certain processes, such
as being transferred to the remote site.
Next, you will export the site definition file
from The Striped Umbrella Web site so
that other users can import the site.
Finally, you will research important copyright issues that affect all Web sites.

Preparing to Publish a Site

Before you publish a site to a remote
server so that it is available to the rest of

the world, it is extremely important that
you test it to make sure the content is
accurate and up to date and that everything is functioning properly. If you use
the Web at all, you have probably felt
frustrated when you click a link that
doesn't work or have to wait for pages
that load slowly because of large graphics
and animations. Remember that a typical
Web viewer has a short attention span
and limited patience. Before you publish
your site, make sure to use the Link
Checker panel to check for broken links
and orphaned files. Make sure that all
image paths are correct and that all
images load quickly and have alternate
text. Verify that all pages have titles, and
remove all Non-Websafe colors. View the
pages in at least two different browsers to
ensure that everything works correctly.
The more you test, the better the chances
that your viewers will have a positive experience and stay at your site. All content
must either be original to the Web site
or have been obtained legally without
violating any copyright laws that protect
Web site content.

Tools You'll Use

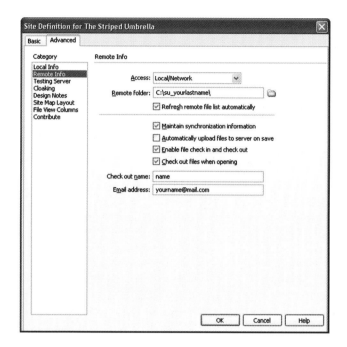

PUBLISH A WEB SITE
AND TRANSFER FILES

What You'll Do

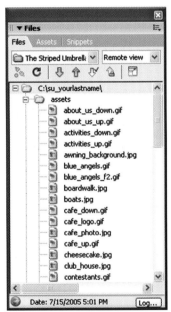

 In this lesson, you will set up remote access to either an FTP folder or a local/network folder for The Striped Umbrella Web site. You will also view a Web site on a remote server, upload files to it, and synchronize the files.

Defining a Remote Site

As you learned in Chapter 1, publishing a site means transferring all files for a site to a Web server. A **Web server** is a computer that is connected to the Internet with an IP (Internet Protocol) address so that it is available on the Internet. Before you can publish a site to a Web server, you must first define the remote site by specifying the Remote Info settings in the Advanced section of the Site Definition dialog box. You can specify remote settings when you first create a new site and define the root folder (as you did in Chapter 1 when you defined the remote access settings for The Striped Umbrella Web site), or you can do it after you have completed all of your pages and are confident that it is ready for public viewing. To specify the remote settings for a site, you must first choose an Access setting, which specifies the type of server you will use. The most common Access setting is FTP (File Transfer Protocol). If you specify FTP, you will need to specify an address for the server and the name of the folder on the FTP site in which your root folder will be stored. You will also need to enter login and password information. Figure 1 shows an

example of FTP settings in the Remote Info category of the Site Definition dialog box.

> **QUICK**TIP
>
> If you do not have access to an FTP site, you can publish a site to a local/network folder. Use the alternate steps provided in this lesson to publish your site to a local/network folder.

Viewing a Remote Site

Once you have defined a site to a remote location, you can then view the remote folder in the Files panel by choosing Remote view from the View list. If your remote site is located on an FTP server, Dreamweaver will connect to it. You will see the File Activity dialog box showing the progress of the connection. You can also use the Connects to remote host button on the Files panel toolbar to connect to the remote site. If you defined your site on a local/network folder, then you don't need to use the Connects to remote host button; the root folder and any files and folders it contains will appear in the Files panel when you switch to Remote view.

Transferring Files to and from a Remote Site

After you define a remote site, you will need to transfer or **upload** your files from the local version of your site to the remote host. To do this, view the site in Local view, select the files you want to upload, then click the Put File(s) button on the Files panel toolbar. Once you click this button, the files will be transferred to the remote site. To view the uploaded files, switch to Remote view, as shown in Figure 2. Or you can expand the Files panel to view both the Remote Site and the Local Files panes.

If a file you select for uploading requires other files, such as graphics, a dialog box will open after you click the Put File(s) button and ask if you want those files (known as **dependent files**) to be uploaded. By clicking Yes, all dependent files in the selected page will be uploaded to the appropriate folder in the remote site. If a file that you wish to upload is located in a folder in the local site, the entire folder will be automatically transferred to the remote site.

QUICKTIP

To upload an entire site to a remote host, select the root folder, then click the Put File(s) button. Sometimes you will need to move the files you want to upload to an intermediary folder before transferring them to the remote site.

If you are developing or maintaining a Web site in a group environment, there might be times when you want to transfer or **download** files that other team members have created from the remote site to your local site. To do this, switch to Remote view,

FIGURE 1
FTP settings in the Site Definition for The Striped Umbrella dialog box

FIGURE 2
Files panel with Remote view selected

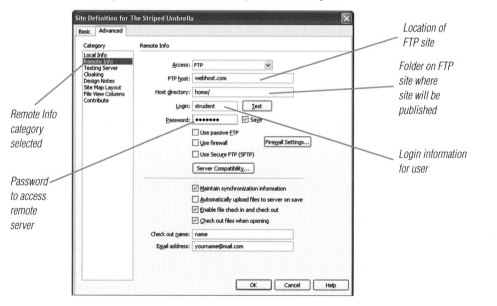

Location of FTP site

Folder on FTP site where site will be published

Remote Info category selected

Password to access remote server

Login information for user

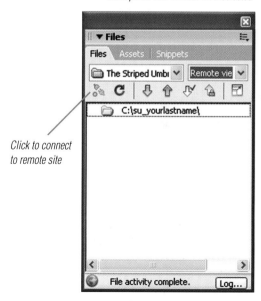

Click to connect to remote site

select the files you want to download, then click the Get File(s) button on the Files panel toolbar.

Synchronizing Files

In order to keep a Web site up to date—especially one that contains several pages and involves several team members—you will need to update and replace files. Team members might make changes to pages on the local version of the site or make additions to the remote site. If many people are involved in maintaining a site, or if you are constantly making changes to the pages, ensuring that both the local and remote sites have the most up-to-date files could get confusing. Thankfully, you can use the Synchronize command to keep things straight. The Synchronize command instructs Dreamweaver to compare the dates of the saved files in both versions of the site, then transfers only the files that have changed. To synchronize files, use the Synchronize Files dialog box, as shown in Figure 3. You can synchronize an entire site or just selected files. You can also specify whether to upload newer files to the remote site, download newer files from the remote site, or both.

FIGURE 3
Synchronize Files dialog box

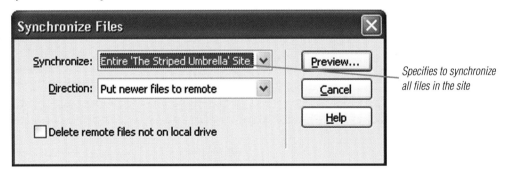

Specifies to synchronize all files in the site

FIGURE 4

FTP settings specified in the Site Definition for The Striped Umbrella dialog box

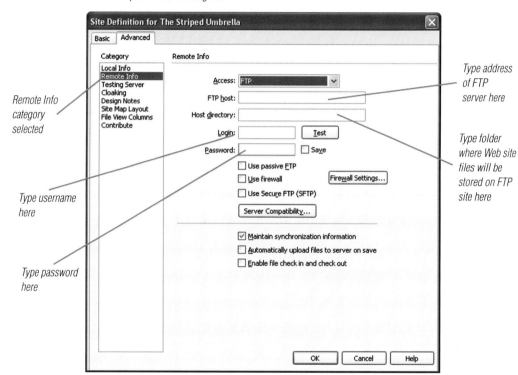

Remote Info category selected

Type username here

Type password here

Type address of FTP server here

Type folder where Web site files will be stored on FTP site here

<div style="float:right">

Set up Web server access on an FTP site

NOTE: Complete these steps only if you know you can store The Striped Umbrella files on an FTP site and you know the login and password information. If you do not have access to an FTP site, complete the exercise called Set up Web server access on a local or network folder on Page 12-8.

1. Open The Striped Umbrella Web site, click **Site** on the menu bar, then click **Manage Sites**.

2. Click **The Striped Umbrella** in the Manage Sites dialog box (if necessary), then click **Edit**.

3. Click the **Advanced tab**, click **Remote Info** in the Category list, click the **Access list arrow**, click **FTP**, then compare your screen to Figure 4.

4. Enter the FTP host, Host directory, Login, and Password information in the dialog box.

    TIP   You must have file and folder permissions to use FTP.

5. Click **OK**, then click **Done** to close the Manage Sites dialog box.

You set up remote access information for The Striped Umbrella Web site using an FTP site folder.

Set up Web server access on a local or network folder

NOTE: Complete these steps if you do not have the ability to post files to an FTP site and could not complete the previous exercise.

1. Using Windows Explorer (Win) or Mac Finder (Mac), create a new folder on your hard drive or on a shared drive named **su_yourlastname**. (For instance, if your last name is Jones, name the folder **su_jones**.)

2. Switch back to Dreamweaver, open The Striped Umbrella Web site, click **Site** on the menu bar, then click **Manage Sites** to open the Manage Sites dialog box.

3. Click **The Striped Umbrella**, click **Edit** to open the Site Definition for The Striped Umbrella dialog box, click the **Advanced tab**, then click **Remote Info** in the Category list.

4. Click the **Access list arrow**, then click **Local/Network**.

5. Click the **Browse for File icon** 📁 next to the Remote folder text box to open the Choose remote root folder for site The Striped Umbrella dialog box, navigate to the folder you created in Step 1, select the folder, click **Open**, then click **Select** (Win) or **Choose** (Mac).

6. Make sure the Refresh remote file list automatically check box is checked, compare your screen to Figure 5, click **OK**, click **OK** to the message about the site cache, then click **Done**.

You created a new folder and specified it as the remote location for The Striped Umbrella Web site, then set up remote access to a local or network folder.

FIGURE 5

Local/Network settings specified in the Site Definition for The Striped Umbrella dialog box

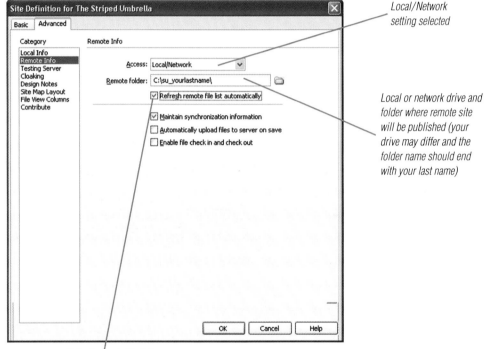

Local/Network setting selected

Local or network drive and folder where remote site will be published (your drive may differ and the folder name should end with your last name)

Refresh remote file list automatically check box

FIGURE 6
Connecting to the remote site

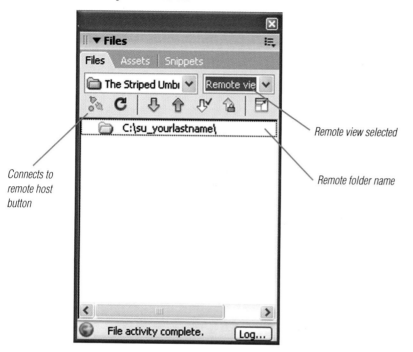

Remote view selected

Remote folder name

Connects to
remote host
button

View a Web site on a remote server

1. Click the **View list arrow** in the Files panel, then click **Remote view**, as shown in Figure 6.

   If you specified your remote access to a local or network folder, then the su_yourlastname folder will appear in the Files panel now. If your remote access is set to an FTP site, Dreamweaver will connect to the host server to see the remote access folder.

2. Click the **Expand to show local and remote sites button** 🗗 to view both the Remote Site and Local Files panes.

   TIP   If you don't see your remote site files, click the Connects to remote host button.

   You used the Files panel to set the view for The Striped Umbrella site to Remote view. You then connected to the remote server to view the contents of the remote folder you specified.

Using a site usability test to test your site

Once you have at least a prototype of the Web site ready to evaluate, it is a good idea to conduct a site usability test. This is a process that involves asking unbiased people, who are not connected to the design process, to use and evaluate the site. A comprehensive usability test will include pre-test questions, participant tasks, a post-test interview, and a post-test survey. This will provide much-needed information as to how usable the site is to those unfamiliar with it. Typical questions include "What are your overall impressions?" "What do you like the best and the least about the site?" and "How easy is it to navigate inside the site?" For more information, go to *www.w3.org* and search for "site usability test".

Upload files to a remote server

1. Click the **about_us.html file**, then click the **Put File(s) button** 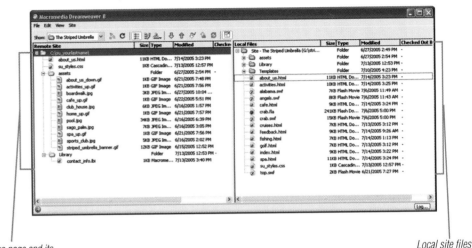 on the Files panel toolbar.

   The Dependent Files dialog box opens, asking if you want to include dependent files.

2. Click **Yes**.

   The about_us file along with all the other image files and the library item used in the about us page are copied to the remote server. The Status dialog box appears and flashes the names of each file as they are uploaded.

3. Expand the assets folder (if necessary), expand the Library folder, then compare your screen to Figure 7.

   The remote site now contains the about us page as well as several images, the library item, and the striped_umbrella external style sheet file, all of which are needed by the about us page.

   | TIP   You might need to expand the su_yourlastname folder in order to view the assets folder.

   You used the Put File(s) button to upload the about_us file and all files that are dependent files of the about us page.

FIGURE 7

Remote view of The Striped Umbrella Web site after uploading the about us page

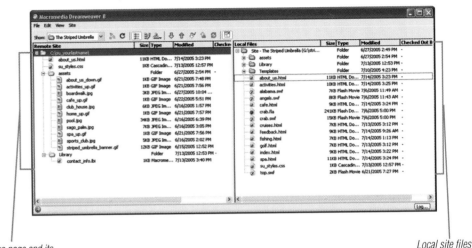

about us page and its
dependent files in
Remote Site

Local site files

FIGURE 8
Synchronize Files dialog box

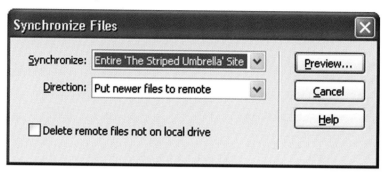

FIGURE 9
Files that need to be uploaded to remote site

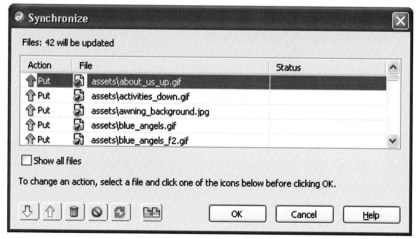

Synchronize files

1. Click **Site** on the Files panel toolbar, click **Synchronize** to open the Synchronize Files dialog box (Win) or click the **Options list arrow**, point to **Site**, then click **Synchronize** to open the Synchronize Files dialog box (Mac).

2. Click the **Synchronize list arrow**, then click **Entire 'The Striped Umbrella' Site**.

3. Click the **Direction list arrow**, click **Put newer files to remote** (if necessary), then compare your screen to Figure 8.

4. Click **Preview**.

   The Status dialog box might appear and flash the names of all the files from the local version of the site that need to be uploaded to the remote site. Then the dialog box shown in Figure 9 opens and lists all the files that need to be uploaded to the remote site.

5. Click **OK**.

   All the files from the local The Striped Umbrella Web site are now contained in the remote version of the site. The dialog box changes to show all the files that were uploaded.

   TIP If you want to keep a record of your synchronizations, you could click Save Log, specify a location and name for the synchronization log, then click Save.

6. Refresh the Files panel to place the files and folders in order.

You synchronized The Striped Umbrella Web site files to copy all remaining files from the local root folder to the remote root folder.

CHECK FILES
OUT AND IN

What You'll Do

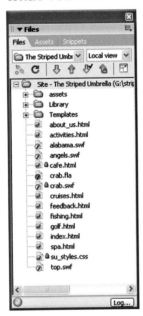

 In this lesson, you will use the Site Definition dialog box to enable the Check In/Check Out feature. You will then check out the cafe page, make a change to it, then check it back in.

Managing a Web Site with a Team

When you work on a large Web site, chances are that many people will be involved in keeping the site up to date. Different individuals will need to make changes or additions to different pages of the site by adding or deleting content, changing graphics, updating information, and so on. If everyone had access to all of the pages at all times, big problems could arise. For instance, what if you and another team member both made edits to the same page at the same time? If you post your edited version of the file to the site after the other team member posts his edited version of the same file, the file that you upload will overwrite his version and none of his changes will be incorporated.

Not good! Fortunately, you can avoid this scenario by using Dreamweaver's collaboration tools.

Checking Out and Checking In Files

Checking in and out files is similar to checking in and out library books. No one else can read a book while you have it checked out. Using Dreamweaver's Check In/Check Out feature will ensure that team members do not overwrite each other's pages. When this feature is enabled, only one person can work on a file at a time. To check out a file, click the file you want to work on in the Files panel, then click the Check Out File(s) button on the Files panel toolbar. Files that you have checked out are marked with green check marks in the Files panel. Files that have been checked in are marked with padlock icons.

After you finish editing a checked-out file, you will need to save and close the file, then click the Check In button to check the file back in and make it available to other users.

When a file is checked in, you cannot make edits to it unless you check it out again. Figure 10 shows the Check Out File(s) and Check In buttons on the Files panel toolbar.

Enabling the Check In/Check Out Feature

In order to use the Check In /Check Out feature with a team of people, you must first enable it. To turn on this feature, check the Enable file check in and check out check box in the Remote Info settings of the Site Definition dialog box.

FIGURE 10

Check Out File(s) and Check In buttons on the Files Panel toolbar

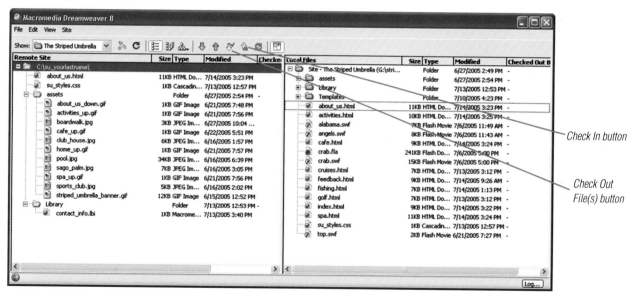

Enable the Check In/Check Out feature

1. Click **Site** on the menu bar, click **Manage Sites** to open the Manage Sites dialog box, click **The Striped Umbrella** in the list, then click **Edit** to open the Site Definition for The Striped Umbrella dialog box.

2. Click **Remote Info** in the Category list, then click the **Enable file check in and check out check box** to select it.

3. Check the **Check out files when opening** check box to select it (if necessary).

4. Type your **name** using lowercase letters and no spaces in the Check out name text box.

5. Type your **e-mail address** in the Email address text box.

6. Compare your screen to Figure 11, click **OK** to close the Site Definition for The Striped Umbrella dialog box, then click **Done** to close the Site dialog box.

You used the sites Definition for The Striped Umbrella dialog box to enable the Check In/Check Out feature and let site collaborators know when you are working with a file in the site.

Check out a file

1. Click the **cafe page** in the Local Files list in the Files panel to select it.

(continued)

FIGURE 11
Enabling the Check In/Check Out feature

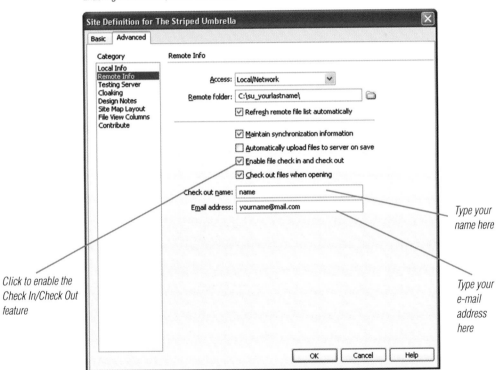

Click to enable the Check In/Check Out feature

Type your name here

Type your e-mail address here

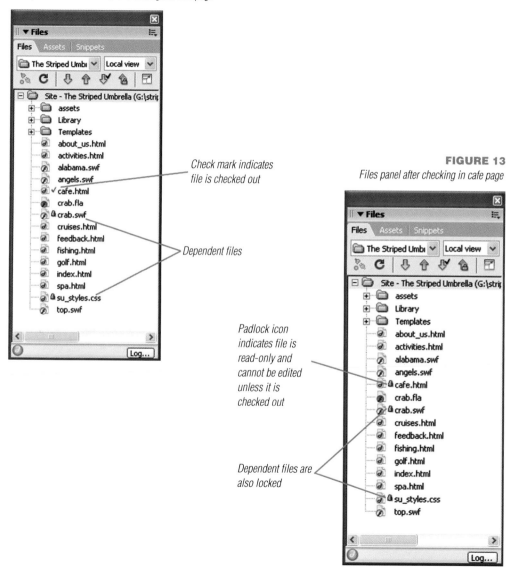

FIGURE 12

Files panel in Local view after checking out cafe page

Check mark indicates
file is checked out

Dependent files

FIGURE 13

Files panel after checking in cafe page

Padlock icon
indicates file is
read-only and
cannot be edited
unless it is
checked out

Dependent files are
also locked

2. Click the **Check Out File(s) button** on the Files panel toolbar.

The Dependent Files dialog box appears, asking if you want to include all files that are needed for the cafe page.

3. Click **Yes**, click another file in the Files panel to deselect the cafe page, collapse the Files panel, switch to Local view, then compare your screen to Figure 12.

The cafe file has a check mark next to it indicating you have checked it out. The dependent files have padlock icons.

> TIP If a dialog box appears asking "Do you wish to overwrite your local copy of cafe.html?", click Yes.

You checked out the cafe page so that no one else can use it.

Check in a file

1. Open the cafe page, change the closing hour for the The Cabana in the nested table to **7:00 p.m.**, then save your changes.

2. Close the cafe page, then click the **cafe page** in the Files panel to select it.

3. Click the **Check In button** on the Files panel toolbar.

The Dependent Files dialog box opens, asking if you want to include dependent files too.

4. Click **Yes**, click another file in the Files panel to deselect the cafe page, then compare your screen to Figure 13.

A padlock icon appears instead of a green check mark next to the cafe page on the Files panel.

You made a content change on the cafe page, then checked in the cafe page, making it available for others to check it out again.

CLOAK FILES

What You'll Do

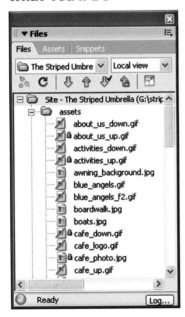

 In this lesson, you will cloak the assets folder so that it is excluded from various operations, such as the Put, Get, Check In, and Check Out commands. You will also use the Site Definition dialog box to cloak all .gif files in the site.

Understanding Cloaking Files

There may be times when you want to exclude a particular file or files from being uploaded to a server. For instance, suppose you have a page that is not quite finished and needs more work before it is ready to be viewed by the rest of the world. You can exclude such files by **cloaking** them, which marks them for exclusion from several commands, including Put, Get, Synchronize, Check In, and Check Out. Cloaked files are also excluded from site-wide operations, such as checking for links or updating a template or library item. You can cloak a folder or specify a type of file to cloak throughout the site.

QUICKTIP

By default, the cloaking feature is enabled. However, if for some reason it is not turned on, open the Site Definition dialog box, click the Advanced tab, click the Cloaking category, then click the Enable cloaking check box.

Cloaking a Folder

There may be times when you want to cloak an entire folder. For instance, if you are not concerned with replacing outdated image files, you might want to cloak the assets folder of a Web site to save time when synchronizing files. To cloak a folder, select the folder, click the Options list arrow in the Files panel, point to site, point to Cloaking, then click Cloak. The folder you cloaked and all the files it contains will appear with red slashes across them, as shown in Figure 14. To uncloak a folder, click the Options list arrow in the Files panel, point to Site, point to Cloaking, then click Uncloak.

QUICKTIP

To uncloak all files in a site, click the Files panel Options list arrow, point to Site, point to Cloaking, then click Uncloak All.

Cloaking Selected File Types

There may be times when you want to cloak a particular type of file, such as a .swf

file. To cloak a particular file type, open the Site Definition dialog box, click the Cloaking category, click the Cloak files ending with check box, then type a file name in the text box below the check box. All files throughout the site that have the specified file extension will be cloaked.

FIGURE 14
Cloaked assets folder in the Files panel

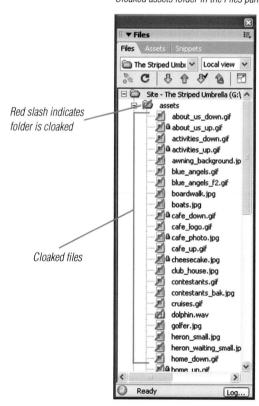

Red slash indicates folder is cloaked

Cloaked files

Cloak and uncloak a folder

1. Verify that Local view is displayed in the Files panel, click **Site** on the menu bar, then click **Manage Sites**.

2. Click **The Striped Umbrella** (if necessary), click **Edit** to open the Site Definition for The Striped Umbrella dialog box, click **Cloaking** in the Category list, verify that the Enable cloaking check box is checked, click **OK**, then click **Done**.

3. Click the **assets folder** in the Files panel, click the **Options list arrow** ☷, point to **Site**, point to **Cloaking**, click **Cloak**, expand the assets folder (if necessary), then compare your screen to Figure 15.

   A red slash now appears on top of the assets folder in the Files panel, indicating that all files in the assets folder are cloaked and will be excluded from putting, getting, checking in, checking out, and many other operations.

   TIP You can also cloak a folder by right-clicking (Win) or [control]-clicking (Mac) the folder, pointing to Cloaking, then clicking Cloak.

4. Right-click (Win) or [control]-click (Mac) the **assets folder**, point to **Cloaking**, then click **Uncloak**.

   The assets folder and all the files it contains no longer appear with red slashes across them, indicating they are no longer cloaked.

You cloaked the assets folder so that this folder and all the files it contains would be excluded from many operations, including uploading and downloading files. You then uncloaked the assets folder.

FIGURE 15
Assets folder after cloaking

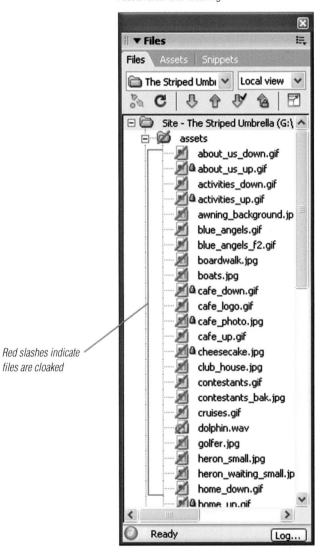

Red slashes indicate
files are cloaked

FIGURE 16
Specifying a file type to cloak

FIGURE 17
Assets folder in Files panel after cloaking .gif files

Assets folder
is not cloaked

Dependent
files for the
cafe page
still show
padlock
icon

All .gif files
are cloaked

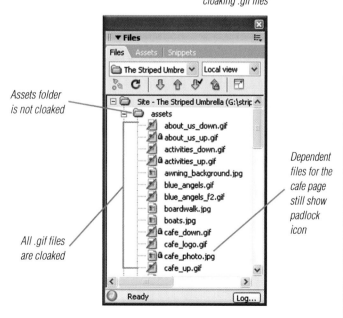

1. Right-click (Win) or [control]-click (Mac) the **assets folder** in the Files panel, point to **Cloaking**, then click **Settings** to open the Site Definition for The Striped Umbrella dialog box with the Cloaking category selected.

2. Click the **Cloak files ending with check box**, select the text in the text box that appears, type **.gif** in the text box, then compare your screen to Figure 16.

3. Click **OK**.

   A dialog box opens, indicating that the site cache will be recreated.

4. Click **OK**, open the assets folder (if necessary), then compare your screen to Figure 17.

   All of the .gif files in the assets folder appear with red slashes across them, indicating that they are cloaked. Notice that the assets folder is not cloaked.

You cloaked all the .gif files in The Striped Umbrella Web site.

IMPORT AND EXPORT
A SITE DEFINITION

What You'll Do

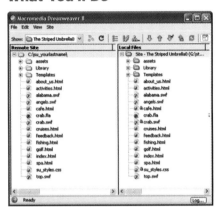

In this lesson, you will export the site definition file for The Striped Umbrella Web site. You will then import The Striped Umbrella Web site.

Exporting a Site Definition

If you work on a Web site for a long time, it's likely that at some point you will want to move it to another machine or share it with other collaborators who will help you maintain it. The site definition for a Web site contains important information about the site, including its URL, preferences that you've specified, and other secure information such as the login and password information. You can use the Export command to export the site definition file to another location. To do this, simply click Site on the menu bar, click Manage Sites, click the site you want to export, then click Export. Because the site definition file contains password information that you will want to keep secret from other site users, you should never save the site definition file in the Web site. Instead, save it in an external file.

Importing a Site Definition

If you want to set up another user with a copy of your Web site, you can import the site definition file. To do this, click Import in the Manage Sites dialog box to open the Import Site dialog box, navigate to the .ste file you want to import, then click Open.

FIGURE 18

Save The Striped Umbrella.ste file in the su_site_definition folder

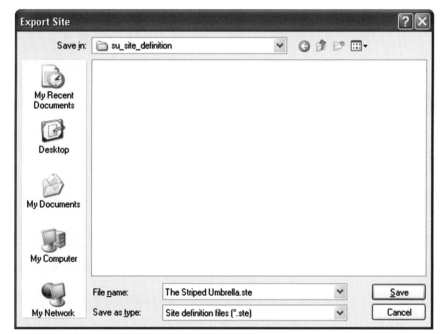

1. Use Windows Explorer (Win) or Finder (Mac) to create a new folder on your hard drive or external drive named **su_site_definition**.

2. Switch back to Dreamweaver, click **Site** on menu bar, click **Manage Sites**, click **The Striped Umbrella**, then click **Export** to open the Export Site dialog box.

3. Navigate to and select the **su_site_definition folder** that you created in Step 1, as shown in Figure 18, click **Save**, then click **Done**.

You used the Export command to create the site definition file and saved it to the su_site_definition folder.

Import a site definition

1. Click **Site** on the menu bar, click **Manage Sites**, click **The Striped Umbrella**, then click **Import** to open the Import Site dialog box.

2. Navigate to the su_site_definition folder, compare your screen to Figure 19, select **The Striped Umbrella.ste**, then click **Open**.

   A dialog box opens and says that a site named The Striped Umbrella already exists. It will name the imported site The Striped Umbrella0 so that it has a unique name.

3. Click **OK**, then click **Done**.

4. Click **Site** on the menu bar, click **Manage Sites**, click **The Striped Umbrella0**, click **Edit**, then compare your screen to Figure 20.

   The settings show that the The Striped Umbrella0 site has the same root folder and default images folder as the The Striped Umbrella site. Both of these settings are specified in the The Striped Umbrella.ste file that you imported. Importing a site in this way makes it possible for multiple users with different computers to work on the same site.

5. Click **OK**, click **OK** to close the warning message, then click **Done**.

   TIP If a dialog box opens warning that the root folder chosen is the same as the folder for the site "The Striped Umbrella," click OK.

You imported The Striped Umbrella.ste file.

FIGURE 19
Import Site dialog box

FIGURE 20
Site Definition for The Striped Umbrella0 dialog box

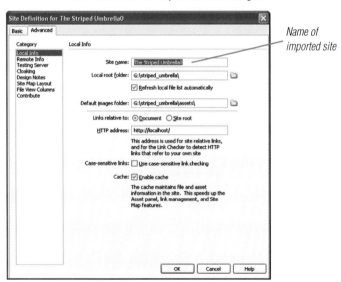

Name of imported site

FIGURE 21

Viewing The Striped Umbrella0 Web site files

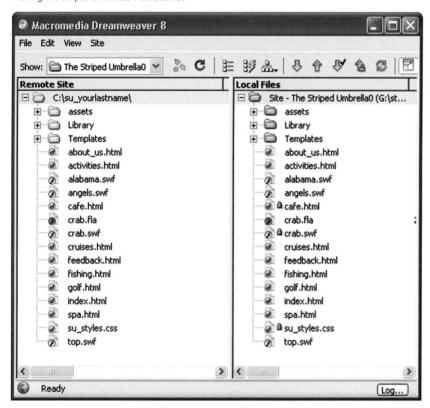

1. Click the **Expand to show local and remote sites button** 🔲 on the Files panel toolbar to expand the Files panel.

2. Expand the Site folder to view the contents (if necessary).

3. Click the **Refresh button** 🄲 to view the files in the Remote Site pane.

   As shown in Figure 21, the site looks identical to the original The Striped Umbrella site, except the name has been changed to The Striped Umbrella0.

   | TIP If you don't see your remote site files, click the Connects to remote host button.

4. Click the **Collapse to show only local or remote site button** 🔲 to collapse the Files panel.

5. Click **Site** on the menu bar, click **Manage Sites**, click **Remove**, click **Yes** to clear the warning dialog box, then click **Done** to delete The Striped Umbrella0 Web site.

You viewed the expanded Files panel for The Striped Umbrella0 Web site and then deleted The Striped Umbrella0 Web site.

EVALUATE WEB CONTENT FOR
LEGAL USE

What You'll Do

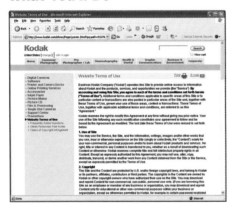

In this lesson, you will examine copyright issues in the context to using content gathered from sources such as the Internet.

Understanding Copyright and Fair Use

The Internet has made it possible to locate compelling and media-rich content for Web sites. A person who has learned to craft searches well can locate a multitude of interesting material, such as graphics, animations, sounds, and text. Just because you can find it easily does not mean that it belongs to you, however. There are several terms that you must understand to prevent violating the law when deciding to use content that has been created and published by someone other than yourself. **Copyright** protects the particular and tangible *expression* of an idea, not the idea itself. If you wrote a story using the facts and idea about aliens crashing in Roswell, New Mexico, no one could copy your story without permission. However, anyone could write a story using a similar plot or characters—the idea of aliens crashing in Roswell is not copyright-protected.

One limitation to copyright is **fair use**. Fair use allows consumers to copy all or part of a copyrighted work in support of their First Amendment rights. For example, you could excerpt short passages of a film or song, or parody a television show, all for noncommercial use. Determining if fair use applies to a work depends on the purpose of its use, the nature of the copyrighted work, how much you want to copy, and the effect on the market or value of the work. Fair use is used as the defense in many copyright infringement cases.

Understanding Intellectual Property

The term "intellectual property" immediately imparts gravitas, even if you have absolutely no idea what it means; but the word "intellectual" simply serves to distinguish this type of property from physical property. **Intellectual property** is a product resulting from human creativity. It can include inventions, movies, songs, designs, clothing, and so on—anything created through intellectual or mental labor, as opposed to being constructed out of physical components. Unlike real property (better known as real estate), or personal property (better known as your stuff), intellectual property refers to intangible assets. For example, if you design a new chair, your design is an **intangible asset**—it conveys the idea of the chair and specifications for how the chair should be built. If you manufacture the chair and sell it to your neighbors, it becomes part of their personal property. Intellectual property law establishes how and when a person and society as a whole can benefit and profit from someone's creation.

What Exactly Does the Copyright Owner Own?

The Copyright Act of 1976 provided the copyright owner with a "bundle" of six rights, consisting of:
1) reproduction
2) creation of **derivative works** (for example, movie version of a book)
3) distribution to the public
4) public performance of literary, musical, dramatic, and choreographic works, pantomimes, and motion pictures and other audio-visual works
5) public display of literary, musical, dramatic, and choreographic works, pantomime, and pictorial, graphic, or sculptural works
6) public performance by digital audio transmission of sound recordings.

By default, only a copyright holder can create a *derivative work* of his or her

original by transforming or adapting it. For example, the film *Hairspray* has gone from movie to musical play, all under the creative guidance of its owner, John Waters.

Understanding Licensing Agreements

In order to decide whether to use a work of intellectual property you find on a Web site, such as an image or a sound file, you must decide whether you can comply with its licensing agreement. A **licensing agreement** is the **permission** given by a copyright holder that conveys the right to use the copyright holder's work. There are many types of licensing agreements: royalty-free or rights-managed, exclusive or nonexclusive.

The rules that a copyright owner uses to establish use of his or her work are known as **terms of use**. For example, an artist grants permission for someone to use the work (license) under certain conditions (terms of use). Figures 22 and 23 are a great example of clear terms of use as stated for the Kodak Web site.

FIGURE 22
The Kodak home page

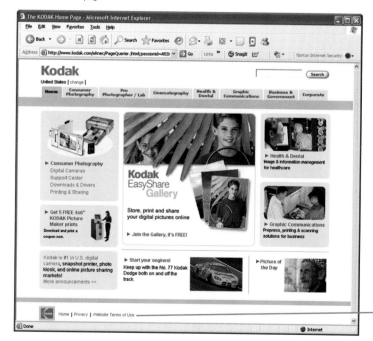

Website Terms of Use link

Obtaining Permission or a License

The **permissions process** is specific to what you want to use (text, photographs, music, trademarks, merchandise, and so on) and how you want to use it (school term paper, personal Web site, book illustration, fabric pattern). And, getting permission from an amateur photographer whose work you found on a photo-sharing Web site is different than getting permission from a large corporation. How you want to use the work will determine the level and scope of permissions you need to secure. The fundamentals, however, are the same. Your request should contain the following:

- Your full name, address, and complete contact information.
- A specific description of your intended use. Sometimes including a sketch, storyboard, or link to a Web site is helpful.
- A signature line for the copyright holder.
- A target date when you would like the copyright holder to respond. This can be important if you're working under deadline.

Posting a Copyright Notice

The familiar © symbol or "Copyright" is no longer required to indicate copyright, nor does it automatically register your work,

FIGURE 23
Kodak Website Terms of Use page

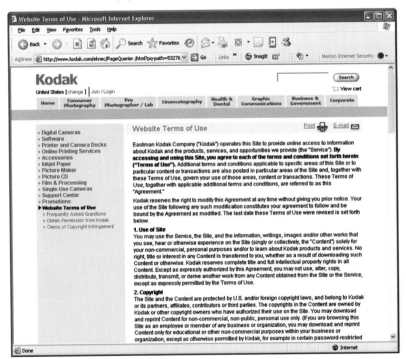

but it does serve a useful purpose. When you post or publish it, you are stating clearly to those who may not know anything about copyright law that this work is claimed by you and is not in the public domain. Your case is made even stronger if someone violates your copyright and your notice is clearly visible. A violator can never claim ignorance of the law as an excuse for infringing. The proper notification can be either:

Copyright 2007
Thomson Course Technology
or © **2007 Thomson Course Technology**
The Web materials you incorporate into your own writings must be cited. This expectation applies even to unsigned material and material that does not display the copyright symbol (©). Moreover, the expectation applies just as certainly to ideas you summarize or paraphrase as to words you quote verbatim.

Here's a list of the elements that make up an APA-style citation of Web-based resources:

- Author's name (if known)
- Date of publication or last revision (if known), in parentheses
- Title of document
- Title of complete work or Website (if applicable), underlined
- URL, in angled brackets
- Date of access, in parentheses

Here are a few examples as they might appear on a references page in your paper:

References
Citation Guides. (1996). UMUC Information and Library Services. **www.umuc.edu/library/citation guides.html** (19 Feb. 2004).

Harnack, A. and Kleppinger, E. (1996). Beyond the MLA handbook. **http://english.ttu.edu/kairos/1.2/inbox/ mla_archive.html** (19 Feb. 2004).

Walker, J. R. and Taylor, T. (1998). *The Columbia Guide to Online Style.* **www.columbia.edu/cu/cup/cgos/ idx_basic.html** (19 Feb. 2004).

Publish a Web site and transfer files.

1. Open the blooms & bulbs Web site.
2. Set up Web server access for the blooms & bulbs Web site on an FTP server or a local/network server (whichever is available to you) using appropriate settings.
3. View the blooms & bulbs remote site in the Files panel.
4. Upload the iris.jpg file to the remote site, then view the remote site.
5. Upload the plant_categories template and all dependent files to the remote site, then view the remote site to make sure all files were transferred.
6. Synchronize all files in the blooms & bulbs Web site, so that all files from the local site are uploaded to the remote site.

Check files out and in.

1. Enable the Check In/Check Out feature.
2. Check out the plants page and all dependent pages.
3. Open the plants page, change the heading style of "Drop by to see our Featured Spring Plants" to seasons, then save your changes.
4. Check in the plants page and all dependent files.

Cloak files.

1. Verify that cloaking is enabled in the blooms & bulbs Web site.
2. Cloak the assets folder, then uncloak it.
3. Cloak all the .jpg files in the blooms & bulbs Web site.

Import and export a site definition.

1. Create a new folder named **blooms_definition** on your hard drive or external drive.
2. Export the blooms & bulbs site definition to the blooms_definition folder.

3. Import the blooms & bulbs site definition to create a new site called blooms & bulbs0.
4. Make sure that all files from the blooms & bulbs Web site appear in the Files panel for the imported site, then compare your screen to Figure 24.

FIGURE 24
Completed Skills Review

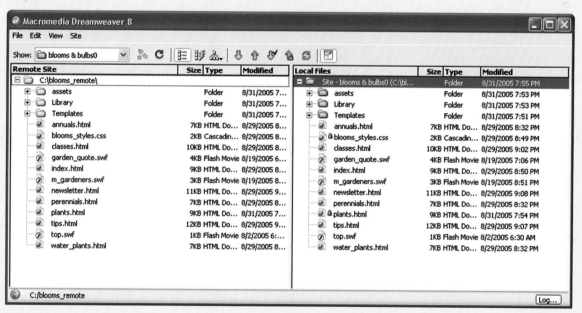

In this Project Builder you will publish the TripSmart Web site that you have developed throughout this book to a remote server or local/network folder. Mike Andrew has provided instructions for where to publish the site on a remote server. You will specify the remote settings for the site, upload files to the remote site, check files out and in, and cloak files. Finally, you will export and import the site definition.

1. Open the TripSmart Web site.
2. If you did not do so in Project Builder 1 in Chapter 1, use the Site Definition dialog box to set up Web server access for a remote site using either an FTP site or a local or network folder.
3. Upload the index page and all dependent files to the remote site.
4. View the remote site to make sure that all files uploaded correctly.
5. Synchronize the files so that all other files on the local TripSmart site are uploaded to the remote site.
6. Enable the Check In/Check Out feature.
7. Check out the index page and all dependent files.
8. Open the index page, change the date on the last updated statement to a date that will automatically update on save, save your

changes, close the index page, then check in the index page and all dependent pages.
9. Cloak all .jpg files in the Web site.
10. Export the site definition to a new folder named **tripsmart_definition**.

FIGURE 25
Sample Project Builder 1

11. Import the tripsmart.ste file to create a new site named TripSmart0.
12. Save your changes, expand the assets folder in the Files panel (if necessary), then compare your screen to Figure 25.

In this Project Builder, you will finish your work on the emma's book bag Web site that you started in Project Builder 2 in Chapter 1. Emma Claire has asked you to publish the emma's book bag Web site to a remote server and transfer all the files from the local site to the remote site. She has also asked you to enable the Check In/Check Out feature so that other staff members may collaborate on the site. Finally, she has asked you to export and import the site definition file.

1. Open the emma's book bag Web site.
2. If you did not do so in Project Builder 2 in Chapter 1, use the Site Definition dialog box to set up Web server access for a remote site using either an FTP site or a local or network folder.
3. Upload the cafe.html page and all dependent files to the remote site.
4. View the remote site to make sure that all files uploaded correctly.
5. Synchronize the files so that all other files on the local emma's book bag site are uploaded to the remote site.
6. Enable the Check In/Check Out feature.
7. Check out the cafe page and all its dependent files.
8. Open the cafe page, then change the opening cafe hours to 10:00.

9. Save your changes, close the page, then check in the cafe page and all dependent pages.
10. Export the site definition to a new folder named **book_bag_definition**.

FIGURE 26
Completed Project Builder 2

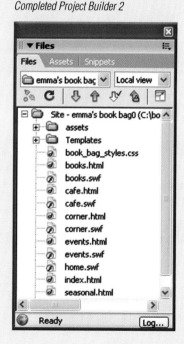

11. Import the emma's book bag.ste file to create a new site named emma's book bag0.
12. Expand the root folder in the Files panel (if necessary), then compare your screen to Figure 26.

Throughout this book you have used Dreamweaver to create and develop several Web sites that contain different elements, many of which are found in popular commercial Web sites. For instance, Figure 27 shows the National Park Service Web site, which contains photos and information on all the national parks in the United States. This Web site contains many types of interactive elements, such as forms, rollovers, Flash content, and tables—all of which you learned to create in this book.

1. Connect to the Internet, navigate to the Online Companion, then select the link for this chapter.
2. Spend some time exploring the pages of this site to familiarize yourself with its elements.
3. Type a list of all the elements in this Web site that you have learned how to create in this book. After each item, write a short description of where and how the element is used in the site.
4. Print out the home page and one or two other pages that contain some of the elements you described and attach it to your list.

FIGURE 27
Source for Design Project

In this project, you will finish your work on the Web site that you created and developed throughout this book.

You will publish your site to a remote server or local or network folder.

1. Before you begin the process of publishing your Web site to a remote server, make sure that it is ready for public viewing. Use Figure 28 to assist you in making sure your Web site is complete. If you find problems, make the necessary changes to finalize the site.

2. Decide where to publish your site. The folder where you will publish your site can be either an FTP site or a local/network folder. If you are publishing to an FTP site, be sure to write down all the information you will need to publish to the site, including the URL of the FTP host, the directory on the FTP server where you will publish your site's root folder, and the login and password information.

3. Use the Site Definition dialog box to specify the remote settings for the site using the information that was decided upon in Step 2.

4. Transfer one of the pages and its dependent files to the remote site, then view the remote site to make sure the appropriate files were transferred.

5. Synchronize the files so that all the remaining local pages and dependent files are uploaded to the remote site.

6. Enable the Check In/Check Out feature.

7. Check out one of the pages. Open the checked-out page, make a change to it, save the change, close the page, then check the page back in.

8. Cloak a particular file type.

9. Export the site definition for the site to a new folder on your hard drive or on an external drive.

10. Import the site to create a new version of the site.

11. Close the imported site, save and close all open pages (if necessary), then exit Dreamweaver.

FIGURE 28
Portfolio Project check list

Web Site Check List

1. Are you satisfied with the content and appearance of every page?
2. Are all paths for all links and images correct?
3. Does each page have a title?
4. Do all images appear?
5. Are all colors Websafe?
6. Do all images have appropriate alternate text?
7. Have you eliminated any orphaned files?
8. Have you deleted any unnecessary files?
9. Have you viewed all pages using at least two different browsers?
10. Does the home page have keywords and a description?

Read the following information carefully.

Find out from your instructor the location where you will store your files.

- To complete many of the chapters in this book, you need to use the Data Files provided on the CD at the back of this book.

- Your instructor will tell you whether you will be working from the CD or copying the files to a drive on your computer or on a server. Your instructor will also tell you where you will store the files you create and modify.

- All the Data Files are organized in folders named after the chapter in which they are used. For instance, all Chapter 1 Data Files are stored in the chapter_1 folder. You should leave all the Data Files in these folders; do not move any Data File out of the folder in which it is originally stored.

Copy and organize your Data Files.

- Copy the folders that contain the Data Files to a USB storage device, network folder, hard drive, or other storage device if you will not be working from the CD.

- As you build each Web site, the exercises in this book will guide you to copy the Data Files you need from the appropriate Data Files folder to the folder where you are storing the Web site. Your Data Files should always remain intact because you are copying (and not moving) them to the Web site.

- Because you will be building a Web site from one chapter to the next, sometimes you will need to use a Data File that is already contained in the Web site you are working on.

Find and keep track of your Data Files and completed files.

- Use the **Data File Supplied** column to make sure you have the files you need before starting the chapter or exercise indicated in the **Chapter** column.

- Sometimes the file listed in the **Data File Supplied** column is one that you created or used in a previous chapter, and that is already part of the Web site you are working on. For instance, if the file book_bag/signings.html is listed in the **Data File Supplied** column, this means that you need to use the signings.html file in the emma's book bag site that you already created.

- Use the **Student Creates File** column to find out the filename you use when saving your new file for the exercise.

DATA FILES LIST

Files used in this book

Macromedia Dreamweaver 8

Chapter	Data File Supplied	Student Creates File	Used In
1	dw1_1.html about_us.swf accommodations.swf activities.swf cafe.swf index.swf shop.swf spa.swf assets/pool.jpg assets/striped_u_background.jpg assets/striped_umbrella_banner.gif		Lesson 2
	dw1_2.html assets/striped_umbrella_banner.gif	about_us.html activities.html cafe.html cruises.html fishing.html spa.html	Lesson 5
	dw1_3.html dw1_4.html assets/blooms_banner.jpg assets/blooms_logo.jpg	annuals.html classes.html newsletter.html perennials.html plants.html tips.html water_plants.html	Skills Review
	dw1_5.html assets/tripsmart_banner.jpg	amazon.html catalog.html destinations.html kenya.html newsletter.html services.html	Project Builder 1
	dw1_6.html assets/book_bag_banner.jpg	books.html cafe.html corner.html events.html seasonal.html signings.html	Project Builder 2

Chapter	Data File Supplied	Student Creates File	Used In
	none		Design Project
	none		Group Project
2	dw2_1.html spa.doc assets/striped_umbrella_banner.gif assets/the_spa.jpg		Lesson 2
	dw2_2.html gardening_tips.doc assets/blooms_banner.jpg assets/garden_tips.jpg		Skills Review
	none		Project Builder 1
	none		Project Builder 2
	none		Design Project
	none		Group Project
3	questions.doc		Lesson 1
		su_styles.css	Lesson 2
	dw3_1.html assets/boardwalk.jpg assets/club_house.jpg assets/pool.jpg assets/sago_palm.jpg assets/sports_club.jpg assets/striped_umbrella_banner.gif		Lesson 4
	assets/stripes_back.gif assets/umbrella_back.gif		Lesson 6
	dw3_2.html assets/blooms_banner.jpg assets/daisies.jpg assets/lantana.jpg assets/petunias.jpg assets/verbena.jpg	blooms_styles.css	Skills Review
	dw3_3.html dw3_4.html assets/tripsmart_banner.jpg assets/lion.jpg assets/zebra_mothers.jpg	tripsmart_styles.css	Project Builder 1

Chapter	Data File Supplied	Student Creates File	Used In
	dw3_5.html dw3_6.html assets/book_bag_banner.jpg assets/reading.jpg	book_bag_styles.css	Project Builder 2
	none		Design Project
	none		Group Project
4	dw4_1.html assets/heron_waiting_small.jpg assets/striped_umbrella_banner.gif assets/two_dolphins_small.jpg		Lesson 1
		top.swf	Lesson 3
	assets/about_us_down.gif assets/about_us_up.gif assets/activities_down.gif assets/activities_up.gif assets/cafe_down.gif assets/cafe_up.gif assets/home_down.gif assets/home_up.gif assets/spa_down.gif assets/spa_up.gif		Lesson 4
	dw4_2.html dw4_3.html assets/boats.jpg assets/heron_small.jpg		Lesson 5
	dw4_4.html dw4_5.html dw4_6.html dw4_7.html assets/b_classes_down.jpg assets/b_classes_up.jpg assets/b_home_down.jpg assets/b_home_up.jpg assets/b_newsletter_down.jpg assets/b_newsletter_up.jpg assets/b_plants_down.jpg assets/b_plants_up.jpg	top.swf	Skills Review

Chapter	Data File Supplied	Student Creates File	Used In
	assets/b_tips_down.jpg assets/b_tips_up.jpg assets/blooms_banner.jpg assets/flower_bed.jpg assets/fuchsia.jpg assets/iris.jpg assets/water_hyacinth.jpg		
	dw4_8.html dw4_9.html dw4_10.html assets/giraffe.jpg assets/parrot.jpg assets/sloth.jpg assets/tripsmart_banner.jpg assets/water_lily.jpg		Project Builder 1
	dw4_11.html dw4_12.html dw4_13.html assets/book_bag_banner.jpg assets/books.jpg assets/grif_stockley.jpg assets/salted_with_fire.jpg		Project Builder 2
	none		Design Project
	none		Group Project
5	assets/cafe_logo.gif assets/cafe_photo.jpg assets/cheesecake.jpg		Lesson 3
	cafe.doc		Lesson 4
	gardeners.doc registration.doc assets/flower_bed.jpg		Skills Review

Chapter	Data File Supplied	Student Creates File	Used In
	assets/hat.jpg assets/pants.jpg assets/vest.jpg		Project Builder 1
	book club.doc assets/muffins.jpg		Project Builder 2
	none		Design Project
	none		Group Project
6	The Striped Umbrella.ste striped_umbrella folder containing these files: about_us.html activities.html cafe.html cruises.html feedback.html fishing.html index.html spa.html su_styles.css top.swf about_us_down.gif about_us_up.gif activities_down.gif activities_up.gif boardwalk.jpg boats.jpg cafe_down.gif cafe_logo.gif cafe_photo.jpg cafe_up.gif cheesecake.jpg club_house.jpg heron_small.jpg hereon_waiting_small.jpg home_down.gif home_up.gif pool.jpg sago_palm.jpg spa_down.gif spa_up.gif		Lesson 1

DREAMWEAVER 6

Chapter	Data File Supplied	Student Creates File	Used In
	sports_club.jpg		
	striped_umbrella_banner.gif		
	the_spa.jpg		
	two_dolphins_small.jpg		
	blooms & bulbs.ste		Skills Review
	blooms folder		
	containing these files:		
	annuals.html		
	blooms_styles.css		
	classes.html		
	index.html		
	newsletter.html		
	perennials.html		
	plants.html		
	tips.html		
	top.swf		
	water_plants.html		
	assets/b_classes_down.jpg		
	assets/b_classes_up.jpg		
	assets/b_home_down.jpg		
	assets/b_home_up.jpg		
	assets/b_newsletter_down.jpg		
	assets/b_newsletter_up.jpg		
	assets/b_plants_down.jpg		
	assets/b_plants_up.jpg		
	assets/b_tips_down.jpg		
	assets/b_tips_up.jpg		
	assets/blooms_banner.jpg		
	assets/flower_bed.jpg		
	assets/fuchsia.jpg		
	assets/garden_tips.jpg		
	assets/iris.jpg		
	assets/lantana.jpg		
	assets/petunias.jpg		
	assets/verbena.jpg		
	assets/water_hyacinth.jpg		
	book_bag folder containing these files:		Project Builder 2
	book_bag_styles.css		
	books.html		

Chapter	Data File Supplied	Student Creates File	Used In
	cafe.html		
	corner.html		
	events.html		
	index.html		
	seasonal.html		
	signings.html		
	assets/book_bag_banner.jpg		
	bookbag.jpg		
	books.jpg		
	grif_stockley.jpg		
	muffings.jpg		
	reading.jpg		
	salted_with_fire.jpg		
	tripsmart folder containing these files:		Project Builder 1
	amazon.html		
	catalog.html		
	destinations.html		
	index.html		
	kenya.html		
	newsletter.html		
	services.html		
	tripsmart_styles.css		
	assets/giraffe.jpg		
	assets/hat.jpg		
	assets/house.jpg		
	assets/lion.jpg		
	assets/pants.jpg		
	assets/parrot.jpg		
	assets/sloth.jpg		
	assets/tripsmart_banner.jpg		
	assets/vest.jpg		
	assets/water_lily.jpg		
	assets/zebra_mothers.jpg		
	none		Design Project
	none		Group Project
7	No files provided		
8	contestants.gif		Lesson 3
	contestants_bak.jpg		
	peaches_small.jpg		Skills Review
	packing_cube.jpg		Project Builder 1
	two_girls.jpg		Project Builder 2

Chapter	Data File Supplied	Student Creates File	Used In
9	crab.fla crab.swf	angels.swf alabama.swf	Lesson 1
	blue_angels.html uss_alabama.html images/.DS_Store images/blue_angels.gif images/blue_angels_f2.gif images/uss_alabama.gif images/uss_alabama_f2.gif		Lesson 2
	dolphin.wav		Lesson 3
	garden_quote.swf garden_tips.html garden_tips.jpg garden_tips_f2.jpg water.wav	m_gardeners.swf	Skills Review
	amazon_map.swf lion.wav		Project Builder 1
		books.swf cafe.swf corner.swf events.swf home.swf	Project Builder 2
10		Templates/activities_pages.dwt	Lesson 1
	golf.doc assets/golfer.jpg	golf.html	Lesson 2
	annuals.doc perennials.doc water_plants.doc	annuals.html water_plants.html Templates/plant_categories.dwt	Skills Review
	assets/headphones.jpg assets/packing_cube.jpg assets/packing_cube_large.jpg assets/passport_holder.jpg	accessories.html clothing.html Templates/catalog_pages.dwt	Project Builder 1
		Templates/main_pages.dwt	Project Builder 2
	none		Design Project
	none		Group Project

Chapter	Data File Supplied	Student Creates File	Used In
11	assets/su_logo.jpg		Lesson 1
	assets/blooms_logo.jpg		Skills Review
	assets/tripsmart_logo.jpg		Project Builder 1
	none		Project Builder 2
	none		Design Project
	none		Group Project
12		The Striped Umbrella.ste	Lesson 4
		blooms & bulbs.ste	Skills Review
		TripSmart.ste	Project Builder 1
		emmas book bag.ste	Project Builder 2
	none		Design Project
	none		Group Project

Absolute path

A path containing an external link that references a link on a Web page outside of the current Web site, and includes the protocol "http" and the URL, or address, of the Web page.

Absolute positioning

The positioning of a layer according to the distance between the layer's upper-left corner and the upper-left corner of the page or layer in which it is contained.

Action

A response to an event trigger that causes a change, such as text changing color.

Action property

Property that specifies the application or script that will process form data.

Alert box

See **popup message**.

Aligning an image

Positioning an image on a Web page in relation to other elements on the page.

Alternate text

Descriptive text that can be set to appear in place of an image while the image is downloading or when a user places the mouse pointer over the image.

ASP

The acronym for Active Server Pages. ASP is a server-side application tool.

Assets folder

A subfolder in a Web site in which you store most of the files that are not Web pages, such as images, audio files, and video clips.

Assets panel

A panel that contains nine categories of assets, such as images, used in a Web site. Clicking a category button will display a list of those assets.

Background color

A color that fills an entire Web page, frame, table, cell, or document.

Background image

A graphic file used in place of a background color.

Banner

Graphic that generally appears across the top of a Web page that can incorporate the company's logo, contact information, and navigation buttons.

Behavior

A preset piece of JavaScript code that can be attached to page elements. A behavior tells the page element to respond in a specific way when an event occurs, such as when the mouse pointer is positioned over the element.

BMP

Bitmapped file. A file format used for images that is based on pixels.

Body

The part of a Web page that is seen when the page is viewed in a browser window.

Border

An outline that surrounds a cell, table, or frame.

Broken links

Links that cannot find the intended destination file for the link.

Browser

Software used to display Web pages, such as Microsoft Internet Explorer or Netscape Navigator.

Bullet

A small raised dot or similar icon.

Bulleted list

The name that is sometimes given to unordered lists using bullets.

Cascading Style Sheet (CSS)
A file used to assign sets of common formatting characteristics to page elements such as text, objects, and tables.

CAST
Acronym for the Center for Applied Special Technology.

Cell padding
The distance between the cell content and cell walls in a table.

Cell spacing
The distance between cells in a table.

Cell walls
The edges surrounding a cell.

Cells
Small boxes within a table that are used to hold text or graphics. Cells are arranged horizontally in rows and vertically in columns.

Checkbox
Form object that can be used on a Web page to let viewers choose from a range of possible options.

Checked out files
Files that are being used by other team members.

Child page
A page at a lower level in a Web hierarchy that links to a parent page.

Class style
See **custom style**.

Client-side scripting
A method used to process information a form collects by using the user's computer.

Clip property
Property that determines the portion of a layer's content that will be visible when displayed in a Web browser.

Cloaked file
File that is marked to be excluded from certain processes, such as being transferred to the remote site.

Code and Design view
A view that is a combination of Code view and Design view.

Code Inspector
A window that works just like Code view except that it is a floating window.

Code snippet
See **snippets**.

Code view
A view that shows the underlying HTML code for the page. Use this view to read or edit the code.

ColdFusion
Development tool that can be used to build data-driven Web applications.

Columns
Table cells arranged vertically.

Comments
Comments are notes of explanation that are inserted into the code and are not visible in the browser window.

Common Gateway Interface (CGI)
Server-side application used for processing data in a form.

Contents
The Macromedia Help feature that lists topics by category.

Copyright
A legal protection for the particular and tangible expression of an idea.

Custom style
A style that can contain a combination of formatting attributes that can be applied to a block of text or other page elements. Custom style names begin with a period (.). Also known as a class style.

Debug
To find and correct coding errors.

Declaration
The property and value of a style in a Cascading Style Sheet.

Default base font
The font that is applied by default to any text that is entered on a page created in Dreamweaver.

Default font color
The color the browser uses to display text if no other color is assigned.

Default link color
The color the browser uses to display links if no other color is assigned. The default link color is blue.

Definition lists
Lists composed of terms with indented descriptions or definitions.

Delimited files
Database or spreadsheet files that have been saved as text files with delimiters.

Delimiter
A comma, tab, colon, semicolon, or similar character that separates tabular data.

Dependent file
File that another file needs in order to be complete, such as an image or navigation bar element.

Derivative work
An adaptation of another work, such as a movie version of a book.

Description
A short summary of Web site content that resides in the head section.

Design view
The view that shows the page as it would appear in a browser and is primarily used when designing and creating a Web page.

Diagonal symmetry
A design principle in which page elements are balanced along the invisible diagonal line of the page.

Document
A page created in Dreamweaver.

Document toolbar
A toolbar that contains buttons for changing the current Web page view, previewing and debugging Web pages, and managing files.

Document window
The large white area in the Dreamweaver workspace where you create and edit Web pages.

Document-relative path
A path referenced in relation to the Web page that is currently displayed.

Domain name
An IP address expressed in letters instead of numbers, usually reflecting the name of the business represented by the Web site.

Down image state
The state of a page element when the element has been clicked.

Download
Transfer a file or files from a remote server to a computer.

Download time
The time it takes to transfer a file to another computer.

DSL
Digital Subscriber Line. A type of high-speed Internet connection.

Editable optional region
An area in a template where users can add or change content, and that users can also choose to show or hide.

Editable region
An area in a template where users of the template can add or change content.

Element
A graphic link that is part of a navigation bar and can have one of four possible appearances.

Embedded CSS style sheet
Styles that are part of an HTML page.

Enable cache
A setting to direct the computer system to use space on the hard drive as temporary memory or cache while you are working in Dreamweaver.

Event trigger
An event, such as a mouse click on an object, that causes a behavior to start.

Expanded Tables mode
A Dreamweaver viewing mode that includes expanded table borders and temporary cell padding and cell spacing.

Export data
To save data that was created in Dreamweaver in a special file format so that you can bring it into another software program.

External CSS style sheet
Collection of rules stored in a separate file that control the formatting of content in a Web page. External CSS style sheets have a .css file extension.

External links
Links that connect to Web pages in other Web sites or to e-mail addresses.

Fair use
Fair use is a concept that allows consumers to copy all or part of a copyrighted work in support of their First Amendment rights.

Favorites
Assets that are used repeatedly in a Web site and are included in their own category in the Assets panel.

Field
See **form object**

Fieldset
HTML tag used to group related form elements together.

File field
Form object that allows viewers to upload files to a Web server.

Files panel
The panel you use to manage your Web site.

Flash button object
Button made from a small, predefined Flash movie that can be inserted on a Web page to provide navigation in a Web site.

Flash player
A free program included with many browsers that allows you to view content created with Macromedia Flash.

Flash text
A vector-based graphic file that contains text.

Font combination
A set of three fonts that specify which fonts a browser should use to display the text on a Web page.

Form control
See **form object**.

Form element
See **form object**.

Form object
An object on a Web page, such as a text box, radio button, or checkbox, that collects information from viewers. Also referred to as **form element**, **form control**, or **field**.

FormName property
Property that specifies a unique name for a form.

Frame
Fixed region in a browser that can display a Web page and act independently from other pages displayed in other frames within the browser window.

Frameset
A document that contains the instructions that tell a browser how to lay out a set of frames showing individual documents on a page, including the size and position of the frames.

Frames panel
Panel in the Advanced Layout panel group that shows a visual representation of the frameset and is used for selecting frames.

FTP
File Transfer Protocol. The process of uploading and downloading files to and from a remote site.

Get
Transferring files from a remote location.

GET method
Method property that specifies that ASCII data collected in a form will be sent to the server appended to the URL or file included in the Action property.

GIF
Graphics interchange format. Type of file format used for images placed on Web pages that can support both transparency and animation.

Graphics
Pictures or design elements that add visual interest to a page.

Head content
The part of a Web page that is not viewed in the browser window. It includes meta tags, which are HTML codes that include information about the page, such as keywords and descriptions.

Headings
Six different styles that can be applied to text: Heading 1 (the largest size) through Heading 6 (the smallest size).

Height property
Property that specifies the height of a layer either in pixels or as a percentage of the screen's height.

Hexadecimal value
A value that represents the amount of red, green, and blue in a color and is based on the Base 16 number system.

Hidden field
Form object that makes it possible to provide information to the Web server and form processing script without the viewer knowing that the information is being sent.

History panel
A panel that lists the steps that have been performed in Dreamweaver while editing and formatting a document.

Home page
Usually the first Web page that appears when viewers visit a Web site.

Horizontal symmetry
A design principle in which page elements are balanced across the page.

Hotspot
An area on a graphic, that, when clicked, links to a different location on the page or to another Web page.

HTML
Hypertext Markup Language. A language Web developers use to create Web pages.

HTML style
A named set of formatting attributes that can be applied to text to ensure consistency for common text elements across all pages of a Web site.

Hyperlink
Graphic or text element on a Web page that users click to display another location on the page, another Web page on the same Web site, or a Web page on a different Web site. Hyperlinks are also known as links.

Image field
Form object used to insert an image in a form.

Image map
A graphic that has been divided into sections, each of which contains a link.

Import data
To bring data created in another software program into an application.

Index
The Macromedia Help feature that displays topics in alphabetical order.

Inline CSS rule
A CSS rule whose code is contained within the body section of the HTML code on a Web page.

Intangible assets
Assets that are referred to as intellectual property.

Intellectual property
A product resulting from human creativity such as a movie or a song.

Interactivity
Allows visitors to your Web site to affect its content.

Insert bar
Groups of buttons for creating and inserting objects arranged by category.

Internal links
Links to Web pages within the same Web site.

IP address
An assigned series of numbers, separated by periods, that designates an address on the Internet.

ISP
Internet Service Provider. A service to which you subscribe in order to be able to connect your computer to the Internet.

JavaScript
A Web-scripting language that interacts with HTML code to create interactive content.

JPEG file
Joint photographic experts group. Type of file format used for images that appear on Web pages, typically used for photographs.

Jump menu
Navigational menu that lets viewers go quickly to different pages in a site or to different sites on the Internet.

Keywords
Words that relate to the content of a Web site and reside in the head content.

Layers
Containers used to divide and arrange the elements of a Web page in a logical front to back order. A layer can contain multiple objects, all of which are managed in the Layers panel.

Layers panel
Panel in the Advanced Layout panel group that is used to control the visibility, name, and Z-Index stacking order of layers on a Web page.

Layout mode
A Dreamweaver mode that is used for drawing tables.

Left property
Property that specifies the distance between the left edge of a layer and the left edge of the page or layer that contains it.

Library item
Content that can contain text or graphics and is saved in a separate file in the Library folder of a Web site.

Licensing agreement
The permission given by a copyright holder that conveys the right to use the copyright holder's work.

Link
See hyperlink.

List
Element on a Web page from which viewers can make a choice from several options. Lists are often used in order forms.

List form object
A form object that lets users choose one or more options from a list of choices.

Locked region
An area on a template that cannot be changed by users of the template.

Macromedia Flash Player
A program that needs to be installed on a computer to view Flash movies.

mailto: link
A common point of contact that viewers with questions or problems can use to contact someone at the company's headquarters.

Menu
Element on a Web page from which Web viewers can make choices. Menus are often used for navigation in a Web site.

Menu bar
A bar located above the document window that includes names of menus, each of which contain Dreamweaver commands.

Menu form object
A form object, commonly used for navigation on a Web site, that lets viewers select a single option from a list of choices.

Menu list
Lists that are very similar to unordered lists.

Merge cells
To combine multiple cells in a table into one cell.

Meta tags
HTML codes that include information about the page, such as keywords and descriptions, and reside in the head content.

Method property
Property that specifies the HyperText Transfer Protocol (HTTP) method used to send form data to a Web server.

Multimedia
Content that combines text, graphics, sound, animation, or interactivity to create a fully engaging experience.

Multiple Document Interface
A Dreamweaver interface choice in which all document windows and panels are positioned within one large application window.

Named anchor
A specific location on a Web page that has a specific name.

Navigation bar
A group of buttons, usually organized in rows or columns, that link to different areas or pages inside or outside a Web site.

Nested layer
Layer whose HTML code is included within another layer's code.

Nested table
A table within a table.

Nested template
A template that is based on another template.

NoFrames content
Alternate content of a Web site that can be viewed without frames.

Non-Websafe colors
Colors that may not be displayed uniformly across computer platforms.

Numbered lists
Lists of items that are presented in a specific order and are preceded by numbers or letters in sequence. Also called ordered lists.

Objects
The individual elements in a document, such as text or images.

Optional region
Region in a template that template users can choose either to show or hide.

Ordered list
List of items that need to be placed in a specific order, where each item is preceded by a number or letter. Also called numbered lists.

Orphaned files
Files that are not linked to any pages in a Web site.

Overflow property
Property that specifies how to handle excess content that does not fit inside a layer.

Over image state
The state of a page element when the mouse pointer is positioned over it.

Over While Down image state
The state of a page element when the mouse pointer is clicked and held over it.

Panel
A window that contains related commands or displays information on a particular topic.

Panel groups
Sets of related panels that are grouped together.

Paragraph style
HTML style that is applied to an entire paragraph.

Parent page
A page at a higher level in a Web hierarchy that links to other pages on a lower level.

Path
The location of a file in relation to other folders in the Web site.

PICS
The acronym for Platform for Internet Content Selection. This is a rating system for Web pages.

PNG
Portable network graphics. A type of file format for graphics.

Point of contact
A place on a Web page that provides viewers a means of contacting a company.

Pop-up menu
A menu that appears when you move the pointer over a trigger image in a browser.

Pop-up message
Message that opens in a browser to either clarify or provide information, or alert viewers of an action that is being taken.

Position property
Property used to define a layer's position on a page.

POST method
Method property that specifies that form data be sent to the processing script as a binary or encrypted file, so that data will be sent securely.

Property inspector
A panel located at the bottom of the Dreamweaver window that lets you view and change the properties of a selected object.

Publish a Web site
To make a Web site available for viewing on the Internet or on an intranet.

Put
Transferring files to a remote location.

Radial symmetry
A design principle in which page elements are balanced from the center of the page outward, like the petals of a flower.

Radio button
Form object that can be used to provide a list of options from which only one selection can be made.

Radio group
A group of radio buttons from which viewers can make only one selection.

Ransom note effect
A phrase that implies that fonts have been randomly used in a document without regard to style.

Reference panel
A panel used to find answers to coding questions, covering topics such as HTML, JavaScript, and Accessibility.

Refresh Local File List Automatically option
A setting that directs Dreamweaver to automatically reflect changes made in your file listings.

Relative path
A path containing a link to a page within a Web site.

Remote server
A Web server that hosts Web sites and is not directly connected to the computer housing the local site.

Remote site
A Web site that has been published to a remote server.

Repeating region
An area in a template whose format is repeated over and over again. Used for presenting information that repeats, such as product listings in a catalog.

Repeating table
A table in a template that has a predefined structure, making it very easy for template users to add content to it.

Required field
A field on a form that must be completed before the form can be processed.

Reset button
A button that, when clicked, will clear data from a form and reset it to its default values.

Resolution
The number of pixels per inch in an image; also refers to an image's clarity and fineness of detail.

Rollover
A special effect that changes the appearance of an object when the mouse rolls over it.

Rollover color
The color in which text will appear when the rollover is taking place.

Rollover image
An image on a Web page that changes its appearance when the mouse pointer is positioned over it.

Root folder (local root folder)
A folder used to store all Web pages or HTML files for the site. The root folder is given a name to describe the site, such as the company name.

Root relative path
A path referenced from a Web site's root folder.

Rows
Table cells arranged horizontally.

Rule of Thirds
The rule of thirds is a design principle that entails dividing a page into nine squares and then placing the page elements of most interest on the intersections of the grid lines.

Rules
Sets of formatting attributes in a Cascading Style Sheet.

Sans-serif fonts
Block-style characters used frequently for headings and subheadings.

Screen reader
A device used by the visually impaired to convert written text on a computer monitor to spoken words.

Search
The Macromedia Help feature that allows you to enter a keyword to begin a search for a topic.

Selection style
HTML style that is applied to selected text.

Selector
The name or the tag to which the style declarations have been assigned.

Serif fonts
Ornate fonts with small extra strokes at the beginning and end of characters. Used frequently for paragraph text in printed materials.

Server-side application
An application that resides on a Web server and interacts with the information collected in a form.

Server-side scripting
A method used to process information a form collects that uses applications that reside on the Web server and interact with the information collected in the form.

Site definition
Information about the site, including the URL, preferences, and password information.

Site map
A graphical representation of the Web pages in a Web site A site map is used to view and edit the navigation structure of your Web site.

Site usability test
A process of using and evaluating a Web site for ease of use.

Snippet
A reusable piece of code that can be inserted on a page to create footers, headers, drop-down menus, and other items.

Split cells
To divide cells into multiple cells.

Standard toolbar
A toolbar that contains buttons you can use to execute frequently used commands also available on the File and Edit menus.

Standard mode
A mode that is used to insert a table using the Insert Table button or command.

States
The four appearances a button can assume in response to a mouse action. These include: Up, Over, Down, and Over While Down.

Status bar
A bar located below the document window that displays HTML tags being used at the insertion point location as well as other information, such as estimated download time for the current page and window size.

Step
Each task performed in the History panel.

Storyboard
A small sketch that represents every page in a Web site.

Styles
Preset attributes, such as size, color, and texture, that you can apply to objects and text. Styles are also called rules.

Style Rendering toolbar
A toolbar with options for rendering a Web page in different media types, such as a handheld device.

Submit button
A button which when clicked, will send the data from a form on a Web page to a Web server to be processed.

Swap
A behavior similar to a rollover effect.

Synchronize files
To synchronize files is to compare the dates of the files in a remote and local site and then transfer only the files that have changed.

Table
Grid of rows and columns that can either be used to hold tabular data on a Web page or can be used as a basic design tool for page layout.

Table header
Text placed at the top or sides of a table on a Web page that is ready by screen readers.

Tabular data
Data that is arranged in columns and rows and separated by a delimiter.

Tag selector
A location on the status bar that displays HTML tags for the various page elements, including tables and cells.

Tags
HTML codes that define the formatting of page elements. They are usually, but not always, written in pairs with beginning and ending tags that surround the affected content in the code.

Target
The location on a Web page that the browser will display in full view when an internal link is clicked, or the frame that will open when a link is clicked.

Target property
Property that specifies the window in which you want form data to be processed.

Template
A template contains the basic layout for pages in Web sites and contains both locked regions, which are areas on the template page that cannot be modified by users of the template, as well as other types of regions that users can change or edit.

Terms of use
The rules that a copyright owner uses to establish use of his work.

Text area field
A text field in a form that can store several lines of text.

Text field
Form object used for collecting a string of characters such as a name, address, or password.

TIFF
Tagged image file format.

Tiled image
A small graphic that repeats across and down a Web page, appearing as individual squares or rectangles.

Top property
Property that specifies the distance between the top edge of a layer and the top edge of the page or layer that contains it.

Tree structure
A diagram that visually represents the way the pages in a Web site are linked to each other.

Unordered lists
Lists of items that do not need to be placed in a specific order and are usually preceded by bullets.

Unvisited links
Links that have not been clicked by the viewer.

Up image state
The state of a page element when the mouse pointer is not on the element.

Upload
Transfer files to a remote server.

URL
Uniform resource locator. An address that determines a route on the Internet or to a Web page.

Vector based graphics
Graphics that are based on mathematical formulas.

Vertical symmetry
A design principle in which page elements are balanced down a page.

Visible property
Property that lets you control whether the selected layer is visible or hidden.

Visited links
Links that have been previously clicked or visited. The default color for visited links is purple.

Web design software
Software for creating interactive Web pages containing text, images, hyperlinks, animation, sounds, and video.

Websafe colors
Colors that are common to both Macintosh, UNIX, and Windows platforms.

Web server
A computer dedicated to hosting Web sites that is connected to the Internet and configured with software to handle requests from browsers.

Web site
A group of related Web pages that are linked together and share a common interface and design.

White space
An area on a Web page that is not filled with text or graphics.

Width property
Property that specifies the width of a layer either in pixels or as a percentage of the screen's width.

Workspace
The area in the Dreamweaver program window where you work with documents, movies, tools, and panels.

WYSIWYG
An acronym for What You See is What You Get, meaning that your Web page should look the same in the browser as it does in the Web editor.

XHTML
The acronym for eXtensible HyperText Markup Language, the most current standard for developing Web pages.

Z-Index property
Property that specifies the vertical stacking order of layers on a page. A Z-Index value of 1 indicates that a layer's position is at the bottom of the stack. A Z-Index position of 3 indicates that the layer is positioned on top of two other layers.